David Owen, Human Rights and the
Remaking of British Foreign Policy

David Owen, Human Rights and the Remaking of British Foreign Policy

David Grealy

BLOOMSBURY ACADEMIC
LONDON • NEW YORK • OXFORD • NEW DELHI • SYDNEY

BLOOMSBURY ACADEMIC
Bloomsbury Publishing Plc
50 Bedford Square, London, WC1B 3DP, UK
1385 Broadway, New York, NY 10018, USA
29 Earlsfort Terrace, Dublin 2, Ireland

BLOOMSBURY, BLOOMSBURY ACADEMIC and the Diana logo are trademarks of
Bloomsbury Publishing Plc

First published in Great Britain 2023
This paperback edition published 2024

Copyright © David Grealy, 2023

David Grealy has asserted his right under the Copyright, Designs and Patents Act, 1988,
to be identified as Author of this work.

For legal purposes the Acknowledgements on p. viii constitute an extension
of this copyright page.

Cover design: Terry Woodley
Cover image © Lord David Owen in his London office. Independent/Alamy Stock Photo.

All rights reserved. No part of this publication may be reproduced or transmitted
in any form or by any means, electronic or mechanical, including photocopying,
recording, or any information storage or retrieval system, without prior permission
in writing from the publishers.

Bloomsbury Publishing Plc does not have any control over, or responsibility for,
any third-party websites referred to or in this book. All internet addresses given in
this book were correct at the time of going to press. The author and publisher regret
any inconvenience caused if addresses have changed or sites have ceased to exist,
but can accept no responsibility for any such changes.

A catalogue record for this book is available from the British Library.

A catalog record for this book is available from the Library of Congress.

ISBN: HB: 978-1-3502-9487-5
PB: 978-1-3502-9490-5
ePDF: 978-1-3502-9488-2
eBook: 978-1-3502-9489-9

Typeset by RefineCatch Ltd, Bungay, Suffolk

To find out more about our authors and books, visit www.bloomsbury.com
and sign up for our newsletters.

Contents

List of Illustrations		vi
List of Abbreviations		vii
Acknowledgements		viii
Introduction		1
1	A Natural Policy for Socialists to Champion: David Owen, Human Rights and New Social Movements in the Long 1960s	11
2	The Morality of Compromise: Selling Arms to El Salvador and Iran	49
3	In Search of a Role: Human Rights and British Relations with the United States and the European Community	85
4	Beyond the Breakthrough: (In)divisible Human Rights and Cold War Contestations	119
5	Lessons from the Balkans: On the Protracted Development of a New World Order	155
Conclusion		185
Bibliography		193
Index		217

Illustrations

1.1 'Pastor to the Foreign Secretary' Mervyn Stockwood, then Bishop of Southwark, addressing an anti-apartheid rally in Trafalgar Square, London, 17 March 1963 (Jim Gray/Keystone/Hulton Archive/Getty Images). 22
2.1 David Owen arriving at 10 Downing Street the day after his unexpected appointment as Foreign Secretary, 22 February 1977 (Fred Mott/Evening Standard/Getty Images). 53
3.1 Patricia Derian, Assistant Secretary of State for Human Rights and Humanitarian Affairs, visits Owen at the Foreign Office, 9 December 1977 (Keystone Pictures USA/Zumapress/Alamy). 96
3.2 Owen chairing a European Community summit at Lancaster House, London, during Britain's presidency of the European Council, 18 April 1977 (Roger Jackson/Stringer/Getty images). 108
5.1 The eponymous architects of the Vance-Owen Peace Plan (VOPP), 2 February 1993. Owen (left) had established a close working relationship with former US Secretary of State Cyrus Vance (right) during his tenure as Foreign Secretary (Rick Maiman/Getty Images). 168

Abbreviations

AAM	Anti-Apartheid Movement
ACP	African, Caribbean and Pacific Countries
CENTO	Central Treaty Organization
CIIR	Catholic Institute for International Relations
CND	Campaign for Nuclear Disarmament
CPRS	Central Policy Review Staff
CSC	Chile Solidarity Campaign
CSCE	Conference on Security and Cooperation in Europe
DOP	Cabinet Committee on Defence and Overseas Policy
EC	European Community
ECHR	European Convention on Human Rights
EEC	European Economic Community
EPC	European Political Cooperation
FCO	Foreign and Commonwealth Office
FFHC	Freedom From Hunger Campaign
FO	Foreign Office
FRG	Federal Republic of Germany
HMG	Her Majesty's Government
ICFY	International Conference on the Former Yugoslavia
ICIHI	Independent Commission on International Humanitarian Issues
ICISS	International Commission on Intervention and State Sovereignty
ICRC	International Committee of the Red Cross
MOD	Ministry of Defence
NATO	North Atlantic Treaty Organization
NCCL	National Council for Civil Liberties
NGO	Non-Governmental Organization
NIEO	New International Economic Order
ODM	Ministry of Overseas Development
OSCE	Organization for Security and Cooperation in Europe
PRC	People's Republic of China
PUS	Permanent Under Secretary at the Foreign and Commonwealth Office
R2P	Responsibility to Protect
SDP	Social Democratic Party
SICOHR	Socialist International Committee on Human Rights
UKMIS	UK Mission to the United Nations
UNCTAD	United Nations Conference on Trade and Development
UNHCR	United Nations High Commissioner for Refugees
VOPP	Vance–Owen Peace Plan
YAH	Youth Against Hunger Campaign

Acknowledgements

This book is based on my PhD, which was funded by the Arts and Humanities Research Council (AHRC). Their generosity has enabled me to pursue my research interests in human rights history and international relations – interests that I owe to the intellectually stimulating experiences of my MA studies in twentieth-century history at the University of Liverpool.

During my PhD, I benefitted immeasurably from the support of my supervisory team. Celia Donert, Michael Hopkins and Anna Bocking-Welch were always there to offer encouragement, read through innumerable drafts, and provide prompt and insightful feedback. I am also extremely grateful to the organizers of the Global Humanitarianism Research Academy (GHRA) for providing me with an opportunity to travel to the Institute of European History in Mainz and to the archives of the International Red Cross in Geneva in July 2017. It was a great privilege to be able to share ideas with both post-graduate and early-career researchers from around the world and to discuss our developing research projects with Fabian Klose, Johannes Paulmann and Andrew Thompson. The AHRC's International Placement Scheme, which brought me to the Library of Congress in Washington, DC, in 2018, likewise requires a special mention. Not only did the experience of studying at the Library's John W. Kluge Center enable me to develop my research in the salubrious confines of the Jefferson building on Capitol Hill, but more importantly, it introduced me to Megan Henvey. I would like to thank her for her kindness and patience, and for keeping me sane and motivated during uncertain times.

While my time at the University of Liverpool has been enriched by too many people to possibly mention here, I would like to take this opportunity to thank Robyn Orr and Michaela Garland for helping me to navigate the voluminous David Owen papers at the Sydney Jones Library. I would also like to acknowledge the support of the University staff members who helped me to organize a conference on human rights and British foreign policy in September 2019, and to thank those responsible for the allocation of the Methodological Innovation and Development Award Scheme and the HSS PGR Development Fund for their role in supporting the event. It is my hope that the conference, to which the Royal Historical Society and the AHRC also made generous donations, has laid the foundations of a burgeoning research network, situated at the intersections of history and policy, that will continue to illuminate the complexities of human rights diplomacy, and the role of human rights promotion in UK foreign policy in the years to come.

Finally, I would like to thank my parents for their unlimited capacity for encouragement and support. This book is dedicated to them.

Introduction

The influence of ethical or moral imperatives within the context of Britain's relations with the wider world during the twentieth century has been the subject of considerable scholarly engagement in recent years. Scholars focusing on the politics and practice of humanitarianism, for example, have illuminated a multiplicity of ways in which humanitarian thinking, often intersecting with colonial or post-colonial discourses, has reflected Britain's changing international role and shaped its interactions with the international community.[1] Several studies have explored the development of rights-based discourse at the nexus of British imperialism and concepts of international governance from the Victorian era to the end of empire in the Cold War.[2] Within the paradigmatic framework of British imperial history, others have found much common ground between the discourses of human rights and humanitarianism, demonstrating the 'entangled' nature of the two fields.[3] Nonetheless, such scholarship has broken

---

[1] See Anna Bocking-Welch, *British Civic Society at the End of Empire: Decolonisation, Globalisation, and International Responsibility* (Manchester: Manchester University Press, 2018); Emily Baughan, 'The Imperial War Relief Fund and the All British Appeal: Commonwealth, Conflict and Conservatism within the British Humanitarian Movement, 1920–1925', *Journal of Imperial and Commonwealth History* 40, No. 5 (December 2012): 845–61; Tehlia Sasson and James Vernon, 'Practising the British way of Famine: Technologies of Relief, 1770–1985', *European Review of History: Revue européenne d'histoire* 22, Issue 6 (2015): 860–72; Matthew Hilton, 'Ken Loach and the Save the Children Film: Humanitarianism, Imperialism, and the Changing Role of Charity in Postwar Britain', *The Journal of Modern History* 87 (June 2015): 357–94; Charlotte Lydia Riley, 'Monstrous predatory vampires and beneficent fairy-godmothers: British post-war colonial development in Africa' (PhD thesis, UCL, 2013), 72–108, available at https://discovery.ucl.ac.uk/id/eprint/1389424/1/Final%2520Thesis.pdf (accessed 25 March 2020).

[2] Kevin Grant, 'The British Empire, International Government, and Human Rights', *History Compass* 11, Issue 8 (August 2013): 573–83. For notable examples of such scholarship, see A.W.B. Simpson, *Human Rights and the End of Empire: Britain and the Genesis of the European Convention* (Oxford: Oxford University Press, 2001); Charles O.H. Parkinson, *Bills of Rights and Decolonization: The Emergence of Domestic Human Rights Instruments in Britain's Overseas Territories* (Oxford: Oxford University Press, 2007); Marco Duranti, *The Conservative Human Rights Revolution: European Identity, Transnational Politics, and the Origins of the European Convention* (Oxford: Oxford University Press, 2017).

[3] Caroline Shaw, *Britannia's Embrace: Modern Humanitarianism and the Imperial Origins of Refugee Relief* (Oxford: Oxford University Press, 2015); Kevin Grant, *A Civilised Savagery: Britain and the New Slaveries in Africa, 1884–1926* (New York: Routledge, 2005); Daniel Gorman, *Imperial Citizenship: Empire and the Question of Belonging* (Manchester: Manchester University Press, 2006); Casper Sylvest, *British Liberal Internationalism, 1880–1930* (Manchester: Manchester University Press, 2009).

'limited' ground regarding the relationship between Britain, the UN, and the evolving international system of human rights.[4]

Indeed, moving beyond Britain's formal retreat from its imperial role, one is struck by the relative dearth of scholarship devoted to unpacking this complex relationship. Notable exceptions include Jan Eckel's masterful exploration of human rights in international politics since the 1940s, which during the course of its analysis, undertakes a comparative investigation of US, Dutch and British foreign policy perspectives on the growing influence of human rights concepts during the 1970s.[5] Grace Livingstone's recently published study on the policies of successive British governments towards the dictatorships of Argentina and Chile from 1973 to 1982, similarly has helped to illuminate the elevation of human rights concerns within the Foreign and Commonwealth Office (FCO) during the late Cold War period, the tensions that human rights considerations created within the FCO and the wider foreign policymaking machinery, and the influential role played by non-governmental organizations (NGOs) and advocacy networks in accelerating this process.[6] Livingstone builds upon the contributions of scholars who, by focusing on the issue of human rights promotion from the perspective of civil society activism and the activities of specific NGOs have, albeit indirectly, shed some much-needed light on the evolution of policymakers' attitudes regarding the perceived efficacy (and desirability) of elevating human rights promotion among the list of British diplomatic imperatives. Tom Buchanan's work on Amnesty International is particularly instructive in this regard, as is much scholarship devoted to the activities of the Chile Solidarity Campaign (CSC) and its role in lobbying the Labour governments of Harold Wilson and Jim Callaghan between 1974 and 1979.[7] Chris Moores, meanwhile, has provided fascinating insight into the evolution of the National Council for Civil Liberties (NCCL – now Liberty) and its engagement with the politics of human rights over the course of its

---

[4] Grant, 'The British Empire', 573.
[5] Jan Eckel, *The Ambivalence of Good: Human Rights and International Politics since the 1940s*, translated by Rachel Ward (Oxford: Oxford University Press, 2019), 190–242.
[6] Grace Livingstone, *Britain and the Dictatorships of Argentina and Chile, 1973-82: Foreign Policy, Corporations and Social Movements* (Basingstoke: Palgrave Macmillan, 2018). See also Sally Morphet, 'British Foreign Policy and Human Rights: From Low to High Politics', in *Human Rights and Comparative Foreign Policy: Foundations of Peace*, ed. David P. Forsythe (New York: UN University, 2000), 87–114.
[7] Tom Buchanan, 'Amnesty International in Crisis, 1966-7', *Twentieth Century British History* 15, No. 3 (2004): 267–89; Tom Buchanan, 'Human Rights Campaigns in Modern Britain', in *NGOs in Contemporary Britain: Non-state Actors in Society and Politics since 1945*, ed. Nick Crowson, Matthew Hilton and James McKay (Basingstoke: Palgrave Macmillan, 2009), 113–28; Tom Buchanan, *Amnesty International and Human Rights Activism in Postwar Britain, 1945-1977* (Oxford: Oxford University Press, 2020); Chris Moores, 'Solidarity for Chile, Transnational Activism and the Evolution of Human Rights', *Moving the Social: Journal of Social History and the History of Social Movements* 51 (2017): 115–36; Shirin Hirsch, 'The United Kingdom: Competing Conceptions of Internationalism', in *European Solidarity with Chile, 1970s–1980s*, ed. Kin Christiaens, Idesbald Goddeeris and Magaly Rodriquez Garcia (Frankfurt: Peter Lang, 2014), 145–62.

eighty-year history, further developing a well-established literature concerning the relationship between human rights and domestic politics within the United Kingdom.[8]

It would also be remiss to overlook the ways in which scholars focusing on British foreign policy through the prisms of their respective research interests have helped to further our understanding of the connections between human rights promotion and the construction of Britain's international role. For instance, in her two-volume study of the Labour Party's approach to foreign affairs, Rhiannon Vickers situates a concern for human rights, and universal moral norms more broadly, as a part of the Party's historic attachment to internationalism.[9] Several studies focusing on Anglo-American relations during the second half of the twentieth century have also yielded some insight into the ways in which human rights promotion has factored into the decision-making of Foreign Office ministers and officials.[10]

A cursory glance at the contents page of any textbook of British foreign policy, however, is still likely to indicate that the emergence of 'ethical' considerations in the context of British foreign policy was a decidedly post-Cold War phenomenon.[11] Closer inspection of the abundant International Relations (IR) scholarship pertaining to the introduction of ethical concerns within the foreign policymaking process in Britain, moreover, reveals a clear focus on the New Labour governments.[12] It is little wonder that the discussion surrounding the 'uncertain merger' of values and interests that currently characterises the UK's engagement with the global community appears strikingly myopic.[13] Developments preceding Robin Cook's (in)famous 'mission statement' of May 1997, in which he outlined an 'ethical dimension' in British foreign

---

[8] Chris Moores, *Civil Liberties and Human Rights in Twentieth-Century Britain* (Cambridge: Cambridge University Press, 2017); Francesca Klug, *Values for a Godless Age: The Story of the United Kingdom's New Bill of Rights* (London: Penguin, 2000); Francesca Klug, *A Magna Carta for All Humanity* (London: Routledge, 2015); Michael Rask Madsen, 'France, the UK, and the "Boomerang" of the Internationalisation of Human Rights (1945–2000)', in *Human Rights Brought Home: Socio-Legal Perspectives on Human Rights in the National Context*, ed. Patrick Schmidt and Simon Halliday (Oxford and Portland, Oregon: Hart Publishing, 2004), 57–86.

[9] Rhiannon Vickers, *The Labour Party and the World, Volume I: The Evolution of Labour's Foreign Policy, 1900–51 & Volume II: Labour's Foreign Policy since 1951* (Manchester: Manchester University Press, 2003; 2011).

[10] See for example James E. Cronin, *Global Rules: America, Britain and a Disordered World* (New Haven, Connecticut & London: Yale University Press, 2014), 63–70; Thomas K. Robb, *Jimmy Carter and the Anglo-American 'Special Relationship'* (Edinburgh: Edinburgh University Press, 2017).

[11] See Robert Self, *British Foreign & Defence Policy since 1945: Challenges and Dilemmas in a Changing World* (Basingstoke: Palgrave Macmillan, 2010); Jamie Gaskarth, *British Foreign Policy* (London: Polity, 2013); Mark Garnett, Simon Mabon and Robert Smith, *British Foreign Policy since 1945* (London: Routledge, 2018).

[12] Nicholas J. Wheeler and Tim Dunne, 'Good International Citizenship: A Third Way for British Foreign Policy', *International Affairs* 74, No. 4 (1998): 847–70; Jamie Gaskarth, 'Ethical Policies or Empty Promises? New Labour and Human Rights in British Foreign Policymaking', *The International Journal of Human Rights* 10, No. 1 (March 2006): 45–60; Jonathan Gilmore, 'Still a "Force for Good"? Good International Citizenship in British Foreign and Security Policy', *BJPIR* 17 (2015): 106–29.

[13] Jonathan Gilmore, 'The Uncertain Merger of Values and Interests in UK Foreign Policy', *International Affairs* 90 (2014): 541–57.

policy, are rarely scrutinized, in spite of their potential to illuminate contemporary policy dilemmas from a broader historical perspective.[14] Notwithstanding the rapid proliferation of human rights scholarship examining the development of the international human rights system and its impact on the recalibration of international politics during the second half of the twentieth century, British foreign policy perspectives on these processes, therefore, remain largely underappreciated.[15]

This book sets out to redress this striking historiographical lacuna by exploring the remaking of British foreign policy in response to the evolution of international human rights norms and institutions through the lens of David Owen's sustained engagement with human rights and humanitarian discourse over the course of his political career. Owen, who was appointed Foreign and Commonwealth Secretary on 21 February 1977 by the Labour Prime Minister, Jim Callaghan, wasted little time in placing a concern for human rights promotion at the heart of British foreign policy, stating during his first major speech that the UK would take a 'stand on human rights in every corner of the globe'.[16] The role of human rights promotion within the British foreign policymaking process duly became a major issue during Owen's tenure as Foreign Secretary between 1977 and 1979, shaping the Callaghan government's response to a wide range of foreign policy questions. The centrality of human rights to his foreign policy outlook was demonstrated by his decision to publish a book on the subject while in office – an exegesis that subsumed topics as seemingly disparate as Eurocommunism and world poverty under the human rights umbrella.[17] Indeed, an appreciation of human rights can be viewed as a 'constant theme' throughout Owen's career in politics thereafter, featuring prominently in his engagement with concepts of international development, humanitarian assistance and collective security during the late Cold War, and in his attempts to cultivate liberal internationalist responses to the ethnic conflicts in Bosnia and Rwanda that erupted during the 1990s.[18]

---

[14] Robin Cook, 'Robin Cook's speech on the government's ethical foreign policy', *Guardian*, 12 May 1997. Notable exceptions include Judi Atkins, 'A Renewed Social Democracy for an "Age of Internationalism": An Interpretivist Account of New Labour's Foreign Policy', *BJPIR* 15 (2013): 175–91; Jamie Gaskarth, 'Interpreting Ethical Foreign Policy: Traditions and Dilemmas for Policymakers', *BJPIR* 15 (2013): 192–209. Robin Cook served as Foreign and Commonwealth Secretary within the Blair government from May 1997 until June 2001.

[15] The academic literature on the rise of human rights as a guiding principle of international affairs is too voluminous to be summarized here, but insightful historiographical reviews detailing the evolution of the field in recent years are provided by Kenneth Cmiel, 'The Recent History of Human Rights', in *The Human Rights Revolution: An International History*, ed. Akira Iriya, Petra Goedde and William I. Hitchcock (Oxford: Oxford University Press, 2012); Devin O. Pendas, 'Towards a New Politics? On the Recent Historiography of Human Rights', *Contemporary European History* 21, No. 1 (2012): 95–111; Robert Brier, 'Beyond the Quest for a "Breakthrough": Reflections on the Recent Historiography on Human Rights', *European History Yearbook* 16 (2015): 155–74; Paul van Trigt, 'Beyond the Last Utopia: About the Historiography of Human Rights', *Tijdschrift voor Geschiedenis* 131, Issue 2 (June 2018): 327–40.

[16] 'Speech by the Rt Hon Dr David Owen MP, Secretary of State for Foreign and Commonwealth Affairs, Prepared for Delivery at the Annual Banquet of the Diplomatic and Commonwealth Writers Association, Thursday 3 March 1977', University of Liverpool Special Collections & Archives, David Owen Papers (hereafter DOP), D709 2/7/2/1.

[17] David Owen, *Human Rights* (London: Jonathan Cape, 1978).

[18] 'Answers from the Rt Hon Dr David Owen MP in Reply to Questions from COSAS Magazine', undated (c. 1984), DOP, D709 3/18/4/66.

Although Owen may be 'one of the most publicly recognized parliamentarians of post-war Britain', he has received surprisingly little in the way of scholarly attention.[19] Existing scholarship, moreover, has tended to focus exclusively on his attempts to reshape social democratic politics within Britain during the 1980s following his decision to break away from the Labour Party and form the Social Democratic Party (SDP) in January 1981, alongside fellow Labour defectors Shirley Williams, Roy Jenkins and Bill Rodgers.[20] Owen's role as leader of the SDP (1983–7) has been the subject of particular scrutiny, with scholars drawing comparisons between the philosophical underpinnings of Owen's SDP and the outlook of the New Labour project that similarly sought to plough a new furrow in the British political landscape; a middle route between Labour and Conservative orthodoxies.[21] As such, it must be said that the notion of David Owen being 'airbrushed out of history' no longer carries the weight it did in 1998 when it was postulated by the journalist David Walker who, upon noticing the similarities between Blair's 'Third Way' and Owen's earlier attempts to carve a new centre-left path in British politics, questioned whether the new label was really necessary.[22] Nonetheless, more needs to be done in order to situate Owen's personal engagement with international human rights within the wealth of scholarship devoted to the growing influence of human rights concepts within international discourse, and to bring his human rights advocacy into conversation with historiographical debates concerning the chronology of human rights history, scrutinizing the development of international human rights norms and practices before, during and after the so-called human rights 'breakthrough' of the 1970s.[23]

[19] Dean Blackburn, 'Facing the Future? David Owen and Social Democracy in the 1980s and Beyond', *Parliamentary Affairs* 64, No. 4 (2011): 643.
[20] Matt Beech, 'David Owen', in *Labour's Thinkers: The Intellectual Roots of Labour from Tawney to Gordon Brown*, ed. Matt Beech and Kevin Hickson (London: I.B. Tauris, 2007), 196–219; Tudor Jones, 'The SDP's Ideological Legacy', *Journal of Liberal Democrat History* 18 (1998): 4–7; Duncan Brack, 'David Owen and the Social Market Economy', *The Political Quarterly* 61, Issue 4 (October 1990): 463–76; Mark Garnett, 'Polemic, Parliament and History: Michael Foot *versus* David Owen', *Parliamentary History* 35, pt. 2 (2016): 171–88.
[21] Beech, 'David Owen', 196–219; Matthew Lakin, 'David Owen, New Labour and the Social Market Economy' (Masters Dissertation published online by the Social Market Foundation, 2009), available at https://www.yumpu.com/en/document/read/51594306/david-owen-new-labour-and-the-social-market-economy-the- (accessed 26 March 2020).
[22] David Walker, 'Tony's ology for sceptics', *Guardian*, 22 September 1998.
[23] See *The Breakthrough: Human Rights in the 1970s*, ed. Jan Eckel and Samuel Moyn (Philadelphia: University of Pennsylvania Press, 2014). Regarding the striking elevation of human rights concepts within international discourse during the 1970s, see also Samuel Moyn, *The Last Utopia: Human Rights in History* (Cambridge, MA: Harvard University Press, 2010). For by far the most in-depth examination of Owen's engagement with human rights discourse during his tenure as Foreign and Commonwealth Secretary see Eckel, *The Ambivalence of Good*, Chapter 7: Human Rights in Western Foreign Policy. However, Eckel's coverage of Owen – and by extension British government policy on human rights promotion – takes place, as the title of the chapter suggests, alongside analysis of the human rights policies of other Western states, chiefly the United States and the Netherlands. As such, the synthetic nature of the task at hand means that extended engagement with Owen's human rights policies is somewhat limited. For a more typical, cursory acknowledgement of Owen's human rights engagement during his time as Foreign Secretary, see Fergus Carr, 'David Owen: Foreign Secretary, 1977–79', in *British Foreign Secretaries since 1974*, ed. Kevin Theakston (London: Routledge, 2004), 96. See also Joseph R. Slaughter, 'Hijacking Human Rights: Neoliberalism, the New Historiography, and the End of the Third World', *Human Rights Quarterly* 40, No. 4 (November 2018): 736.

As a means of uncovering not only David Owen's multifaceted personal engagement with human rights discourse, but also the imperatives of the institutions he was operating within and those he sought to influence through his advocacy, this study draws upon a wide range of primary source material. The David Owen papers at the University of Liverpool's Special Collections & Archives have been an invaluable resource, laying bare the evolution of Owen's political philosophy and the origins of his attachment to human rights, as well as revealing his connections with a host of NGOs engaged in the development of human rights and humanitarianism over the course of his political career. Abundant materials from collections housed at the National Archives in Kew have also been consulted in order to appropriately situate Owen's human rights commitment against the backdrop of changing institutional perspectives. The majority of this material has been sourced from the files of the FCO, although documents originating from the Ministry of Overseas Development and the Prime Minister's Office have also been consulted, as have the minutes of Cabinet meetings. Additional institutional perspectives have been explored through the archives of the SDP at the University of Essex and the collections of the Labour History & Study Centre at the People's History Museum in Manchester, which have not only provided a means of exploring the deliberations of the Labour Party's Research Department, but have also yielded insights into the activities of human rights advocacy groups such as the Chile Solidarity Campaign. Personal papers, including those belonging to Margaret Thatcher, Judith Hart (Minister for Overseas Development) and Peter Jay (British Ambassador to the United States), have also served to illuminate the flexibility of human rights as a normative concept in international relations and its situation within the context of Britain's evolving international role.[24]

The records of debates within the House of Commons and the House of Lords have been utilized in conjunction with several newspaper and magazine collections. Digitized US State Department files have also provided this study with an international dimension, buttressed by research undertaken in the Manuscript Division at the Library of Congress in Washington, DC, which has helped to bring into focus British human rights policies at key junctures from the perspective of Owen's contemporaries within the US foreign policy establishment. A Postgraduate Vibeke Sørensen Grant has enabled me to examine European Community perspectives on Britain's human rights polices during Owen's tenure as Foreign Secretary by exploring the Historical Archives of the European Union at the European University Institute, Florence. Printed sources, such as the diaries and memoirs of Owen's peers, have tempered this archival material with more personal insights and reflections. To this end, this study has also benefitted immeasurably from the insights of oral history. The vast collection of digitized oral history interview transcripts curated by the British Diplomatic Oral History

---

[24] The papers of Judith Hart, who held the position of Minister for Overseas Development on three occasions (1969–70, 1974–5, 1977–9), are held at the People's History Museum, Manchester. The papers of Thatcher and Jay (British Ambassador to the United States, 1977–9) are both situated at Churchill College, Cambridge, although selected papers from the Thatcher collection have also been digitized by the Margaret Thatcher Foundation https://www.margaretthatcher.org/archive (accessed 10 August 2020).

Programme (BDOHP) based at Churchill College, Cambridge, has provided an opportunity to explore the recollections of British diplomats spanning several generations and numerous institutional specializations. Interviews conducted by the author, including interviews with Owen himself, his political adviser David Stephen, Assistant Private Secretary Stephen Wall, and Minister of State for Foreign Affairs Frank Judd, have also been indispensable sources of information.

This study follows a broadly chronological structure. For the sake of analytical clarity, however, a thematic approach has also been adopted: each chapter focuses on a particular aspect of Owen's engagement with human rights, exploring how this spoke to, and intersected with, wider debates concerning the development of international human rights concepts and the construction of Britain's foreign policy approach against the backdrop of its evolving role within the international community. As such, a unique component of his political outlook will be illuminated within each of the five chapters, pertaining to the factors that shaped its early development, its subsequent evolution, and its praxis. In so doing, this study draws inspiration from the 'biographical turn' and from recent complementary developments within human rights historiography, in which scholars have drawn attention to the highly contingent nature of human rights history, uncovering the translation of international human rights concepts into highly specific contexts by historical actors which resulted in the creation of human rights 'vernaculars' – local interpretations of human rights 'which were laced with the ideas historical actors brought to them'.[25]

By tracing the development of Owen's political philosophy prior to his unexpected appointment as Foreign and Commonwealth Secretary in February 1977, Chapter 1 seeks to contextualize his public adoption of the human rights cause, exploring how human rights came to be seen, in his eyes, as a 'natural policy for socialists to champion'.[26] Owen, imbued with the conviction that politics needed to be based on sturdy moral foundations through his exposure to the Christian socialism of Mervyn Stockwood during the course of his undergraduate studies at Cambridge, came to regard the hollow managerialism of Harold Wilson's first Labour government (1964–70) as a betrayal of the radical tradition from which the Labour Party had developed. As Owen's disappointment encouraged him to search for novel means of re-establishing

---

[25] Brier, 'Beyond the Quest for a "Breakthrough"': 165; Mark Philip Bradley, 'American Vernaculars: The United States and the Global Human Rights Imagination', *Diplomatic History* 38, No. 1 (2014): 1–21. See also Stefan-Ludwig Hoffmann, 'Introduction: Genealogies of Human Rights,' in *Human Rights in the Twentieth Century*, ed. Stefan-Ludwig Hoffmann (Cambridge: Cambridge University Press, 2011), 1–26; Steven L.B. Jensen and Roland Burke, 'From the Normative to the Transnational: Methods in the Study of Human Rights History', in *Research Methods in Human Rights: A Handbook*, ed. Bärd A. Andreassen, Hans-Otto Sano and Siobhán McInerney-Lankford (Cheltenham: Edward Elgar, 2017), 117–40. For explorations of the 'biographical turn' and its relationship to the broader trends of microhistory, see Hans Renders and Binnie de Haan, 'Introduction: The Challenges of Biographical Studies', in *Theoretical Discussions of Biography: Approaches from History, Microhistory, and Life Writing*, ed. Hans Renders and Binnie de Haan (Leiden: Brill, 2004), 1–8; Barbara Caine, *Biography and History* (New York: Palgrave Macmillan, 2010); Hans Renders, Binnie de Haan and Jonne Harmsma, 'The Biographical Turn: Biography as Critical Method in the Humanities and in Society', in *The Biographical Turn: Lives in History*, ed. Hans Renders, Binnie de Haan and Jonne Harmsma (New York: Routledge, 2017), 3–11.

[26] Owen, *Human Rights*, 13.

the Party's radical credentials, ultimately leading him to advocate for rapprochement with the intellectual currents of the 'new left', these currents were contemporaneously shaping the context in which groups such as the Campaign for Nuclear Disarmament (CND) and the Anti-Apartheid Movement (AAM) operated. The internationalist outlook of activists engaging with the politics of security and racial equality consequently became more closely associated with a left-wing framework of solidarity. These visions of solidarity, which competed against a more apolitical human rights tradition within the transnational activist networks that began to develop during the late 1960s, helped to establish a particular left-wing human rights vernacular within Britain and internationally during the 1970s, which became particularly visible in the international response to the Chilean coup of September 1973. It was this distinctive stirring of extra-parliamentary internationalism that Owen's human rights advocacy sought to 'bind' to the state in order to revitalize Labour Party politics following his appointment as Foreign Secretary.[27]

Chapter 2, the first chapter to engage directly with the human rights policy advanced by Owen during his tenure as Foreign Secretary, focuses on how his human rights advocacy impacted Britain's bilateral relationships, chiefly with countries whose human rights records were deemed to be less than satisfactory, with El Salvador and Iran serving as case studies. Analysis builds upon the previous chapter's engagement with Britain's growing human rights network, and its interactions with the British foreign policy establishment during the human rights 'breakthrough' by examining a highly effective lobbying campaign, spearheaded by the Catholic Institute for International Relations (CIIR), that yielded the cancellation of an armoured vehicles contract with the government of El Salvador in January 1978. The contemporaneous trajectory of British policy towards the Shah of Iran, however, demonstrates clearly the narrow parameters within which human rights considerations were able to shape the formulation of policy during this pivotal juncture, underscoring the role of deeply embedded economic and geopolitical concerns in marginalising human rights issues within Anglo–Iranian relations. Sensitive to Iran's significance as a pro-Western power in the Middle East and appreciative of the opportunities that the Shah's custom provided for British business, Owen tried to champion human rights promotion as a central pillar of Britain's international affairs while the Callaghan government simultaneously provided support to the Shah's failing dictatorship. In his attempts to rationalize and justify, unsuccessfully, this selective application of his human rights initiative, Owen constructed a 'morality of compromise' that drew inspiration from the concept of value pluralism elucidated by the philosopher Isaiah Berlin.[28]

Developing the previous chapter's attempts to delineate the policy space in which human rights activism was capable of shaping decision-making during Owen's tenure as Foreign Secretary, Chapter 3 examines how Owen's amplification of Britain's human rights policy factored into the recalibration Britain's international role during a particularly introspective moment in British post-war history. Analysis focuses on Owen's attempts to amplify British influence in the human rights field in concert with

[27] Eckel, *The Ambivalence of Good*, 196.
[28] David Owen, 'The Morality of Compromise', *The Times*, 29 April 1978.

the Carter administration in the US and through the fora of the European Community (EC) while exploring the generational specificities of his 'Churchillian' conception of Britain's international role, which held there to be no conflict between the pursuit of European integration and Anglo-American cooperation on foreign policy issues. The Callaghan government was able to synchronize its policy positions with Washington, notably on the issue of Rhodesian independence, but also on other pressing human rights issues such as the Conference on Security and Cooperation in Europe (CSCE) and the reform of the United Nations' human rights architecture. Within the EC, however, Owen's enthusiastic endorsement of Carter's foreign policy approach only exacerbated the transatlantic tensions that had been developing on account of Carter's heavy-handed management of the human rights issue within the context of East–West dialogue. Nonetheless, this chapter demonstrates that Britain was by no means indifferent to the promotion of human rights within the European Community. On the contrary, British representatives at this time were by far the most vocal proponents of the idea to codify human rights concerns in the renegotiated Lomé Convention, which governed the EC's economic relations with African, Caribbean and Pacific (ACP) countries.

Chapter 4 moves beyond Owen's tenure as Foreign Secretary by undertaking an analysis of the evolution of Britain's human rights policy during the Conservative governments of Margaret Thatcher, illuminating the ideological schism that divided Labour and the Conservative Party on the issue of human rights and its appropriate situation within the British foreign policymaking process. While David Owen and Margaret Thatcher were united in their weaponization of human rights within the context of East–West relations, this point of agreement belied a fundamental divergence. Whereas Owen's human rights vision – and indeed the conception of human rights advanced by fellow Labour ministers Judith Hart and Frank Judd – encompassed a concern for both political and civil liberties *and* socio-economic rights, the conception of human rights that predominated within the Thatcher ministries was far more circumscribed and reflective of a 'neoliberal' world view. Consequently, while human rights policy during the Callaghan government came to impinge upon issues concerning overseas development and Britain's constructive involvement with the politics of the North–South dialogue more broadly, the more constrained human rights vision that emerged during the 1980s tended to preclude British engagement with initiatives championed by the Global South. Instead, under Thatcher, the human rights–British foreign policy nexus became more exclusively associated with the ideological struggle of the Cold War. As the 1980s progressed, and human rights discourse appeared ever more entangled with concepts of democratic promotion and free-market economics, Owen can be seen – through his membership of the Independent Commission on International Humanitarian Issues (ICIHI) – to gravitate towards humanitarianism: a movement that seemed more capable of furthering a common understanding of humanity by tackling the pressing issues facing the developing world.

Finally, Chapter 5 moves into the post-Cold War landscape, assessing Owen's role as EU Co-Chairman of the Conference on the Former Yugoslavia, and his attempts to negotiate a peace settlement that would bring an end to the Bosnian War (1992–5). Here it is posited that a different picture of Owen's 'Balkan Odyssey' emerges when it is placed within its broader context.[29] Owen was one of the most vocal proponents of Western military intervention in Bosnia during the early stages of the conflict – a conviction that was buttressed by his continued engagement with concepts of global governance. While the apparent moderation of Owen's interventionist position during the peace negotiations themselves has come in for justifiable criticism, this chapter demonstrates that, following his ignominious departure from the Balkans, Owen can clearly be situated within a broader interventionist milieu in which it is possible to observe the development of a protean 'Responsibility to Protect' (R2P) ethic. The lobbying efforts undertaken by Owen on behalf of the Carnegie Commission on Preventing Deadly Conflict (which ran from 1994 to 1998), moreover, are shown to exert a perceptible influence on key figures within the New Labour government of Tony Blair following its landslide victory in the general election of May 1997, shaping its attitudes towards conflict prevention and the reform of the United Nations' security apparatus.

By exploring the ways in which Owen's human rights advocacy shaped, reflected, and at times rejected the prevailing wisdom of British diplomacy as it pertained to international human rights promotion, this book historicizes the emergence of the 'ethical' dimension in British foreign policy, provides fresh insight into the elevation of human rights considerations within foreign policy decision-making internationally, and brings its unique observations to bear on broader questions surrounding human rights' contested 'breakthrough' during the 1970s and their influence in international relations thereafter. Moreover, a new perspective on David Owen's political philosophy and his relationship to the broader currents of British politics during the second half of the twentieth century also emerges over the course of the analysis, problematizing accounts which tend to marginalize Owen and his influence on the British political landscape by framing him as 'Dr Death' – a Sisyphean figure whose apparent attraction to lost causes (and his capacity to destroy those to which he attached himself) left him stranded in the political wilderness by the time he decided to retire from party politics in 1991: 'not so much a yesterday's man as a day before yesterday's man. A politician remembered more as a Spitting Image puppet than as a real person.'[30] Certainly, Owen's tendency to champion political causes before they had acquired a stable foothold in the wider body politic often left him isolated. However, while Owen's engagement with the discourses of human rights and humanitarianism can be reconciled partially with this broad characterisation, this study will demonstrate that his championing of these concepts, both within the confines of Whitehall and without, nonetheless served to shape British foreign policy decision-making at key junctures during the late Cold War and early post-Cold War periods, and provides a unique prism through which to interrogate the intersections between British foreign policy and broader international developments concerning human rights promotion, and Britain's changing role in the world, during the period in question.

---

[29] David Owen, *Balkan Odyssey*, 2nd edn (London: Indigo, 1996).
[30] John Crace, 'Dr Death tells the chilling tale of the Great Plot Against Britain', *Guardian*, 19 May 2016.

1

A Natural Policy for Socialists to Champion

David Owen, Human Rights and New Social Movements in the Long 1960s

Following the untimely death of Foreign and Commonwealth Secretary Anthony Crosland on 19 February 1977, David Owen, who had served under Crosland in a ministerial capacity at the Foreign Office since September 1976, was unexpectedly appointed in his stead. The move was labelled as 'a remarkable stroke of radicalism' on the part of the Prime Minister by the *Guardian*'s political editor, Ian Aitken.[1] Meanwhile Peter Jenkins was even more effusive in his attempts to contextualize this most unlikely promotion:

> The Foreign Office, though somewhat diminished in importance, remains the most glamorous of all of the great offices of state, a job still fit for a golden boy, and when a young man not yet in the Cabinet finds himself at once not only in the Cabinet but Her Britannic Majesty's Principal Secretary of State for Foreign and Commonwealth Affairs, sixth no less in the pecking order of protocol, and all this two years before his fortieth birthday then that is the stuff political fairy tales are made of.[2]

Naturally, attention soon turned to the task of deciphering the significance of this development – what drove the man who now found himself, at a mere thirty-eight years of age, 'suddenly and beyond prediction' occupying the top spot at the Foreign Office?[3] As regards Owen's political outlook, there was seemingly little to be gleaned from his meteoric ascension to the upper echelons of British politics. Although Nigel Hawkes of the *Observer* noted that 'the political company David Owen keeps is on the Right of the party', Owen himself avoided 'falling into easy categories'.[4] Owen clearly shared some of his predecessor's intellectual strengths. According to the *Guardian*, however, these were 'not quantifiable purely in terms of left and right'.[5] Those who

---

[1] Ian Aitken, 'Owen replaces Crosland, and Healey stays', *Guardian*, 22 February 1977.
[2] Peter Jenkins, 'Healey factor', *Guardian*, 23 February 1977.
[3] 'At last, a gamble on youth', *Guardian*, 23 February 1977
[4] Nigel Hawkes, 'Ambitious "locum" at the FO', *Observer*, 20 February 1977.
[5] 'At last, a gamble on youth', *Guardian*.

attempted to identify his proclivities in oppositional terms were also left frustrated: 'For a man who has risen so fast, David Owen has few political enemies'.[6] He was, it seems, for all intents and purposes 'a blank canvas'.[7]

These contemporary assessments certainly did little to presage the radical steps that Owen would take in formulating a human rights-based foreign policy agenda that would come to define his tenure as Foreign Secretary. To be sure, Labour had begun to adopt a more positive attitude to human rights promotion within the United Nations during their time in government from 1964–70. Following Labour's return to power in 1974, moreover, steps were taken to address the concerns of human rights campaigns targeting abuses in Latin America, yielding dramatic changes in Britain's bilateral relations with the Chilean government of Augusto Pinochet, whose forces had deposed the democratic socialist leader Salvador Allende in September 1973. As Jan Eckel notes, however, it was under Owen's initiative that Britain first declared human rights promotion to be the *raison d'être* of its foreign affairs outside of the United Nations.[8] Indeed, Owen wasted little time in charting this ambitious new course, declaring before the House of Commons on 1 March that Britain must take a 'stand' on human rights violations

> in any corner of the globe. We must not discriminate. We will apply the same standards and judgments to Chile as we do to Communist countries or to Uganda, or to South Africa. For, without respect for human rights, we cannot hope for peace and stability in the long run. It is not a question of interfering in other people's internal affairs. The United Nations Charter, the Universal Declaration of Human Rights, and the UN Covenants on Human Rights demonstrate clearly that abuses of human rights, wherever they may occur, are the legitimate subject of international concern.[9]

Subsequent chapters will examine the steps that were taken to turn Owen's rhetoric into a political reality, exploring how human rights promotion impacted Britain's bilateral relations with nations guilty of gross human rights violations and shaped its relationships with the United States and the EC, situating these developments within the wider international context of the late 1970s – widely regarded as a transformative 'breakthrough' moment in the history of human rights.[10] This chapter, however, will seek to explain *why* the enigmatic Owen came to regard the promotion of international human rights as an appealing and potentially electorally propitious project. More specifically, it will explore how human rights came to be seen, in Owen's eyes, as a 'natural policy for socialists to champion' that may help to reconnect the increasingly moribund Labour Party with the radicalism embodied by emerging extra-parliamentary campaigns and initiatives associated with the new social movements that had developed

---

[6] Hawkes, 'Ambitious "locum" at the FO', *Observer*.
[7] Stephen Fay, 'What makes David run?' *Sunday Times*, 27 February 1977.
[8] Eckel, *The Ambivalence of Good*, 192.
[9] 'Foreign Affairs', 1 March 1977, *Hansard: House of Commons*, Volume 927, Column 209.
[10] See *The Breakthrough*, ed. Eckel and Moyn; Moyn, *The Last Utopia*.

during the 1960s.¹¹ Owen's adoption of human rights was, as Eckel notes, 'deeply influenced' by tactical considerations, 'aiming to bind the internationalist engagement, which was stirring ever more forcefully outside parliament to the state'.¹² But how did Owen – who was somewhat detached from the intellectual foundations of Labourism according to conventional wisdom – become so receptive to the societal concerns that were beginning to exert a greater influence over the formulation of foreign policy?¹³ And how did human rights become so readily associated with the internationalist outlook which Owen sought to 'bind' to the state as a means of galvanising British democratic socialism? After all, such ideational connections had certainly not been axiomatic for much of the post-war period, with conservative forces predominating in human rights engagement throughout Europe and the United States in the context of the early years of the Cold War.¹⁴

By investigating how Owen's political philosophy evolved *alongside* the development of extra-parliamentary groups seeking a reappraisal of Britain's overseas role over the course of the 'long' 1960s, however, the answers to both questions become clear.¹⁵ Owen, imbued with the conviction that politics needed to be based on sturdy moral foundations through his exposure to the Christian socialism of Mervyn Stockwood during the course of his undergraduate studies at Cambridge, became increasingly disenchanted by a creeping sense of amorality that cast a pall over Harold Wilson's first Labour government (1964–70). Organizations such as CND and the AAM, which called for Britain to take a moral lead in world affairs, meanwhile, were similarly disappointed by a Wilson government that had promised much but ultimately delivered little when it came to satisfying their demands. As Owen's disappointment encouraged him to search for novel means of re-establishing the Party's radical credentials which had been lost during the 'White Heat' of Wilson's technocratic revolution, and ultimately led him to advocate for rapprochement with the intellectual currents of the 'new left', these currents were contemporaneously shaping the context in which groups such as CND and the AAM operated. The internationalist outlook of activists engaging with the politics of security and racial equality became more closely associated with a left-wing framework of solidarity as a result. These visions of solidarity competed for primacy against a more apolitical human rights tradition

---

¹¹ Owen, *Human Rights*, 13.
¹² Eckel, *The Ambivalence of Good*, 196.
¹³ Blackburn, 'Facing the Future?'; Beech, 'David Owen', 196–219; Roy Jenkins, *A Life at the Centre* (London: Macmillan, 1991), 617; Eckel, *The Ambivalence of Good*, 196.
¹⁴ See Moyn, *The Last Utopia*, 74–83; Samuel Moyn, *Christian Human Rights* (Philadelphia: University of Pennsylvania Press, 2015); Duranti, *The Conservative Human Rights Revolution*.
¹⁵ The literature on the 'long' 1960s is voluminous, with historians contending from a wide variety of perspectives that, in order to appropriately contextualize the processes of social and political change associated with the decade, we ought to consider developments that do not necessarily fall neatly between 1960-9. See for example Arthur Marwick, *The Sixties: Social and Cultural Transformation in Britain, France, Italy and the United States, 1958–74* (Oxford: Oxford University Press, 1998); Simon Hall, 'Protest Movements in the 1970s: The Long 1960s', *Journal of Contemporary History* 43, No. 4 (2008): 655–72; Kathryn Schumaker, *Troublemakers: Students' Rights and Racial Justice in the Long 1960s* (New York: New York University Press, 2019); Mia Lee, *Utopia and Dissent in West Germany: The Resurgence of the Politics of Everyday Life in the Long 1960s* (Abingdon and New York: Routledge, 2019).

within the transnational activist networks that began to develop during the late 1960s, facilitating the emergence of a left-wing human rights 'vernacular' within Britain and internationally during the 1970s, which became particularly visible in the transnational campaigns that sprang up in response to the Chilean coup of September 1973.[16] It was this distinctive stirring of extra-parliamentary internationalism that Owen's human rights advocacy sought to 'bind' to the state in order to revitalise Labour Party politics following his appointment as Foreign Secretary.

This chapter, therefore, will not only challenge widely-held assumptions regarding Owen's political philosophy, but will also build upon recent scholarship concerning the development of civic engagement in post-war Britain and the evolution of the new social movements that emerged during the 1960s, postulating a reassessment of the British '68 in the process. The British experience of 1968 is well known for its apparent failure to ignite with the same explosiveness as the 'Paris May'.[17] Yet this chapter argues that a more complete picture of the impact of 1968 on British political culture emerges if a wider focus is adopted, allowing for a greater appreciation of the ways in which the nature of human rights engagement within Britain during the 1970s was shaped by the political and social activist networks of the 'new left' which had emerged during the preceding decade. Consequently, this chapter will also speak to ongoing debates concerning the chronology of human rights history, problematizing the identification of 'breakthrough' moments while underscoring the significance of appropriate contextualization in the writing of human rights histories.[18]

Pastor to the Foreign Secretary

Although 'not divorced entirely from politics', Owen's upbringing in Devon did little to prefigure his political development.[19] The 'Welsh radical political tradition' through which Owen traces his roots may have served to place certain parameters on the development of a political outlook: 'It was always considered perfectly natural by my family that when I did start to commit myself politically it would not be to the Conservative Party'.[20] Beyond the presence of this apparently self-evident aversion, however, Owen's milieu was seemingly detached from partisan politics. His father,

---

[16] See Bradley, 'American Vernaculars', 1–21.
[17] For rare examples of scholarly interest in British contributions to the transnational protest movements that reached their peak in 1968, see Ronald Fraser, *1968: A Student Generation in Revolt* (London: Chatto and Windus, 1988), 272–3; Holger Nehring, 'Great Britain', in *1968 in Europe: A History of Protest and Activism, 1956–1977*, ed. Martin Klimke and Joachim Scharloth (Basingstoke: Palgrave Macmillan, 2008), 125–36. Indeed, it is possible to observe a conspicuous lack of substantive engagement with the British experience of 1968 within several volumes devoted to the analysis of the protest movements in their transnational context. This is particularly apparent in *1968: The World Transformed*, ed. Carole Fink, Philipp Gassert and Detlef Junker (Cambridge: Cambridge University Press, 1999).
[18] See for example Bradley, 'American Vernaculars'; Lora Wildenthal, *The Language of Human Rights in West Germany* (Philadelphia: University of Pennsylvania Press, 2012).
[19] Fay, 'What makes David run?' *Sunday Times*.
[20] David Owen, *Time to Declare* (London: Penguin, 1992), 18.

John, served as chairman of the parish council in Plympton as an independent, having disavowed party politics soon after returning from military service in 1945.[21] Owen's mother, Molly, meanwhile, displayed a campaigning zeal that left a lasting impression, raising awareness for people with mental disabilities through the Health Committee on Devon County Council and the Plymouth Hospital Management Committee. When Molly Owen became a Devon County Councillor in 1957, however, she did so as 'a genuine independent', canvassing (with David's help) on the slogan 'Keep politics out of local government'.[22]

As such, while Owen's memoirs attribute a degree of influence to his parents that he had previously tended to overlook by describing his entry into politics as an 'accident', this influence is perhaps best understood in broad terms as an appreciation of social service and the championing of the disadvantaged.[23] Owen's schooling at Mount House in Tavistock and later at Bradfield College did seemingly little to mould these proclivities into something more refined. Although Owen's involvement with Bradfield's debating club, the 1952 Society, was 'a stretching experience where one learnt the art of argument and felt the excitement of ideas', at this point in his life it is still important to point out that, in Owen's mind, engaging with broad ethical and moral questions was merely a stimulating intellectual exercise that fell short of informing a burgeoning political outlook.[24] As Owen himself has stated unequivocally: 'I wasn't at all political at that stage.'[25] Following his enrolment as a medical student at Sidney Sussex College, Cambridge, in September 1956, however, politics quickly became impossible to ignore: 'Within a few weeks of term starting the British, French and Israeli forces went into Suez at the very moment that Hungary was being raped by the Russians.'[26]

It is with considerable justification that 1956 is viewed as a watershed moment in post-war British political history. The capitulation of Anthony Eden's Conservative government in the face of widespread international condemnation, amplified by the opprobrium of the Eisenhower administration in the United States, and the subsequent withdrawal of British troops following the abortive attempt to take back control of the recently nationalized Suez Canal in alliance with France and Israel, has been widely regarded as a fatal blow to Britain's international reputation – the unmistakable confirmation that Britain was no longer a world power.[27] Moreover, while the folly of Suez was undoubtedly a 'disastrous defeat for the old imperialist powers', the near-contemporaneous repression of the Hungarian uprising by Soviet tanks was equally deleterious as far as communism's international credibility was concerned, resulting in the virtual implosion of the Communist Party of Great Britain (CPGB) at the 'moment

---

[21] See ibid., 15.
[22] Ibid., 16.
[23] Ibid.
[24] Ibid., 21.
[25] 'Afternoon South-West: Interview with David Owen – Radio Devon', audio cassette, undated, DOP, D709 3/22/2/2/1.
[26] Owen, *Time to Declare*, 43.
[27] See for example David Reynolds, *Britannia Overruled: British Policy and World Power in the Twentieth Century*, 2nd edn (Harlow: Pearson, 2000), especially Chapter 8: Circles, 1955–70; Martin Woollacott, *After Suez: Adrift in the American Century* (London & New York: I.B. Tauris, 2006); Keith Kyle, *Suez: Britain's End of Empire in the Middle East* (London & New York: I.B. Tauris, 2011).

of its greatest opportunity'.[28] The 'painful symmetry' between Suez and Hungary, however, would engender the establishment of a 'new' left: 'a non-aligned socialist politics rejecting both orthodox communism and western social democracy' that sought to define itself in opposition to the 'polarities of the Cold War'.[29]

Can a young David Owen be situated within this 'new oppositional space' that was 'gradually claimed by a loose coalition of disaffected communists, independent socialists and student radicals' following the 'double exposure' of 1956?[30] Well, not exactly. On the one hand, Owen recalls that academic pursuits were set aside and, like many other Cambridge undergraduates, he 'plunged into the frenzy of political debate'.[31] And yet Owen also notes with some surprise that the cataclysmic developments of 1956, and the response they evoked, did not lead to him becoming deeply involved in student politics at Cambridge.[32] Indeed, Owen is rather dismissive of his political engagement prior to joining the Labour Party – a decision that was made with considerable urgency in late 1959 during his medical training at London's St Thomas' Hospital. Owen's autobiographical collaboration with Kenneth Harris, *Personally Speaking* (1987), records the abrupt nature of this development:

> It came about in a very sudden, unexpected, and – for me – dramatic kind of a way ... I can't be sure whether I heard the words in a broadcast, or read them in a newspaper, but they were the words of Hugh Gaitskell, and the words, two in number, were 'armchair socialists'. He was urging those who cared for social justice, giving people a better way of life, to get out of their armchairs and *do* something about it ... I decided there and then to join the Labour Party and see what I could do to answer Gaitskell's call.[33]

The fact that Gaitskell was able to strike such a chord, however, should indicate that Owen's political leanings had become more pronounced over the course of his studies – Gaitskell's appeal was targeted explicitly towards those whose latent socialist affinities had not *yet* found an outlet.

As a matter of fact, over the course of the three years Owen spent at Cambridge he was influenced profoundly by the charismatic figure of Mervyn Stockwood, who, prior

---

[28] Geoff Eley, *Forging Democracy: The History of the Left in Europe, 1850–2000* (Oxford: Oxford University Press, 2002), 335; Francis Beckett and Tony Russell, *1956: The Year that Changed Britain* (London: Biteback, 2015), 280.

[29] Eley, *Forging Democracy*, 332; Madeleine Davis, '"Among the Ordinary People": New Left Involvement in Working-Class Political Mobilization 1956–68', *History Workshop Journal* 86 (Autumn 2018): 133; Paul Blackledge, 'The New Left: Beyond Stalinism and Social Democracy?' in *Against the Grain: The British Far Left from 1956*, ed. Evan Smith and Matthew Worley (Manchester: Manchester University Press, 2014), 45. See also Peter Sedgwick, 'The Two New Lefts', in *The Left in Britain, 1956–1968*, ed. David Widgery (London: Penguin, 1976), 131–51; Stuart Hall, 'Life and Times of the First New Left', *New Left Review* 61 (January/February 2010), available at https://newleftreview.org/issues/II61/articles/stuart-hall-life-and-times-of-the-first-new-left (accessed 30 March 2020).

[30] Eley, *Forging Democracy*, 332; Davis, '"Among the Ordinary People"', 133; David Widgery, 'The Double Exposure: Suez and Hungary', in *The Left in Britain, 1956–1968*, ed. Widgery, 43.

[31] Owen, *Time to Declare*, 43.

[32] Ibid.

[33] David Owen, *Personally Speaking to Kenneth Harris* (London: Weidenfeld & Nicolson, 1987), 23.

to his appointment as the Anglican Bishop of Southwark in 1959 (a position he would occupy until 1980), thrilled Cambridge undergraduates at the church of Great St Mary's during a veritable renaissance of spiritual engagement at the University. As Murray Irvine recalls, the 1950s were 'boom years for Christianity in Cambridge. Undergraduates were more interested in religion than in politics'.[34] For some members of his enraptured audience, however, it appeared that Stockwood's sermons had the effect of erasing this distinction. John Collins, for instance, recalls the dynamism that characterized Stockwood's tenure at the parish, which saw St. Mary's practically

> overflowing ... each Sunday with undergraduates and townspeople who came to hear Christianity made more relevant ... Mervyn Stockwood gave us a whole new way of looking at our faith – taking for example the Lord's Prayer and asking what we meant by 'thy kingdom come, thy will be done, on earth as it is in heaven'. From there it was but a short step to the issues of the day – Suez, *Look Back in Anger*, Harold Macmillan's 'You've never had it so good'.[35]

Collins would later add: 'I shall always be grateful to Mervyn for showing me the Christian road to socialism'.[36] Stockwood's sermons had a similar impact on Owen. In the aftermath of Suez and Hungary, 'Cambridge was in total ferment', and 'there was a deep-seated anxiety about the situation that was developing day by day'.[37] But Stockwood 'led us through the moral quagmire that faced us ... his words to me were electric ... they had none of the moral equivocation which I tended to associate with the Church of England'.[38] This was, Owen recalls, a 'kind of Christianity which may have inspired me to move later to the Labour Party'.[39]

Although admittedly influenced by the writings of Marx, the 'kind of Christianity' that Stockwood impressed upon his congregation was deeply rooted in the British Christian socialist tradition – a form of Protestant liberation theology that developed during the late nineteenth century, and which found 'its voice in a thin black line of young Anglican priests and activists who found themselves exposed to the near impossibility of urban mission'.[40] While Owen may not have been a *tabula rasa* in a spiritual sense – he had in fact been imbued with an interest in theology from an early age by his grandfather, Gear – it is clear that Owen's exposure to Stockwood had

---

[34] Rev. Murray Irvine, 21 March 1995, quoted in Michael De-La-Noy, *Mervyn Stockwood: A Lonely Life* (Mowbray: London, 1996), 121.
[35] John Collins, February 1995, quoted in ibid., 86.
[36] John Collins, March 1995, quoted in ibid.
[37] David Owen, Speech on Mervyn Stockwood: 'The Ministry of Mervyn Stockwood' (edited version included in *History of Great St Mary's*, edited by John Binns), circa 1996, DOP, D709 5/2/27.
[38] Ibid.
[39] Owen, *Personally Speaking to Kenneth Harris*, 13.
[40] Mervyn Stockwood, *The Cross and the Sickle* (London: Sheldon Press, 1978), 7–8; Robert Colls, 'The Forgotten World of Christian Socialism', *History Today* 65, Issue 3 (March 2015): 37. See also Peter d'Alroy Jones, *The Christian Socialist Revival, 1877–1914: Religion Class, and Social Conscience in Late Victorian England* (Princeton: Princeton University Press, 1968); Paul T. Phillips, *A Kingdom on Earth: Anglo-American Social Christianity, 1880–1940* (University Park: The Pennsylvania State University Press, 1996); Alan Wilkinson, *Christian Socialism: Scott Holland to Tony Blair* (London: SCM Press, 1998).

political implications. Great St Mary's was, Owen recalls, 'the closest I came to finding a political forum in Cambridge'.[41] Stockwood's sermons seemed to initiate a process of prolonged introspection wherein Owen struggled to reconcile the complexities of the stimulating environment surrounding him: 'Looking through my [student] notebooks ... I find that they reflect a constant adolescent debate between materialism and idealism, sexuality and celibacy, all overlaid by a pretty strong Christian commitment.'[42] By the time of the 1959 general election – after which Gaitskell would issue his clarion call – it would appear that this struggle had set in motion a qualitative shift away from the apolitical theology of his grandfather towards an understanding that politics ought to be underpinned by moral virtue: 'Can any party have won an election on a more immoral slogan ["You've never had it so good"], a positive disgrace and a sign of the moral depravity of our life? People seem to vote on their bellies ... I cannot go on stomaching the Conservative complacency, the "life's better" touch, so it bloody well ought to be, but *much* better.'[43]

It was certainly not uncommon to bemoan the apparent lack of moral fibre in British politics at this particular juncture. Labour's third successive defeat to the Conservatives in 1959 came to be seen by many on the left as an indication that, in light of the profound socio-economic transformations of the post-war period and the emergence of the 'affluent society' christened by J.K. Galbraith in 1958, the Party had been cut adrift from the British people.[44] Still, as Lawrence Black notes, 'the left's relationship to affluence was not predetermined – it unfolded between contested readings of social change'.[45] While the Party leadership chose to concentrate much of their 1959 campaign on economic issues – a decision which, as Steven Fielding posits, merely played to the strengths of the Tory government – voices within both the 'Gaitskellite' and 'Bevanite' wings of the Party, and also within the emerging new left, often looked to tackle the problem of affluence from an ethical perspective, with responses ranging from guarded suspicion to outspoken hostility on the grounds that affluence was 'morally and culturally corrupt'.[46]

Owen's sudden compulsion to join the Party as a consequence of moral outrage, however, was somewhat atypical in the sense that, during the so-called age of affluence, Labour found it particularly difficult to appeal to young Britons who, if they did indeed harbour socialist affinities, were more likely to find the new left milieu of coffee shops and jazz bars more attractive than a Party that was struggling to shake associations of deterioration and decrepitude – 'still at the penny-farthing stage in a jet-propelled

---

[41] Owen, *Times to Declare*, 3–5, 45.
[42] Ibid., 50.
[43] Ibid., 54–5. Emphasis in the original text.
[44] John Kenneth Galbraith, *The Affluent Society* (Boston: Houghton Mifflin, 1958).
[45] Lawrence Black, *The Political Culture of the Left in Affluent Britain, 1951–64* (Basingstoke: Palgrave Macmillan, 2003), 10.
[46] Ibid., 124. See Steven Fielding, *The Labour Governments 1964–1970, Volume I: Labour and Cultural Change* (Manchester: Manchester University Press, 2003), 61–5; Madeleine Davis, 'Arguing Affluence: New Left Contributions to the Socialist Debate 1957–63', *Twentieth Century British History* 23, No. 4 (2012): 496–528; Madeleine Davis, 'Edward Thompson's Ethics and Activism 1956–1963: Reflections on the Political Formation of The Making of the English Working Class', *Contemporary British History* 28, No. 4 (2014): 438–56.

era'.⁴⁷ An appreciation of Stockwood's role in providing a bridge between Christianity and politics that Owen would eventually cross, therefore, serves to underscore the already well-documented uptick in religious engagement among young Britons during the 1950s.⁴⁸ It also speaks to recent developments concerning the need to adopt a nuanced interpretation of post-war secularization, moving away from a narrow focus on the decline of religious observance in Britain during the second half of the twentieth century, towards a greater appreciation of the ways in which religion was being 'transformed', its 'changing visibility in political and public life', and 'the ways in which the institutions, practices, and discourses of the church continued to play a meaningful role in the lives of many Britons'.⁴⁹ Indeed, in addition to politicising a generation of Cambridge undergraduates from his pulpit at Great St Mary's, Stockwood can also be situated within a broader coalition of left-wing activists in which Christian voices were some of the loudest in advocating for a reappraisal of Britain's international role and the adoption of a progressive self-image that would serve as the basis for Britain's ongoing 'greatness' in light of its diminished military capability.

Holger Nehring's study of CND, for example, suggests that a Christian ethic permeated the organization to such an extent that 'to observers today, CND might very well appear a kind of radical revivalism'.⁵⁰ Meanwhile, regarding the contemporaneous growth of the AAM in Britain during the mid-to-late 1950s prior to its official establishment in 1960, Rob Skinner notes how the organization was similarly shaped to a significant degree by the moral fervour of its Christian adherents, developing 'at the intersections between the webs of Christian, anti-colonial and international Left networks'.⁵¹ The connection between these two groups, however, was much deeper than the overlap in membership, evidenced by the presence of leading figures within the Anglican Church in both.⁵² Rather, CND and the AAM can be viewed as constitutive

---

47 Lawrence Black, '"Still at the Penny-Farthing Stage in a Jet-Propelled Era": Branch Life in 1950s Socialism', *Labour History Review* 65 (2000): 203. See also Catherine Ellis, 'The Younger Generation: The Labour Party and the 1959 Youth Commission', *Journal of British Studies* 41, No. 2 (April 2002): 205–31.
48 See Callum G. Brown, *The Death of Christian Britain: Understanding Secularisation, 1800–2000* (London: Routledge, 2001); Ian Jones, *The Local Church and Generational Change in Birmingham, 1945–2000* (Woodbridge: Boydell Press, 2012); Callum G. Brown, *The Battle for Christian Britain: Sex, Humanists and Secularisation, 1945–1980* (Cambridge: Cambridge University Press, 2019). For a more sceptical assessment of the notion that a religious revival took place during the decade see Clive D. Field, *Britain's Last Religious Revival? Quantifying Belonging, Behaving, and Believing in the Long 1950s* (Basingstoke: Palgrave Pivot, 2015).
49 Bocking-Welch, *British Civic Society at the End of Empire*, 155. For narratives focusing on the decline of religious observance in the post-war period, see Steve Bruce, *Religion in the Modern World: From Cathedrals to Cults* (Oxford: Oxford University Press, 1996); Brown, *The Death of Christian Britain*; Brown, *The Battle for Christian Britain*. C.f. Jane Garnett et al, 'Introduction', in *Redefining Christian Britain: Post-1945 Perspectives*, ed. Jane Garnett et al (London: SCM Press, 2006), 1–18; Jeremy Morris, 'The Strange Death of Christian Britain: Another Look at the Secularization Debate', *Historical Journal* 46, No. 4 (2003): 963–76.
50 Holger Nehring, '"The Long Night is Over": The Campaign for Nuclear Disarmament, "Generation" and the Politics of Religion (1957–1964)', in *Redefining Christian Britain*, ed. Garnett et al, 140.
51 Rob Skinner, *The Foundations of Anti-Apartheid: Liberal Humanitarianism and Traditional Activists in Britain and the United States, c. 1919–64* (Basingstoke: Palgrave Macmillan, 2010), 5.
52 Canon John Collins, for instance, held an executive role in both organizations. Trevor Huddleston, and Donald Soper, similarly, were Anglican priests who participated in both CND and the AAM. See Skinner, *The Foundations of Anti-Apartheid*, 3, 152, 166.

elements of a broader 'shift in British civil society', in which these groups adopted an active role in 'shaping the contours of the debate about what Britain was, and what it should be, in a post-imperial age'.[53] This has been most clearly illuminated by Jodi Burkett's study of radical extra-parliamentary groups during the 'long' 1960s, which explores the ways in which CND, the AAM – and also the National Union of Students (NUS) and the Northern Ireland Civil Rights Movement – sought in their own unique ways to reconcile the belief that empire was an 'outdated notion' with Britain's enduring pretensions to 'great' power status.[54] Certainly, British involvement in the burgeoning AAM exuded a moralistic tone that was perhaps reflective of a political culture that privileges 'morally inspired protest', and the movement clearly viewed the maintenance of Britain's international prestige as a prerequisite for its early campaigns.[55] It was from within CND, however, that the clearest arguments for Britain's ongoing 'greatness' based on moral superiority emanated, according to Burkett. CND saw the end of empire and the 'creation of a modern post-imperial, Britain' as an opportunity for the nation to 'reclaim its position as moral compass of the world'.[56]

During Stockwood's tenure at Great St. Mary's, he became closely affiliated with high-profile members of both CND and the AAM through the cultivation of a Christian socialist network which would frequently meet in Bloomsbury, where the likes of Canon John Collins, Tom Driberg and Donald Soper 'thrashed out their differences' on international issues.[57] His support of unilateral nuclear disarmament and his condemnation of apartheid South Africa, moreover, was made abundantly clear when, at the third annual CND Easter march in April 1960, he called upon Harold Macmillan to speak up for 'all that is best in Britain' and 'set an example to the world by renouncing the hydrogen bomb' in the same way that the Prime Minister had condemned racial apartheid.[58] Stockwood's engagement with debates concerning the reconstruction of Britain's international role based on setting a moral example, however, clearly preceded the establishment of either CND or the AAM. In 1953, for instance, Stockwood gave his sign of approval (along with Driberg and Collins) to a pamphlet written by Labour MPs Richard Acland, Fenner Brockway and Leslie Hale entitled *Waging Peace: The Need for a Change in British Policy*, in which the authors 're-examined the assumptions upon which Britain's foreign and military policies have been based since the winter of 1950–51' and found that they were 'no longer valid'.[59] While it was now not feasible to entertain the notion that Britain could act as a 'third force' alongside the two global superpowers of the US and USSR, the UK, so the trio

---

[53] Skinner, *The Foundations of Anti-Apartheid*, 166; Jodi Burkett, *Constructing Post-Imperial Britain: Britishness, 'Race' and the Radical Left in the 1960s* (Basingstoke: Palgrave Macmillan, 2013), 11.
[54] Burkett, *Constructing Post-Imperial Britain*, 20.
[55] Skinner, *The Foundations of Anti-Apartheid*, 2. See Burkett, *Constructing Post-Imperial Britain*, 27–8.
[56] Burkett, *Constructing Post-Imperial Britain*, 21–4.
[57] De-La-Noy, *Mervyn Stockwood*, 97.
[58] 'On This Day, 1960: Thousands protest against H-bomb', 18 April 1960, BBC News, available at http://news.bbc.co.uk/onthisday/hi/dates/stories/april/18/newsid_2909000/2909881.stm (accessed 3 May 2020).
[59] Richard Acland, MP, Fenner Brockway, MP, Leslie Hale, MP, *Waging Peace: The Need for a Change in British Policy* (London: Halcyon Press, 1953), 1.

of MPs suggested, could still provide an influential 'third voice' on world affairs.[60] In this capacity, Britain could lead the way in shining a spotlight on the gross disparities of the global economic system and the emerging 'world-wide social revolution caused by the awakening of about one and a half billion people ... who still live in centuries-old poverty but have learned from what they see in the West that their poverty is not inevitable'.[61] In other words:

> We must now start waging peace. We must proclaim to the world that in our view the economic social and moral dangers are today greater, and in the long run enormously greater, than the military. We ought, therefore, vigorously and purposefully to set about the business of winding up what is left of the old imperialism and starting the war on want on a significant and expanding scale ... For both of these purposes we should make substantial reductions in our arms expenditure.[62]

Moreover, as a means of providing conceptual clarity to this multi-faceted moral mission and underscoring the need for Britain to set an example that other nations could follow, the authors stated that it was impossible to 'over-emphasise the importance of the conception of Human Rights as a positive objective if we are now to succeed in waging peace'.[63] The realization of the principles enshrined by the Universal Declaration of Human Rights signed in 1948, more specifically, was identified as 'an immediate goal; and we should strive towards it, even at the cost of risk, more courageously and resolutely than ever before'.[64] Such an ambitious remit would be, as the authors concluded, tantamount to a 'moral and spiritual revolution. But why not? We shall not survive the challenge of this century without one'.[65]

There is, therefore, much to support Brian Harrison's suggestion that Stockwood's politicized sermons on issues such as the Suez Crisis ought to be viewed as part of a broader debate concerning the reconceptualization of Britain's international responsibilities.[66] Situated alongside the pioneering roles played by the likes of Trevor Huddleston and Canon John Collins in the development of the AAM and CND, they similarly contributed to a sense that, after decades of frustrated attempts, Christians in Britain had begun to demonstrate 'their "relevance" in political and reforming activism'.[67] Indeed, upon closer inspection, Stockwood's sermon on the consequences of Suez, delivered on 4 November 1956 with Owen in attendance, gives us perhaps the clearest indication of the heady mix of Christian ethics and internationalist principles

---

[60] Ibid., 8.
[61] Ibid., 3.
[62] Ibid., 8.
[63] Ibid., 10.
[64] Ibid., 11.
[65] Ibid., 18.
[66] See Brian Harrison, *Seeking a Role: The United Kingdom 1951–1970* (Oxford: Oxford University Press, 2009), 344.
[67] Ibid.

Figure 1.1 'Pastor to the Foreign Secretary' Mervyn Stockwood, then Bishop of Southwark, addressing an anti-apartheid rally in Trafalgar Square, London, 17 March 1963 (Jim Gray/Keystone/Hulton Archive/Getty Images).

that he sought to impress upon his student congregation, underlining his desire for Britain to set a moral example on the world stage:

> Britain, thought to be leading the world towards a new international conception of law and order, upon which the future of civilisation depends, stands convicted by sixty-four nations, and we find ourselves in the dock alongside Soviet Russia. People like myself who grew up in the First World War ... and then lived through

Abyssinia, Mussolini, Hitler, 1939 and more bereavements and Hiroshima, believed that with the United Nations something had been born which, though like all children is weakly and immature, would grow up to give hope to this sad, tormented war-weary world. And our sin last week, and as a Christian I advisedly use the word sin, is that we did our best to kill the child.[68]

Stockwood's excoriation of Eden's folly clearly left a deep impression on Owen, who recalls the lasting sense of 'outrage' that the sermon imparted in his memoirs.[69] It is worth noting, however, that while Stockwood played an integral part in the development of what Owen describes as a 'searching' for morality in politics, this burgeoning interest emerged on the fringes of the aforementioned activist networks in which Stockwood himself participated: 'Despite this moral questioning', Owen reveals, he 'never felt the remotest temptation to join CND or any of the student peace movements', believing that their campaigns failed to appreciate the complexity of the debates they were confronting.[70] Moreover, although Owen has come to view the upheavals of 1956, and the ways in which they were imbued with particular moral and political significance by Stockwood, as the genesis of a broad interest in human rights issues, it is also worth noting that this retrospective ascription risks obscuring the fact that, during this formative period in Owen's life, the language of human rights, both internationally and domestically, was perhaps as elusive and even more quicksilver than his nascent political inclinations.[71]

Although slow to gain 'widespread acceptance' in Britain during the post-war years, Tom Buchanan's analysis of Amnesty International suggests that a new human rights 'sensibility' began to emerge in some quarters during the 1950s, driven largely by campaigns on the left concerning political imprisonment in the right-wing dictatorships of Spain and Portugal.[72] It was in this context that prototypical human rights advocacy groups like Justice and PEN developed, laying the foundation for the establishment of Amnesty International by Peter Benenson in 1961.[73] As Buchanan notes, it was 'precisely this politicization that Benenson sought to transcend when launching his "Appeal for Amnesty" by emphasizing *the fact of political imprisonment for a belief* rather than the cause for which the prisoner was imprisoned'.[74] However, notwithstanding the largely *parti pris* left-wing engagement with the issue of political prisoners in fascist dictatorships, the adoption of the human rights idea in *Waging Peace* as a means of advancing an avowedly 'socialist' view of international politics – a lens through which a progressive, post-imperial conception of Britain's engagement with the international community could be brought into focus – was somewhat of an anomaly for the period.[75] Samuel Moyn, for example, has described how, during the

---

[68] Mervyn Stockwood, *Cambridge Sermons* (London: Hodder and Stoughton, 1959), 65–6.
[69] Owen, *Time to Declare*, 45.
[70] David Owen, interview with the author, 6 December 2017; Owen, *Time to Declare*, 45.
[71] Owen interview, 6 December 2017.
[72] Buchanan, 'Human Rights Campaigns in Modern Britain', 113–18, 113, 117.
[73] See ibid., 117–18; Tom Buchanan, '"The Truth Will Set You Free": The Making of Amnesty International', *Journal of Contemporary History* 37, No. 4 (2002): 578–81.
[74] Buchanan, '"The Truth Will Set You Free"', 579. Emphasis in the original text.
[75] Acland, Brockway, Hale, *Waging Peace*, 19.

post-war period, conservative (and in many cases Christian conservative) forces were among the most influential in the incubation and shaping of human rights discourse, a reflection perhaps of the 'remarkable hegemony of centre-right politics' that took hold over a continent exhausted by war, pacified by consumerism and welfare capitalism, and constrained by the 'straitjacket of the Cold War'.[76] Arguments concerning conservatism's hegemonic influence over the evolutionary trajectory of human rights during this period also find clear support in Marco Duranti's radical reinterpretation of the European Convention on Human Rights (ECHR), wherein the author amply demonstrates that conservative forces within Britain and France viewed the treaty as a potential bulwark against the prospective policies of radical socialist governments should they be elected in either country.[77] If nothing else, then, the fact that the ECHR came into force during the same year that *Waging Peace* sought to present human rights as a natural socialist project capable of articulating internationalist principles in more affective terms, certainly speaks to Buchanan's observation that 'despite the Universal Declaration of 1948', a 'common language of human rights' did not exist during the 1950s.[78]

But perhaps the search for commonality is not the most instructive means of exploring the development of the human rights idea throughout history after all. In fact, these coexisting and competing visions of human rights can be seen to illuminate much broader debates concerning the historicity of human rights and the highly contingent nature of its evolution. As Stefan-Ludwig Hoffmann posits, for example, the rapid development of human rights as a norm in international relations during the second half of the twentieth century was driven largely by its politicization; only achieving the status of 'doxa' once the concept had 'provided a language for political claim making and counter-claims'.[79] Moreover, while Hoffmann proffers a framework of 'competing universalism' which may help to bring some analytical clarity to such contests, Jan Eckel, similarly, can be seen to eschew assumptions of universal understanding by suggesting that an epistemological framework attentive to asynchronous, polycentric developments and multiple chronologies may provide the most effective means of exploring the concept's evolution since the 1940s.[80] Furthermore, Mark Philip Bradley has echoed Kenneth Cmiel in underscoring the importance of appropriately situating the development of human rights ideas within their specific cultural and political settings, suggesting that the development of human rights may be best understood as a series of 'vernaculars' which were 'laced with the

---

[76] Martin Conway, 'The Rise and Fall of Western Europe's Democratic Age, 1945–1973', *Contemporary European History* 13, No. 1 (February 2004): 81, 68. See Moyn, *The Last Utopia*, 74–83; Moyn, *Christian Human Rights*. For notable examples of scholarship exploring the fusion of Christianity and Cold War politics on either side of the Atlantic, see Andrew Preston, 'Introduction: The Religious Cold War', in *Religion and the Cold War: A Global Perspective*, ed. Philip E. Muelenbeck (Nashville: Vanderbilt University Press, 2012), xi–xxii; Diane Kirby, 'Anglo-American Relations and the Religious Cold War', *Journal of Transatlantic Studies* 10, No. 2 (June 2012): 167–81.
[77] Duranti, *The Conservative Human Rights Revolution*.
[78] Buchanan, '"The Truth Will Set You Free"', 579.
[79] Hoffmann, 'Introduction', in *Human Rights in the Twentieth Century*, ed. Hoffmann, 2.
[80] Ibid., 13–25, 13. See Eckel, *The Ambivalence of Good*.

ideas historical actors brought to them'.[81] By exploring how, over the course of the 1960s, Owen's political philosophy continued to develop *alongside* the growth of CND and the AAM – the two 'planks' of a 'new wave of political radicalism' that would sustain student politics for over a decade – the remainder of this chapter will seek to illuminate the emergence of one such human rights 'vernacular', as the concept was slowly but surely extricated from the conservative hegemony of post-war Europe and established, within Britain and elsewhere, as a language of left-wing solidarity and protest during the 1970s – 'a natural policy for socialists to champion', as Owen came to see it.[82] The first step in this process requires a careful analysis of how Owen and the aforementioned protest movements responded to a shared stimulus: a Labour government who promised much in the way of moral conviction, but ultimately delivered little.

Decade of disillusion

Bearing in mind the impact he had on the development of Owen's incipient political outlook, it is ironic that Mervyn Stockwood should have reacted with disbelief to the news that Owen was running for election in the constituency of Torrington as a Labour MP in 1964: 'When he told me he was standing, I said, "what? As a Tory?" I had always thought of him as an enlightened Tory and that those were his natural roots. And when he said "No, Labour", I was astonished.'[83] In fairness to Stockwood, it can hardly be suggested that Owen was, at this stage, steeped in the thinking of socialist intellectuals. By the time he found himself driving to meet the selection committee at Torrington in the spring of 1962, Owen claimed to have read Tawney, G.D.H. Cole and Titmuss.[84] However, it seems that the prospect of cross-examination at the hands of these more qualified comrades served to cast a spotlight on the lacunae of his socialist credentials. As such, Owen broke his journey to purchase the latest copy of the *New Statesman* in the hopes that some last-minute cramming might spare his blushes.[85] Owen's electoral campaign would prove to be unsuccessful, but the concern he exhibited for society's *moral* wellbeing betrays the fact that more fundamental convictions permeated the admittedly derivative 'Gaitskellite' platform on which he campaigned: 'As in 1945 the mood in Britain is demanding a new attitude, a new awakening. Allied with this wish is the realisation that it requires a change of government. We need new ideas ... a reassertion of standards of morality and service that we all know have sadly lapsed ... The Labour Party is nothing if it is not a moral crusade, its policies are founded in idealism.'[86]

---

[81] Cmiel, 'The Recent History of Human Rights', 29–36; Bradley, 'American Vernaculars': 4; Brier, 'Beyond the Quest for a "Breakthrough"', 165.
[82] Skinner, *The Foundations of Anti-Apartheid*, 166; Owen, *Human Rights*, 13.
[83] Mervyn Stockwood quoted in Michael Cockerill, 'To Thine Owen Self be True', *The Listener*, 12 September 1985.
[84] Owen, *Personally Speaking to Kenneth Harris*, 26.
[85] Ibid.
[86] David Owen, '"New Spirit": Speech delivered at Bideford on Wednesday 21 July 1964', DOP, D709 2/1/1/8.

Although the roots of this moralistic approach can undoubtedly be traced back to Cambridge, it is also important to note that Owen was marching in lockstep with Gaitskell's successor, Harold Wilson. Prior to becoming Labour leader following Gaitskell's death in 1963, Wilson had, while serving as Labour Party Chairman, declared before the Party Conference in October 1962 that '[t]his Party is a moral crusade or it is nothing'.[87] This phrase, which Wilson would repeat during the successful 1964 general election campaign that made him the first Labour Prime Minister for thirteen years, struck a chord with Owen, and, by the time the pair met for the first time at Plymouth North Road Railway Station twelve days before the March 1966 general election, Owen had begun to view his Prime Minister as 'something of a miracle worker and even a hero'.[88]

Owen initially found Wilson to be emblematic of the age, and his proposed technological revolution 'seemed to match the needs of the country'.[89] But it did not take long for disillusionment to set in, as Owen laments: 'Purpose became drift. Planning collapsed with the National Plan. Priorities were abandoned with deflation, and partnership went down with the trade union reform package. By 1967 my belief in this rhetoric, and my original high hopes were all dashed.'[90] It was at this stage that Owen gained a degree of notoriety for voicing his dissatisfaction with the Wilson government alongside fellow Labour MPs David Marquand and John Mackintosh in *Change Gear!* This 'statement', conceived as a supplement to *Socialist Commentary* in October 1967, drew historical comparisons between the Wilson government and its stalling programme of reform with the Liberals of 1906 and the American Democratic Party of Franklin D. Roosevelt; both having 'passed through temporary periods of doubt and uncertainty two or three years after coming to power'.[91] The Labour Party itself had faced a similar struggle after 1945, but it too had been able to 'recover the initiative' and institute 'revolutionary changes'.[92] In all three cases, the trio of MPs argued, decline was successfully arrested not by 'continuing along their old path or at their old speeds', rather by 'decisively changing direction – or changing gear'.[93] As is made clear in the title of the statement, Owen, Marquand and Mackintosh did not deem it appropriate to call for the former – the government's aims 'are our aims; its values are our values'.[94] Their contention, instead, was concerned with the 'speed' and 'tempo' of the government's attack 'on the evils against which the Labour movement has struggled since its foundation'.[95]

A notebook entry from January 1968, however, indicates that something deeper lay behind Owen's despondency – that calling for a change of *direction* may have been more in tune with his conscience:

---

[87] 'The Chairman's Address', *The Times*, 2 October 1962.
[88] Owen, *Time to Declare*, 90.
[89] Ibid., 88.
[90] Ibid., 91.
[91] 'Change Gear! Towards a Socialist Strategy: A Statement by David Marquand MP, John Mackintosh MP, David Owen MP', Supplement to *Socialist Commentary*, October 1967, DOP, D709 2/2/3/1, iii.
[92] Ibid.
[93] Ibid.
[94] Ibid., xiv
[95] Ibid.

I can't help doubting if HW will still be PM by 1969 and for the first time ever I wish fervently that we could get rid of him. Of course it's a long story the disillusionment. In a way I'd prefer to think it was just the mundane process of getting to know and seeing the way he operates. Since the enthusiasm of 1966 it is as if an age has passed and I wonder to myself why I ever did it. At this moment, even allowing for flu, I feel *shabby* – no other word really describes it.[96]

It ought to be noted that Owen's disenchantment with the Wilson government was rooted primarily in his divergent interpretation of key economic issues, which came to the fore following Wilson's introduction of the 'July measures' in 1966: 'a deflationary package which some of us in the party were horrified by.'[97] Nonetheless, it is also possible to infer from Owen's dejection a sense that Wilson had failed him on a more fundamental level.

As far as Owen was concerned, the inspirational quality of democratic socialism – its ability to speak to the moral and ethical precepts that gave politics meaning – was not merely desirable; its success as a political doctrine depended upon it. A handwritten essay in Owen's papers at the University of Liverpool spells out this concern in relation to Max Weber's seminal essay *Politics as a Vocation* (1918). Politics on the left, Owen wrote, was accompanied by an 'ever-present danger' that it will 'cease to inspire, cease to dream'.[98] However, for those attempting 'to establish a political belief on the realities of political action', a balancing act of sorts was required between an 'ethic of ultimate ends' and an 'ethic of responsibility'.[99] Unrelenting pursuit of the former entailed the rejection of compromise and therefore made 'little practical sense'.[100] Owen noted with sadness, however, that although the ethic of responsibility may be 'prepared to live in the world as it is', the prevailing belief in the short-term efficacy of this outlook had 'led to the total abandonment of the ethic of ultimate ends'.[101] Owen's deep dissatisfaction with Wilson's premiership becomes clearer when viewed in relation to this Weberian binary. During the two years that followed his successful election campaign in 1966, Owen had witnessed his once beloved Prime Minister drift towards an acceptance of the ethic of responsibility which became increasingly hollow and devoid of deeper meaning. Owen's detachment from Harold Wilson was not then, as Dean Blackburn suggests, due to the former's 'detachment from Labourism', and we should certainly think twice before accepting Michael Foot's assertion that Owen's criticism of Wilson owed more to his unbridled ambition for high office than any principled convictions he may have held.[102] Indeed, as Mark Garnett has recently noted, 'Owen's archive at Liverpool University bears eloquent witness to the extent of his alienation from "this government"'.[103] The development of Owen's political philosophy under Wilson was in

---

[96] Reproduced in Owen, *Time to Declare*, 91.
[97] Owen, *Personally Speaking to Kenneth Harris*, 39. See also Garnett, 'Polemic, Parliament and History', 174.
[98] David Owen, 'Essay on the "Left"', undated (circa 1968), DOP, D709 1/2/6.
[99] Ibid.
[100] Ibid.
[101] Ibid.
[102] Blackburn, 'Facing the Future?': 637; Garnett, 'Polemic, Parliament and History': 171–88.
[103] Garnett, 'Polemic, Parliament and History': 181.

fact characterized by the further entrenchment of those principles to which he already cleaved: chiefly, the conviction that the mode of democratic socialist politics with which he identified could not survive in a moral vacuum, and derived its strength from the cultivation of inspirational ideals.

Owen's reaction to the first Wilson government was far from unique. In the eyes of some contemporary commentators, Wilson's reign came to typify a 'Decade of Disillusion', a verdict that has put down deep roots in the scholarly literature devoted to his leadership.[104] Owen's frustration with Wilson's tendency towards pragmatism was certainly echoed within some sections of the Labour Cabinet.[105] Moreover, as the scales were falling from Owen's eyes on account of the disparity between the rhetoric and the reality of Wilson's administration, extra-parliamentary pressure groups such as CND and the AAM were similarly becoming disenchanted as Wilson appeared unable, or perhaps unwilling, to meet their demands in the international arena. As Burkett posits, for such organizations, 'the goal of the late 1950s and early 1960s was to get a Labour government re-elected'.[106] However, within 'six months of Wilson's election the hope within the left that he would take the country down a new, more moral path was beginning to dissipate'.[107] Wilson's determination to maintain Britain's nuclear weapons capabilities, along with a reluctance to curtail Britain's military presence 'East of Suez' and the adoption of an apparently subservient attitude towards Washington, dashed the hopes of CND.[108] Meanwhile, the AAM, encouraged by the support of the Labour movement during its period in opposition and buoyed by Wilson's condemnation of Tory policy in March 1963, was soon to be disappointed by the rather limited arms embargo that the Wilson government placed on the apartheid regime in South Africa, which did not inhibit the fulfilment of existing contracts.[109] Wilson's failure to respond effectively to the renegade white minority regime in Rhodesia following the decision of its leader, Ian Smith, to unilaterally declare independence from the United Kingdom in November 1965, only served to reinforce the AAM's sense of 'betrayal' – Wilson's less than exemplary efforts to bring Smith to the negotiating table were seen by many as 'a sanctioning of white domination and apartheid'.[110] While these groups sought to

---

[104] See *Decade of Disillusion: British Politics in the Sixties*, ed. David McKie and Chris Cook (Basingstoke: Palgrave Macmillan, 1972). See also Austen Morgan, *Harold Wilson* (London: Pluto, 1992). For more charitable accounts, see for example Ben Pimlott, *Harold Wilson* (London: HarperCollins, 1992); Philip Ziegler, *Wilson: The Authorised Life of Lord Wilson of Rievaulx* (London: Wiedenfeld and Nicolson, 1993). Conventional wisdom regarding the apparently 'unprincipled' nature of Wilson's leadership, however, has seemingly endured, as evidenced by more recent attempts to re-examine his legacy including *Harold Wilson: The Unprincipled Prime Minister? Reappraising Harold Wilson*, ed. Andrew Crines and Kevin Hickson (London: Biteback, 2016).
[105] See Richard Crossman, diary entry, 17 July 1966, in Richard Crossman, *The Diaries of a Cabinet Minister, Volume I: Minister of Housing, 1964–66* (London: BCA, 1976), 42–3.
[106] Burkett, *Constructing Post-Imperial Britain*, 113.
[107] Ibid., 31.
[108] See ibid, 115–16; Kate Hudson, *CND: Now More than Ever: The Story of a Peace Movement* (London: Vision, 2005), 65–6, 95–6; Paul Byrne, *The Campaign for Nuclear Disarmament* (London: Routledge, 1988), 50–1.
[109] See Skinner, *The Foundations of Anti-Apartheid*, 167–8, 194–8; Håkan Thörn, *Anti-Apartheid and the Emergence of a Global Civil Society* (Basingstoke: Palgrave Macmillan, 2006), 75.
[110] Burkett, *Constructing Post-Imperial Britain*, 117.

impress particular agendas upon the Wilson government, their responses to its shortcomings were, according to Burkett, united by a shared perception of moral deficiency: 'Wilson specifically, had failed to provide moral leadership.'[111]

From the perspective of the AAM, this perceived lack of moral fibre was brought into sharper focus as the organization began to articulate its demands through the language of international human rights with an increasing degree of regularity as the 1960s progressed. The British arm of the AAM which, from 1965 onwards, played a prominent role in the 'co-ordination of the transnational anti-apartheid network, continued to refer to apartheid as a human rights issue in the internationally distributed *AA News* in the 1960s'.[112] The AAM also participated in the establishment of the UK Committee on Human Rights in 1967 and, in the following year, it responded to the United Nations' decision to designate 1968 international 'Human Rights Year' by sending a circular letter to 'all organizations in the international anti-apartheid network, urging them to campaign about the apartheid issue as a violation of human rights'.[113] This establishment of connections between human rights norms and the politics of racial equality was, it must be said, not especially novel. It is, in fact, possible to note the existence of a complementary or even symbiotic relationship between the development of the anti-apartheid network and a growing level of human rights awareness in international politics that can be traced back to the 1940s.[114] Scholars of the anti-apartheid network have also been eager to point out that human rights norms and campaigns against institutionalized racism have 'long historical roots reaching back to nineteenth century humanitarianism'.[115] There is, however, clearly much to support Håkan Thörn's assertion that a new relationship was being forged between human rights discourse and anti-apartheid campaigns during the 1960s, with the emergence of transnational anti-apartheid campaigns helping to transform the power of human rights in international discourse.[116] Thörn frames this development as a manifestation of a wider sociological trend illuminated by the path-breaking scholarship of Margaret E. Keck and Kathryn Sikkink, which focuses on the establishment of transnational advocacy networks at this juncture.[117] What was developing here, Keck and Sikkink maintain, was 'a new kind of global politics (or civil society), which grew as a cultural legacy of the 1960s' and served to elevate human rights discourse to a level of influence hitherto unseen in international politics.[118]

---

[111] Ibid., 118.
[112] Thörn, *Anti-Apartheid and the Emergence of a Global Civil Society*, 7.
[113] Ibid. See also Burkett, *Constructing Post-Imperial Britain*, 180.
[114] See for example Skinner, *The Foundations of Anti-Apartheid*, 2–3, 59, 79.
[115] Ibid., 6.
[116] See Thörn, *Anti-Apartheid and the Emergence of a Global Civil Society*. For further examination of the relationship between the development of anti-apartheid networks and international human rights norms, see also Audie Klotz, *Norms in International Relations: The Struggle Against Apartheid* (Ithaca: Cornell University Press, 1995).
[117] See Thörn, *Anti-Apartheid and the Emergence of a Global Civil Society*, 6–7.
[118] Margaret E. Keck and Kathryn Sikkink, 'Transnational Advocacy Networks in International and Regional Politics', *International Social Science Journal* 68, Issue 227–8 (March–June 2018): 69 (reprinted from *International Social Science Journal* 51, Issue 159 (March 1999): 89–101). See also Margaret E. Keck and Kathryn Sikkink, *Activists Beyond Borders: Advocacy Networks in International Politics* (Ithaca: Cornell University Press, 1998).

While the moral impetus of CND did not necessarily translate into the same overt engagement with international human rights, the development of the organization during the 1960s can nonetheless be seen to mirror that of the AAM in certain key respects, with both groups adopting an increasingly internationalist outlook reflective of the emergent global civil society elucidated by Keck and Sikkink. Against the backdrop of disappointment engendered by the Wilson government, both CND and the AAM began to place less importance on the supposedly unique character of their British audience, and instead opted to couch their moral arguments in appeals to an overarching sense of shared humanity.[119] This change in emphasis was also accompanied by the adoption of a more expansive modus operandi in both cases which was largely driven by younger members of both groups who had become active in radical student politics. As Burkett notes, CND, the AAM, and indeed other extra-parliamentary organisations on the left such as the National Union of Students, 'succumbed to the demands of some of their membership to campaign on a wider variety of issues', and began 'more actively to promote the connections between their main focus, be it the bomb, apartheid or student welfare, and a wide variety of social and economic issues'.[120] The ways in which the internationalist outlook of these groups was shaped at the intersections of traditional civic engagement and networks constitutive of an incipient global civil society – in which radical student politics played a key role – will be explored in greater depth later in the chapter. Before analysing how these intellectual and sociological stimuli continued to contour the evolution of transnational activists concerned with the recalibration of Britain's overseas role during the late 1960s and into the 1970s, however, it is worth taking note of the steps that *were* being taken by the Wilson government to re-evaluate Britain's engagement with the international community, which included a significant reappraisal of British engagement with human rights diplomacy at the United Nations.

The impetus behind this decision to adopt a more positive attitude towards the promotion of human rights within the fora of the UN, it would appear, was provided largely by a solitary letter sent to Wilson's Foreign Secretary, Patrick Gordon Walker, during the first week of his premiership by respected human rights lawyer and former Deputy Director of the UN Human Rights Division, Egon Schwelb.[121] The letter detailed Britain's regrettable transformation from one of the most vocal human rights advocates on the international stage during the late 1940s to 'one of the most restrictive and conservative forces' in the human rights field, and urged the newly elected Wilson government to implement a thorough reassessment of UK human rights policy.[122] As one FCO official later revealed, Schwelb's letter found a receptive audience, triggering a review of UK policy towards human rights the following year which, in turn, led to the adoption of 'a more positive interpretation of Articles 55 and 56 of the UN

---

[119] See Burkett, *Constructing Post-Imperial Britain*, 108–10.
[120] Ibid., 145.
[121] See Steven L.B. Jensen, *The Making of International Human Rights: The 1960s, Decolonization, and the Reconstruction of Global Values* (Cambridge: Cambridge University Press, 2016), 91–2.
[122] 'Letter of October 19, 1964 from Mr E. Schwelb to the Foreign Secretary', The National Archives, Kew (hereafter TNA), FCO 58/4423.

Charter'.¹²³ This modification of UK policy towards the two Articles – which imposed on UN member states an obligation to promote respect for and observance of human rights, and to cooperate with the UN to achieve this end – had potentially far-reaching foreign policy implications.¹²⁴ Not only did it place condemnation of the South African government's policy of racial apartheid on firmer legal footing; it also afforded the UK government the opportunity to criticize the 'continual failure by Communist Governments to promote many of the rights and freedoms contained in the Universal Declaration of Human Rights'.¹²⁵

Although Schwelb's letter certainly hastened a reassessment of the UK's policy on human rights, Foreign Office (FO) documents also seem to suggest that a burgeoning interest in this matter was already developing prior to his intervention. Two days before to the arrival of Schwelb's letter, for instance, the FO's UN Department received a telegram from the UK's New York Mission regarding a human rights seminar scheduled to take place in Belgrade the following June. 'On balance', the UK's participation was seen as a net positive within the Department, and the FO's adoption of a more positive approach to human rights promotion became clearer as the seminar drew closer.¹²⁶ On 16 March 1965, for instance, it was suggested that the UK government should be represented, for the first time at such an event, by a Minister of State.¹²⁷ In 'accordance with the Government's policy of playing a more active role in the human rights field', the UK also proposed to host a UN seminar on the subject of human rights in 1968.¹²⁸

This being said, any attempts to appropriately contextualize the Wilson government's engagement with international human rights must take into consideration the contemporaneous removal of colonial impediments which had previously dictated Britain's defensive approach to human rights issues. As highlighted by Fabian Klose, although colonial powers such as Britain and France played a prominent role in the construction of 'the human rights regime' in the post-war years, the maintenance of their colonial territories – which included the implementation of intensely brutal counterinsurgency campaigns – increasingly undermined their claims of moral authority in the eyes of the international community.¹²⁹ A.W.B. Simpson, furthermore, contends that the relationship between Britain's imperial responsibilities and its support for international human rights was inversely proportional: 'There was, after

---

[123] S. Foulds to Mr Jones, 'Human Rights Policy at the UN', 17 September 1986, TNA, FCO 58/4423.
[124] See Charter of the United Nations, Chapter IX: International Economic and Social Co-operation (Articles 55–60), available at https://www.un.org/en/sections/un-charter/chapter-ix/index.html (accessed 9 December 2019).
[125] Mr Stewart to Lord Caradon (New York), 'Policy towards United Nations Human Rights Activities', 22 April 1966, TNA, FCO 58/4423.
[126] J.G. Taylor to J.E. Powell-Jones, 17 October 1964, TNA, FO 371/178441.
[127] K.R.C. Pridham, 'U.N. Programme of Advisory Services in Human Rights', 16 March 1964, TNA, FO 371/183656.
[128] C.A. Axworthy to Mr Jerrom, 20 September 1964, TNA, CO 936/758.
[129] Fabian Klose, '"Source of Embarrassment": Human Rights, State of Emergency, and the Wars of Decolonization', in *Human Rights in the Twentieth Century*, ed. Hoffmann, 237. See also Huw Bennett, *Fighting the Mau Mau: The British Army and Counter-Insurgency in the Kenya Emergency* (Cambridge: Cambridge University Press, 2012); Brian Drohan, *Brutality in an Age of Human Rights: Activism and Counterinsurgency at the End of the British Empire* (Ithaca and London: Cornell University Press, 2017).

1966, no Colonial Office to preach caution lest human rights instruments should be used as a political weapon by colonial "agitators", or encourage usurpations of power by the United Nations.'[130] It was, Simpson notes, 'no accident that it was in 1966, with most of the colonies gone, and the Colonial Office a guttering candle, that the British government first recognized a right of individual petition under the European Convention [on Human Rights]'.[131]

To be sure, Britain's colonial concerns can be seen to impart a degree of caution as the FO began to make plans for the aforementioned 1968 UN human rights seminar, informing the decision to focus the seminar's discussion on the topic of 'freedom of association' – a subject that raised less difficult questions than the suggested alternatives, chiefly the protection of human rights in the administration of colonial justice.[132] Nonetheless, it is clear that such concerns were no longer paramount and, by becoming the first of the 'four great powers' to host such an event during the United Nations' Human Rights Year, the UK had not only achieved a public relations coup, but had also begun to build an incipient human rights bureaucracy in the process.[133] As the Lord Chancellor Gerald Gardiner described while addressing the seminar on 18 June 1968:

> In early 1966 a meeting was convened in London of distinguished persons in the field of human rights which decided to establish a National Committee to organise a programme for Human Rights Year. This committee, to which more than 160 national organisations are affiliated, has stimulated the formation of more than a hundred local human rights committees – ordinary people coming together to exercise their rights of freedom of association and to pursue political, social and other goals in the field of human rights. Their activity is beginning to show practical benefits in all kinds of ways, and it will leave a permanent impress on the United Kingdom. Your seminar is an important manifestation of Human Rights Year, and it will be keenly followed as such by the human rights bodies I have described.[134]

At an institutional level, however, Britain's rediscovery of human rights advocacy was not as all-encompassing as Gardiner maintained. According to Sir John Coles, to whom human rights responsibilities were delegated following his introduction to the UN Economic and Social Department of the Foreign Office in 1964, human rights promotion did not rank highly among the FO's list of priorities: 'looking back, it's really rather remarkable. I was really the only person in the Foreign Office dealing with human rights,

---

[130] Simpson, *Human Rights and the End of Empire*, 299.
[131] Ibid.
[132] See C.A. Axworthy to Mr Jerrom, 20 September 1964; T.C.D. Jerrom to Mr Carter; Mr Roberts; Sir Francis Herchenroder; Mr Eastwood, 22 September 1965, TNA, CO 936/758; C.A. Axworthy to Mr Jerrom, 31 January 1966, TNA, CO 936/758.
[133] 'Draft speech by the Lord Chancellor to the UN Seminar on Freedom of Association, 11.00 a.m. approx., on Tuesday, 18 June 1968, at the Royal Garden Hotel, Kensington', TNA, FCO 61/246.
[134] Ibid. On the designation of 'Human Rights Year', see The UNESCO Courier, '1968: International Year for Human Rights', XXI (January 1968), available at https://unesdoc.unesco.org/ark:/48223/pf0000078234 (accessed 8 January 2020).

and I can't say anybody else was very interested in it'.[135] Furthermore, Wilson's foreign policy record was punctuated by a series of incidents that demonstrated clearly the disparity between rhetoric and reality as far as the promotion of international human rights was concerned. The protracted failure of the Wilson government to deal effectively with the intransigence of the Smith regime in Rhodesia – which was identified by the Prime Minister himself as a human rights issue – was perhaps the primary reason behind much of the opprobrium heaped upon his government's foreign policy, which promised a lot, and delivered little.[136] Moreover, as Tom Buchanan highlights, revelations regarding the use of torture in the British colony of Aden in 1966 were viewed as a particularly bitter disappointment by Amnesty International's Peter Benenson.[137] There was also the decision of the Wilson government to normalize its relations with the Greek dictatorship, which had taken control of the country in April 1967, demonstrating in no uncertain terms that commercial interests and the geopolitical concerns of Cold War diplomacy took precedence over human rights imperatives.[138] Likewise, against the backdrop of humanitarian catastrophe that accompanied the Nigerian civil war, contested between the government of Nigeria and the secessionist state of Biafra (1967–70), assessments of the Wilson government and its perceived indifference indicated that the British Prime Minister had, through his own rhetorical commitment to human rights promotion, made a rod for his own back: 'What About Their Human Rights, Mr Wilson?' asked one particularly pointed critique of government policy in *Tribune* magazine.[139]

Nonetheless, taken together, the progress made by the Wilson government towards reconceptualizing Britain's human rights engagement under the auspices of the UN, and the emergence of transnational advocacy networks during the 1960s that, according to Jan Eckel, 'created a crucial precondition' for the subsequent development of human rights activism, indicates that the 1960s ought to be more carefully considered as a formative moment in the history of human rights.[140] Indeed, this is the argument

---

[135] Sir John Coles, interview with Malcolm McBain for the British Diplomatic Oral History Programme, Churchill College Cambridge (hereafter BDOHP), 24 November 1999, available at https://www.chu.cam.ac.uk/media/uploads/files/Coles.pdf (accessed 9 December 2019).

[136] See 'Human Rights Year', 13 February 1968, *Hansard: House of Commons*, Volume 758, Column 1137. For a contemporary critique of Wilson's Rhodesian policy, see John Rex, 'The Race Relations Catastrophe', in *Matters of Principle: Labour's Last Chance*, Tyrell Burgess et al (London: Penguin, 1968), 70–82. For a more general account of the Wilson government's foreign policy (and its shortcomings), see Chris Wrigley, 'Now you See it, Now you Don't: Harold Wilson and Labour's Foreign Policy 1964–70', in *The Wilson Government, 1964–1970*, ed. Richard Coopey, Steven Fielding and Nick Tiratsoo (London: Pinter Publishers, 1993), 123–35.

[137] Buchanan, 'Amnesty International in Crisis, 1966–7': 271.

[138] Effie G.H. Pedaliu, 'Human Rights and Foreign Policy: Wilson and the Greek Dictators, 1967–1970', *Diplomacy and Statecraft* 18 (2007): 185–214.

[139] Joan Mellors, 'What About Their Human Rights, Mr Wilson?' *Tribune*, 18 October 1968, cited in Lasse Heerten, 'The Dystopia of Postcolonial Catastrophe: Self-Determination, the Biafran War of Secession, and the 1970s Human Rights Movement', in *The Breakthrough*, ed. Eckel and Moyn, 20. For an example of Wilson's public pronouncements on the subject of human rights promotion, see Harold Wilson, Leader's Speech at the Labour Party Conference, Blackpool, 1 October 1968, available at http://www.britishpoliticalspeech.org/speech-archive.htm?speech=166 (accessed 12 May 2020): 'We are the Party of human rights. The only Party of human rights that will be speaking from this platform this month. Human rights: this has been the central theme of this Government's actions from the day we took office.'

[140] Eckel, *The Ambivalence of Good*, 156.

made by Steven L.B. Jensen, who posits that the 1960s prefigured the so-called human rights 'breakthrough' of the following decade.[141] Although Jensen's argumentation revolves largely around the hitherto underappreciated role of human rights advocates in the Global South in the development of the human rights regime, his assertion that 1968 can be regarded as 'a bridge between the international human rights efforts of the 1960s and the 1970s', can also be supported by analysing Britain's evolving human rights network through the prism of this crucial juncture.[142] Although the radical protest movements that constituted the British '68 did not reach the same high-pitched crescendo as some of their continental counterparts, by exploring the lasting influence of their intellectual and sociological inducements on the landscape of transnational activism we are able to understand more clearly the processes through which concepts of internationalism and left-wing solidarity became so readily associated with the language of human rights during the 1970s. By exploring these developments alongside the continuation of Owen's political education and the deepening dissatisfaction that led him to entertain more radical solutions to the problems of government, the political capital that Owen came to invest in human rights will also be examined. By the time that he became Foreign Secretary, Owen saw in the adoption of the human rights cause an opportunity to 'bind the internationalist engagement, which was stirring ever more forcefully outside parliament, to the state', and to a Labour Party that had long since abrogated its responsibility to appeal to moral convictions.[143]

The echoes of 1968

Notwithstanding the UN's decision to mark the twentieth anniversary of the Universal Declaration of Human Rights by labelling 1968 'Human Rights Year', in the collective consciousness, 1968 has become more closely associated with the international spirit of protest that united seemingly disparate activist movements across the globe in an overarching struggle against perceived injustice and oppression. In fact, as Jan Eckel describes:

> Little could have expressed the position of human rights policy in the late sixties more clearly than the fact that the anniversary was simply drowned out by the uproar of that year, and that it has subsequently – we should perhaps say consequently – vanished from historical representation. Whichever political events were occupying international public attention in 1968 – the student protests, the Tet Offensive in Vietnam, the murders of Martin Luther King and Robert Kennedy, the

---

[141] See Jensen, *The Making of International Human Rights*. Regarding the significance of the 1960s as a formative decade in human rights history, see also Roland Burke, *Decolonization and the Evolution of International Human Rights* (Philadelphia: University of Pennsylvania Press, 2010); Sarah B. Snyder, *From Selma to Moscow: How Human Rights Activists Transformed U.S. Foreign Policy* (New York: Columbia University Press, 2018).

[142] Jensen, *The Making of International Human Rights*, 176.

[143] Eckel, *The Ambivalence of Good*, 196.

Soviet invasion of Czechoslovakia, tensions in the Middle East after the Six Day War, or civil war in Nigeria – human rights were not among them.[144]

The International Conference on Human Rights in Tehran which took place across April and May of that year, moreover, did not so much provide a 'high point' of the anniversary celebrations as indicate a 'new low in international human rights policy, marked by government wrangling, political manoeuvring, and empty rhetoric'.[145]

It is perhaps unsurprising, then, to find that Catholics in Northern Ireland who marched on the streets of Derry/Londonderry in opposition to the Stormont government viewed the UN designation with a considerable degree of ironic detachment.[146] Northern Ireland's '68 was replete with student activists who drew inspiration from the civil rights movement in the United States, and the perceived interconnectedness of their struggle has certainly been reflected by scholarly coverage of the 'global 1968'.[147] In some instances, however, national boundaries felt distinctly material. In France, for example, what began as a revolt by a small group of students in the Parisian suburb of Nanterre, 'quickly developed into a general strike that paralyzed the entire country', causing a political crisis that 'threatened to topple the Gaullist system'.[148] By contrast, although Britain witnessed its largest and most violent post-war demonstration on 17 March 1968 as between 10,000 and 20,000 activists gathered in front of the American Embassy on London's Grosvenor Square, revolution never seemed to be 'an immediate prospect'.[149] They may have looked across the Channel in admiration, wishing that such revolutionary spirit was as keenly felt in Britain as it was in Paris, but student leaders such as Pete Gowan were 'aware that what was going on there was worlds away from the everyday realities of the British student movement'.[150] In the absence of the chronic and acute repression that emanated from the de Gaulle regime, the British '68 failed to ignite. What was intended to mark its apogee – a march on Downing Street on 27 October 1968 – resulted in a decidedly peaceful affair that stood in stark contrast to the events in France months earlier.[151]

---

[144] Ibid., 115.
[145] Ibid., 114. See also Roland Burke, 'From Individual Rights to National Development: The First UN International Conference on Human Rights, Tehran, 1968', *Journal of World History* 19 (2008): 275–96.
[146] Patrick Corrigan, '1968: Year of Human Rights', Amnesty International UK/blogs, available at https://www.amnesty.org.uk/blogs/belfast-and-beyond/1968-year-human-rights (accessed 9 December 2019).
[147] See for example Arthur Marwick, 'The Cultural Revolution of the Long Sixties: Voices of Reaction, Protest, and Permeation', *The International History Review* 27, No. 4 (2005): 780–806; *The Global Revolutions of 1968: A Norton Casebook in History*, ed. Jeremi Suri (New York: W.W. Norton & Company, 2007); Timothy S. Brown, '1968. Transnational and Global Perspectives', *Docupedia-Zeitgeschichte*, 11 June 2012, available at www.docupedia.de/zg/1968 (accessed 9 December 2019).
[148] Ingrid Gilcher-Holtey, 'May 1968 in France: The Rise and Fall of a New Social Movement', in *1968*, ed. Fink, Gassert and Junker, 259.
[149] Fraser, *1968*, 272.
[150] Pete Gowan interview in ibid., 272–3.
[151] 'Police win the day against militant few in march', *The Times*, 28 October 1968; 'The Day the Police were Wonderful', *Daily Mirror*, 28 October 1968; 'Struggle to keep march together', *Guardian*, 28 October 1968

As demonstrated by Chris Moores' work on the National Council for Civil Liberties (NCCL) and its involvement with the 1968 protests in London, however, it seems that there is more to be gleaned from the British '68 if one looks beyond its failure to catch fire. The two hundred NCCL observers who, according to Moores, 'attempted to place themselves where the police and protesters were likely to clash' in order to ensure the protesters' right to 'freedom of assembly', for example, tell us something about the schismatic character of left-wing politics in Great Britain at that time:

> The location of these activists between police and protesters symbolizes the Council's wider positioning in this period. Politically, it occupied a space between the formal left, represented by the Labour governments, and developing manifestations of a new left associated with extra-parliamentary movements and the emerging counter-culture. This sense of 'in-betweenness' led Tony Smythe, the Council's General Secretary between 1966 and 1972, to suggest it occupied a 'curious no-man's land'.[152]

Moores draws from Geoff Eley's broader depiction of 'two parallel lefts' that became discernible across Europe at this point: 'one following a new social movements paradigm including feminism, ecology, peace, Third World solidarities, gay/lesbian rights and anti-racism, and another consisting of the formal political party aiming to win elections'.[153] In Britain, the NCCL constituted merely one of several 'progressive professional' groups which came to occupy space between the two movements during the 1960s and the 1970s, combining 'an enthusiasm for these "new" issues with their pursuance in a professional manner representative of their membership's socio-economic status'.[154] Because of their historic concern for civil liberties, however, the NCCL found it particularly easy 'to blend supposedly older civil liberties concerns with the new rhetoric of rights associated with new social movements'.[155] For Moores, this process played a crucial role in shaping concepts of human rights within the United Kingdom during this period with civil liberties NGOs acting as the 'vital interlocutors' that translated global human rights into national settings: 'it was NGOs like the NCCL that sought to translate the moral and utopian language of human rights, as best they could, into the everyday'.[156] This new emphasis on rights was not merely symptomatic of the new politics; it was seen by some as its lingua franca – 'Just as civil liberties stood at the confluence of liberal and socialist thought during the 1930s, rights politics had the potential to offer a shared landscape for a broad set of organisations and social movements to find "agreement"'.[157] Although this galvanizing influence may not have satisfied Britain's most ardent *soixante-huitards*, Moores maintains that the evolution of the NCCL during this period is demonstrative of the

---

[152] Chris Moores, 'The Progressive Professionals: The National Council for Civil Liberties and the Politics of Activism in the 1960s', *Twentieth Century British History* 20, Issue 4 (2009): 539.
[153] Ibid., 550. See Eley, *Forging Democracy*, 460–1.
[154] Moores, 'The Progressive Professionals', 540.
[155] Ibid.
[156] Moores, *Civil Liberties and Human Rights in Twentieth Century Britain*, 10.
[157] Ibid., 148.

fact that there was undoubtedly 'some permeation of new left thought beyond the large protest movement during the 1970s'.[158]

Indeed, this process can also be observed in the development of the British response to the violent deposition of Salvador Allende by the right-wing forces of Augusto Pinochet in September 1973. The Chilean coup is widely recognized by human rights historians as a defining moment in the evolution of international human rights advocacy, prompting a truly transnational display of solidarity that brought together a multiplicity of diverse constituents.[159] In Britain, the non-governmental response to the coup was spearheaded by the Chile Solidarity Campaign (CSC), although it is necessary to situate it within a network of NGOs in the human rights space that seemed to open up in the aftermath of the Pinochet takeover. Certainly, Peter Benenson's establishment of Amnesty International in 1961 – and indeed his role in founding Justice in 1956–7 – was instrumental in the development of NGO-driven human rights advocacy in the UK.[160] Nonetheless, as Julian Filochowski of the Catholic Institute for International Relations (CIIR) recalls, this process was greatly expedited by Allende's usurpation: 'In Britain, I see – certainly in the ... NGO area that I patrolled – I see the Pinochet coup as being the thing which started the process which woke up a lot of people.'[161] This much is supported by the fact that the CIIR, along with Amnesty, the NCCL, the British Council for Aid to Refugees, Christian Aid, Academics for Chile, and War on Want, coordinated their fundraising efforts with the CSC and discussed such issues as the entry of Chilean refugees into the UK in concert with the aforementioned organizations.[162]

However, while the Chilean coup certainly captured the imagination of myriad NGOs, the CSC itself made no bones about its political orientation. It was an avowedly left-wing group that made a conscious effort to cultivate relationships with the Labour Party, the trade unionist movement, the CPGB, and 'the principal Trotskyist groups'.[163] David Stephen, who travelled to Chile on a 'fact-finding mission' on behalf of the Labour Party in the aftermath of the coup, is in no doubt that Chile immediately became 'a left wing issue'.[164] Following his return from Chile, moreover, Stephen – who would later be appointed as David Owen's political adviser in the FCO – noted with some interest the presence of prominent figures of the British '68 who had apparently taken their place in the vanguard of the protest movement directed against the Pinochet regime: 'I went to Chile three weeks after the coup, and, on my return, went to a demonstration in London

---

[158] Ibid., 218. For a damning account of the legacy (or lack thereof) of the British '68 from the perspective of an active figure within student politics at the time, see Peter Sedgwick, 'Farewell, Grosvenor Square', in *The Left in Britain*, ed. Widgery, 32: 'If the movements generated in these successive waves had possessed any capacity to educate in wider political horizons, the United Kingdom would now have a permanent cadre of several hundred thousand left-wing activists.'

[159] See Jan Eckel, 'Allende's Shadow, Leftist Furor, and Human Rights: The Pinochet Dictatorship in International Politics', in *European Solidarity with Chile*, ed. Christiaens, Goddeeris and Garcia, 76.

[160] See Buchanan, 'Human Rights Campaigns in Modern Britain', 113–24.

[161] Julian Filochowski, interview with the author, 17 May 2019.

[162] Wendy Tyndale to Judith Hart, 23 January 1974, People's History Museum, Manchester (hereafter PHM), HART/04/07.

[163] Mike Gatehouse, circular to all foreign committees, 10 January 1974, PHM, CSC/13/5.

[164] David Stephen, interview with the author, 16 May 2019.

which was led by Tariq Ali, and the slogan of the march was "solidarity with the armed resistance".[165] Chile therefore, not only became a cause célèbre for the British left, broadly speaking; it was, Stephen recalls, an issue taken up with particular vigour by the 'new left', of which Tariq Ali was perhaps the most recognizable constituent.[166] Ali, a leading figure in the International Marxist Group (IMG) and founder and editor of the radical newspaper *Black Dwarf*, had established his new left credentials alongside the likes of Rudi Dutschke, Joschka Fischer and Daniel Cohn-Bendit during the student protests of 1968. However, whereas the momentum of his continental counterparts had long since stalled, by the time of the Pinochet coup Ali found himself at the forefront of a political movement that seemed to be in the ascendency, a remarkable change in fortunes given the relative passivity of the British '68 experience.[167] As a matter of fact, less than twelve months prior to the Pinochet coup, Ali felt sufficiently emboldened by this apparent uptick in radicalism to presage a 'Coming British Revolution'.[168] As far as he was concerned, the 'only real alternative to capitalist policies' was 'provided by the revolutionary left groups as a whole. Despite their smallness and despite their many failings they represent the only way forward'.[169]

It is little wonder, therefore, that Ali's presence within the anti-Pinochet movement led many contemporary observers to suspect that the Chilean issue was being used as a Trojan horse of sorts – a vehicle for advancing radical left-wing politics in the UK. Such concerns were frequently addressed to then Shadow Minister for Overseas Development, Judith Hart, an outspoken critic of the Pinochet regime who corresponded frequently with the CSC and later became the Labour Party's representative on their committee.[170] Referring to Hart's calls for Britain to accept Chilean refugees, a letter from Evelyn Bamberger lays bare these anxieties while also indicating that the rhetoric of 'rights' had become highly politicized in this context: 'Dear Mrs. Hart, I think thousands of people are completely sick of you and your left-wingers who are always standing up "for rights" of unsavoury people to stay in this country, more especially when they come in under some cloak of disguise, in most cases real trouble makers and communists.'[171] Hart's support for the Chilean refugees drew particularly animated correspondence from her own constituents, who regarded those seeking asylum as 'scruffy little commies' and suggested that ulterior motives lay behind her attachment to their cause: 'Double standards of course. It is quite right if the Russians annex small nations like Hungary and Czechoslovakia but if the real friends of this country do anything, it is a safe bet that the Labour Party ... Peter Hain and that great British subject with the old English name of Tariq Ali will shout their heads off.'[172]

---

[165] Ibid.
[166] Ibid.
[167] See Evan Smith and Matthew Worley, 'Introduction: The Far Left in Britain from 1956', in *Against the Grain*, ed. Smith and Worley, 1–22.
[168] Tariq Ali, *The Coming British Revolution* (London: Jonathan Cape, 1972).
[169] Ibid., 10, quoted in Smith and Worley, 'Introduction', 1.
[170] See for example Wendy Tyndale to Judith Hart and Leslie Hirst, 28 December 1973, PHM, HART/04/07; Wendy Tyndale to Judith Hart, 28 January 1974, PHM, HART 04/07.
[171] Evelyn Bamberger to Judith Hart, 17 January 1973, PHM, HART/04/13.
[172] James Sawyer to Judith Hart, 24 September 1973, PHM, HART/04/13.

Indeed, the association of Hart (as a representative of the Labour Party) with leading figures within the British new left such as Ali and Hain – the young South African exile who had rapidly established himself as a leading figure within student politics and the Anti-Apartheid Movement upon his arrival in Britain during the late 1960s – appeared to strike an ominous chord that rang in many ears.[173]

Upon closer inspection, the apparent conflation of human rights concerns and radical left-wing politics evidenced by such correspondence was not the result of mere circumstance. Certainly, the Chilean coup was uniquely capable of uniting extra-parliamentary forces on the left because it featured the forceful deposition of a democratic socialist leader – in whom such high hopes were invested – by what would become a brutal right-wing dictatorial regime.[174] However, taking a broader view, it is possible to observe how the politics of Chile were prefigured by the evolution of extra-parliamentary campaigns on the left concerning issues of international security and racial equality during the late 1960s, which took on increasingly radical connotations as traditional civic engagement began to dissolve into a potent blend of left-wing radicalism, typified by the new social movements and the leading lights of student politics in Britain. According to Burkett, as the 1960s progressed, the radical left in Britain increasingly felt the need to create 'a cross-cutting organisation like the "Radical Alliance" created by Tariq Ali in 1965'.[175] It was this tendency towards synthesis, Burkett posits, that 'helped to shape the context' in which pressure groups such as CND and the AAM existed.[176] Simon Stevens' examination of the AAM bears eloquent witness to this process, demonstrating the growing influence of radical student groups such as the Young Liberals therein, and the role that key activists such as Peter Hain played in establishing the Stop the Seventy Tour Committee (STST), which successfully campaigned for the cancellation of the South African cricket team's scheduled tour of Britain in 1970.[177] Holger Nehring's analysis of the 'politics of security' in Britain and West Germany between 1945 and 1970, similarly, attests to this transformative process – of traditional forms of civic engagement and morally inspired protest being transformed, co-opted, and conflated with the political imperatives of new social movements that developed during the 1960s, acquiring a more radical persuasion as a result.[178]

Consequently, the objectives of these groups were often reframed in a discourse of solidarity – which, as Keck and Sikkink posit, developed alongside the 'human rights

---

[173] See also Mrs. V.C.L. George to Judith Hart, 23 February 1974, PHM, HART/04/13. For Hain's recollections of his entry into student politics, and the ways in which his anti-apartheid activism was shaped by the outlook and modus operandi of the 'new left', see Peter Hain, *Outside In* (London: Biteback, 2012), 49–50.

[174] See Eckel, 'Allende's Shadow, Leftist Furor, and Human Rights'; Moores, 'Solidarity for Chile, Transnational Activism and the Evolution of Human Rights': 115–36; Patrick William Kelly, 'The 1973 Chilean Coup and the Origins of Transnational Human Rights Activism', *Journal of Global History* 8, Issue 1 (2013): 165–86.

[175] Burkett, *Constructing Post-Imperial Britain*, 145.

[176] Ibid.

[177] Simon Stevens, 'Why South Africa? The Politics of Anti-Apartheid Activism in the Long 1970s', in *The Breakthrough*, ed. Eckel and Moyn, 211–15.

[178] Holger Nehring, *The Politics of Security: British and West German Protest Movements and the Early Cold War, 1945–1970* (Oxford: Oxford University Press, 2013), 247–301.

tradition' as the 'second main pattern for international advocacy among NGOs' post-1968, and often competed against it for ideational primacy within the spaces occupied by such networks.[179] While the frameworks of human rights and solidarity both 'involve relationships between oppressed peoples and those in a position to support them', they are separated by 'important conceptual differences'.[180] For instance, solidarity is said to involve 'a substantive dimension that right-based activism does not, that is, support based on a conviction of defending a just cause. Human rights appeals, on the other hand, raise the more procedural claims that violations of personhood or of recognized civil or legal norms and procedures are always unacceptable, whatever the victim's beliefs'.[181] The relationship between the two frameworks, moreover, has not always been complementary. In fact, despite 'considerable collaboration', human rights organizations have occasionally struggled to 'capture political space in advocacy networks for an approach that many schooled in a leftist solidarity tradition condemned as apolitical'.[182]

Closer inspection of the political debates vitiating the CSC lends support to this notion. Having donned their 'blue jeans and T-shirts' in order to infiltrate a meeting of the CSC at the London School of Economics in November 1974, Foreign Office officials were struck by the mood of the spectators and the questions that were put to the speakers, providing them 'with a vivid picture of the attitude of the militants who have captured the leadership of the Chile Solidarity Campaign'.[183] As the Campaign entered the New Year, the increasingly schismatic nature of its support was underscored by Christopher D. Crabbie of the FCO's Latin America Department, who informed the British Embassy in Santiago that Tariq Ali's IMG was attempting to force the Campaign's Committee, chiefly the moderates identified within the 'pre-Moscow group', into accepting a 'radical political manifesto based on the argument that the defeat of President Allende proves that true socialism cannot come to real power through parliamentary means'.[184] The IMG, Crabbie maintained, was 'determined not to let the Campaign become simply a pressure group on human rights'.[185]

Crabbie's despatch may have highlighted this 'internecine warfare' with an unmistakable hint of *Schadenfreude*.[186] Nonetheless, in spite of this fragmentation, and in spite of the fears emanating from the CSC's hierarchy concerning the Campaign's loss of momentum due to the international normalization of the Pinochet regime, the protest movement to which the CSC provided a great deal of impetus had already begun to shape government policy towards Chile following the electoral victory of the Labour Party – once again led by Harold Wilson – over Edward Heath's Conservative

---

[179] Keck and Sikkink, *Activists Beyond Borders*, 95.
[180] Ibid.
[181] Ibid.
[182] Ibid.
[183] C.D. Crabbie to P.W. Summerscale, 'A Public Meeting about Chile', 28 November 1974, TNA, FCO 7/2608.
[184] C.D. Crabbie to M.I.P. Webb, 'The Chile Solidarity Campaign', 15 January 1975, TNA, FCO 7/2795.
[185] Ibid.
[186] Ibid: 'As Chile vanishes into the inside pages of the British press, the conflict between these two groups is likely to intensify according to the law of left-wing fissility ... In the next few months I expect the Campaign to come under increasing pressure from the extreme left wing groups, and this will inevitably mean a decline in its coherence and influence.'

government on 28 February 1974.[187] As Grace Livingstone highlights, Wilson's victory, situated against a backdrop of trade union militancy and a multiplicity of NGO campaigns, provided the platform on which a prototypical 'ethical' foreign policy could be erected.[188] Although, as Livingstone notes, this description is somewhat 'anachronistic' given that the 'ethical' prefix became widely used in discussions of British foreign policy only during Robin Cook's tenure as Foreign Secretary (1997–2001), the Labour governments of Harold Wilson and Jim Callaghan nonetheless implemented radical policies towards the Pinochet regime in response to its flagrant human rights abuses: an arms embargo, acceptance of Chilean refugees, the cutting of export credits and the removal of the British Ambassador from the Embassy in Santiago.[189]

In so doing, Labour encountered stiff opposition from a phalanx of FCO officials who believed that the Pinochet regime provided greater opportunities for British business than the deposed Allende government.[190] By illuminating this tension, Livingstone raises a crucial question regarding the 'power of the elected official versus the bureaucrat'.[191] Indeed, Julian Filochowski's recollections certainly speak to a sense of deeply entrenched realism that guided the operations of the FCO. Shortly after arriving at the CIIR in 1973, Filochowski experienced his first 'encounter' with the FCO when he sought to bring a UN Security Council Resolution regarding the Panama Canal – then under US ownership – to the attention of the head of the FCO's Latin American Department. The UK, Filochowski maintained, surely ought to support Panama's aspirations for 'effective sovereignty, over all its territory'.[192] Filochowski's case was simple: 'in the end, surely morally speaking, we should be voting for this.'[193] The FCO response was withering: 'my dear young man, morality has got nothing to do with foreign policy.'[194] The question of the FCO's attachment to this proposition, and the ways in which it militated against the institutionalization of human rights concerns within the UK's foreign policymaking machinery, will be explored in greater depth within subsequent chapters of this book. Nonetheless, at this juncture, it is still worth underlining that the re-election of Wilson marked the arrival of a government more attuned to the human rights concerns being brought to their attention by a burgeoning network of human rights-focused NGOs. As Filochowski recalls: 'all the time people were interacting with the Foreign Office and the government and ... getting a much more sympathetic response than they'd ever done under Heath.'[195]

By the time of Owen's appointment as Foreign and Commonwealth Secretary, then, it seems that the human rights concerns amplified by pressure groups such as the CSC

---

[187] C.D. Crabbie to P.W. Summerscale, 'The Chile Solidarity Campaign', 6 December 1974, TNA, FCO 7/2608.
[188] Livingstone, *Britain and the Dictatorships of Argentina and Chile, 1973–82*, 2.
[189] Ibid., 18.
[190] See ibid., particularly Chapter Four: Ethical Foreign Policy? Labour Versus the Foreign Office (1974–1979).
[191] Ibid., 4.
[192] Filochowski interview; Richard Severo, 'U.S. in U.N. Council Vetoes Panama Canal Resolution', *New York Times*, 22 March 1973.
[193] Filochowski interview.
[194] Ibid.
[195] Ibid.

were beginning to make their mark on the formulation of British policy. The contemporaneous evolution of David Owen's political philosophy during the CSC's lobbying campaign, moreover, can be seen to mirror certain political imperatives of the Campaign, and of the NCCL. For example, while both can be seen as bridges of sorts between the established institutions of left-wing politics in Britain and newer forms of activism that first became visible during the late 1960s, Owen's meditations on the state of British socialism during the four years Labour had spent in opposition indicate a belief that the broadening of Labour's appeal across such generational and ideational boundaries was sorely needed.[196] Although Owen's brief engagement with the Justice for Rhodesia Campaign in early 1973 – which brought together pressure groups on the left, including the AAM and the Africa Bureau, and sought to impress upon the UK government its 'moral and historical obligations' towards the people of Rhodesia – may be taken as an indication that his personal sensitivity to issues regarding oppression and racial equality was becoming more acute, it was Owen's desire to appeal to emerging radical left-wing energies that would arguably play a more central role in determining his public adoption of the human rights cause.[197]

Having joined the 1963 Club (an offshoot of the Gaitskellite Campaign for Democratic Socialism) upon his entry into Parliament in 1966, Owen continued to associate himself with a group of high-profile Labour politicians on the right of the Party who supported Roy Jenkins' bid for Party leadership during the interregnum that separated the two Wilson governments.[198] The development of Owen's political outlook during Labour's time in opposition, however, is not so easily reconciled with Owen's membership of the 1963 Club, whose constituents, as Patrick Bell notes, were generally resistant to the attempts by the National Executive Committee (NEC) to institute a more radical socialist programme that would propel the Party back into office.[199] The dashed hopes of Wilson's premiership may have meant that Owen's re-election in the general election of 1970 'felt very hollow', but Owen's despondency did not lead to an abandonment or moderation of his principles.[200] Instead, the years following Labour's 1970 defeat witnessed Owen attempting to seize the initiative by casting off the prevailing 'negative' image of Labour and redefining it as a natural home for disaffected radicals. In August 1973, a month prior to the upheavals that would grip Chile and captivate transnational advocacy networks, Owen saw an opportunity to do precisely that:

---

[196] Moores, 'Solidarity for Chile, Transnational Activism and the Evolution of Human Rights', 117.

[197] Peter Mackay, '1973 Justice for Rhodesia Campaign: Press Statement', 30 January 1973, DOP, D709 2/15/2/3. See also David Owen to Peter Mackay, 5 February 1973, DOP, D709 2/15/2/3; Newsbrief: Rhodesia '73, published by the Africa Bureau for the 1973 Justice of Rhodesia Campaign, Vol. 1, No, 1, February 1973, DOP, D709 2/15/2/3.

[198] See Patrick Bell, *The Labour Party in Opposition, 1970–1974* (London: Routledge, 2004), 193–4. For Owen's recollections of how he came to be affiliated with this group, whose membership included Roy Jenkins, Anthony Crosland, Bill Rodgers and Roy Hattersley, see Owen, *Personally Speaking to Kenneth Harris*, 39–40; Owen, *Time to Declare*, 94–5. For analysis of this group and its influence within the Labour Party, see Leopoldo Brivati, 'The Campaign for Democratic Socialism 1960-1964' (PhD thesis, Queen Mary University of London, 1992).

[199] See Bell, *The Labour Party in Opposition*.

[200] Owen, *Time to Declare*, 164.

The anxieties, confusions and doubts of many of the electorate are apparent for all to see ... As a Party, we can always respond to this situation by increasing the volume of our verbal assault on the Government and simply including in our condemnation the Liberal Party for good measure. Sadly, there are already signs that this will be the dominant response, yet such a response will only strengthen the Party's identification in the minds of many electors as an increasingly negative one in British politics ... How can the Labour Party's position be improved? One way would be to recognise frankly that some, at least, of the present Liberal vote is a radical vote and that this radical vote is a crucial percentage of Liberal support for the Labour Party to attract, if it is to form a majority Government.[201]

To capture this radical vote, however, a re-evaluation of the Party's modus operandi was required. Instead of a reliance on 'traditional socialist solutions', an exploration of 'what is loosely called "the New Left"' was called for; 'we need ... to discover our radicalism'.[202] According to the journalist Stephen Fay, this proclamation would have occurred around the time that Owen discovered the work of the French utopian socialist Pierre Proudhon. Supposedly, Owen found Proudhon's handling of the 'compromise between control by the state and anarchy attractive, and it broadened his Christian socialism'.[203] In light of Owen's philosophical development hitherto, it would perhaps be more accurate to say that his reading of Proudhon – if he did in fact find this experience as impactful as Fay suggests – *refined* his outlook, adding further intellectual ballast to his long-standing convictions while training his eye on those elements of left-wing politics that were increasingly seeking an outlet through extra-parliamentary means of expression.

Owen's solicitation of these radical political forces speaks to the historic complexity of the relationship between the Labour Party and the new left, particularly as it pertains to the former's capacity to view the latter as a source of 'ideological renewal' (on the rare occasions that it sought to engage with it), and the latter's tendency to regard the Labour Party with 'ambivalence' if not hostility – 'a positive obstacle to the development of the authentically socialist politics it sought to foster'.[204] Moreover, when viewed alongside the contemporaneous development of a British human rights network in the aftermath of the Chilean coup, which had not only effected a change in the relationship

---

[201] David Owen, Speech at the St Aubyn Labour Party Hall, Devonport, Plymouth, 6 August 1973, DOP, D709 2/9/1.
[202] Ibid.
[203] Fay, 'What makes David run?' *Sunday Times*.
[204] Madeleine Davis, 'Can One Nation Labour Learn from the New Left?' *Renewal* 21, Issue 1 (Spring 2013): 5; Madeleine Davis, '"Labourism" and the New Left', in *Interpreting the Labour Party: Approaches to Labour Politics and History*, ed. John Callaghan, Steven Fielding and Steve Ludlam (Manchester: Manchester University Press, 2003), 39. For additional coverage of the relationship between the new left and Labour politics, see Geoffrey Foote, *The Labour Party's Political Thought: A History* (Basingstoke: Palgrave Macmillan, 1985); Ben Jackson, *Equality and the British Left* (Manchester: Manchester University Press, 2007); David Fowler, 'From "Danny the Red" to British Student Power: Labour and the International Student Revolts of the 1960s', in *The British Labour Party and the Wider World*, ed. Paul Corthorn and Jonathan Davis (London and New York: Tauris Academic Studies, 2008), 167–189.

between social movements and Britain's diplomatic machinery, but had clearly exhibited the influence of new left radicals schooled in a tradition of internationalist left-wing solidarity, these philosophical musings help us to understand why Owen was so attentive to the internationalist engagement that was, by the time of his appointment as Foreign Secretary in February 1977, 'stirring ever more forcefully outside parliament', and appreciative of the fact that appeals couched in the language of human rights were capable of galvanising such forces.[205] Of course, the politics of Chile were by no means the only factor which had served to elevate human rights to a degree of prominence hitherto unseen in international affairs by the time of Owen's appointment. For instance, as Owen notes in *Human Rights* – his exegesis on the subject and its myriad foreign policy applications published in August 1978 – the thawing of Cold War tensions and the 'establishment of a dialogue between the advanced industrialised nations and those of the developing world' along with the 'appalling violations of human rights in a number of countries' including Chile, had since the 'beginning of the decade ... helped to sharpen public concern in many different countries and continents about the condition of human rights worldwide'.[206] The book's opening chapter ('Human Rights in Britain'), however, is clearly illustrative of the political capital that Owen had come to invest in the human rights cause, and can be seen to reflect the key tenets of a political philosophy that had been decades in the making.

Owen begins by taking the reader though his interpretation of post-war British politics on the left, in which the foundational ideas of British socialism had been repeatedly buffeted by the forces of materialism and undermined by an increasing acceptance of pragmatism. This began when the prosperity of the 1950s and 'the apparently ever-rising living standards of the population led many to conclude that the bad old days had gone forever, and with them the relevance of socialist values'.[207] Seeping insidiously into socialist thought through the assumption that the solutions to the problems of inequality should be conceptualized exclusively in terms of economic growth, this belief had apparently calcified by the early 1960s.[208] Labour, Owen posited in an October 1977 interview, had also made the mistake of 'thinking there was a link between size and socialism', a connection Owen disavowed, arguing that 'size breeds bureaucracy, and bureaucracy militates against change'.[209] This was not merely undesirable; it also constituted, in Owen's estimation, a subversion of the 'British' tradition of democratic socialism, rooted in concepts of 'community co-operation, participation, workers' democracy', and 'de-centralised decision-making'.[210] In Owen's view, the 'essential value of socialism' was altruism, a virtue that could be cultivated and given fresh meaning if articulated in the language of human rights: 'Socialism means nurturing the instinct to help one's neighbour to live as part of a community, it means answering basic human wishes to influence their destiny. Socialism means enlarging

---

[205] Eckel, *The Ambivalence of Good*, 196.
[206] Owen, *Human Rights*, 14.
[207] Ibid., 5.
[208] See ibid., 6.
[209] Interview with William Wolff, *Evening News*, 5 October 1977, DOP, D709 2/7/6/7.
[210] Owen, *Human Rights*, 4.

and nurturing the altruistic element in us all. The espousal of human rights is a radical policy, a natural policy for socialists to champion.'²¹¹

In 'Human Rights in Britain', the target of Owen's treatise is also made abundantly clear: namely, those disaffected souls who had, in the wake of 1968, disavowed party politics but continued to seek extra-parliamentary outlets through which they could express their concerns. 'Some of the energies, idealism and commitment of the traditional centre socialist', Owen noted, were 'already finding their outlet beyond the framework of conventional politics' in the form of pressure groups such as 'the Disablement Income Group, the Child Poverty Action Group, Shelter, Oxfam and the Friends of the Earth'.²¹² Radical thinking in Britain, therefore, was not dead: 'The wish to change society remains – particularly amongst the young', but it had largely been 'strangled by committees' and then deadened by the 'bureaucratic embrace' of Whitehall.²¹³ Much of current political language, moreover, was 'ritually divisive and so polarised that it strikes very few sparks and fails to stimulate commitment in the young … is rarely inspiring and though inevitably technical infrequently draws on underlying values'.²¹⁴

Upon publication, Owen's book was understandably criticized in some quarters for politicizing human rights overtly. Owen had, in the eyes of some contemporary commentators, positioned himself as 'a socialist faith healer' with 'principles as binding as the Ten Commandments but somehow less realistic'.²¹⁵ General Secretary of Amnesty International Martin Ennals accordingly sounded a cautionary note in his review of the book. *Human Rights* was a commendable effort in some respects. After all, 'it is rare for a British Foreign Minister to try to explain publicly and in writing the basis of his thinking … it is not often clear that there is any theoretical basis to British foreign policy other than a hopscotch pattern of isolated interest points'.²¹⁶ What Ennals found 'disappointing', however, was that much of the book's opening chapter was 'devoted to showing the high ethical values of democratic socialism rather than the importance of a human rights approach from whatever political angle one has chosen. Human rights is the paper objective of all parties and indeed all politicians. It is not helpful for the overall debate to try to identify them with one particular moral philosophy'.²¹⁷

Conclusion

By exploring how the key tenets of David Owen's political philosophy developed along parallel tracks to the evolving internationalist engagement of British extra-parliamentary pressure campaigns such as CND and the AAM during the 'long 1960s',

---

²¹¹ Ibid., 10, 13.
²¹² Ibid., 8.
²¹³ Ibid., 9.
²¹⁴ Ibid.
²¹⁵ Gordon Brook-Shepherd, 'Human ills that Dr Owen cannot cure', *Sunday Telegraph*, 3 September 1978; Norman Cook, 'Big Jim's little disaster', *Liverpool Daily Post*, 24 August 1978, DOP, D709 2/9/6.
²¹⁶ Martin Ennals, 'Politics and Human Rights', *Socialist Commentator* (November 1978), TNA, FCO 58/1414.
²¹⁷ Ibid.

this chapter has attempted to provide some much-needed context to Ennals' critique, explaining *how* and *why* David Owen was able and willing to frame human rights as a 'natural policy for socialists to champion' by the time of his unlikely appointment as Foreign Secretary in February 1977. It has been posited that Owen's adoption of the human rights cause was, although motivated by strategic considerations, entirely consonant with a political outlook that had been decades in the making. Imbued with the conviction that politics – and particularly democratic socialist politics – could not survive in a moral vacuum on account of his exposure to the Christian socialism of Mervyn Stockwood during his student days at Cambridge, this strongly held belief became more deeply entrenched during the 1960s as the Wilson government drifted towards managerialism, and the Labour Party became increasingly detached from its radical foundations. This process of disenchantment, moreover, would lead Owen to search for rapprochement with the spirit of left-wing radicalism associated with the new left as a means of reconnecting Labour with its radical roots. Meanwhile, the internationalist commitments of British extra-parliamentary groups on the left such as CND and the AAM, which had exhibited a concern for the moral character of Britain's international role since the 1950s, were being shaped by their exposure to the new social movements that would emerge over the course of the following decade, a development that led activists concerned with the politics of security and racial equality to situate their engagement within a framework of left-wing solidarity. These intersections help us to understand how a particular human rights 'vernacular' coalesced around the politics of Chile in the aftermath of Salvador Allende's deposition in September 1973, and became closely associated with prominent figures within the British new left. Indeed, while concepts of human rights and solidarity are not one and the same, these ideational frameworks developed alongside each other within the spaces occupied by the transnational advocacy networks that began to emerge during the late 1960s, often competed for activists' attention, and, as evidenced by the case of the CSC, led to the apparent conflation of the two. Hence, as Owen was attempting to build bridges between the parliamentary Labour Party and the grassroots political campaigns that were increasingly seeking extra-parliamentary modes of expression, the language of human rights was demonstrating an ability to captivate and galvanize the internationalist sentiments that sprang up alongside the new social movements with which Owen sought reconciliation.

Consequently, this chapter has approached the subject of David Owen's political outlook from a fresh perspective, challenging the notion that his criticisms of the Wilson government – and his affiliation with groups and individuals on the right of the Labour Party – were somehow symptomatic of a general detachment from the intellectual foundations of Labourism. By building upon recent scholarship concerning civic engagement in post-war Britain and the emergence of the new social movements of the 1960s, the preceding paragraphs have also problematized conventional narratives regarding the trajectory of the British '68. By looking beyond its failure to ignite, we are able to observe the lasting influence that the intellectual currents of the British new left exerted over activist networks in ways that prefigured the development of human rights activism in Britain during the 1970s. As such, we are able to see the validity in Jan Eckel's assertion that, instead of focusing on the ways in which the upheavals of 1968 underscored the somewhat peripheral status of human rights as an international discourse (the 'human rightsless' interpretation of 1968), historians should appreciate the ways in which the 'rapid upsurge that ideas of human rights would experience in the following decade had a great deal to do with what happened in that year'.[218] Accordingly, this chapter has also lent its support to Eckel's contention that the 1970s, while undoubtedly a moment of substantive 'transformation' in the history of human rights, ought not to be separated from the formative moments that came before.[219]

In its attempts to underscore the significance of contextualization in the writing of human rights history, amply demonstrated by scholars such as Lora Wildenthal and Mark Philip Bradley, this chapter has only briefly alluded to some of the key international developments which served to elevate human rights as a global discourse during the 1970s.[220] The following chapter, however, will begin to explore in more depth the altered geopolitical climate within which David Owen's human rights-based approach to foreign affairs was constructed, assess how the growing influence of actors within civil society shaped Owen's approach to human rights promotion, and analyse how structural imperatives and Owen's personal proclivities came together to define the parameters within which human rights concerns could alter the trajectory of British foreign policy during his tenure as Foreign and Commonwealth Secretary.

---

[218] Eckel, *The Ambivalence of Good*, 115.
[219] Ibid., 8.
[220] Wildenthal, *The Language of Human Rights in West German*; Bradley, 'American Vernaculars'.

2

The Morality of Compromise

Selling Arms to El Salvador and Iran

Clearly, we ought to regard Samuel Moyn's assertion that human rights 'emerged in the 1970s seemingly from nowhere' with a degree of caution – the human rights advocacy that would become increasingly prominent over the course of the decade had been prefigured by the emergence of transnational activist networks during the 1960s.[1] Nonetheless, the aforementioned 'explosion of international civil society' can be seen as a constitutive aspect of a much broader phenomenon that opened 'a new window of opportunity for international human rights' during the 1970s.[2] While NGOs operating within transnational advocacy networks served to sharpen international responses to human rights violations in Chile following the deposition of Salvador Allende in September 1973, the evolution of such networks was both a reflection and an accelerant of an increasingly interconnected international order in which the suffering of individuals in distant lands became at once more visible and potentially treatable.[3] The emergence of these 'new affective bonds between the individual, the state and the world community' was, in part, the result of recent and far-reaching technological innovations which 'made communications faster and cheaper, with the result that news of humanitarian crises travelled more quickly than ever before'.[4] It was also a consequence of momentous political developments. Détente between East and West and the codification of human rights provisions through the CSCE – a forum for dialogue and negotiation consisting of thirty-three European nations, the United States and

---

[1] Moyn, *The Last Utopia*, 3.
[2] Michael Cotey Morgan, 'The Seventies and the Rebirth of Human Rights', in *The Shock of the Global: The 1970s in Perspective*, ed. Niall Ferguson, Charles S. Maier, Erez Manela and Daniel J. Sargent (Cambridge, MA: Belknap Press of Harvard University Press, 2011), 240.
[3] For examples of scholarship concerning the increasingly interconnected nature of the international system in the 1970s (real or perceived), see Akira Iriye, *Global Community: The Role of International Organizations in the Making of the Contemporary World* (Berkeley: University of California Press, 2002); Daniel J. Sargent, 'The United States and Globalization in the 1970s', in *The Shock of the Global*, ed. Ferguson, Maier, Manela and Sargent, 49–64; Matthew Connelly, 'Future Shock: The End of the World as They Knew it', in ibid., 337–50.
[4] Mark Philip Bradley, 'The Origins of the 1970s Global Human Rights Imagination', in *The Long 1970s: Human Rights, East–West Détente and Transnational Relations*, ed. Poul Villaume, Rasmus Mariager, and Helle Porsdam (London: Routledge, 2016), 17; Morgan, 'The Seventies and the Rebirth of Human Rights', 240.

Canada – served to situate human rights firmly within the context of Cold War politics, undermining principles of non-interference and the primacy of state sovereignty, and creating an institutional framework around which activist movements on both sides of the Iron Curtain could coalesce.[5] Furthermore, the entry into force of the two UN Human Rights Covenants concerning Civil and Political Rights and Economic, Social and Cultural Rights in 1976 signalled the increasing institutionalization of human rights concerns within international politics.[6]

Several factors, then, 'converged in the mid-1970s which together signalled a step-change in the human rights regime and which challenged realist assumptions about the nature of international relations'.[7] This convergence, moreover, yielded perhaps the clearest indication of the recent elevation of human rights within international discourse: 'the intrusion of human rights into the diplomacy of western states'.[8] In their attempts to translate rhetorical commitments to international human rights promotion from theory into practice, however, policymakers recapitulated age-old debates concerning the realist-idealist schism within international relations.[9] Thus, noting the ubiquity of human rights concerns within international discourse, typified by the crusading example set by the Carter administration in the US (1977–81), Hans J. Morgenthau – philosopher and international relations theorist of the realist tradition – felt compelled to shine a withering spotlight on the eternal difficulties attendant to the advancement of what may be deemed an 'ethical' foreign policy:

> the United States is a great power with manifold interests throughout the world, of which human rights is only one and not the most important one, and the United States is incapable of consistently following the path of the defence of human rights without manoeuvring itself into a Quixotic position ... the principle of the defence of human rights cannot be consistently applied in foreign policy because it can and it must come [into] conflict with other interests that may be more important than the defense of human rights in a particular instance.[10]

---

[5] See for example Daniel C. Thomas, *The Helsinki Effect: International Norms, Human Rights, and the Demise of Communism* (Princeton: Princeton University Press, 2001); Sarah B. Snyder, *Human Rights Activism and the End of the Cold War: A Transnational History of the Helsinki Network* (Cambridge: Cambridge University Press, 2011); *The CSCE and the End of the Cold War: Diplomacy, Societies and Human Rights, 1972–1990*, ed. Nicholas Badalassi and Sarah B. Snyder (New York and Oxford: Berghahn, 2019).

[6] Jack Donnelly, 'The Social Construction of International Human Rights', in *Human Rights in Global Politics*, ed. Tim Dunne and Nicholas J. Wheeler, (Cambridge: Cambridge University Press, 1999), 76.

[7] Tim Dunne and Marianne Hanson, 'Human Rights in International Relations', in *Human Rights: Politics and Practice*, ed. Michael Goodhart, 3rd edn (Oxford: Oxford University Press, 2016), 48.

[8] Ibid., 49.

[9] For a general exposition of theoretical and practical issues concerning the situation of ethical imperatives within the foreign policies of nation states, see Karen E. Smith and Margot Light, 'Introduction', in *Ethics and Foreign Policy*, ed. Karen E. Smith and Margot Light (Cambridge: Cambridge University Press, 2001), 1–11; Jack Donnelly, *Universal Human Rights: In Theory and Practice*, 2nd edn (New York: Cornell University Press, 2003), 155–72; Mike W. Doyle, 'Ethics and Foreign Policy: a Speculative Essay', in *New Labour's Foreign Policy*, ed. Richard Little and Mark Wickham-Jones (Manchester: Manchester University Press, 2000), 49–60; R.J. Vincent, *Human Rights and International Relations* (Cambridge: Cambridge University Press, 1986), 111–52.

[10] Hans J. Morgenthau, *Human Rights and Foreign Policy* (New York: Council on Religion and Foreign Affairs, 1979), 4–7.

This chapter will explore how British diplomatic perspectives on the human rights 'breakthrough' of the 1970s can help to further illuminate these debates, exploring the spaces within which human rights promotion began to shape British foreign policymaking during this highly significant moment in the history of human rights and international relations. Following an examination of the steps that were taken to establish more consistent, formalized processes of human rights promotion within the FCO during the weeks and months leading up to David Owen's appointment as Foreign Secretary in February 1977, this chapter will address how British policymakers sought to reconcile the conflicting imperatives of human rights advocacy and the pursuit of economic and strategic interests in the context of Britain's bilateral relations. This will be undertaken by focusing on two case studies concerning the supply of arms to well-known violators of human rights: the repressive Salvadoran government of Carlos Humberto Romero, and the Republic of Iran, governed by the autocratic rule of Shah Mohammad Reza Pahlavi. These two examples have been selected because they each serve to define, in their own unique way, the narrow parameters within which human rights concerns were able to exert an influence over the formulation of British foreign policy during Owen's tenure as Foreign Secretary.

By investigating the decision to cancel the sale of armoured vehicles to the government of El Salvador in January 1978, this chapter will, in turn, continue to assess the evolving relationship between NGOs participating in transnational advocacy networks and the British foreign policy establishment, detailing the highly effective lobbying campaign spearheaded by the Catholic Institute for International Relations (CIIR). Indeed, by revealing how the CIIR was able to leverage human rights concerns by bringing the combined pressure of sympathetic journalists, parliamentarians, civil servants, and representatives of the Catholic Church within Britain to bear on the foreign policy establishment, the El Salvador case study demonstrates that bureaucratic inertia within Whitehall was not an insurmountable obstacle on the path towards a more 'ethical' approach to foreign policy. Nonetheless, this case study also serves to lay bare the prevalence of economic concerns within Whitehall, and the ways in which such interests – typified by the British arms lobby – militated against the promotion of human rights in British foreign policy at this particular juncture.[11] The oppositional nature of this relationship will be underscored by demonstrating how Owen's public adoption of the human rights cause served, in more ways than one, to problematize British–Iranian relations during his time at the Foreign Office. Sensitive to Iran's significance as a pro-Western power in the Middle East and appreciative of the opportunities that the Shah's custom provided for British business, Owen would continue to champion human rights promotion as a guiding principle of British foreign policy while simultaneously supporting the Shah's dictatorial regime, which was struggling to quell the civil unrest that would eventually topple his empire in early 1979.

---

[11] Regarding the influence of the British arms industry during the 1970s, see for example Nikolas Gardner, 'The Harold Wilson Government, Airwork Services Limited, and the Saudi Arabian Air Defence Scheme, 1965–1973', *Journal of Contemporary History* 42, No. 2 (2007): 345–63; Malcolm M. Craig, '"I Think We Cannot Refuse the Order": Britain, America, Nuclear Non-Proliferation, and the Indian Jaguar Deal', *Cold War History* 16, No. 1 (2016): 61–81; Okhan Erciyas, 'British Dilemmas: Arms Sales and Human Rights in Anglo-Iranian Relations (1968–1979)' (PhD thesis, University of Leicester, 2020).

This chapter, therefore, will begin to situate hitherto neglected British diplomatic perspectives on the so-called human rights 'breakthrough' of the 1970s within the rapidly expanding scholarly literature on human rights and international relations. It will also develop the previous chapter's engagement with transnational advocacy networks by exploring their ability to subvert, complicate or bypass traditional modes of policy formulation, in addition to building upon recent scholarship concerning the FCO's interest in trade promotion during the twentieth century.[12] Moreover, by exploring how Owen – in lieu of a clear and objective FCO policy on human rights promotion – grappled with the ad hoc reconciliation of competing ethical and strategic imperatives, this chapter will not only address enduring debates surrounding the appropriate situation of ethical concerns within the foreign policies of nation states, but will also examine the philosophical foundations on which the Foreign Secretary sought to construct a human rights policy capable of synthesising matters of principle and expediency.

Human rights in the FCO: The human rights comparative assessment

David Owen's public commitment to the elevation of human rights considerations within British foreign policy, initially outlined during his maiden speech as Foreign and Commonwealth Secretary in the House of Commons on 1 March 1977, was underlined days later when he addressed the annual banquet of the Diplomatic and Commonwealth Writers Association.[13] Owen – in an oblique reference to the extra-parliamentary expressions of internationalist solidarity and human rights engagement highlighted in Chapter 1 – reiterated his conviction that foreign policy should 'reflect the values of society', and argued that 'those who conduct foreign affairs should respond positively to the weight of public opinion and concern'.[14] Consequently, Owen stated, Britain would take a 'stand on human rights in every corner of the globe'.[15] Certainly, it is worth exercising caution in ascribing the speech's intellectual content to Owen in its entirety – as John Dickie notes, no Foreign Secretary 'ever starts with a clean slate'.[16] This particular speech was due to be delivered by Owen's predecessor, Anthony Crosland, who had spent a great deal of time working on earlier drafts during the weeks leading up to his untimely death on 19 February.[17] The speech also reflected the input of myriad Foreign Office officials.[18]

---

[12] See *The Foreign Office, Commerce and British Foreign Policy in the Twentieth Century*, ed. John Fisher, Effie Pedaliu and Richard Smith (Basingstoke: Palgrave Macmillan, 2016).
[13] See 'Foreign Affairs', 1 March 1977, *Hansard: House of Commons*, Volume 927.
[14] Annual Banquet of the Diplomatic and Commonwealth Writers Association speech, 3 March 1977.
[15] Ibid.
[16] John Dickie, *Inside the Foreign Office* (London: Chapman, 1992), 288.
[17] See Owen, *Time to Declare*, 281; Sir Brian Lee Crowe, interview with Gwenda Scarlett, BDOHP, 15 October 2003, Churchill College, Cambridge, available at https://www.chu.cam.ac.uk/media/uploads/files/Crowe.pdf (last accessed 9 January 2020).
[18] Bernard D. Nossiter, 'Britain Backs Carter on Human Rights', *Washington Post*, 6 March 1977.

Figure 2.1 David Owen arriving at 10 Downing Street the day after his unexpected appointment as Foreign Secretary, 22 February 1977 (Fred Mott/Evening Standard/Getty Images).

Nevertheless, by suggesting that the 'Foreign Office types had put into Owen's mouth a sophisticated view of détente and rights', and that 'Owen's principal contribution to the speech' was to 'edit down some of the repetition and delete a De Tocqueville quote that was more in keeping with the intellectual style of his predecessor', Bernard D. Nossiter of the *Washington Post* drastically understates Owen's influence.[19] In fact, a record of a meeting in which a draft of the speech was discussed reveals that Owen, feeling that the government was not doing enough to align itself with public opinion on human rights issues, 'said that he would consider taking a stronger line than hitherto on human rights and might wish to write this part of the speech himself'.[20] This version of events is substantiated by a despatch from the US Embassy in London: 'A source close to the Prime Minister has told us that Dr. Owen's March 3 speech on human rights was very much his own idea. It is a cause to which the Foreign Secretary is personally committed.'[21] As such, it appears that the *Guardian*'s Patrick Keatley was

[19] Ibid.
[20] 'Secretary of State's Meeting to Discuss his Speech to the Diplomatic and Commonwealth Writer's Association (3 March) Wednesday 23 February at 12 Noon', TNA, FCO 58/1143.
[21] London Embassy to State Department, 'HMG and Human Rights', 7 March 1977, The National Archives, College Park, MD., Central Foreign Policy Files, Record Group 59 – General Records of the Department of State, Electronic Telegrams, 1977, available at https://aad.archives.gov/aad/create pdf?rid=47775&dt=2532&dl=1629 (last accessed 9 January 2020).

more accurate in his assessment of the speech and the ways in which it 'bore the personal stamp of the new Foreign Secretary'.[22]

As demonstrated within the previous chapter, Owen's adoption of the human rights cause was not only influenced by his desire to 'bind' growing expressions of internationalist engagement within Britain to the state; it was entirely consonant with the key tenets of his political philosophy, which had been decades in the making.[23] It is, however, also important to note that the example set by Jimmy Carter's Democratic administration following his victory in the US presidential election of 1976 had undoubtedly rendered the promotion of international human rights a more feasible and propitious endeavour. Carter had campaigned for the presidency attempting to infuse a sense of morality into the conduct of US foreign policy though the promotion of international human rights – a concern Carter would underline in his inaugural address of 20 January 1977: 'Because we are free,' Carter stated, 'we can never be indifferent to the fate of freedom elsewhere. Our moral sense dictates a clear-cut preference for those societies which share with us an abiding respect for individual human rights'.[24] Reflecting on the impact and timing of the Carter administration's statement of intent, Owen concedes that 'we were in their slipstream in many respects, if the truth be told'.[25] Contemporary commentators, therefore, were understandably quick to interpret Owen's public adoption of a human rights-based approach to foreign affairs as a mere adjunct to that of the Carter administration, undertaken as a means of ingratiating the Callaghan government with the recently elected President before Owen and his Prime Minister departed for Washington the following week.[26] However, although Owen's *amplification* of human rights concerns within the context of British foreign policy had certainly been influenced by the US President's moralistic approach to foreign affairs, suggestions that this represented a case of jumping on the Carter bandwagon at an auspicious moment can only be pushed so far. As Foreign Office officials were at pains to point out when briefing the Washington Embassy for a meeting with Carter's Assistant Secretary of State for Human Rights and Humanitarian Affairs in April 1977, attempts to formalize the FCO's human rights commitments were already at an advanced stage.[27]

Dismissing the 'very limited amount of ill-formed criticism' that suggested Owen's speech 'represented a me-too approach by the Secretary of State after Carter's inaugural speech', Michael Simpson-Orlebar of the FCO's UN Department referred to an

---

[22] Patrick Keatley, 'Owen champions human rights', *Guardian*, 4 March 1977.
[23] Eckel, *The Ambivalence of Good*, 196.
[24] 'Inaugural Address of President Jimmy Carter', *Public Papers of the Presidents of the United States, Jimmy Carter, 1977, Book I* (Washington, DC.: United States Government Printing Office, 1977), 3. For Carter's statements on human rights and US foreign policy prior to his election, see *Foreign Relations of the United States, 1977–1980, Volume I, Foundations of Foreign Policy, 1974–1980*, ed. Kristin L. Ahlberg (Washington, DC.: Government Printing Office, 2014), documents 2, 4, 6, 9.
[25] Owen interview, 6 December 2017.
[26] See for example Vincent Ryder, 'Human Rights Basic to Foreign Policy, Says Owen', *Daily Telegraph*, 4 March 1977; Bernard D. Nossiter, 'Britain Supports Carter Stand on Human Rights: Britain Backs Carter's View on Human Rights Question', *Washington Post*, 4 March 1977; Jurek Martin, 'U.S. welcomes Owen's human rights speech', *Financial Times*, 5 March 1977.
[27] See M.K.O. Simpson-Orlebar to C.W. Squire, 'Human Rights', 21 April 1977, TNA, FCO 58/1143.

'assessments exercise, which showed a heightened concern by HMG for human rights', pointing out that this 'was put in hand by Ministers well before Carter had emerged as the Presidential candidate most likely to succeed'.[28] In light of the measures taken by Labour governments to heed the concerns of human rights campaigners vis-à-vis the governments of South Africa and Chile, human rights concerns had in fact begun to gather momentum within the Foreign Office from early 1976 onwards.[29] Summarizing a letter sent by Amnesty International's Martin Ennals to his brother David – then Minister of State for Foreign and Commonwealth Affairs – on 4 February 1976, P.M. Maxey records that the former had enquired about 'the possibility of the FCO initiating a procedure, such as the US State Department recently established, whereby our Embassies would report on the human rights situation in countries with which we have diplomatic relations'.[30] Initially, Ennals' suggestion that this procedure could inform the formulation and implementation of UK aid programmes did not find a receptive audience. Although conceding that '[a]ll ways in which Britain could help promote human rights in the world deserve careful consideration', Maxey concluded that 'the disadvantages of Mr Ennals' suggestion outweigh the possible advantages'.[31] This message was duly conveyed in David Ennals' response on 9 March.[32]

Resistance to the notion of inserting human rights criteria into Britain's overseas aid policy, however, would face a much sterner test following the seemingly unilateral decision of the Minister of State for Overseas Development, Reginald Prentice, to do just that. Prentice, according to a record of a telephone conversation with Parliamentary Secretary of State, Evan Luard, had 'firmly decided' in early 1976 that 'a country's human rights record must be taken into account in determining aid'.[33] When it became clear that 'Mr Prentice would not be budged from this position', Luard decided to 'let the matter drop' and, during the weeks and months that followed, the debate concerning the appropriate situation of human rights considerations alongside Britain's pre-existing foreign policy imperatives continued apace.[34] During a 28 July meeting of FCO ministers, the decision was made to publish two papers, 'one to be produced by the FCO Planning Staff to consider the means by which some comparative assessment of human rights infringement might be made and the other by the ODM [Ministry of Overseas Development] to consider the ways in which human rights factors might be

---

[28] Ibid.
[29] See 'Record of a Meeting held at the State Department on 20 June 1977 at 2:00 PM', DOP, D709 2/7/15/2.
[30] P.M. Maxey to Mr Weir; Mr Green, 25 February 1976, TNA, FCO 58/1009.
[31] Ibid.
[32] D. Ennals to M. Ennals, 9 March 1976, TNA, FCO 58/1009: 'First, I should assure you that our Embassies already cover the human rights field in their reporting. There would be little advantage and some extra cost in turning this into a systematic routine.' Alongside such logistical considerations, Ennals expressed concerns regarding the 'principle of relating aid to a government's performance in the human rights field', noting that if 'after adopting the policy you suggest, we wished to sustain the level of our aid to a particular country ... we could be misinterpreted as giving a seal of approval to a government whose human rights record was unsatisfactory'.
[33] A.F. Green to Mr Dales, 'Oral Question for the ODM about Aid to Indonesia', 14 June 1976, TNA, FCO 58/1009.
[34] Ibid.; D. Williams to Reg Prentice, 'Human Rights & Aid', 22 June 1976, TNA, FCO 58/1010.

taken into account in the administration of the aid programme'.³⁵ Luard quickly became a vocal proponent of the former.

In this capacity, Luard encountered stiff opposition from Michael Palliser, Permanent Under-Secretary of State and Head of the Diplomatic Service. Palliser's Steering Committee discussed the two papers on 6 October and concluded that attempts to codify human rights provisions within the FCO would be destined to fail because they 'would be unqualified and based upon partial information', providing 'a subjective and possibly misleading picture' that 'would in turn add to our foreign policy problems'.³⁶ This interpretation was clearly not shared by Luard. In fact, on the same day that Palliser articulated his concerns regarding the efficacy of the comparative assessment, Luard wrote to the Foreign and Commonwealth Secretary, summarising his attached paper as follows: 'In brief the paper concludes that, while there would be significant difficulties, it would be possible to undertake such an assessment, based on a system of marking by qualified observers from within the Diplomatic Service'.³⁷ Underscoring the viability of such an exercise by citing the recent precedent set by the US government, Luard concluded his message with a forceful contention: 'the concern on human rights questions is as great in this country as in the US ... there is as much demand that this concern should be reflected in our foreign policy'.³⁸ There was, therefore, 'no reason why we should not attempt ourselves at least the type of comparative assessment which is the pre-condition for taking account of such questions in our policy'.³⁹

While Palliser's Steering Committee, in keeping with his aforementioned reservations, advised ministers not to proceed with the exercise, 'this advice was submitted and rejected'.⁴⁰ This sense of divergence between ministers and officials as regards the perceived efficacy – or indeed, desirability – of instituting a comparative human rights assessment was clearly articulated in B.L. Crowe's minute to M.S. Weir on 26 January 1977:

> As you know, I share your concern. I do not, however, think we can stop this wagon rolling until we have some solid road block to put in its way. The PUS has expressed his own and the Steering Committee's serious doubts about the human rights exercise to Mr Luard, but Ministers have determined to go ahead with it and generally to study human rights in the foreign policy context. They will not be dissuaded by officials sniping from the sidelines; indeed their resistance to official advice might be increased. They will feel that, with the Americans already more active, at least publicly, than we are in examining human rights issues and with the prospect of this activity becoming even greater under the new Administration, there is every reason for HMG to study the matter in some depth.⁴¹

---

³⁵ Undated minute addressed to Minister for Overseas Development with attached draft paper, 'Human Rights and Aid', TNA, FCO 58/1010.
³⁶ Michael Palliser to Mr Luard, 'Proposed Comparative Assessment of the Human Rights Performance of Foreign Governments', 13 October 1976, TNA, FCO 58/1143.
³⁷ Evan Luard to Anthony Crosland, 13 October 1976, TNA, FCO 58/1143.
³⁸ Ibid.
³⁹ Ibid.
⁴⁰ J.O. Kerr to Mr Weir, 'Human Rights and Foreign Policy', 7 February 1977, TNA, FCO 8/2997.
⁴¹ B.L. Crowe to Mr Weir, 'Human Rights in Foreign Policy', 26 January 1977, TNA, FCO 8/2997.

Such misgivings clearly lend support to the notion that the British diplomatic machinery tends to regard innovative initiatives with suspicion. Although there is a widespread acknowledgment among scholars of political institutions that bureaucracies concerned with foreign policymaking tend towards the maintenance of the status quo, making the 'embedding' of novel ideas a difficult task, the British diplomatic machinery in particular has been noted for its innate conservatism and its aversion to 'visionary thinking'.[42] As William Wallace posited in 1977, this bureaucratic inertia was rooted in the self-image cultivated by civil servants working within the FCO: 'they see themselves as defending the continuity of British policy vis-à-vis politicians whose perspective is often no longer than the next election … they are in a real sense protectors of the national interest against the immediate pressures of party interests'.[43] Similarly, Derek Heater noted at the time that senior members of the FCO are 'rightly proud of their professional experience and skill, their knowledge and judgement representing the cumulative intellectual wealth of a working lifetime immersed in foreign affairs. Most Foreign Secretaries, on the other hand, spend only a limited proportion of their political careers in that office and tend to be looked upon as mere amateurs by their Foreign Office Staff'.[44] There was, therefore, 'considerable potential for political tension' in the relationship between ministers and officials within the FCO.[45]

Moreover, tensions between ministers and officials have, on occasion, become particularly pronounced when the latter have been confronted with a Labour government intent on broadening the definition of the British 'national interest' to include moral or ethical considerations.[46] For instance, as Geoffrey Moorhouse's 1977 study of the FCO recorded: 'Most people left of centre who have had dealings with the Foreign Office claim that the diplomats take a very restricted view of what is British self-interest, usually adding that it generally seems to be limited to immediate economic returns. The diplomats, for their part, become very impatient with an emphasis on morality purveyed by Labour politicians, and what they regard as naïve notions about the brotherhood of man'.[47] The accounts of George Brown, who served as Foreign Secretary from 1966–8 during the first Wilson government, and of Joe Haines – Wilson's press secretary – certainly lend credence to the oppositional character of ministerial-official relations during periods of Labour government.[48] Nicholas ('Nico')

---

[42] See Daniel W. Drezner, 'Ideas, Bureaucratic Politics, and the Crafting of Foreign Policy', *American Journal of Political Science* 44, No. 4 (October 2000): 733–49, 735; John Coles, *Making Foreign Policy: A Certain Idea of Britain* (London: John Murray, 2000), 45.
[43] William Wallace, *The Foreign Policy Process in Britain* (London: Royal Institute of International Affairs, 1977), 9.
[44] Derek Heater, *Britain and the Outside World* (London: Longman, 1976), 67.
[45] Ibid.
[46] See for example Kevin Theakston, 'New Labour and the Foreign Office', in *New Labour's Foreign Policy*, ed. Little and Wickham-Jones, 112–13. For a more general discussion of the divergent foreign policy traditions that have animated Labour and Conservative policy (and the FCO's historic discomfort with the former's tendency towards internationalism), see Vickers, *The Labour Party and the World*, Volumes I & II.
[47] Geoffrey Moorhouse, *The Diplomats: The Foreign Office Today* (London: Jonathan Cape, 1977), 157.
[48] See George Brown, *In My Way* (London: Victor Gollancz, 1971), 129; Joe Haines, *The Politics of Power* (London: Jonathan Cape, 1977), 72.

Henderson's reflections on his diplomatic career, in which he served as Assistant Private Secretary and Principal Private Secretary to five Foreign Secretaries, similarly attest to this clash of philosophies, and to the FCO taking a rather dim view of the idea, championed by Labour ministers, that Britain ought to set a moral example for other nations to follow.[49] For his part, Henderson clearly regarded the FCO as a repository of timeless wisdom that ought to be protected from the whims of transient ministers, as evidenced by a revealing anecdote provided by Lord Butler of Brockwell:

> When I was still in the Treasury, reasonably young, I found myself sitting next to Nico Henderson at a dinner... Nico said to me, 'You guys in the Treasury: what do you do when your ministers do not accept the departmental line?' I said, 'We do our very best to persuade and advise them and so on, but if in the end they decide differently, we regard it as our responsibility to carry out those decisions as conscientiously as we can.' He said, 'That is not what we do in the Foreign Office. If we find a minister who does not accept our departmental line, we wait until we get a minister who will.'[50]

Nonetheless, official scepticism notwithstanding, work on the human rights comparative assessment had, by the time Crowe came to express his concerns, already become public knowledge following Anthony Crosland's appearance on the BBC's *Panorama* programme on 17 January 1977. When questioned by David Dimbleby about the human rights stance of the incoming Carter administration and the notion that America's allies would be pressured into adopting a similar position, Crosland revealed that the FCO already had a head-start as far as human rights were concerned: 'I don't know whether that will happen and this is a very worrying problem. I'm trying to get the Foreign Office to work out a sort of index – if you like, an index of human rights and democratic rights.'[51] Crosland's disclosure may have had the effect of prompting a greater level of engagement with the issue of turning the comparative assessment into concrete policy proscriptions.[52] Still, by the time of Owen's appointment, little had apparently been done to bridge this gap – a point that was conceded by Luard in a message to Owen following the completion of the assessment:

> My first comment is that I think that this has been a successful exercise. As a result we certainly now have a far more reliable and objective picture of the human rights situation in countries throughout the world than we had before. This should enable

---

[49] See Nicholas Henderson, *The Private Office: A Personal View of Five Foreign Secretaries and of Government from the Inside* (London: Weidenfeld and Nicolson, 1984), 89–91.
[50] 'Decision Making in Foreign Policy', FCO Historians and Oxford University Press Learning from History Seminar, 21 February 2013, 29, available at https://issuu.com/fcohistorians/docs/learning_from_history_seminar (accessed 18 May 2020).
[51] 'Excerpt of a transcript from Anthony Crosland's BBC "Panorama" interview with David Dimbleby', TNA, FCO 58/1143.
[52] See 'Record of a Meeting between Mr Luard, Parliamentary Under-Secretary at the Foreign and Commonwealth Office, and Mr Meacher, Parliamentary Under Secretary of State at the Department of Trade, in the Foreign and Commonwealth Office on 18 January 1977 at 4 PM', TNA, FCO 8/2997.

us to be more consistent and better informed in our statements and actions on human rights matters than we could previously ... The difficult question remains: now that we have obtained this more reliable information, what use should we make of it in terms of policy? Can a vigorous stance on human rights questions, which I certainly hope we shall continue to maintain, be reconciled with safeguarding our national interests in our relations with particular governments?[53]

The following section of this chapter will explore how this dilemma was brought into sharp focus following Owen's discovery in October 1977 that the UK government was about to ship a consignment of armoured vehicles to the repressive regime in El Salvador. By reconstructing the steps leading up to the eventual cancellation of the contract in early 1978, the proceeding paragraphs will begin to examine in greater detail how institutional inertia militated against the elevation of human rights concerns within British foreign policy at this juncture. By exploring the Salvadoran episode, however, we are also able to illuminate the ways in which actors within the emerging transnational advocacy networks introduced during the previous chapter were able to exert a tangible influence over the British foreign policymaking process, making it more receptive to the growing human rights concerns of extra-parliamentary groups by subverting traditional methods of policy formulation in Whitehall.

Armoured cars and archbishops: The curious case of El Salvador

Owen was alerted to the imminent shipment of British armoured vehicles (twelve Saladin and three Ferret scout cars) to El Salvador on 4 October 1977 by Minister of State for Foreign and Commonwealth Affairs, Ted Rowlands.[54] The contract, valued at approximately £850,000, had been granted political clearance in January, concluding negotiations dating back to June 1976.[55] Upon receiving word of this predicament, Owen was in no doubt that the issue ought to be tackled head-on: 'I suddenly find that we're about to ship the bloody things ... we now face a situation where [the] contracts have all been signed, vehicles just about to go, and, you know, this is outrageous! We've got to somehow stop it.'[56] Attitudes within official circles, however, were decidedly less bullish. For instance, a 23 September despatch from San Salvador in which the recently appointed British Ambassador articulated his concern that the vehicles could be used by the government of El Salvador to quell internal opposition – in addition to the prospect that they could also be utilized against British troops stationed in Belize if El Salvador chose to support Guatemala's claim to the territory – was met with a

---

[53] Evan Luard to David Owen, 'Human Rights and Foreign Policy', 3 May 1977, TNA, FCO 58/1143.
[54] Ted Rowland's minute (drafted for Secretary of State), 'Supply of Armoured Vehicles to El Salvador', 4 October 1977, TNA, FCO 99/51.
[55] See J.W.R. Shakespeare to PS/Mr Rowland, 'Sale of Armoured Vehicles to El Salvador', 16 September 1977, TNA, FCO 99/51.
[56] Owen interview, 6 December 2017.

sympathetic but ultimately inflexible response from A. Collins of the FCO's Mexico and Caribbean Department.[57] Rowlands' disquiet, likewise, was given short shrift. Referring to both the Ambassador's telegram and a 22 September minute from Rowland's Private Secretary, J.W.R. Shakespeare stressed that, as regards the 'human rights aspects' of the sale, there could be 'no comparison between the situation in El Salvador and that which has obtained in Chile, the only country in Latin America where sales of defence equipment have been brought to an end due to the abuses of human rights of the regime in power'.[58]

In making his case, Shakespeare invoked the human rights assessment provided by the Embassy earlier in the year, which 'had the effect of putting El Salvador in middle band 4'.[59] This appeal to the human rights comparative assessment, however, rings slightly hollow, as it is followed by Shakespeare's concession that '[w]ere we now faced with a request for political clearance ... we would certainly wish to consider the human rights situation in the country as well as the Belize angle'.[60] Indeed, the minute concludes by reaffirming the economic considerations of the sale that clearly superseded such concerns.[61] Shakespeare subsequently elucidated the potential economic impact of cancellation on 3 October. Although El Salvador had 'publicly expressed support for Guatemala in the Belize dispute', and the 'mildly reforming impetus of 1974–76' had given way to a more repressive approach, it would still be 'inadvisable to cancel or postpone this particular contract ... A large sum of money would have to be repaid to El Salvador and MOD [Ministry of Defence] would be liable to incur substantial charges from the shipper'.[62] There was also the risk of the manufacturer taking

> wider damage to their hard won business in Latin America. The fact that abuses of human rights are worse elsewhere, including in all probability in Argentina, would be confusing and would cause further uncertainty about our reliability as a supplier throughout Latin America ... We would not be justified in asking MOD (at Ministerial level) to cancel or otherwise impede the contract ... But we should take diplomatic action to safeguard our interests (in respect of both grounds for concern).[63]

Following Owen's submission of a formal request to the Secretary of State for Defence, Fred Mulley, to cancel the contract on 7 October, the battle would largely be contested at an inter-departmental level.[64] Mulley, and Secretary of State for Trade,

---

[57] See A. Collins to Priority San Salvador, 'YOUR TELNO 65: Military Equipment for El Salvador', undated, TNA, FCO 99/51.
[58] Mr Shakespeare to PS/Mr Rowlands, 'Supply of Arms to El Salvador', 27 September 1977, TNA, FCO 99/51.
[59] Ibid.
[60] Ibid.
[61] Ibid.
[62] J.W.R. Shakespeare to Mr Hall; PS/Mr Rowlands, 'Supply of Armoured Vehicles to El Salvador', 3 October 1977, TNA, FCO 99/51.
[63] Ibid.
[64] See David Owen to Secretary of State for Defence, 'Supply of Armoured Vehicles to El Salvador', 7 October 1977, TNA, FCO 99/51.

Edmund Dell, put up a united front in defence of the contract, stressing the economic implications of cancellation at the eleventh hour, and raising the point that this would set a dangerous precedent.[65] Unconvinced by the arguments of Mulley and Dell, Owen went on the offensive: 'We must have a system of tightening up on MOD contracts ... Why did this contract ever get this far? Who agreed to supply El Salvador? I want more details and explanation, and quickly please.'[66] When the contract was discussed at a Cabinet Committee on Defence and Overseas Policy (DOP) meeting on 15 November, however, arguments appealing to the 'national interest' clearly won the day, and the decision to proceed with the sale of the armoured vehicles – subject to Salvadoran assurances that the vehicles would not be used against Belize – was duly reported in *The Times* as a victory for the MOD over the FCO.[67]

The fact that the DOP's verdict became public knowledge caused a great deal of alarm within Whitehall, leading to an inquest into how and why the decision got into the hands of the Press. Recalling his dealings with a representative of the Press Association, V.J. Henderson concluded that information must have been leaked shortly after the meeting.[68] This was indeed the case, although contrary to Mulley's suspicions that the leak came from the FCO, the source of the leak was in fact an official within the MOD, who forwarded the details of the contract and the DOP decision to the Catholic Institute for International Relations (CIIR).[69] 'The leak was to us', recalls Julian Filochowski, who described to the author the ways in which the CIIR subsequently attempted to exert pressure on the government through sympathetic journalists such as Hugh O'Shaughnessy, 'a member of CIIR's Education Committee which oversaw the work we [the CIIR] were engaged with on Central America'.[70] The CIIR's influence had grown within Britain's burgeoning human rights network in the aftermath of Salvador Allende's usurpation in 1973, and the organization was particularly attentive to the increasing persecution of El Salvador's Catholic community by the Romero regime, which viewed the Church as a subversive presence.[71] Furthermore, in what may be described retrospectively as a demonstration of the

---

[65] Fred Mulley to David Owen, 'Supply of Armoured Vehicles to El Salvador', 14 October 1977, TNA, FCO 99/51; Edmund Dell to David Owen, 'Supply of Armoured Vehicles to El Salvador', 19 October 1977, TNA, FCO 99/51.

[66] J.S. Wall to Mr Shakespeare, 'Supply of Armoured Vehicles to El Salvador', 31 October 1977, TNA, FCO 99/51. See also David Owen to Fred Mulley, 'Supply of Armoured Vehicles to El Salvador', 19 October 1977, TNA, FCO 99/51.

[67] '£850,000 Sale', *The Times*, 17 November 1977.

[68] V.J. Henderson to Mr Collins; Mr Shakespeare, 'El Salvador: Armoured Vehicles Contract Press Association Story', 16 November 1977, TNA, FCO 99/52.

[69] J.S. Wall to Mr Whyte, 'El Salvador: Armoured Vehicles Contract', 22 November 1977, TNA, FCO 99/52; Filochowski interview.

[70] Julian Filochowski, personal correspondence with the author, 30 June 2019.

[71] Established by Archbishop of Westminster Cardinal Hinsley in 1940 as 'The Sword of the Spirit', the organization adopted the name 'The Catholic Institute for International Relations' in 1965 before being renamed 'Progressio' in 2006. It ceased operations in 2017. Regarding the political activity of the Catholic Church in El Salvador and the persecution of Salvadoran Catholics, see for example William M. LeoGrande, *Our Own Backyard: The United States in Central America, 1977-1992* (Chapel Hill: University of North Carolina Press, 1998), Chapter Two: The Dragons' Teeth of War; Alan McPherson, *Intimate Ties, Bitter Struggles: The United States and Latin America since 1945* (Washington, DC: Potomac Books, 2006), 82-6.

'boomerang' model of transnational activism, Filochowski was able to quickly acquire information from the CIIR's Salvadoran contacts regarding the state's use of violence against Catholic reformers, and present that information to FCO ministers.[72]

Although distressed by the leak, officials soon began to exhibit an almost hubristic sense of equanimity: 'in the event, this looks like being a storm in a teacup!' reads one handwritten note referring to the coverage of the DOP decision in the Press.[73] Such optimism, however, was misplaced. Like-minded journalists were not the only weapons Filochowski and the CIIR had up their sleeves – 'We started doing things in parliament'.[74] The 'key man' in this regard, Filochowski recalls, was Lord Chitnis, a Liberal peer and head of the Joseph Rowntree Trust, who agreed to raise the matter of the El Salvador contract in his maiden question in the House of Lords.[75] Filochowski canvassed enthusiastically for support of Chitnis, but was nonetheless taken aback by the reaction elicited by Chitnis' question when it was delivered on 8 December:

> Pratap [Chitnis] asks his question; he gets the answer exactly verbatim that we'd said he would get... he asks his supplementary question; he gets fobbed off, as we also expected. So then, straight way, from one of the front benches... [someone] said, 'Minister you're not answering the noble Lord's question', something we'd not anticipated, he'd got support... and so people we'd not anticipated were standing up... and these questions kept coming![76]

By this stage, Lord Goronwy-Roberts – the minister tasked with rebuffing Lord Chitnis and his sympathizers – was defending a weakened position. The Salvadoran assurances on which the contract rested had been granted but were not as comprehensive as those requested by the DOP.[77] Cardinal Basil Hume, the Archbishop of Westminster, had also begun to exert his considerable influence on proceedings.

Hume had written to Owen on 28 September, highlighting the 'very difficult situation that the Church has faced in El Salvador since the beginning of the year' and urging HMG to 'make the strongest representations through the British Ambassador to the government there regarding the infringements of basic human rights'.[78] The Cardinal received an encouraging reply. While conditions in El Salvador could not be improved, Owen argued, 'without a change of mind and heart on the part of the

---

[72] Keck and Sikkink, *Activists Beyond Borders*, 13. See for example Julian Filochowski to Ted Rowlands, 23 September 1977, TNA, FCO 99/54; 'Record of a Meeting between the Minister of State for Foreign & Commonwealth Affairs and Representatives of the Catholic Institute for International Relations and Other Organisations: On 8 December at 10.00 AM', TNA, FCO 99/52.

[73] The handwritten note is dated 17 November 1977 and appears on V.J. Henderson to Mr Collins; Mr Shakespeare, 'El Salvador: Armoured Vehicles Contract Press Association Story', 16 November 1977, TNA, FCO 99/52.

[74] Filochowski interview.

[75] Ibid. See also Trevor Smith, 'Lord Chitnis Obituary', *Guardian*, 14 July 2013.

[76] 'Filochowski interview'. See also, 'El Salvador: Military Equipment Sales', 8 December 1977, *Hansard: House of Lords*, Volume 387.

[77] See A.J. Collins to Mr Hall; PS/Mr Rowlands, 'Supply of Armoured Vehicles to El Salvador', 1 December 1977, TNA, FCO 99/52. The assurances did not rule out the possibility that the armoured vehicles could be used against Belize when British troops were no longer stationed there.

[78] Cardinal Hume to David Owen, 28 September 1977, TNA, FCO 99/54.

land-owners and the business community in general', this process could be 'aided by expressions of concern from major developed countries with which El Salvador maintains links'.[79] In this respect, Owen reassured the Cardinal that he would 'not hesitate to express to the Salvadorean authorities the British Government's concern about abuses of human rights, at a suitable opportunity'.[80]

As such, Hume was understandably disappointed by Owen's acquiescence following the DOP meeting in mid-November. Upon corresponding with Filochowski, Owen's political adviser, David Stephen, told the Foreign Secretary that CIIR members had 'found the Government's decision very depressing, and that Cardinal Hume felt particularly "let down" because you had previously written to him in such positive terms about this'.[81] Hume would articulate his displeasure on 1 December in a letter to the Prime Minister, quoting from Owen before 'respectfully suggesting' that the cancellation of the armoured vehicles contract would 'provide "a suitable opportunity" for the British Government to express its concern over the situation of human rights in El Salvador'.[82] An anonymous handwritten note from 12 December, moreover, reveals that the pressure – typified by the Cardinal's intervention – was beginning to tell: 'Now overtaken by events the PM has briefly acknowledged the Archbishop's letter saying that the S[ecretary] of S[tate] will send a considered response.'[83] Indeed, Owen's reply revealed a moderation of the government's position, specifying that '[w]e will not for the future allow any further sales until there has been clear evidence of a marked change in the situation in El Salvador regarding human rights.'[84] Nonetheless, the deal was still set to proceed in accordance with the terms set out by the DOP. Unmoved, the Cardinal applied yet more pressure on the government during the New Year.

Although Filochowski has dismissed the FCO's contention that Cardinal Hume involved himself in the debate at the behest of the CIIR, there was clearly some degree of coordination between them.[85] For instance, prior to Cardinal Hume's press release of 13 January 1978 in which he once again urged the government to reconsider the sale of the armoured vehicles, Filochowski telephoned Stephen Wall (Owen's Assistant Private Secretary) informing him of Hume's intentions.[86] The Cardinal's decisive contribution to the El Salvador saga, however, would take a more surreptitious form – a private letter sent to Jim Callaghan on the eve of a follow-up DOP Committee meeting scheduled for 18 January, during which the El Salvador contract was to be revisited. As Owen recalls, 'the Cabinet Subcommittee opens on this thing and Jim says, "I thought perhaps before we all got any further we should ... I've just had a letter"'.[87] As Callaghan

---

[79] David Owen to Cardinal Hume, 20 October 1977, TNA, FCO 99/54.
[80] Ibid.
[81] David Stephen to David Owen, 'Arms to El Salvador', 24 November 1977, TNA, FCO 73/438.
[82] Cardinal Hume to James Callaghan, 1 December 1977, TNA, FCO 99/54.
[83] Anonymous handwritten note, 12 December 1977, TNA, FCO 99/54.
[84] David Owen to Cardinal Hume, 14 December 1977, TNA, FCO 99/53.
[85] D. Joy to Mr Hall; Private Secretary', Supply of Armoured Vehicles to El Salvador', 16 January 1978, TNA, FCO 99/204; Filochowski correspondence.
[86] See Baden Hickman, 'Cardinal urges arms ban', *Guardian*, 13 January 1978; David Stephen to Mr Wall, 'Arms for El Salvador', 12 January 1978, TNA, FCO 99/204.
[87] Owen interview, 6 December 2017.

proceeded to retrieve the letter – visibly 'well-thumbed' – from his pocket, Owen quickly realized that Callaghan's mind had been made up. For those who had lobbied the government to reconsider the sale of armoured vehicles to El Salvador, it was 'game, set, and match'.[88]

But to what extent could Owen be counted as an ally of the CIIR, Cardinal Hume and Lord Chitnis, or of those members of the Cardiff Justice & Peace Group whose weekly vigils held in front of Callaghan's constituency surgery served to keep the El Salvador issue at the forefront of the Prime Minister's mind?[89] In an email exchange with Julian Filochowski, Maggie Smart – Owen's personal secretary – recounts a version of events that would suggest that Owen was very much in favour of cancellation. More than this, he was party to the Cardinal's modus operandi:

> My memory is that the actual decision to sell the vehicles was taken by Lord Owen's predecessor, Tony Crosland, in January 1977. David Owen had no alternative but to defend this position on coming into office but he was unhappy with it from the start and my memory from Private Office which he agrees with is that there was a conspiracy to ensure that Cardinal Hume's letter arrived on the eve of the all-important Committee meeting with Callaghan in the chair in which you, David Stephen and probably Tom McNally [Callaghan's political adviser] were complicit. David Owen describes the meeting opening with Callaghan slowly reading out Cardinal Hume's letter which he finished and looked around the table and said – does anyone still want to continue to sell armoured vehicles to El Salvador (with a grin on his face) and there were no takers to argue the case to continue with the sale.[90]

While Filochowski confirmed that this account tallied with his, it is nearly impossible to discern the veracity of this claim through an analysis of the relevant FCO files at the National Archives.[91] As regards Owen's 'co-conspirators', it would certainly appear that Tom McNally became more skittish and increasingly receptive to the CIIR's lobbying efforts following the publication of a 3 January article in the *Guardian* which called into question the sincerity of the Salvadoran assurances.[92] David Stephen, for his part, came under scrutiny in the aftermath of the cancellation on account of his connections with Filochowski, receiving an obliquely accusatory minute from G.E. Hall on 19 January.[93]

As for Owen, while definitive accounts of this conspiracy may forever remain in his custody, and in the recollections of those select few who may have played a crucial role behind the scenes in bringing sufficient pressure to bear on the Prime Minister, there

---

[88] Ibid.
[89] Julian Filochowski to Maggie Smart, 22 March 2019.
[90] Maggie Smart to Julian Filochowski, 21 March 2019.
[91] Filochowski to Smart, 22 March 2019.
[92] David Owen, interview with the author, 19 March 2019. For the article in question, see 'Pledge on arms refused', *Guardian*, 3 January 1978. McNally's growing concern can be seen in Tom McNally to David Stephen, 4 January 1978, TNA, FCO 99/204; Julian Filochowski to Tom McNally, 12 January 1978, TNA, FCO 73/438; Tom McNally to David Stephen, 16 January 1978, TNA, FCO 73/438; David Stephen to Private Secretary, 'Arms Sales', 17 January 1978, TNA, FCO 73/438.
[93] G.E. Hall to David Stephen, 'Mr Julian Filochowski', 19 January 1978, TNA, FCO 99/205.

exists sufficient documentary evidence bearing witness to his dissatisfaction with the El Salvador contract and his committed efforts to obstruct the deal to substantiate the notion that his public acceptance of the DOP's initial verdict masked his true feelings. Following the DOP decision in mid-November, for example, Owen explored the legal ramifications pertaining to the insertion of 'break clauses' in arms sales contracts, and, in the lead-up to the second DOP meeting in January, Owen can be seen arguing for a postponement of the sale, pending the completion of a report by the Human Rights Commission of the Organization of American States.[94] Whether positive or negative, this report could 'either give some defence against attacks on human rights grounds in the UK for a subsequent delivery or would provide the basis for a cancellation on human rights grounds'.[95] While the final decision was Callaghan's to make, this tactic, Filochowski insists, played a crucial role in keeping the option of cancellation on the table: 'David [Stephen] sort of implied to me afterwards that David Owen had secured it . . . in fact it couldn't possibly have been cancelled without David [Owen] suggesting that it would be postponed.'[96]

In any case, it would appear that the assumption – implicit in existing coverage of the episode – that the pressures exerted on policymakers emanated exclusively from beyond the walls of Whitehall, is only partially substantiated in the final analysis.[97] To be sure, officials were surprised by the degree of public concern over the human rights implications of the El Salvador contract.[98] There can also be no doubt that religious lobbying groups, and the CIIR in particular, had the effect of amplifying this sense of outrage, and at key moments. Their lobbying efforts, however, would not have yielded the cancellation of the armoured vehicles contract had it not been for the fact that they found a receptive audience *within* foreign policymaking circles, from the unnamed MOD official who leaked sensitive information to the CIIR following the first DOP meeting, to the Foreign Secretary himself. As such, the El Salvador case study is difficult to reconcile with traditional conceptions of British foreign policy formulation described by the 'Westminster model' – a 'hierarchical, institutionalized process centred on Westminster and Whitehall' in which the role of civil servants is 'idealised as being the sole source of advice on policy' solicited by ministers.[99] Similarly, the CIIR's

---

[94] See Attorney General to Secretary of State for Defence, 'Arms Sales', 23 November 1977, TNA, FCO 99/52; E.A.J. Fergusson to Mr Wilberforce, 'Arms Sales', 28 November 1977, TNA, FCO 99/52; A. Parry to PS/Secretary of State, 'Arms Sales', 30 November 1977, TNA, FCO 99/52.

[95] 'Brief for the Secretary of State's use at the DOP Meeting on Wednesday 18 January 1978', attached to D. Joy to Mr Hall; Mr Wall, 'Supply of Armoured Vehicles to El Salvador', 17 January 1978, TNA, FCO 99/204.

[96] Filochowski interview.

[97] See Mark Phythian, *The Politics of British Arms Sales Since 1964* (Manchester: Manchester University Press, 2000), 137–40.

[98] Hugh O' Shaughnessy, 'Salvador arms deal in doubt', *Financial Times*, 15 December 1977. See also D. Joy to A.S. Papadopolous, 'Armoured Vehicles', 26 January 1978, TNA, FCO 99/205.

[99] Gaskarth, *British Foreign Policy*, 42; Francesca Gains and Gerry Stoker, 'Special Advisers and the Transmission of Ideas from the Policy Primeval Soup', *Policy & Politics* 39, No. 4 (2011): 490. For a recent analysis of the 'Westminster model' and its limitations, see Meg Russell and Ruxandra Serban, 'The Muddle of the "Westminster Model": A Concept Stretched Beyond Repair', *Government and Opposition* (2020): 1–21

cultivation of parliamentary engagement with its endeavours – which utilized contacts within Labour, as well as the Liberal and Conservative Parties – draws our attention to the benefits of broadening our focus beyond the minister-official duopoly, necessitating perhaps the adoption of a 'differentiated polity model' of policy analysis, appreciative of the 'fragmented and conflictual nature of policymaking', and the 'particular individual or organizational interests' that policymakers may be inclined to pursue.[100]

Indeed, the merits of a differentiated polity model of policy formulation – wherein policy is 'constructed not by hierarchies of governmental actors but instead through networks that bring together interested parties from the public, the private and the voluntary sectors' – become even more apparent when we consider the role played by political advisers throughout the El Salvador episode.[101] Although Tom McNally has distanced himself from Owen's 'conspiracy', there is no doubt that David Stephen – his interests in human rights and Latin America well-known and his attendant expertise highly-valued – often acted as an interlocutor between the CIIR and Owen's Office.[102] This transmission of information was not, according to Filochowski at least, a one-way process: '[Stephen] in his own way was leaking, you know, telling us where things were ... these political assistants, advisers, they went with the ministers to a lot of these meetings'.[103] Stephen, moreover, was perhaps not the only political adviser passing information on to the CIIR – Filochowski has also suggested that Roger Darlington, political adviser to Merlyn Rees, kept the CIIR abreast of key developments pertaining to the contract.[104]

The curious case of El Salvador, therefore, not only suggests that the prominence of religious activists within Britain's burgeoning human rights network – and perhaps the role of religious activists in the development of the international human rights regime in a much broader sense during this critical juncture in human rights history – is deserving of more sustained scholarly engagement; it also illuminates the capacity of political advisers to subvert the traditional power structures that have militated against challenges to the status quo and marginalized human rights advocates.[105] Furthermore, by demonstrating the connections linking activists within the CIIR to political

---

[100] Gaskarth, *British Foreign Policy*, 47. For further reading on the 'Differentiated Polity Model', see for example R.A.W. Rhodes, *Network Governance and the Differentiated Polity: Selected Essays, Volume I* (Oxford: Oxford University Press, 2017).

[101] Gaskarth, *British Foreign Policy*, 47.

[102] Tom McNally, interview with the author, 19 February 2019. According to Owen, Stephen, who had worked with the human rights charity the Runnymede Trust prior to his appointment as Owen's political adviser in September 1977, had 'a distinguished knowledge of Latin America even though a young man'. Owen, moreover, recalls that he 'was not happy with the type of advice we were getting from the Foreign Office, which seemed to me to be very casual and uncommitted on human rights in Latin America' and that if 'David wanted me to override it I tended to find in favour of David frankly' (Owen interview, 19 March 2019).

[103] Filochowski interview.

[104] Ibid. The author contacted Darlington on 12 June 2019 seeking to corroborate Filochowski's recollection of events. Darlington does not recall being involved with the El Salvador contract debate in any capacity.

[105] As discussed in the previous chapter, historians of human rights have previously explored Christian conservative perspectives during the postwar period (see Moyn, *Christian Human Rights*). For an example of recent scholarship that broadens the focus on religious human rights perspectives to include ecumenical engagement with anti-racist solidarity and transnational social justice movements, see Bastiaan Bouwman, 'From Religious Freedom to Social Justice: The Human Rights

advisers, sympathetic parliamentarians and influential public figures, the El Salvador episode also casts a spotlight on the ways in which NGOs operating within broader transnational advocacy networks have been capable of connecting public concern over morally dubious policy with the instruments of government. When viewed from this perspective, the key role that the CIIR played in securing the cancellation of the Salvadoran contract speaks clearly to Margaret E. Keck and Kathryn Sikkink's definition of such advocacy networks and the ways in which they operate.[106]

Nonetheless, the notion that the El Salvador case study can be seen to usher in a new era of British diplomacy, transcending the framework of the 'Westminster model' and the bureaucratic inertia of Whitehall, can only be pushed so far. On the one hand, the manner in which the influence of the CIIR had grown within the corridors of power accords with broader trends concerning the 'politics of expertise' that became an increasingly recognizable feature of British politics during the second half of the twentieth century, as politicians began to seek out expert forms of knowledge beyond Whitehall, and NGOs became increasingly professionalized and 'political', scaling up their lobbying and advocacy work during the 1970s.[107] On the other, the institutional inertia exhibited by FCO officials represents its own form of 'expertise', one that acted as a bulwark against these processes. As the merits of cancellation were being debated, official scepticism was still tangible – seeing themselves as guardians of the 'national interest', FCO officials felt it necessary to educate the idealistic ministers whose ambitions did not always take into account the 'facts of the matter'.[108] This tension, moreover, can be read into the decision taken by senior officials to have the Secret Service (MI5) 'put a tail' on Filochowski, clearly perturbed by his perceived influence on proceedings.[109] This move certainly contributed little towards cultivating connections between the foreign policymaking establishment and human rights NGOs, a notion that had been deemed favourable by Evan Luard during a seminar on human rights and foreign policy in June 1977, and by Ted Rowlands during a meeting with Filochowski in December.[110] It would also be a mistake to regard the cancellation of the armoured vehicles contract as an unequivocal victory for human rights and a

---

Engagement of the Ecumenical Movement from the 1940s to the 1970s', *Journal of Global History* 13, Issue 2 (2018): 252–73. On the role of special advisers, see Stephen Robert Hanney, 'Special Advisers: Their Place in British Government' (PhD thesis, Brunel University, February 1993); Nigel Wicks, 'Defining the Boundary within the Executive: Ministers, Special Advisers and the Permanent Civil Service', The ninth report of the Committee on Standards in Public Life, April 2003, available at https://www.gov.uk/government/publications/defining-the-boundaries-within-the-executive-ministers-special-advisers-and-the-permanent-civil-service (accessed 19 May 2020); Gains and Stoker, 'Special Advisers and the Transmission of Ideas from the Policy Primeval Soup': 485–98.

[106] See Keck and Sikkink, *Activists Beyond Borders*, 1–38.

[107] Matthew Hilton, James McKay, Nicholas Crowson and Jean-François Mouhot, *The Politics of Expertise: How NGOs Shaped Modern Britain* (Oxford: Oxford University Press, 2013), esp. Chapter Five: The Pressure of Politics: Walking the Corridors of Power. See also *NGOs in Contemporary Britain*, ed. Crowson, Hilton, McKay.

[108] A.J. Collins to Mr Yarnold, 'Supply of Armoured Vehicles to El Salvador', 10 November 1977, TNA, FCO 99/51.

[109] Stephen interview, 16 May 2019.

[110] See 'Mr Evan Luard's Seminar on Human Rights: Oxford, 24–25 June, 1977', TNA, FCO 58/1150; 'Record of a Meeting between the Minister of State for Foreign & Commonwealth Affairs and Representatives of the Catholic Institute for International Relations and Other Organisations'.

confirmation of the recent elevation of human rights considerations among British diplomatic imperatives, evidenced ostensibly by the FCO's recent attempts to establish more objective human rights criteria to guide their operations.

The El Salvador case, in fact, can be seen to highlight the striking limitations of the human rights comparative assessment. An exchange between Luard and G.E. Hall in December, for instance, reveals that interpretations of the assessment and its appropriate policy applications could be massively divergent. 'I do not think it necessarily follows', Luard posited, 'that, if we publicly use human rights grounds as a reason for halting future sales to El Salvador, we must immediately halt arms sales to any country where the situation may be as bad'.[111] Referring to the examples Hall provided of countries which could be affected by the adoption of such a policy – 'presumably those which are at least as low in our human rights league table' – Luard concluded by advocating for a selective application of the comparative assessment: 'if we were to demand total consistency in our policy it could of course lead to the conclusion that we should never use human rights as a criterion in such questions.'[112] Hall was quick to counter:

> Mr Luard says that our human rights table is inherently fallible. I do not think that anyone has any doubts about this, but it is the only attempt we have made to have objective criteria and it is certainly much less fallible than subjective judgement on a case by case basis. This attempt to reach objective criteria supports my own subjective judgement that Mr Luard is, with respect, mistaken in believing that the human rights situation in El Salvador is worse than in Jordan, Zambia, Nigeria, Egypt, Pakistan, Oman, Iran and Tanzania. It is true that Ministerial criteria (not 'total consistency') could lead to the conclusion that we should reconsider arms sales to those countries as well as to El Salvador and I indeed said so in my minute ('it could well be that there is a good case on human rights grounds for deciding not to sell arms to a majority of these countries') ... a decision one way or another on this issue should not be pre-empted by action which would tend to make the human rights situation in El Salvador a criterion for the denial of sales of arms.[113]

The concerns articulated by Hall regarding the setting of potentially punitive precedents, buttressed it seems by doubts concerning the efficacy of stressing the human rights aspects of the El Salvador sale, often led those in favour of cancellation to emphasize the Belize issue in the construction of their arguments.[114] However, while

---

[111] Evan Luard to Mr Rowlands, 'Human Rights and Arms Sales', 20 December 1977, TNA, FCO 99/53.
[112] Ibid.
[113] G.E. Hall to PS/Mr Luard, 'Human Rights and Arms Sales', 21 December 1977, TNA, FCO 99/53.
[114] See for example Owen's Private Office to Priority Certain Missions and Dependent Territories TELNO GUIDANCE 10, 'Supply of Armoured Vehicles to El Salvador', 20 January 1978, TNA, FCO 99/205: 'Although human rights issues were part of the decision to cancel, it was considered wise to play down this aspect to avoid entering into arguments about the relationship between human rights and arms sales which are necessarily very complex and which must be argued in detail on a case by case basis and not pre-empted by the sort of simplistic statement which would have been necessary in this case'; J.W.R. Shakespeare to PS/PUS; PS/Lord Goronwy-Roberts; Private Secretary, 'Supply of Armoured Vehicles to El Salvador', 2 November 1977, TNA, FCO 99/51: '[T]he Secretary of State has not used El Salvador's human rights record as a justification for his request to the Defence Secretary that the contract should be cancelled.'

Achilles Papadopolous, the British Ambassador to El Salvador, was expressing his relief that 'we managed to avoid explicitly relating the cancellation – as distinct from future sales – to the human rights situation', events elsewhere were conspiring to make the connection between human rights and the thorny issue of arms sales unavoidable.[115] Indeed, when it came to the management of British–Iranian relations during the twilight of Shah Mohammad Reza Pahlavi's autocratic rule, the economic and geopolitical factors that had led successive British governments to court the Shah as a patron of the British armaments industry would see the Callaghan government offer its unquestioning support to the Shah in the face of growing internal opposition, leaving little doubt as to the peripheral role that human rights concerns would play in the formulation of British policy. The following paragraphs will explore how Owen struggled to reconcile these two conflicting imperatives before examining how his attempts to square this particular circle led him to search for philosophical grounds on which he could defend the apparent inconsistencies of British human rights policy.

'The price to pay was a little inconsistency': Appeasing the Shah of Iran

Iran's status as a protector of Western interests in the Middle East had grown considerably following Britain's withdrawal from the Persian Gulf in 1968 and the subsequent adoption of the 'twin pillars' policy by the Nixon administration in the United States, which sought to establish Iran and Saudi Arabia as the guarantors of regional stability and bulwarks against Soviet expansionism.[116] The Shah quickly became a shining example of this aspect of the Nixon Doctrine, which gave military and financial aid to countries that protected US interests, crushing a Marxist rebellion in Oman's Dhufar province between 1972 and 1975.[117] The geostrategic significance of maintaining cordial relations with Iran – a reliable supplier of crude oil – gave the Shah an enormous degree of leverage in his dealings with Western allies, transforming him from a 'submissive client into a semi-independent partner'.[118] Contemporaneously, Britain's worsening balance of payments situation increasingly rendered exports a 'political priority', with high-profile inquiries – Plowden, Duncan and Berrill – serving to push trade promotion 'up the Foreign Office agenda'.[119] The promotion of Britain's economic interests, which accounted for approximately thirty percent of the FCO's budget in 1975–6, moreover, was highlighted as a particular priority vis-à-vis oil producing nations with whom 'past associations and military ties meant there were still

---

[115] Achilles Papadopolous to D. Joy, 'Armoured Vehicles Contracts', 1 February 1978, TNA, FCO 99/205.
[116] See Roham Alvandi, *Nixon, Kissinger, and the Shah: The United States and Iran in the Cold War* (New York: Oxford University Press, 2014); Claudia Castiglioni, 'No Longer a Client, Not Yet a Partner: The US-Iranian Alliance in the Johnson Years', *Cold War History* 15, No. 5 (2015): 491–509.
[117] See James F. Goode, 'Assisting Our Brothers, Defending Ourselves: The Iranian Intervention in Oman, 1972–75', *Iranian Studies* 47, Issue 3 (May 2014): 441–62.
[118] Vittorio Felci, '"A Latter-Day Hitler": Anti-Shah Activism and British Policy towards Iran, 1974–1976', *Diplomacy and Statecraft* 30, No. 1 (2019): 517.
[119] John Fisher, Effie Pedaliu and Richard Smith, 'Introduction', in *The Foreign Office, Commerce and British Foreign Policy in the Twentieth Century*, ed. Fisher, Pedaliu and Smith, 2.

opportunities' to secure British trade.¹²⁰ Iran, as Richard Smith notes, 'was at the top of the list as one of the UK's top 20 export markets and the largest in the Middle East'.¹²¹ Indeed, while his predecessor estimated that as much as eighty percent of his time was devoted to commercial work, Anthony Parsons' tenure as British Ambassador to Tehran (1974–9) arguably witnessed an even deeper entrenchment of British economic interests in the activities of the Embassy.¹²²

As recent scholarship on British policy towards Iran during the 1970s has made clear, Britain's unquestioning support of the Shah's dictatorship, engendered by an appreciation of these economic and geopolitical concerns, began to pose particular problems for the Labour governments of Harold Wilson and Jim Callaghan (1974–9). The Shah's modernizing programme known as the 'White Revolution' did not yield greater political liberalization. Furthermore, the response of Iran's secret police, intelligence and security force (SAVAK) to internal protest against the Shah's reforms was characterized by mass arrests, unfair trials, the physical and psychological torture of detainees, and mass surveillance of Iranian citizens.¹²³ In response to these developments, the radicalization of Iranian opposition to the Shah within Britain – spearheaded by Iranian students studying at UK universities – served to amplify criticism of Britain's relationship with Iran.¹²⁴ This increasing animosity towards the Iranian regime was also undergirded by the growing influence of the 'new social movements' identified within the previous chapter, and by the permeation of this sentiment within the Labour Party itself, which led to increasingly polyphonic debates on foreign policy within the Party as the radical left came to control the National Executive Committee (NEC) and the Labour Party Conference by the mid-1970s, while the centre-right of Party predominated within the Cabinet.¹²⁵ The striking elevation of human rights concerns within international discourse, and a particular emphasis on campaigns against repressive state action against the individual that became discernible during the 1970s, reinforced and became 'intertwined' with these currents of anti-Shah activism, highlighting the human rights question, and its appropriate situation in the context of Anglo-Iranian relations, as a cause for concern within foreign policymaking circles prior to Owen's appointment as Foreign Secretary.¹²⁶

Indeed, Crosland's disclosure of the human rights comparative assessment during his *Panorama* appearance seems to have initiated a dialogue between Foreign Office

---

¹²⁰ Richard Smith, '"Paying Our Way in the World": The FCO, Export Promotion and Iran in the 1970s', in *The Foreign Office, Commerce and British Foreign Policy in the Twentieth Century*, ed. Fisher, Pedaliu and Smith, 488–9.
¹²¹ Ibid., 490.
¹²² See Fisher, Pedaliu and Smith, 'Introduction', 9; Smith, '"Paying Our Way in the World"', 493. For Parsons' recollections of his tenure as Ambassador to Tehran and the predominantly economic focus of his activities, see Anthony Parsons, *The Pride and the Fall: Iran, 1974–79* (London: Jonathan Cape, 1984); Sir Anthony (Derrick) Parsons interview with Jane Barder, BDOHP, 22 March 1996, available at https://www.chu.cam.ac.uk/media/uploads/files/Parsons_Anthony.pdf (accessed 20 May 2020).
¹²³ See for example Matthew K. Shannon, *Losing Hearts and Minds: American-Iranian Relations and International Education during the Cold War* (Ithaca, New York and London: Cornell University Press, 2017), 131–44.
¹²⁴ See Felci, '"A Latter-Day Hitler"': 520–24.
¹²⁵ Ibid.: 520.
¹²⁶ Ibid.: 519.

and Embassy officials regarding the potential fallout of the Foreign Secretary's admission, and the ways in which the institutionalization of human rights concerns within the FCO could complicate British policy towards Iran, limiting opportunities for British business. As M.S. Weir warned Michael Palliser on 31 January, the 'key element in our economic relationship with Iran is that all major business is decided by the Shah himself', and nothing would 'jeopardise that relationship more rapidly or effectively than the news that HMG had joined the anti-Shah lobby on the human rights issue'.[127] Such considerations were clearly not lost on Owen, then serving as Crosland's Minister of State – on the same day, he responded to a letter seeking clarification of the government's position on the sale of defence equipment to Iran in which he implicitly conceded that the human rights situation in Iran was a legitimate cause for concern. Nonetheless, if the United Kingdom 'sold arms only to countries whose internal policies were 100% to our liking', Owen argued, 'we should have few customers and few allies'.[128] British–Iranian relations were, Owen continued, underpinned by 'certain obligations as an ally in the Central Treaty Organization (CENTO), which we regard as an important force for stability in the Middle East'.[129] It was clear, however, that economic considerations were paramount: 'We have to bear in mind the importance which Iran has for our economy. Last year Iran supplied 23% of our oil imports and took exports valued at around £500 million. There are, in addition, many large contracts under discussion which could give a further substantial boost to our trade and create yet more jobs for British workers.'[130]

Had it not been for Crosland's untimely passing which facilitated Owen's unexpected promotion, Owen would have been obligated to present these economic realities – and the ways in which they informed Britain's unquestioning approach to the Shah's autocratic tendencies – to a deputation of Labour MPs led by the young and idealistic Member for Edinburgh Central, Robin Cook. Cook had written to Crosland in December 1976 in an attempt to draw the Foreign Secretary's attention to a recently published Amnesty International report on Iran 'which documented the use of torture and arbitrary arrest as part of widespread political repression'.[131] As 'one of Iran's major defence allies and economic partners', Cook argued that Britain had 'a duty to respond by making representations to the Government of Iran concerning its infringement of basic human rights', and requested a meeting with either Crosland or 'the appropriate minister at the Foreign Office to discuss the Government's response to the report'.[132] The meeting was initially scheduled for February, and, according to the FCO's Michael James, Owen's briefing was geared towards maintaining good relations with Iran 'in proper perspective'.[133] This would be achieved, James suggested to his contacts at the

---

[127] M.S. Weir to PUS, 'Human Rights in Foreign Policy', 31 January 1977, TNA, FCO 8/2997.
[128] David Owen to A.E. Rawlinson, 31 January 1977, TNA, FCO 8/2991.
[129] Ibid.
[130] Ibid.
[131] Robin Cook, et al, to Anthony Crosland, 20 December 1976, TNA, FCO 8/2997.
[132] Ibid.
[133] 'Amnesty International Campaign against Iran', 10 February 1977, The National Archives, College Park, MD., Central Foreign Policy Files, Record Group 59 – General Records of the Department of State, Electronic Telegrams, 1977, available at https://aad.archives.gov/aad/createpdf?rid=32076&dt =2532&dl=1629 (accessed 9 January 2020).

US Embassy in London, by contending that 'allegations in the AI report are out of date and that figures for political prisoners are exaggerated'.[134] The FCO briefing paper, moreover, would 'note that the Shah's record in human rights is improving, go into the good side of the remarkable social and economic progress made by his regime, and point up the Shah's known determination to spread Iran's wealth around'.[135] This line, it would appear, was also supported by the Embassy in Tehran, which provided 'ample material for a robust brief for Dr David Owen' in preparation of his scheduled meeting with Cook's deputation.[136] The postponement of the meeting – and the delegation of ministerial responsibility to Frank Judd – did little to alter this approach as Judd was presented with a brief punctuated with subheadings that reinforced the '[c]onstraints on HMG's Freedom of Action', cast aspersions on the veracity of the 'Amnesty Report and Reliability of Evidence', stressed the need to consider 'Iran in Context', and underlined the '[i]mportance of Iran to [the] UK'.[137]

Owen's public pronouncements on the subject of human rights, in which he clearly positioned the British government shoulder-to-shoulder with the Carter administration, however, appear to have exerted a moderating effect on the exigencies of Anglo–Iranian trade, and the ways in which these were weaponized by the British arms lobby. With the Carter administration's arms sales to Iran on hold pending the completion of PD-13, a presidential directive that would lay out specific guidance on conventional arms transfer policy, some officials anticipated an opportunity to break the US monopoly on the supply of aircraft to the Iranian air force.[138] In response to Parsons' suggestion that the entrepreneurial instincts of the defence industry ought to be curbed in this instance, lest they damage Anglo–American relations, B.A. Major asserted that 'we are living in a highly competitive commercial world, and the American industrialists at least must understand our aircraft manufacturers' desire to penetrate the lucrative Iranian market'.[139] Nonetheless, the Defence Department, as summarized

---

[134] Ibid.
[135] Ibid.
[136] Anthony Parsons to Ivor Lucas, 6 February 1977, TNA, FCO 8/2997.
[137] See I.T.M. Lucas to Mr Lipsey; Mr Weir; PS/Mr Judd, 'Iran: Amnesty Report', with attached brief 'Iran: Meeting of Minister of State and MPs to Discuss the Amnesty Report, 23 March 1977', 15 March 1977, TNA, FCO 8/2997. See also David Lipsey to Mr Lucas, 'Iran: Amnesty Report', 16 March 1977, TNA, FCO 8/2998.
[138] See 'PD-13: Conventional Arms Transfer Policy', 13 May 1977, The Jimmy Carter Presidential Library and Museum, available at https://www.jimmycarterlibrary.gov/assets/documents/directives/pd13.pdf (accessed 20 May 2020). In the event, although PD-13 placed certain restrictions on the transfer of US weapons technologies, the decision of the Carter administration to provide the Shah with sophisticated surveillance aircraft (AWACS) in April 1977 can be seen as 'an early, if not the earliest, indication that Carter's idealism was on a collision course with Cold War Reality' (Stephen McGlinchey and Robert W. Murray, 'Jimmy Carter and the Sales of the AWACS to Iran in 1977', *Diplomacy and Statecraft* 8, No. 2 (2017): 255). See also Luca Trenta, 'The Champion of Human Rights meets the King of Kings: Jimmy Carter, the Shah, and Iranian Illusions and Rage', *Diplomacy and Statecraft* 24, No. 3 (2013): 476–98. For the US Ambassador to Tehran's account of the AWACS saga and its implications, see William H. Sullivan, *Mission to Iran* (New York & London: W.W. Norton & Company, 1981), 114–23.
[139] B.A. Major to Miss Darling; Mr Clay, 'Defence Sales to Iran: Competition with the Americans', 21 March 1977, TNA, FCO 8/2991. See also See A.D. Parsons to Mr Weir, 'Defence Sales – IAFF', 6 March 1977, TNA, FCO 8/2991.

by P. Yarnold's response, sided with Parsons, admitting that Britain could not be seen to capitalize on the US decision in light of the supportive stance adopted by Owen. Attempts to leverage Carter's moratorium would leave the UK vulnerable to criticism and charges of hypocrisy 'in view of the Government's expressions of support for President Carter's human rights policy'.[140] With some degree of reluctance, Ivor Lucas of the FCO's Middle East Department concurred: 'It would be wise for us to avoid any possible suggestion that we were cashing in on American embarrassment, and we must also avoid criticism and accusation[s] of bad faith so soon after our own Government's expressions of support for President Carter's pronouncement on human rights and arms limitation'.[141] But if Owen's human rights initiative prevented the British arms industry from occupying the space left by the temporary US withdrawal from the lucrative Iranian market, it soon became clear that this moderating influence had its limits.

During Judd's meeting with Cook's deputation on 23 March, for instance, Judd cited Owen's speech at the annual banquet of the Diplomatic and Commonwealth Writers Association, framing Owen's human rights initiative as a complicating factor in British-Iranian relations, but one that could certainly be reconciled with long-standing strategic imperatives.[142] Indeed, Owen's speech had been interpreted by the *Guardian*'s political editor, Peter Jenkins, as an attempt to strike a 'practical and moral balance' that was more attentive to the nuances of international relations than President Carter's decidedly evangelical approach.[143] Margaret Van Hatten of the *Financial Times*, likewise, took note of Owen's moderation: 'While following in principle the Carter administration's policy on human rights, the British approach indicated in Dr. Owen's speech is more cautious, stressing the need to take measures which "stand a chance of being effective", rather than provoking "counter-productive reaction"'.[144] While this was not, according to Judd, 'an excuse for dodging the issue', Owen's human rights agenda was clearly interpreted as a malleable entity – 'The watchword was commitment in principle, pragmatism in action'.[145]

The policy implications of this approach became apparent during Owen's summit in Tehran with the Shah weeks later. In anticipation of the meeting, the suggestion that Owen should raise the issue of independent observers attending criminal trials with the Shah was dismissed by Parsons on the grounds that this would give the question of human rights observance 'disproportionate prominence in relation to the whole spectrum' of British–Iranian relations, and would likely get the Foreign Secretary's

---

[140] P. Yarnold to Mr Major, 'Defence Sales to Iran: Competition with the Americans', 22 March 1977, TNA, FCO 8/2991.
[141] I.T.M. Lucas to Mr Weir, 'Defence Sales to Iran: Competition with the Americans', 22 March 1977, TNA, FCO 8/2991.
[142] 'Human Rights in Iran: Record of Meeting between the Minister of State and Labour MPs held in the Foreign and Commonwealth Office on Wednesday, 23 March 1977 at 4.30 P.M.', TNA, FCO 58/1164.
[143] Peter Jenkins, 'Delicate Balance', *Guardian*, 4 March 1977.
[144] Margaret Van Hatten, 'Owen gives strong support to Carter's human rights stand', *Financial Times*, 4 March 1977.
[145] 'Human Rights in Iran: Record of Meeting between the Minister of State and Labour MPs'.

relationship with the Shah 'off to a bad start'.[146] These fears were compounded by the timing of the meeting. Martin Ennals of Amnesty International was also planning a visit to Tehran, and Ivor Lucas was concerned that 'the Iranians will wrongly deduce that the British Government is in collusion with Amnesty to conduct a campaign on the subject [human rights] against the Iranian authorities'.[147] Judd, however, believed that Owen's public adoption of a human rights-based approach to foreign affairs meant that he could not afford to appear evasive on the issue: 'In view of his Human Rights initiative it may be difficult for the Secretary of State to say on [his] return that he had not raised this with the Shah.'[148] Still, although Owen duly raised the 'difficult question of human rights' during his meeting with the Shah on 14 May, and again with the Iranian Minister of Foreign Affairs the following day, according to Parsons – who witnessed Owen's encounter with the Iranian monarch – the Foreign Secretary proceeded with caution: 'the truth is that Owen spoke one very mildly worded sentence and then changed the subject.'[149]

In fact, the application of Owen's public pronouncements on international human rights promotion to Anglo–Iranian relations during the final days of the Pahlavi dynasty conforms to the policy of appeasement that had already put down roots in the FCO and the British Embassy in Tehran, which sought to rejuvenate the Shah's public image in Britain while downplaying reports concerning the human rights violations suffered by Iranian citizens.[150] During a November 1977 interview with Vanya Kewley for the BBC's *Everyman* programme, for example, Owen embraced the official line that the Shah's nascent experiment in liberalization was yielding some positive results in terms of the human rights situation in Iran.[151] Owen would subsequently put this argument to Jenny Little (head of the Labour Research Department) in February 1978 after Little had brought to Owen's attention a resolution on Iran, remitted by the Standing Orders Committee of the Party. 'The resolution is based on a questionable premise', Owen began. 'It seems to me a gross exaggeration to say that Iran has an international reputation for "ruthless political repression and torture"', he continued. 'If I may quote myself, answering a question on this subject in a television interview last November, "I think you have to look at the culture, the tradition, the history, the whole business of the authority of the Shah in its origins in Persian history, if you are going to

---

[146] Anthony Parsons to Ivor Lucas, 'TELNO 188: Amnesty's Report on Iran', 28 March 1977, FCO, TNA, FCO 8/2998.
[147] I.T.M. Lucas minute, 1 April 1977, TNA, FCO 58/1164.
[148] M.H. D'Ath to Mr Lucas, 'Human Rights in Iran: Minister of State's Meeting with Labour MPs on 23 March', 4 April 1977, TNA, FCO 58/1164. Emphasis in the original text.
[149] 'Record of Discussion between the Foreign and Commonwealth Secretary and His Imperial Majesty Mohammed Reza Pahlavi, Shahanshah Aryamehr at Niavaran Palace on Saturday, 14 May 1977 at 6 pm', TNA, FCO 58/1164; 'Record of a Meeting between the Secretary of State for Foreign and Commonwealth Affairs and Dr Khalatbari, Iranian Minister of Foreign Affairs, held in Tehran on 15 May at 10.30 am', TNA, FCO 58/1164; Anthony Parsons' comment in Nicholas W. Browne, 'British Policy and Iran 1974–1978 (post mortem on Iran)', 1981, TNA, FCO 8/4029, 86.
[150] See Felci, ' "A Latter-Day Hitler" ': 527-30..
[151] See D.E. Tatham to H.D.A.C. Miers, 'BBC Interview with Dr Owen', 29 November 1977, TNA, FCO 8/2999. As regards Owen's response reflecting that of the Embassy, see for example Anthony Parsons, 'Human Rights in Iran', Foreign and Commonwealth Office, Diplomatic Report No. 175/177, 12 April 1977, TNA, FCO 58/1164.

really take a balanced view'".[152] In the face of criticism emanating from within his own party, Owen still felt that is was possible to reconcile the conflicting imperatives of supporting the Shah and promoting human rights: 'None of this affects the deep concern I feel and have expressed about the human rights issues in Iran and elsewhere.'[153]

Owen's continued pursuit of both ends, however, was increasingly becoming a hostage to fortune. By early 1978, growing civil unrest was threatening to undermine the Shah's authority in a way that previous waves of protest had not. According to Nicholas Browne's exhaustive investigation into British policy towards Iran during this period, the regime's decision to denounce the Ayatollah Khomeini as an 'adventurer and non-believer' in January 'provoked a riot in the religious centre of Qom' that marked 'the beginning of an accelerated cycle of violent protest'.[154] Concomitantly, FCO ministers pondered whether a recalibration of HMG's approach was in order; maybe British-Iranian relations should no longer be conducted, as they had been for so many years, 'on the basis of bootlicking'.[155] Callaghan, meanwhile, apparently became increasingly reluctant to 'kowtow to the Shah'.[156] Analysis of the forces militating against the Shah, however, soon put paid to this indifference, finding 'little prospect of a liberal pro-Western regime and no particularly friendly opposition group to cultivate'.[157] The most efficacious policy, therefore, was to 'support the Shah warts and all, while occasionally offering treatment for the warts'.[158] The acceptance of this fact led the government to agree to the supply of CS gas and crowd control equipment to the Shah during the summer.[159] Owen's agreement to the sale was in no small part a response to the developing internal situation in Iran; a recognition that the Shah's prospective usurpers were unlikely to serve Britain's economic interests or advance the cause of human rights more enthusiastically than the Shah himself. It was also indicative, perhaps, of the limits of Callaghan's attenuated support of Owen's human rights policy. It would certainly comport with the account of Tom McNally, who recalls that the Prime Minister, who was broadly sceptical of championing human rights within a foreign policy context, was willing to let Owen take a more enthusiastic position, but was also quick to preach caution if and when significant strategic and economic interests were at risk.[160] In seeking to understand Owen's readiness to heed such concerns, however, it is also important to note that he was simultaneously seeking out philosophical premises with which he could frame his human rights initiative, insulating it from accusations of inconsistency and hypocrisy. Or so he hoped.

---

[152] David Owen to Jenny Little, 7 February 1978, TNA, FCO 8/3210.
[153] Ibid.
[154] Browne, 'British Policy and Iran 1974-1978', 5.
[155] Ibid., 55.
[156] Ibid.
[157] Ibid., 56.
[158] Ibid. See also Edward Posnett, 'Treating His Imperial Majesty's Warts: British Policy towards Iran, 1977-79', *Iranian Studies* 45, No. 1 (January 2012): 129-37; Erciyas, 'British Dilemmas', 187-93.
[159] For Owen's record of the decision taken to provide the Shah with CS gas, see Owen, *Personally Speaking to Kenneth Harris*, 151-2.
[160] McNally interview. See also Henry Brandon, 'Interview File: Callaghan, James, 1978', Library of Congress, Washington, DC., Manuscript Division (hereafter LOC), Henry Brandon Papers, Box 16: Folder 10.

During the annual meeting of the CENTO Ministerial Council in April 1978, Ivor Lucas recalls that Owen, while contributing to the proceedings with the 'appropriate comment here and there', was clearly preoccupied: 'I noticed that he was scribbling away, and assumed that he was making notes for his summing up of the meeting. Then I saw that he was consulting some books on the table in front of him, and glancing at these I realised that they were hardly germane to the topics under discussion: one of them was Paul Johnson's *History of Christianity*.'[161] Having left the meeting somewhat perplexed, the purpose of Owen's extra-curricular activities revealed itself to Lucas as he opened his copy of *The Times* a few days later to find 'an extract from an address given by Dr Owen in a Plymouth church on the subject of "The Morality of Compromise"; in the course of it, he quoted Paul Johnson!'[162] Owen had, in February 1978, embraced the idea of compromise more directly than he had during earlier statements relating to human rights while addressing the Zionist Foundation.[163] The address featured in *The Times*, however, constituted by far the most in-depth exposition on the issue of compromise and its integral role in the implementation of human rights policy to date.

Beginning with generalities, Owen's opening gambit asserted that '[w]e all of us compromise in our private lives. No family man or woman can possibly for one moment exist in a family without giving as well as taking; without holding a view and finding it needs to be changed; without bending to the collective will of the family.'[164] Compromise in public life, Owen bemoaned, was judged by a different standard: 'The politician's compromises are very obvious, can be seen by everyone, can be dissected, can be editorialized upon, can be scathingly attacked. Indeed, there has been a tendency to elevate, possibly to an unrealistic height, the attraction of the man in public life who is the man of principle, the man of consistency, the man of unbending views.'[165] Framing this as a false dichotomy, Owen argued that 'as in private so in public the man who is prepared to modify his views, to come together in collective decisions, to support sometimes publicly things which he may have argued against privately, to hold to his principles but not to the extent that they cannot be modified, is not someone who should be criticized'.[166] This conviction had its roots in 'much more fundamental attitudes and a much more fundamental issue', namely a disavowal of 'absolute values [being] ultimately compatible with one another'.[167] By way of explaining the genesis of

---

[161] Ivor Lucas, *A Road to Damascus: Mainly Diplomatic Memoirs from the Middle East* (London: The Radcliffe Press, 1997), 145.
[162] Ibid.
[163] See 'Secretary of State's Speech to the Zionist Foundation on 1 February 1978', TNA, FCO 73/484: 'Sometimes what Governments have to say over individual cases may cause distress and raise difficulties in our inter-governmental relations, affect our business relations, our financial relations and therefore our own prosperity and employment prospects at home. This does not mean that we should keep silent it means that we have to be sensible and not provoke unnecessary damage ... At the governmental level, therefore, the question of human rights has to be seen in this wider perspective.'
[164] Owen, 'The Morality of Compromise', *The Times*.
[165] Ibid.
[166] Ibid.
[167] Ibid.

this belief, Owen posited that his medical background had disposed him to the notion that 'human nature and its values, though profound, and even sacred to the individual, are so personal, and those values so unique to the individual that there is not nor can there be absolutes in values'.[168] Following the publication of *Human Rights* in August, however, it became clear that this inclination had been buttressed by the philosophy expounded by Isaiah Berlin: 'I have been profoundly influenced by the writings of Sir Isaiah Berlin and his most recent book, *Russian Thinkers* (Hogarth Press, 1978).'[169] Indeed, while direct references to Berlin are absent in the address featured in *The Times*, sections of the 'Morality of Compromise' undoubtedly signify an appreciation of Berlin's oeuvre.

As Owen reveals in his memoirs, Berlin's seminal essay *The Hedgehog and the Fox*, which distils the world's thinkers into two categories – hedgehogs, who 'relate everything to a single central vision, one system ... a single universal organising principle'; and foxes, 'who pursue many ends, often unrelated and even contradictory' – clearly resonated with him during his student days in Cambridge.[170] Owen quickly identified with the latter, 'distrusting those who knew one big idea'.[171] This is not, however, the strand of Berlin's philosophy that predominated in Owen's speech. Rather, Berlin's conviction 'that human goods are irreducibly plural, frequently incompatible, and sometimes incommensurable with one another' – his championing of 'value pluralism' – is the aspect of his philosophical outlook which seems to have played the key role in the construction of Owen's 'Morality of Compromise'.[172] There was, in Owen's view, 'an inevitable conflict of values and what is more an inevitable conflict in the interpretation of values ... within the human system ... If you accept this then you come to the fact, as I see it, that compromise is the bridge. Compromise, far from being the enemy of morality, is its friend'.[173] This premise, it would appear, provided Owen with sufficient philosophical justification for advancing a human rights-based approach to foreign affairs that would not, indeed could not, be applied with complete consistency:

> I do not believe that a country can operate in the world without trying to project its own ethical values, its own moral principles. Once you believe that, and once you say that, you become a victim for those people to whom consistency is itself an absolute value, to whom any deviation from principle is somehow seen as weakness and to those who want to elevate to an unnatural level an inflexible and rigid hierarchy of values. When I began to speak out for human rights and a policy of human rights to permeate our whole foreign policy, I warned that there was a price to pay – that price was a little inconsistency from time to time ... I would no longer say a little inconsistency, I would say a very great deal of inconsistency ... I do not

---

[168] Ibid.
[169] Owen, *Human Rights*, 2.
[170] Isaiah Berlin, *Russian Thinkers*, revised edn (London: Penguin, 2008), 24; Owen, *Time to Declare*, 51.
[171] Ibid.
[172] George Crowder, 'Pluralism, Relativism and Liberalism in Isaiah Berlin', refereed paper presented to the Australasian Political Studies Association Conference, University of Tasmania, Hobart, 29 September–1 October 2003, available at http://berlin.wolf.ox.ac.uk/ (accessed 9 January 2020).
[173] Owen, 'The Morality of Compromise', *The Times*.

support attacks on the compromiser and the compromise. I do not understate the value of at times the use of expedience or expediency. I do not uphold as an absolute value criticism of the inconsistent or of the inconsistencies. I do not believe that contradiction is always wrong.[174]

The fact that a British Foreign Secretary should find political capital in Berlin's philosophical output is eminently understandable. Berlin had in fact been courted by the British political establishment during the early years of the Cold War with a view to providing the ideological struggle with a degree of philosophical clarity.[175] Moreover, although Berlin rebuffed these overtures, his conception of value pluralism, and its perceived ability to provide the reconciliation of divergent ethical and strategic imperatives with philosophical ballast, has exhibited an enduring influence in Western political discourse.[176] As Jan-Werner Müller notes, in the eyes of his many admirers, Berlin has much to offer those facing difficult intellectual-political decisions, helping them 'to resist an attitude where one positively revels in a sense of moral certainty'.[177] It therefore follows that Owen's increasing exposure to the underlying realities of British–Iranian relations led him towards a greater appreciation of Berlin's writings on the concept of value pluralism. It is important to point out, however, that while Owen's engagement with Berlin's thinking dated back to his student days in Cambridge, his *re-engagement* with Berlin was, in part, a consequence of a wider search for philosophical material pertaining to the ethics of compromise, undertaken as the conflicting imperatives of human rights promotion and the pursuit of British economic and strategic interests vis-à-vis Iran were becoming increasingly stark. For example, Owen not only sifted through Paul Johnson's *History of Christianity* (1976) in order to substantiate his 'morality of compromise' (a search that likely yielded the references within the speech to the writings of Søren Kierkegaard); correspondence in his private papers seems to suggest that he also sought out John Morley's *On Compromise* (1874).[178] Morley's book, as Byron Dexter wrote shortly after the end of the Second World War, may have provided 'the textbook' for a generation of Victorian reformers, but it also spoke to the contemporary need to locate 'the boundaries of compromise in international relations'.[179] *On Compromise*, Dexter continued, 'was essentially a theoretical statement of the relationship of principle and expediency in the affairs of the world', in which Morley 'wished to allot to principle the greatest possible share in

---

[174] Ibid.
[175] Anne Deighton, 'Don and Diplomat: Isaiah Berlin and Britain's Early Cold War', *Cold War History* 13, No. 4 (2013): 525–40.
[176] See Jan-Werner Müller, 'Introduction: Concepts, Character, and the Specter of New Cold Wars', in *Isaiah Berlin's Cold War Liberalism*, ed. Jan-Werner Müller (Singapore: Palgrave Macmillan, 2019), 1–10.
[177] Ibid., 3.
[178] David Owen to Sergeant Wilson, 21 July 1978, DOP, D709 2/7/1/6: 'Thank you very much for returning the book "On Compromise" by John Morley [to the Foreign Office library] which I had given up for lost. I am most grateful to you.'
[179] Byron Dexter, 'Morley and Compromise', *Foreign Affairs* 26, No. 2 (January 1948): 336.

setting the boundaries, and for that reason he took pains to make principle an extension of the search for a practicable solution to problems, not the enemy of it'.[180]

Owen's 'Morality of Compromise', however, not only inverted Morley's interpretation of the relationship between principle and expediency (taking expediency as an extension of principle); it could also be argued that Owen – as a consequence of engaging with Berlin's output with at least one eye on justifying the inconsistencies of his human rights policy – distorted Berlin's understanding of value pluralism as it pertained to the protection of human rights. While Berlin's views on human rights were complicated to say the least, it has been suggested that his views on liberal pluralism 'in which his tragic value pluralism is embedded within, and constrained by other ingredients of, a common moral horizon that gives priority to the value of human survival', and 'to a minimum core of human rights distributed and sanctioned by such rules', point to Berlin's implicit conviction that some fundamental values ought not to be sacrificed in the name of expediency.[181] It is therefore understandable that while some readers deemed Owen's sincerity refreshing and even laudable, many found cause for concern.[182] Professor Stephen Haseler of Georgetown University, for example, commended Owen for a 'sophisticated defence of the politician's necessary art of compromise free from the bogus pomposity that so often suffuses the world of statecraft', but nonetheless found it troubling that 'Dr Owen at no point in his published remarks' addressed 'the question as to when compromise should stop'. 'Surely', Haseler wrote:

> There has to be a point beyond which a man who holds to certain values (perhaps Dr Owen's 'man of unbending views') can no longer compromise them if they are under attack? Here is the gaping void, the fatal flaw, in Owen's submission. To elevate compromise itself into a morality, or at a lower level to proselytize on its merits, not only holds up one to the charge of holding no values (obviously not the case for Dr Owen) but, more seriously, sends a terrifying message to one's opponents. That message, put simply, is that they can always win if they push hard enough.[183]

As regards his approach towards the Shah, however, Owen clearly did not reach the outer limits of his compromise ethic. Moreover, attempts to justify his increasingly pragmatic approach to human rights promotion internationally served to amplify

---

[180] Ibid., 341.
[181] Jonathan Riley, 'Liberal Pluralism and Common Decency', in *Isaiah Berlin's Cold War Liberalism*, ed. Müller, 57–91, 57. Regarding Berlin's stance on human rights, see for example Deighton, 'Don and Diplomat': 536. Deighton notes how, in the process of rebuffing a Foreign Office invitation to provide Western efforts in the ideological struggle of the Cold War with some philosophical heft, Berlin referred 'scathingly' to the Universal Declaration of Human Rights, which had been mooted as a potential pillar around which a Western sense of ideological purpose could be constructed. See also Bryan Magee, *Men of Ideas* (New York: The Viking Press, 1978), 17–18.
[182] See for example, Randolph Wise, 'Morality of Compromise', *The Times*, 10 May 1978; Eric James, 'Morality of Compromise', *The Times*, 12 May 1978.
[183] Stephen M. Haseler, 'Morality of Compromise', *The Times*, 9 May 1978. See also David Maud, 'Morality of Compromise', *The Times*, 6 May 1978.

criticism of the Labour government's policy of appeasement, exacerbating the schism between the Labour left and the centre-right Labour Cabinet, and eroding public trust in 'Dr David "Human Rights" Owen' and the selective application of his principled rhetoric.[184]

The decision taken to provide the Iranian authorities with crowd control equipment during the summer of 1978 was followed by another cycle of protests. President Carter's reaffirmation of his administration's support for the Shah on 10 September, and the arrival of the Ayatollah in Paris two weeks later only served to perpetuate and exacerbate this civil unrest. 'It was about this time', Owen recalls, 'that my views on Iran involved me personally in domestic political flak'.[185] The source of Owen's troubles were comments that he had made following an interview with Brian Walden. The interview itself was primarily concerned with African affairs, but, after the cameras had stopped rolling, the conversation turned to events in Iran. Owen told Walden 'how necessary it was that Britain backed the Shah, and gave him the reasons. He asked me if I would repeat them on television. I said I would. But like a fool, I agreed to record them there and then'.[186] Owen's comments were eventually televized on 22 October during an edition of *Weekend World* devoted to Iran – by this stage, 'the situation had much deteriorated'.[187] The programme itself 'described the number of Labour MPs who abominated the regime; the secret police; the supply of arms ... implied Chieftain tanks were being used to shoot down Iranian democrats in the streets; and painted a grim picture of the Shah's tyrannical regime'.[188] Owen's comments to the effect that pushing the Shah too firmly towards liberalization would only serve to embolden elements of the opposition who were themselves 'opposed to modernization and liberalization', were consequently framed as unflatteringly as possible by Walden:

> After I had finished, Brian Walden said: 'This is one of the bluntest answers I think I have ever heard any government spokesman give on Iran.' He ended the programme with: 'Iran is far from being the only country in which a regime Britain supports is abusing rights. In Africa, Asia and Latin America, we're relying on lots of very brutal friends to protect our interests. They'll doubtless all be glad to learn that Britain's concern for human rights is at the moment running a poor second to the need to defend British interests.'[189]

The interview, as Owen recalls, dealt a fatal blow to his relationship with the Labour left and, following the broadcast, Stan Newens, Labour MP for Harlow, and Frank Allaun, chairman of the Labour Action for Peace group, took the opportunity to write to the Prime Minister, pointing out that 'the Labour Party took an entirely different view of the Iranian disturbances from the Government and was highly critical

---

[184] Edward Mortimer, 'The "Iranian Values" which Keep the Shah in Power', *The Times*, 26 October 1978.
[185] Owen, *Personally Speaking to Kenneth Harris*, 154.
[186] Ibid.
[187] Ibid.
[188] Ibid.
[189] Ibid., 155.

of the Shah's methods'.[190] As Owen makes clear, however, he did not regret the comments he gave during the interview itself, 'only the timing of its release'.[191] Indeed, a 4 October minute from David Stephen indicates that Owen was well aware that the government's Iranian policy would likely come under increasing scrutiny during the coming months, but was nonetheless 'prepared to take this on'.[192] As such, Owen stood by the decision to supply the Shah with another shipment of CS gas, reiterating the justification that featured in his interview with Walden in the Commons on 6 November.[193] But his words were beginning to sound ever more hollow, and although Owen had not yet reached the point at which principle and expediency could no longer be reconciled, his attempts to square the circle were, it seems, becoming increasingly galling. Following the arrest of Iranian opposition leader, Dr Karim Sanjabi, for example, the *Tribune* took the opportunity to comment on the recent publication of Owen's *Human Rights*, in which large sections of his thesis on the 'Morality of Compromise' are reproduced verbatim:

> In his book, *Human Rights* (which we are happy to report, is not selling well), our Foreign Secretary, David Owen writes: 'I am sometimes criticised for talking too much about moral values, for trying to draw attention to the latent altruism that I believe exists in most individuals and which is not fully tapped' ... Now really this joke has gone too far ... Few people will be surprised to find a British Foreign Secretary sticking up for a tyrant like the Shah of Iran. To do so is completely consistent with everything we know about the conduct of British foreign and commercial affairs. What does turn the stomach slightly is the constant posturing and moralising we get from David Owen.[194]

Nonetheless, as 1978 drew to a close, Owen saw little cause for an alteration of the government's approach. As Browne records, on 20 December 'the Foreign Secretary conducted a further review of British policy. He concluded that it would be best to follow the old naval maxim: "In a fog slow down but do not change course".'[195] The Shah fled from Iran on 16 January and the Ayatollah arrived in Tehran to fill the power vacuum two weeks later. Subsequent events, however, only served to reinforce Owen's conviction that Britain had made the correct decision – in terms of protecting its interests *and* promoting human rights: 'I was right when I said that if the Shah fell, the mullahs would take over, and their regime on human rights would be far worse ... British interests were at stake and when the Shah was toppled we suffered and are still

---

[190] Regarding the impact of the *Weekend World* interview on Owen's relationship with the Labour left, see ibid. The letter from Newens and Allaun is quoted in 'Dr Owen sees danger if the Shah is ousted', *The Times*, 23 October 1978.
[191] Ibid.
[192] David Stephen to Mr Tomkys, 4 October 1978, TNA, FCO 73/484.
[193] See I.T.M. Lucas to Mr Weir, 'Arms Sales to Iran: Call by Mr Newens', 27 November 1978 with attached brief 'Arms Sales to Iran – Call on Mr Judd by Stanley Newens MP 28 November', TNA, FCO 8/3124; 'Iran', 6 November 1978, *Hansard: House of Commons*, Volume 957.
[194] 'Human Rights: Sanjabi arrested in Iran but no public protest from David Owen', *Tribune*, 17 November 1978, TNA, FCO 73/484.
[195] Browne, 'British Policy and Iran 1974–78', 59.

suffering.'[196] While Owen's continued support for the Shah was undoubtedly shaped by these assumptions (better the devil you know …) the preceding paragraphs have posited that an appreciation of Owen's 'Morality of Compromise' helps us to understand why Owen did not jettison his human rights initiative or disavow his emphatic public pronouncements on the subject, and instead felt emboldened to pursue the reconciliation of two imperatives that were bound to conflict with each other – the pursuit of British interests, be they economic or strategic, and the elevation of human rights within the context of British foreign policy.

Conclusion

In response to an emergent international human rights zeitgeist that gathered speed during the 1970s, the FCO made tentative steps towards the institutionalization of human rights concerns in the British foreign policymaking process. Work on the human rights comparative assessment, for instance, began well before Jimmy Carter had articulated his human rights commitment on the global stage. David Owen, through his public statements, subsequently amplified the nascent human rights dimension in British foreign policy following his appointment as Foreign Secretary in February 1977. Owen's human rights initiative, moreover, exerted a perceptible influence over Britain's bilateral relationships. This was clearly observable with regard to El Salvador, where Owen's human rights-based approach to foreign affairs helped to create the space in which a powerful human rights lobby, spearheaded by the CIIR, could operate and bring sufficient pressure to bear on the Callaghan government to warrant the cancellation of a military contract. While certainly less influential in the context of British–Iranian relations, Owen's statements on the subject of human rights nonetheless had the effect of partially constraining the entrepreneurial instincts of the British arms industry.

Both case studies, however, have ultimately served to define the narrow parameters within which human rights interests could shape the formulation and implementation of policy during David Owen's tenure as Foreign and Commonwealth Secretary. It would be potentially misleading, for example, to state that the sale of armoured vehicles to El Salvador was cancelled on human rights grounds. Human rights considerations played a key role, to be sure, but it would appear that strategic considerations regarding Belize also had to be leveraged in order to cancel the contract. Official explanations also make clear that Whitehall preferred to emphasise the Belize angle, lest a dangerous precedent be set whereby human rights campaigns could be expected to yield the cancellation of contracts with human rights offenders whose pocketbooks were at lot larger than the government of El Salvador's. While the lobbying efforts of the CIIR – which found a sympathetic audience within policymaking circles – were able to overcome FCO inertia, these deeply embedded economic interests, compounded by geopolitical concerns, led to the subordination of Owen's principled rhetoric to the

---

[196] Owen, *Personally Speaking to Kenneth Harris*, 155.

maintenance of cordial relations with the Shah's dictatorship during the twilight of the Pahlavi dynasty. In the process of exploring the marginalization of human rights concerns within the context of Anglo–Iranian relations, which became evident prior to Owen's appointment as Foreign Secretary, but continued during his stewardship of the Foreign Office, the Iranian case study also revealed another aspect of Owen's political outlook – a compromise ethic that rejected moral monism and drew inspiration from the concept of value pluralism elucidated by Isaiah Berlin. Owen hoped that this would allow him to pursue a human rights-based foreign policy that would also be able to accommodate the more unsavoury aspects of Britain's 'national interest'. In the event, while Owen may have embarked upon his radical reframing of Britain's human rights commitments with a view to building bridges between extra-parliamentary activists and the Labour Party, this strategy merely served to amplify criticism of the government's policy of appeasement and exacerbate the schism that had been developing between the left of the Party and the centre-right Cabinet. Indeed, if Owen intended to bind the internationalist sentiment that was stirring outside of parliament to the state through his public adoption of the human rights cause, by the time the Pahlavi dynasty experienced its ignominious denouement, his attempts to rationalize the contradictions of his human rights initiative had communicated to his audience another message entirely – that 'grand rhetoric is a sign of an interest having a lower value in practice than policy pronouncements suggest'.[197] They also reflected the wisdom of Zbigniew Brzezinski, President Carter's National Security Adviser and acolyte of Hans Morgenthau: 'Principle and expediency obviously collide, though one can always find some formula for rationalizing the supremacy of one over the other.'[198]

The limitations that were placed on human rights promotion within the context of British foreign policy during Owen's tenure as Foreign Secretary – boundaries that were defined by deeply embedded institutional concerns, the failure to adequately institutionalise human rights commitments within the FCO machinery, and by Owen's philosophical outlook – have therefore been clearly delineated. However, while this chapter sought to illuminate such complicating factors by focusing on Britain's bilateral relationships with human rights offenders – of which the case studies of El Salvador and Iran served as particularly illustrative examples – the following chapter will continue to explore the spaces within which human rights advocacy impacted British foreign policy, and the factors that confined them, by assessing how policymakers approached the pursuit of human rights imperatives in concert with their allies in the United States and the European Community during this 'breakthrough' period in the history of human rights and international relations.

---

[197] Donnelly, *Universal Human Rights*, 171.
[198] Zbigniew Brzezinski, 'The New Dimensions of Human Rights', Fourteenth Morgenthau Memorial Lecture on Ethics and Foreign Policy, 26 May 1995, available at https://www.carnegiecouncil.org/publications/archive/morgenthau/269 (accessed 9 January 2020).

3

In Search of a Role

Human Rights and British Relations with the United States and the European Community

Introducing the topic of human rights and comparative foreign policy, David P. Forsythe highlighted national 'self-image' as a key factor that 'affects attention to human rights, both at home and in foreign policy'.[1] Indeed, as demonstrated by the abundant scholarship devoted to the human rights-based foreign policy advanced by President Carter, the elevation of human rights concerns within the realm of foreign policy ought to be viewed as the result of 'a two-level game' in which 'domestic values and pressures combine with international standards and pressures to produce a given policy in a given situation for a given time'.[2] Perceptions of accelerating globalization and the emergence of 'an increasingly complex international system' that loomed large during the 1970s may have provided a novel ideational framework within which the Carter administration situated its foreign policy approach.[3] Nonetheless, the explosion in American human rights engagement during the 1970s – typified by Carter's moralistic foreign policy – also grew out of a desire to salve the psychological wounds inflicted upon the American psyche by the catastrophe of the Vietnam War, and the moral bankruptcy of the Nixon era: 'As Americans entered the 1970s, many felt that they were standing on quicksand. Old certainties, beliefs, and standards – about America's role in the world and the nature of the world at large – had crumbled. The promotion of international human rights was one of the ideas that helped Americans to make sense of the new global terrain.'[4] The task of appropriately situating hitherto-neglected British diplomatic perspectives on the so-called human rights 'breakthrough' of the 1970s amid the rapidly expanding historiography, therefore, requires careful consideration of the ways in which human rights promotion may have reflected domestic debates surrounding the (re)definition of Britain's role within an increasingly interconnected international system. After all, David Owen's public adoption of the

---

[1] David P. Forsythe, 'Introduction', in *Human Rights and Comparative Foreign Policy*, ed. Forsythe, 2.
[2] Ibid.
[3] Jerel A. Rosati, *The Carter Administration's Quest for Global Community: Beliefs and their Impact on Behaviour* (Columbia, SC: University of South Carolina Press, 1987), 40.
[4] Barbara Keys, *Reclaiming American Virtue: The Human Rights Revolution of the 1970s* (Cambridge, MA: Harvard University Press, 2014), 3.

human rights cause appears to have coincided with a particularly introspective moment, in which the prospective recalibration of the nation's overseas role became subject to intense scrutiny.

In some quarters, Dean Acheson's incisive critique of British intransigence – the notion that Great Britain had 'lost an Empire' and had 'not yet found a role' – was still regarded as a fitting summary of the post-war British experience.[5] For example, Lord Harlech, Chairman of the Main Study Group at Chatham House, which set out in October 1977 to appropriately define Britain's international responsibilities by asking whether Britain's once expansive horizons should undergo a contraction commensurate with her economic misfortunes, bemoaned Britain's apparent inability to come to terms with its reduced international status: 'after fifty years of self-delusion, can we find a broad role to measure it with our reduced circumstances? That I suggest is the task that Chatham House has set itself with this study and that is the formidable task my colleagues and I will try to perform.'[6] Nonetheless, in suggesting that Britain's socio-economic woes were largely self-inflicted and reversible, Lord Harlech seemed to envisage a rosier future for Britain abroad than the one intimated by the report of the Central Policy Review Staff (CPRS) months earlier.[7]

The Berrill Report, as it is perhaps better known, advocated 'a drastic cut in, and changed role for, British overseas representation' predicated on what it called 'a more realistic and modest concept of the UK's role in the world'.[8] Lord Harlech was not alone in criticizing the CPRS's conclusion that 'excellence is bad and mediocrity should be clasped to our bosom, as befits a medium sized power'.[9] The report's fatalistic tone was also roundly criticized in the Lords when it was debated in November 1977. Written in a 'minor key', it was a 'dismal diagnosis' at odds with Lord Ballantrae's experience of the diplomatic service, which was 'continually focusing on the years that lie ahead, without loss of dignity, without loss of prestige, and, above all, without that spirit of defeatism which seems to me to run through this whole Review'.[10] Lord Home, likewise, condemned the 'charter for pessimism and defeatism' and urged Owen to dismiss its findings: 'The report is introspective, which is the last thing, in our present situation, that this country ought to be. I hope that the Foreign and Commonwealth Secretary, and his successors in that office, will have confidence in himself and his ambassadors.'[11] Owen obliged. Not only did he dismiss Berrill's diagnosis; he would also, throughout his tenure as Foreign Secretary, seek to drive home the message that defeatism and 'finding a role' were not one and the same: 'It is time for us to stop selling ourselves

---

[5] Dean Acheson, 'Our Atlantic Alliance: The Political and Economic Strands', speech delivered at the United States Military Academy, West Point, New York, 5 December 1962. Reprinted in *Vital Speeches of the Day* 29, No. 6 (1 January 1963): 163.
[6] Lord Harlech, 'Future of British Foreign Policy', 18 October 1977, Chatham House Online Archive, RIIA/8/3854.
[7] Ibid.
[8] Brian Harrison, *Finding a Role? The United Kingdom, 1970–1990* (Oxford: Oxford University Press, 2010), 21–2; Central Policy Review Staff, *Review of Overseas Representation* (1977), cited in ibid., 22.
[9] Lord Harlech, 'Future of British Foreign Policy'.
[10] 'CPRS: "Review of Overseas Representation"', 23 November 1977, *Hansard: House of Lords*, Volume 387, Column 854.
[11] Ibid., Column 888–9.

short and to end our present mood of introspection and self-denigration. We need more self-confidence, more national buoyancy. We are in danger of exaggerating our weaknesses and of underplaying our potential. We have considerable strengths.'[12]

By looking beyond 'traditionalist' accounts of British post-war foreign policy and adopting instead a 'transformationalist' approach that is more attentive to the ways in which historical actors sought to arrest – or even reverse – Britain's relative decline within the international community, this chapter will explore how Owen's human rights advocacy reflected his optimistic assessment of Britain's capacity to influence international affairs.[13] Disregarding the prevailing wisdom of senior FCO officials, who maintained that Britain's future lay firmly within the European Community (EC), and that romanticized notions of its 'special relationship' with the United States only served to obscure this reality, Owen viewed Britain's relationships with the United States and the EC as mutually reinforcing, and sought to play an active role in the promotion of international human rights in concert with both.

As it pertained to the former, human rights promotion served to situate the Callaghan government shoulder-to-shoulder with the Carter administration, thus facilitating the continued rapprochement between the two nations following a subtle downgrading of the transatlantic partnership during the early 1970s. Owen's attempts to champion human rights within an essentially 'Churchillian' conception of Britain's international role, however, served to problematize EC cooperation on foreign policy issues. Carter's stance on human rights caused a significant degree of consternation within the Community, with member states sensing that the President's human rights crusade – and by extension, Owen's – could disrupt détente and stymie continental cooperation between East and West. Britain's EC partners were also unwilling to push as hard as Owen was for the inclusion of human rights provisions in the renegotiated Lomé Convention, a trade and aid agreement between the EC and African, Caribbean and Pacific (ACP) countries. By the time it was voted out of office in May 1979, the Callaghan government cut an isolated figure within the Community, even though its energetic attempts to institutionalize human rights provisions within the foreign policy apparatus of the EC cannot be easily reconciled with conventional narratives of British (or Labour Party) Euroscepticism. By examining these transatlantic tensions, this chapter will not only continue to situate British diplomatic perspectives within the vast historiography concerning the human rights 'breakthrough' of the 1970s, but will also address long-standing debates surrounding Britain's search for a post-imperial role in the international arena, approach the subject of Anglo-American relations from a fresh perspective, and contribute to timely conversations concerning Britain's complex relationship with the European Union and its forebears. Furthermore, by illuminating the generational specificity of Owen's conception of Britain's overseas role and its capacity to exert a progressive influence on world affairs, this chapter will reveal yet more of Owen's worldview and the ways in which it prefigured his human rights advocacy.

---

[12] Owen, *Human Rights*, 17–18. For Owen's view of the Berrill Report, see Owen, *Time to Declare*, 264–5.
[13] See Self, *British Foreign and Defence Policy since 1945*, 7–12, 7.

A return to the 'special relationship'

Anglo-American relations had worsened significantly during the early 1970s under the premiership of Edward Heath, who made no secret of his deeply-held conviction that Britain ought to prioritise the cultivation of its European connections. The subtle downgrading of the 'special relationship' to a 'natural relationship' under Heath was certainly accelerated by his failure to strike up a rapport with President Richard Nixon.[14] Faltering interpersonal relations, moreover, were compounded by disagreements between the two countries over the Yom Kippur War of 1973 and by the shockwaves sent through the global economy in the aftermath of the OPEC oil crisis of the same year.[15] Heath's campaign to integrate the UK into the European Community, however, had arguably the most deleterious effect on Anglo–American relations during this period, eroding 'still further what remained of Anglo-American contacts at the highest level'.[16] Simply put: 'Heath's vision of the future did not include an Anglo-American special relationship.'[17]

Owen fundamentally rejected this outlook. A matter of weeks after his appointment as Foreign Secretary, he was interviewed by journalist and son-in-law of the Prime Minister, Peter Jay, for the BBC's *Weekend World*, revealing in the process his far-reaching conception of Britain's overseas role. At its core, Owen saw no conflict between the pursuit of British interests via the European Community and a 'unique access to the United States'.[18] Furthermore, the exploitation of the latter would add weight to British concerns if they pertained to issues where Britain could claim some form of 'historical involvement and expertise', particularly where there was 'a Commonwealth connection'.[19] Owen, then, can be seen to iterate an essentially 'Churchillian' diplomatic framework in which Britain could exercise a unique influence on the international stage by dint of its position at the nexus of three interconnected spheres of influence: Europe, the United States and the Commonwealth.[20] Owen, however, felt that this triumvirate had become imbalanced, as emphasis had shifted towards Britain's increasing integration into the EC following its entry in 1973. As myriad historians of British diplomacy have recorded, the drive towards greater European involvement was, to some degree, based on the perception that Britain's relationships with the other two

---

[14] C.J. Bartlett, *"The Special Relationship": A Political History of Anglo-American Relations since 1945* (Harlow: Longman, 1992), 130. See also John Dumbrell, *A Special Relationship: Anglo-American Relations from the Cold War to Iraq* (Basingstoke: Palgrave Macmillan, 2006), 75.

[15] See for example Bartlett, *"The Special Relationship"*, 132–4; Self, *British Foreign and Defence Policy since 1945*, 87; Michael F. Hopkins, 'Introduction,' in *The Washington Embassy: British Ambassadors to the United States, 1939–77*, ed. Michael F. Hopkins, Saul Kelly and John W. Young, (Basingstoke: Palgrave Macmillan, 2009), 11–12.

[16] Bartlett, *"The Special Relationship"*, 130.

[17] Alan P. Dobson, *Anglo-American Relations in the Twentieth Century: of Friendship, Conflict and the Rise and Decline of Superpowers* (New York: Routledge, 1995), 141. See also David Dimbleby and David Reynolds, *An Ocean Apart: The Relationship Between Britain and America in the Twentieth Century* (London: Hodder & Stoughton, 1988), 266–87.

[18] David Owen, interview for BBC's *Weekend World*, 3 April 1977, DOP, D709 2/7/2/2.

[19] Ibid.

[20] For a summary of the Churchill doctrine, see for example David Sanders, *Losing an Empire, Finding a Role: British Foreign Policy since 1945* (Basingstoke: Palgrave Macmillan, 1990), 1.

'spheres' could no longer be leveraged sufficiently as a means of retaining international influence.[21] As such, it should come as little surprise to find that Owen interpreted the prevailing Eurocentrism as an outgrowth of a wider pessimism which needed addressing: 'We have got into a mood of self-denigration and a feeling that we have lost our buoyancy. In the very necessary reorientation of our policy towards Europe, we have swung the pendulum so that there is a danger of restricting our horizons.'[22] This impression had been reinforced during the early days of his tenure as Foreign Secretary, through his encounters with senior diplomats who seemingly embodied this synthesis of Eurocentrism and defeatism:

> My main task [upon accepting the position of Foreign Secretary] ... was to brief myself thoroughly on the European Community. As I did, it dawned on me that the UK really did have a lousy deal. Yet talking to Foreign Office officials, with some notable exceptions, I found the senior diplomats so dismissive, even light-hearted, about these realities that I soon despaired of being able to develop a tough negotiating stance which we would stick to ... Too many of the Euro-diplomats were reluctant to embark on any course which put us at serious loggerheads with the majority of Community members. They were intelligent people but they never had the tenacity to fight for British interests in the same way as the French diplomats fought at every level for France. Many of the British diplomats by contrast are Euro-federalists, believe in an eventual United States of Europe and do think this is a higher calling than the more mundane task of fighting the British corner.[23]

Although Stephen Wall (who served as Owen's Assistant Private Secretary at the FCO) is somewhat dismissive of Owen's characterization of these diplomats as 'Euro-federalists', he concedes that there existed during this period a vanguard of 'senior diplomats who had got used to having a campaigning role over the European Community', and were therefore unwilling to pursue policies which may be seen as combative or obstreperous within the Community.[24] Perhaps understandably, then, Owen quickly subsumed these encounters within a broader narrative of generational conflict. Indeed, Owen's phraseology – that Britain ought to 'have grown out of' such masochistic tendencies, for example – betrayed his strongly-held belief that Britain had reached a fork in the road.[25] The myopia exhibited by the 'Euro-federalists' in the

---

[21] See Philip Murphy, 'Britain and the Commonwealth: Confronting the Past – Imagining the Future', *The Round Table* 100, No. 414 (June 2011): 271. Regarding the stresses and strains placed on Anglo-American relations during this period, see for example Sanders, *Losing an Empire*, 174–7; Bartlett, *"The Special Relationship"*; Dumbrell, *A Special Relationship*.
[22] 'Wanted: a Bolder Britain', David Owen interview in *The Sunday Times*, 12 September 1977.
[23] Owen, *Time to Declare*, 245–6.
[24] Sir Stephen Wall, interview with Thomas Raineau (Universite de Paris – Sorbonne), part 1, 12 December 2010; part 2, 28 February 2012, BDOHP, available at https://www.chu.cam.ac.uk/media/uploads/files/Wall.pdf (accessed 1 September 2017); Owen, *Time to Declare*, 248.
[25] 'Speech Prepared for Delivery by the Foreign and Commonwealth Secretary, the RT Hon Dr David Owen MP, to the International Press Association, Brussels', 24 May 1977, DOP, D709 2/7/2/1.

Foreign Office was to be rejected by an incoming generation of Britons who could not comprehend – and much less countenance – their single-minded Eurocentrism.

Owen's decision to appoint the aforementioned Jay as British Ambassador to the United States in May 1977 in place of Peter Ramsbotham, moreover, can be interpreted as a manifestation of this outlook – a self-assured image of Britain propagated by a generation who simultaneously rejected notions of pre-war imperial grandeur and fatalistic readings of Britain's decline from world power. Certainly, we ought to be wary of generalising based on Owen's example. As Owen himself has noted, his concerns regarding the perceived Eurocentrism of senior FCO officials were not widely shared by his contemporaries within Whitehall. Narratives of generational schism, therefore, may be of limited utility in terms of bringing Britain's multifaceted engagement with the EC into focus.[26] Nonetheless, in explaining Jay's appointment, Owen would repeatedly underscore this sense of generational division and its implications regarding the construction of a more optimistic vision of British foreign policy. Consider, for example, this excerpt from Owen's press briefing following Jay's appointment: 'I made the decision ... because I believe he has outstanding ability. In my view he is one of the most able of my generation ... He will bring to his new job new ideas, new attitudes, and present an intelligent, realistic and confident image of Britain in the US.'[27] This notion of a generational watershed was also present in Owen's explanatory letter to US Secretary of State, Cyrus Vance.[28] Likewise, in defending his decision during a September 1977 interview with *The Sunday Times*, Owen once again framed Jay's appointment within a broader, generational shift, which brought with it a fresh outlook:

> I want to project a more optimistic and confident image of Britain. I felt that here I was, a young Foreign Secretary, and I wanted to have somebody who spoke for my generation, and, therefore, I put [forward] somebody who was able and competent to project an image of Britain which was, I think, one that I would like to project ... Timidity and caution have been ... the reasons, I think, why Britain has lacked something in the last few decades. We need more get up and go, we need a slightly more dynamic attitude if we are to pull through and assert our true place in the world.[29]

Entrusted with conveying this new-found optimism to the Carter administration, Jay wasted little time in reassuring his Embassy staff that a bright and prosperous future lay ahead: 'I do not believe that Britain is doomed – on the contrary, I think it is on the forefront of the most exciting and challenging battle over political, social and economic adjustments which face all the democratic industrialised countries equally and that Britain is probably further advanced than most of them towards pioneering fruitful

---

[26] Owen interview, 6 December 2017.
[27] 'Excerpt from the Secretary of State's Press Briefing Today on Mr Jay's Appointment', 11 May 1977, DOP, D709 2/7/2/2.
[28] 'Letter from David Owen to Cyrus Vance' 2 May 1977, Peter Jay Papers, Churchill College, Cambridge (hereafter PJAY) 2/24.
[29] 'Wanted: a Bolder Britain', *The Sunday Times*.

solutions to these problems.'³⁰ In seeking to contextualize Jay's ebullience, we should certainly not overlook the contemporaneous revival of Britain's economic fortunes. In contrast to the sense of restricted horizons which had prevailed during the majority of Ramsbotham's tenure, Jay had arrived in the American capital at a 'happier moment' according to the *Washington Post*, 'as North Sea oil begins to balance Britain's international accounts, strengthen the pound and lift the spirits of British diplomacy'.³¹ The fundamental argument of the 1977 CPRS Report – that 'the continued deterioration in Britain's economic position over the past eight years has directly and unavoidably weakened Britain's international standing' – had therefore been undermined by the recent easing of financial restrictions.³² Jay's sense of optimism, however, was not just a consequence of a recent 'balancing of the books'; it was, it seems, rooted in the perception that a more fundamental transformation was taking place within British society.

Speaking to the National Press Club on 7 September 1977, for example, Jay declared that a 'new era' was beginning to take shape.³³ A 'new realism' had begun to spread through the nation which went far deeper than the 'favourable cyclical trends' of stock market recovery and the increased foreign investment that had served to assuage economic anxieties. This reflected 'a change of heart' which was, to some extent, 'a product of a new generation in all parts of our national life who never knew the era of Empire and great-power status and so have no hankerings to go back to an irrecoverable past, who caught the American preference for success over the most elegantly justified failure'.³⁴ For Jay, as with Owen, the upshot of this generational schism from a foreign policy perspective boiled down to the revival of Churchillian diplomacy: 'The decision of the British people in 1975 to confirm their membership of the Common Market was decisive ... This has given new and practical significance to Winston Churchill's old saw about Britain's unique position at the natural intersection of European, Commonwealth and Atlantic relationships'.³⁵ The emergence of this more assertive attitude in British politics, which had permeated the sphere of foreign policy, moreover, was identified by Jay as a root cause of the Callaghan government's decision to provide 'steadfast and prompt British support for President Carter's stand on human rights'.³⁶

This rejection of the Eurocentrism that, in Owen's view, had put down deep roots within the FCO, and the concomitant desire to project a more self-assured image of Britain in the US provides further support to the historiographical reappraisal of the Callaghan government and its role in cultivating UK–US cooperation. Indeed, in their analyses of the Labour governments of 1974–9, several historians have challenged the popular belief that a revival of Anglo-American relations did not occur until the following decade on account of the partnership forged between Margaret Thatcher and

---

30 'Remarks by HM Ambassador to Embassy Staff', 25 July 1977, PJAY 5/3/1.
31 'Special Relations', *Washington Post*, 14 May 1977.
32 William Wallace, 'After Berrill: Whitehall and the Management of British Diplomacy', *International Affairs* 54, Issue 2 (1978): 224–5.
33 'Speech by the British Ambassador, Mr. Peter Jay at the National Press Club, Washington', 7 September 1977, PJAY 5/3/1.
34 Ibid.
35 Ibid.
36 Ibid.

Ronald Reagan.[37] Anne Lane, for instance, offers a strong appraisal of Callaghan's role, both as Foreign Secretary (1974–6) and as Prime Minister (1976–9), in engendering transatlantic rapprochement.[38] Similarly, David Reynolds highlights how Callaghan's rejection of Heath's exclusive Europeanism, clearly elucidated in his first major speech as Foreign Secretary in March 1974, 'set the pattern for the remaining Labour years – coolness towards Europe matched by a renewed cultivation of the "special relationship"'.[39] John Dumbrell also notes how, in contrast to the frostiness of the Heath–Nixon years, 'Callaghan developed a cordial personal relationship' with Jimmy Carter following his victory in the presidential election of 1976, and points out how Peter Jay became one of Carter's most vocal champions following his arrival in Washington.[40] However, as it pertained to the cultivation of the Anglo–American relationship, the effect of the Callaghan government's stance on human rights issues – and the impact of David Owen's human rights advocacy more specifically – has been largely underappreciated.

One notable exception is provided by John Dickie: 'Owen and Callaghan made their mark quickly with Carter and [Secretary of State, Cyrus] Vance. In his first public speech as Foreign Secretary, Owen paved the way for a warm reception at the White House for Callaghan the following week by giving human rights the top priority accorded to them by Carter as an integral part of foreign policy.'[41] As noted in the previous chapter, contemporary coverage of Owen's address to the Diplomatic and Commonwealth Writers Association on 3 March 1977 both overlooked the FCO's attempts to establish formalized human rights criteria (an undertaking that predated the emergence of Carter onto the global stage), and vastly underestimated Owen's personal commitment to the human rights issue. Furthermore, it appears that Owen's speech initiated a private dialogue between the two governments on the subject of human rights, providing further evidence that public relations concerns played only a partial role in its formulation. Correspondence between Callaghan and Carter days prior to their Washington summit, for instance, reveals that human rights concerns had been placed firmly on the agenda.[42] Peter Ramsbotham's reflections on their preliminary discussions at the White House also note that Callaghan and Carter 'soon found themselves to be talking on the same wavelength on the major issues of the world economy, East–West relations and morality in foreign policy ... the principal subjects of discussion'.[43] The harmony that existed behind the scenes, moreover, was

---

[37] For an example of this interpretation (particularly of Thatcher's significance with regard to the revival of the 'special relationship'), see Sanders, *Losing an Empire*.
[38] Anne Lane, 'Foreign and Defence Policy', in *New Labour, Old Labour: The Wilson and Callaghan Governments, 1974–79*, ed. Anthony Seldon and Kevin Hickson (London: Routledge, 2004), 154–69.
[39] Reynolds, *Britannia Overruled*, 236.
[40] Dumbrell, *Special Relationship*, 101.
[41] John Dickie, *'Special' No More, Anglo-American Relations: Rhetoric and Reality* (London: Weidenfeld & Nicolson, 1994), 160.
[42] Jimmy Carter, 'Message for Prime Minister Callaghan', 8 March 1977, TNA, FCO 73/289: 'Dear Mr. Prime Minister, Thank you for your prompt reply to my message about our meetings in Washington this week. You have proposed an excellent agenda ... I will of course want to discuss human rights'.
[43] Peter Ramsbotham to David Owen, 'The "Special Relationship" Revived: Visit to Washington by the Prime Minister and the Secretary of State, 9–12 March 1977', 18 March 1977, TNA, FCO 73/289.

clearly reflected in public as, in their effusive resurrection of the 'special relationship', both Callaghan and Carter seemed at pains to underscore a shared worldview based on a commonality of ethical precepts.[44]

Thomas K. Robb's recently published study on Anglo-American relations during the Carter administration, however, takes a rather dismissive view of the extent to which such pronouncements of common purpose yielded any substantive cooperation between the two governments in the human rights field. Rather, Robb asserts that Owen's public statements on human rights belied official reservations regarding the wisdom of Carter's moralistic approach to international affairs: 'such concerns about the president's foreign policy gained strength throughout British policy making circles and became a key area of concern for officials within both the FCO and Treasury.'[45] Robb also casts aspersions on the sincerity of the Foreign Secretary's human rights advocacy, asserting in a footnote that 'Owen provides the *misleading* impression in his memoirs that he was fully supportive of promoting international human rights'.[46] The previous chapter has indeed made clear that the elevation of human rights among Britain's diplomatic imperatives was viewed as a problematic development within some sections of Whitehall. It is also true that Owen himself was eager to establish a degree of critical distance between his own human rights approach and that of President Carter. Before departing for Washington to meet with the President for the first time, for instance, Owen informed the Charge and Political Counsellor of the US Embassy in London that he wanted to discuss with Carter the 'small print reservations' on human rights contained in his 3 March speech.[47] These were, Owen stated, 'serious points' which he wanted to 'amplify in Washington'.[48]

Callaghan, similarly, was initially sceptical of Carter's evangelical disposition.[49] Nonetheless, the Prime Minister's concern that Carter's human rights policy was a hostage to spiritual inclinations was seemingly allayed by their exchanges in Washington. As Callaghan conveyed to the House of Commons following his return: 'President Carter and I discussed at length the subject of human rights, on which, as the House knows, the President feels deeply and has expressed his views in a forthright manner. It

---

[44] See for example E.A.J. Fergusson to Patrick Wright, 'The Prime Minister's reply to President Carter's Speech of Welcome at the Official White House Dinner', 8 March 1977, TNA, FCO 73/289; Jimmy Carter, 'London, England: Remarks on Arrival at Heathrow Airport', 5 May 1977, The American Presidency Project, available at https://www.presidency.ucsb.edu/documents/london-england-remarks-arrival-heathrow-airport (accessed 3 January 2020); Jimmy Carter, 'Newcastle-Upon-Tyne, England – Remarks at the Newcastle Civic Centre', 6 May 1977, The American Presidency Project, available at https://www.presidency.ucsb.edu/documents/newcastle-upon-tyne-england-remarks-the-newcastle-civic-centre (accessed 3 January 2020).

[45] Robb, *Jimmy Carter and the Anglo-American 'Special Relationship'*, 44.

[46] Ibid., 28, footnote 15. Emphasis added by author.

[47] 'Foreign Secretary's Preview of Visit to Washington, March 10–11', 7 March 1977, The National Archives, College Park, MD., Central Foreign Policy Files, Record Group 59 – General Records of the Department of State, Electronic Telegrams, 1977, available at https://aad.archives.gov/aad/create pdf?rid=47779&dt=2532&dl=1629 (accessed 3 January 2020).

[48] Ibid. Regarding British concerns over Carter's human rights commitments and their international implications, see also Umberto Tulli, *A Precarious Equilibrium: Human Rights and Détente in Jimmy Carter's Soviet Policy* (Manchester: Manchester University Press, 2020), 97–8.

[49] See for example Bernard Donoughue, *Downing Street Diary, Volume II: with James Callaghan in No. 10* (London: Jonathan Cape, 2008), 159.

was clear that President Carter had given very careful thought to his approach to this matter, and he welcomed the speech made recently by the Foreign and Commonwealth Secretary.[50] Indeed, according to Ramsbotham's despatch addressed to the Foreign Secretary, both Owen and Callaghan left Washington disabused of the notion that Carter was prone to 'shooting from the hip': 'One of the strongest impressions which the Prime Minister and you derived from your talks with him was that he is not a man who acts on impulse (contrary to the apprehensions of some of our allies), but that his various moves on foreign affairs since his inauguration have been carefully thought out.'[51] Consequently, US Ambassador to the UK Kingman Brewster Jr – who struck up a close relationship with Owen, enabling Embassy officials to circumvent traditional Foreign Office contacts by engaging with the Foreign Secretary directly – was moved to reflect upon the dissipation of British anxieties in his assessment of the 'British Factor in American Policy', submitted to the State Department in September 1977:

> the UK and other European allies were uncertain how candidate Carter's statements on such central issues as non-proliferation, strategic arms control, conventional arms transfers, and human rights would be affected by the realities of presidential office. After eight months, the British have been largely reassured. The UK watched approvingly as Washington returned the focus of US diplomatic attention to its closest allies and renewed the importance of the Anglo-American relationship ... This is not to say that the British have abandoned their right to disagree. For example, HMG thought that too much zeal for non-proliferation and human rights could be self-defeating. But it is also our impression that their concern is now largely dissipated, though they are still sometimes sceptical about our means. As long as British interests are protected, however, they are generally willing to try to help us toward our ends.[52]

Certainly, Britain's adoption of the human rights cause was subject to more constrictive restraints than the US iteration on account of its relative economic and military frailty. As a Foreign Office document explained: 'The United States is influential, strong and self-sufficient enough to take the risk of giving offence to third countries. With our much greater dependence on international trade, our much smaller influence on other countries and the weakness of the British economy, it behoves us to be more careful, and in particular to be sure that we are not taking stands which weaken our competitive position vis-à-vis our major trading rivals in Europe and Japan.'[53] With

---

[50] 'United States and Canada' (Prime Minister's Visit)', 15 March 1977, *Hansard: House of Commons*, Volume 928, Column 219.

[51] Ramsbotham to Owen, 18 March 1977.

[52] 'British Factor in American Policy', 23 September 1977, The National Archives, College Park, MD., Central Foreign Policy Files, Record Group 59 – General Records of the Department of State, Electronic Telegrams, 1977, available at https://aad.archives.gov/aad/createpdf?rid=220932&dt=2532&dl=1629 (accessed 3 January 2020). Regarding Brewster's close working relationship with Owen, see Alex Spelling, 'Ambassadors Richardson, Armstrong and Brewster, 1975–81', in *The Embassy in Grosvenor Square: American Ambassadors to the United Kingdom, 1938–2008*, ed. Alison R. Holmes and J. Simon Rofe (Basingstoke: Palgrave Macmillan, 2012), 202–3.

[53] Appendix A in PUS to PS/Mr Luard; Private Secretary, 'Human Rights and Foreign Policy', undated (received 10 May 1977), TNA, FCO 58/1143.

such considerations in mind, Michael Simpson-Orlebar informed Christopher Squire at the Washington Embassy that while Owen's public statements on human rights promotion had 'demonstrated that British and American objectives in the field of human rights' were 'identical', disagreements over 'tactics' would not be unexpected.[54] It is also possible to note operational differences between the two countries' human rights policies at an institutional level. Whereas human rights responsibilities at the FCO were delegated to pre-existing departments and subsumed within broader remits, the Carter administration established a specialized Bureau of Human Rights and Humanitarian Affairs at the State Department, headed by an Assistant Secretary of State dealing specifically with these issues.[55] The methodological similarities between the US and UK in the compilation of their annual human rights assessments of foreign countries, likewise, should not be overstated.[56]

Nonetheless, as regards the formulation of major policy positions, such as the appropriate stance to take on human rights issues during the CSCE follow-up conference in Belgrade when it opened in October 1977, experts in Washington saw ample ground for the synchronization of an Anglo-American approach based on close and candid consultation and so many shared 'assumptions and perceptions'.[57] Owen clearly reciprocated. For instance, State Department documents reveal that, on 'British initiative', Owen met with Assistant Secretary of State for Human Rights and Humanitarian Affairs Patricia Derian at the FCO on 9 December 1977 to ask 'where the US thought the UK could do more' on the human rights front, before inviting Derian 'to inform him of any human rights problems on which the USG would like British assistance or a more active British stance'.[58] A constructive dialogue between the pair had clearly been established at a NATO Ministerial meeting in Brussels days

---

[54] M.K.O. Simpson-Orlebar to C.W. Squire, 'Human Rights', 21 April 1977, TNA, FCO 58/1143.

[55] Indeed, these institutional peculiarities were laid bare during an Anglo-American seminar on human rights and foreign policy held at the Foreign Office in November 1978. See 'Remarks made at November 1978 US/UK Briefing on Human Rights and Foreign Policy', PHM, HART 08/47. For examples of scholarship addressing the bureaucratisation of the Carter administration's human rights policy see Isabella Borshoff, 'What is a Human Rights Foreign Policy: Definitions, Double Standards, and the Carter Administration', *Historian* 78, Issue 4 (Winter 2016): 710–32; Itai Nartzizenfield Sneh, *The Future Almost Arrived: How Jimmy Carter Failed to Change U.S. Foreign Policy* (New York: Peter Lang, 2008), 66–100; Joshua Muravchik, *The Uncertain Crusade: Jimmy Carter and the Dilemmas of Human Rights Policy* (Washington, DC: American Enterprise Institute for Public Policy Research, 1991), 40–1.

[56] See for example Appendix C in PUS to PS/Mr Luard; Private Secretary, 'Human Rights and Foreign Policy', undated (received 10 May 1977), TNA, FCO 58/1143: 'There is no parallel between our league table and the American approach to the human rights performance of individual countries … under the previous Administration they specifically rejected a league table approach and to the best of our knowledge they are not considering one under the new Administration'.

[57] 'PARM – Annual Policy and Resource Assessment – Part 1', 31 March 1977, The National Archives, College Park, MD., Central Foreign Policy Files, Record Group 59 – General Records of the Department of State, Electronic Telegrams, 1977, available at https://aad.archives.gov/aad/createpdf?rid=63575&dt=2532&dl=1629 (accessed 3 January 2020). Regarding the development of a 'Western' approach to the Belgrade conference, see for example Tulli, *A Precarious Equilibrium*, 98–111.

[58] 'Human Rights: Meeting Between Asst Secretary Derian and Foreign Secretary Owen', 12 December 1977, The National Archives, College Park, MD., Central Foreign Policy Files, Record Group 59 – General Records of the Department of State, Electronic Telegrams, 1977, available at https://aad.archives.gov/aad/createpdf?rid=289834&dt=2532&dl=1629 (accessed 3 January 2020).

Figure 3.1 Patricia Derian, Assistant Secretary of State for Human Rights and Humanitarian Affairs, visits Owen at the Foreign Office, 9 December 1977 (Keystone Pictures USA/Zumapress/Alamy).

earlier, as evidenced by Derian's letter to Owen on 23 December, which sought the UK's acceptance of Indochinese refugees while reaffirming a shared commitment to international human rights issues: 'I found our discussion productive and hope to continue with you a dialogue on human rights issues of mutual importance.'[59] Similar efforts to coordinate an Anglo-American approach on human rights issues can also be observed with regard to United Nations fora. On 18 July 1977, for example, Evan Luard and Owen's Minister of State for Overseas Affairs, Frank Judd, met with US Ambassador to the UN Andrew Young to discuss President Carter's proposals for reforming the UN human rights machinery, chiefly those relating to more frequent meetings of the Human Rights Commission and the strengthening of the '1503 procedure' through which member states could bring human rights complaints to the attention of the Commission.[60] These suggestions were welcomed by Luard and both sides 'agreed on

---

[59] 'Indochinese Refugees: Letter from Assistant Secretary Derian to Foreign Secretary Owen', 23 December 1977, The National Archives, College Park, MD., Central Foreign Policy Files, Record Group 59 – General Records of the Department of State, Electronic Telegrams, 1977, available at https://aad.archives.gov/aad/createpdf?rid=301832&dt=2532&dl=1629 (accessed 3 January 2020).

[60] See 'Record of Second Session of Anglo-US Talks on the UN held in Mr Luard's Office on 18 July, 1977, at 3.15 PM', TNA, FCO 58/1145.

the need for a general consensus on a broader concept of human rights (political, civil, economic, social)' in order to allay the fears of developing countries that human rights was little more than an ideological weapon at the disposal of the industrialized Western democracies.[61]

Cooperation between the two governments on international human rights promotion even served to mitigate US criticism of the Callaghan government over the suspension of civil liberties in Northern Ireland. Robb may be correct in suggesting 'British officials feared that Carter's human rights agenda would encourage the President to become embroiled in events in Northern Ireland as these were coming under closer scrutiny by human rights activists'.[62] Concerns over the suspension of civil liberties in Northern Ireland, and the international response to such measures which had been amplified by the case brought before the European Commission on Human Rights by the Irish government in 1970-1, had certainly provided a catalyst for British engagement with human rights.[63] It is also evident that the limitations that British policy in Northern Ireland placed on the government's claims to moral authority on the international stage were clearly understood by Owen.[64] However, by the time of Owen's unexpected appointment as Foreign Secretary following the death of Anthony Crosland, the government had already taken steps to defuse the situation, publicly abandoning the 'five techniques' of detention and interrogation that constituted inhumane treatment and torture in the eyes of the European Commission on Human Rights in January 1976.[65] Any such concerns, moreover, would certainly have been assuaged by the sympathetic assessment of the Callaghan government's Northern Ireland policy included in the annual congressional human rights report of 1977.[66] In fact, as one US diplomat recalls, the report incensed the 'Irish lobby' in Washington, such was the charitable nature of its assessment of Britain's approach to the ongoing sectarian struggles in the region:

---

[61] 'US-UK Pre-UNGA Consultations', 19 July 1977, The National Archives, College Park, MD., Central Foreign Policy Files, Record Group 59 – General Records of the Department of State, Electronic Telegrams, 1977, available at https://aad.archives.gov/aad/createpdf?rid=164875&dt=2532&dl=1629 (accessed 3 January 2020).

[62] Robb, *Jimmy Carter and the Anglo-American 'Special Relationship'*, 44.

[63] See for example Cronin, *Global Rules*, 63-70.

[64] These concerns, for example, can be observed within bilateral exchanges between London and Tehran, with Owen recognising that Britain too had 'skeletons' in its cupboard due to past actions in Northern Ireland, which imparted a note of moderation when criticizing the Shah of Iran's treatment of dissidents. See Erciyas, *British Dilemmas*, 122.

[65] See Charles Townshend, 'Northern Ireland', in R.J. Vincent (ed.), *Foreign Policy and Human Rights: Issues and Responses* (Cambridge: Cambridge University Press, 1986), 132-40. Regarding the increasing scrutiny accorded to Britain's policies of detention and interrogation in Northern Ireland by human rights activists and international human rights institutions during the 1970s, see also Brice Dickson, *The European Convention on Human Rights and the Northern Ireland Conflict* (Oxford: Oxford University Press, 2010), 147-53; Ed Bates, *The Evolution of the European Convention on Human Rights from its Inception to the Creation of a Permanent Court of Human Rights* (Oxford: Oxford University Press, 2010), 271-7; Ian Cobain, *Cruel Britannia: A Secret History of Torture* (London: Portobello Books, 2012), 166-203.

[66] 'Human Rights', 12 November 1977, The National Archives, College Park, MD., Central Foreign Policy Files, Record Group 59 – General Records of the Department of State, Electronic Telegrams, 1977, available at https://aad.archives.gov/aad/createpdf?rid=262860&dt=2532&dl=1629 (accessed 3 January 2020).

The report on Great Britain included Northern Ireland, and I remember, as this was being done, having people make an appointment with me who were Americans but basically were Irish radicals. They sat in my office, three of them, berating the Department of State for not understanding the terrible human rights atrocities being perpetuated against the poor Irish Catholics ... These people's eyes were flashing and their faces were flushed, and there was a young woman there who was just leaning forward bitterly condemning what we were not recognizing in our report.[67]

Simply put, the Carter administration, according to the recollections of another State Department official, did not get 'too much involved in the UK's problem in Ireland'.[68] Upon closer inspection, in fact, it appears that an implicit understanding that the UK had little to learn from the US when it came to human rights promotion underpinned the Carter administration's reticence. As John W. Kimball, who worked closely with the London Embassy as a Political Officer between 1977–80, reveals: 'The Embassy was ... quite involved in consultations about Northern Ireland. We were able, if I may say so, to avoid meddling on human rights grounds. We were interested in having Northern Ireland come out right, that is peacefully and fairly for both communities. But we were very careful not to tell the British what to do or to imply that it was a so-called humanitarian issue. For one thing, we would have been preaching to the converted about human rights.'[69] This combination of doubts regarding the perceived efficacy of interference, and a sense of shared understanding around the promotion of human rights worldwide – in other words, an acceptance that prompting would have been surplus to requirements – is also clearly visible in Cyrus Vance's November 1977 assessment of Britain's human rights policy, accompanied in this instance by a sense of gratitude to the UK for positioning itself so clearly alongside the Carter administration on matters concerning human rights and international affairs.[70]

---

[67] Robert S. Steven, interview with Charles Stuart Kennedy for the Association for Diplomatic Studies and Training Foreign Affairs Oral History Project (hereafter ADST), 3 August 2001, available at https://www.adst.org/OH%20TOCs/Steven,%20Robert%20S.toc.pdf (accessed 14 January 2020).
[68] Ward Barmon, ADST interview with Charles Stuart Kennedy, 27 July 1998, available at https://www.adst.org/OH%20TOCs/Barmon,%20Ward.toc.pdf (accessed 14 January 2020).
[69] John W. Kimball, ADST interview with Charles Stuart Kennedy, 24 May 1999, available at https://www.adst.org/OH%20TOCs/Kimball,%20John%20W.toc.pdf (accessed 14 January 2020).
[70] 'Human Rights', 12 November 1977: 'HMG is engaged in a delicate balancing act between the requirements of security and human rights. Our primary objective is to encourage – or at least not complicate – HMG's own efforts at political reconciliation between the two communities in Ulster ... Any interference would of course also be regarded as interference by the British government (and the opposition), would be resented by a majority of those in Northern Ireland, and would be viewed by all informed Britons as destabilizing to HMG's own delicate efforts to bring the two sides together ... In view of this likely reaction, it is extremely doubtful that any US intervention would produce an improvement in the human rights situation ... The UK was one of the first major countries to come out vigorously in support of the Carter administration's human rights policy, and we should be able to continue to expect support from HMG on a broad range of human rights issues.'

Tackling the Rhodesian impasse

Anglo-American entente, moreover, had been further reinforced subsequent to Callaghan and Owen's US visit by the coordination of a united approach towards the issue of Rhodesian independence. The resolution of Rhodesia's protracted constitutional crisis – set in motion by Rhodesian Prime Minister Ian Smith's Unilateral Declaration of Independence (UDI) from British rule in November 1965 – had in fact been the most pressing item on Owen's agenda when he departed for Washington with his Prime Minister.[71] Notwithstanding the sobering realization that the Rhodesian problem had endured in spite of several high-profile diplomatic initiatives, chiefly those orchestrated by Harold Wilson aboard HMS *Tiger* and HMS *Fearless* in 1966 and 1968 respectively, Owen was more than willing to stake his political reputation on resolving the crisis that had claimed the 'scalps' of British diplomats 'high and low'.[72] Key to Owen's optimistic outlook was his assessment of the Carter administration's intentions in the region. Multilateral attempts to tackle the Rhodesian impasse through the Geneva conference (28 October–14 December 1976) had recently failed to provide a viable solution to the problem, but Owen travelled to the US capital in the knowledge that the new administration was willing to pay greater attention to the problems of Southern Africa than previous US governments: 'We knew that Carter, and his Secretary of State, Cy Vance, wanted very much to be more involved in Africa.'[73] This being said, Owen was nonetheless surprised by the speed at which he was able to come to an agreement with his American counterpart regarding the approach that the two governments would pursue. As Owen recounts in his 'Rhodesia diary', it took less than fifteen minutes to establish a framework for Anglo–US co-operation on Rhodesia which was formally endorsed by Callaghan and Carter shortly thereafter.[74]

As the *Observer* was quick to note, the Anglo-American approach Owen toured across Africa during the intensive schedule of shuttle diplomacy that followed constituted 'a radically different approach to the Rhodesian crisis from anything adopted by any one of his predecessors during the 11 years since the Smith regime declared its independence'.[75] Whereas previous initiatives had been 'directed towards finding a compromise settlement acceptable to both the Smith regime and its black challengers', Britain – with the much-needed support of the US – was 'now more ready to move ahead in drafting an independence constitution' irrespective of Mr. Smith's intransigence.[76] Those who worked closely with Owen on the formulation of Rhodesian policy, moreover, have suggested that this fundamental recalibration did more than merely 'add new links to the chain of

---

[71] See for example 'Foreign Secretary's Preview of Visit to Washington, March 10–11'.
[72] Nicholas Carroll, 'Flying doctor a tonic for embittered Africa', *The Sunday Times*, 17 April 1977. For an examination of Wilson's attempts to overcome the Rhodesian impasse, see Manuele Facchini, '"The Millstone Around Our Necks": Harold Wilson and the HMS Fearless Conference (9–13 October 1968)', *Contemporary British History* 28, No. 3 (2014): 274–93.
[73] Owen, *Personally Speaking to Kenneth Harris*, 77. For an analysis of the US approach to the Rhodesian question prior to Carter's inauguration, see for example Anthony Lake, *The 'Tar Baby' Option: American Policy Toward Southern Rhodesia* (New York: Colombia University Press, 1976).
[74] David Owen, 'Rhodesia Diary', undated, DOP, D709 2/7/3/1.
[75] Colin Legum, 'Owen goes off to rob Smith's veto', *Observer*, 10 April 1977.
[76] Ibid.

events' that would eventually lead to the creation of the Republic of Zimbabwe; it introduced fundamental provisions that would lay the very foundations of the Lancaster House Agreement signed by Owen's successor, Lord Carrington, on 21 December 1979.[77] This contention is supported by Nancy Mitchell, who notes how Carrington's 'bravura performance' at Lancaster House and 'the myth of Margaret Thatcher – the Iron Lady who broke the mold' has obscured the fact that the Lancaster House Agreement was 'almost identical to the Anglo-American proposals' in its fundamental elements: 'a constitution, a transitional period of direct British rule, and elections.'[78]

Upon closer inspection, it appears that the two allies were united in this venture by a common pursuit of human rights imperatives, largely driven by the outward projection of domestic anxieties surrounding 'race'. Mitchell's analysis of the Carter administration's African policy, for instance, describes how it was 'much less treacherous for American politicians to discuss the racial politics of a faraway African country' such as Rhodesia than 'to wade into the explosive domestic topics of busing and affirmative action'.[79] Indeed, Carter's Vice-President, Walter Mondale, revealed to Mitchell that the analogy between the codified racism of Ian Smith's white minority government and the grievances of the civil rights movement in the US informed 'everything' the Carter administration did in Southern Africa.[80] Owen's enthusiastic attempts to tackle the Rhodesian impasse were similarly reflective of concerns regarding race relations at home. Before an audience gathered in Labour's Cardiff West constituency on 3 March 1978, for example, Owen not only suggested that race 'is likely to be one of the dominant issues in world politics in the remaining decades of this century', he also sought to impress upon those in attendance that it

> is vital that we in this country understand this now. Otherwise there is a grave danger that through overly-hasty and ill-considered responses to the twin challenges of race and immigration at home and racial equality and discrimination in Southern Africa this country will cease to be taken seriously as a source of political and moral leadership in the world. We cannot speak with one voice in this country and another abroad. Our stand on racism inside the country will affect our posture in the world and vice versa ... Unless we succeed we shall set the world against us and simply hasten this country's decline into selfish parochialism and irrelevance.[81]

---

[77] David Martin and Phillis Johnson, *The Struggle for Zimbabwe: The Chimurenga War* (London: Faber & Faber, 1981), 264. Lord Frank Judd, interview with the author, 15 January 2018: Frank Judd served as Minister of State for Foreign and Commonwealth Affairs under Owen, and maintains that Owen 'really set up, made possible' the pragmatic solution that was eventually overseen by Carrington and Thatcher; Sir Stephen Wall, interview with the author, 23 August 2018: Stephen Wall (Owen's Assistant Private Secretary) posits that, 'fundamentally [it was] the Vance-Owen policy that Carrington implemented when he became Foreign Secretary'.

[78] Nancy Mitchell, *Jimmy Carter in Africa: Race and the Cold War* (Washington, DC: Woodrow Wilson Press, 2016), 645.

[79] Ibid., 8.

[80] Ibid., 13.

[81] David Owen, 'Extracts from a Speech by the Secretary of State for Foreign and Commonwealth Affairs, Dr David Owen MP, to Cardiff West Constituency Labour Party', 3 March 1978, DOP, D709 2/7/2/2.

Owen's framing of issues concerning British race relations within a global context was, it must be stated, nothing new. Kennetta Hammond Perry and Elizabeth Buettner, for example, have demonstrated that flashpoints of racial tension such as the Notting Hill riots of 1958 and Peter Griffiths' racist campaign in the Smethwick constituency during the 1964 general election became imbued with international significance, undermining Britain's capacity to portray itself as a progressive voice in global affairs.[82] Owen's anxieties in this regard, and the ways in which they were reflected in his Rhodesian initiative, however, are particularly noteworthy. Not only do they speak to the centrality of discussions concerning 'race' in the construction of Britain's post-imperial identity, they also ought to be considered alongside debates regarding the metropolitan impact of decolonisation – part of Britain's 'new' imperial history – and its paradoxical effect on a generation of young Britons who may have identified themselves as post-imperial, but whose interactions with the international community were nonetheless shaped by enduring narratives of British imperial beneficence and colonial responsibility.[83] This was particularly evident in youth NGO engagement in the humanitarian sector during the post-war period.

While the entangled histories of humanitarianism and empire have been amply demonstrated, British youth engagement with humanitarian NGOs became 'a way of finding a new role for the nation and its people in the aftermath of empire, and an attempt by a new generation to distance itself from the legacies of empire'.[84] However, as illustrated by Anna Bocking-Welch's analysis of British engagement with the United Nations' Freedom From Hunger Campaign (FFHC) during the 1960s, the separation between colonial and post-colonial was far less clear cut than contemporaries tended to perceive it. Although young Britons participating in the Campaign under the auspices of Youth Against Hunger (YAH) 'came to symbolise the possibility of a positive global role for Britain, one untainted by difficult colonial legacies', youth campaigns such as YAH signalled, in many respects, a continuation of colonial-era humanitarianism, reflecting the same 'principles of imperial benevolence and

---

[82] See Kennetta Hammond Perry, *London Is the Place for Me: Black Britons, Citizenship and the Politics of Race* (Oxford: Oxford University Press, 2015), 91–124; Elizabeth Buettner, '"This is Staffordshire not Alabama": Racial Geographies of Commonwealth Immigration in Early 1960s Britain', *The Journal of Imperial and Commonwealth History* 42, No. 4 (2014): 710–40.

[83] See for example Burkett, *Constructing Post-Imperial Britain*; Bill Schwarz, '"The Only White Man in There": The Re-Racialisation of England, 1956–1968', *Race and Class* 38, No. 1 (1996): 65–78; Sarah Stockwell, 'Ends of Empire', in *The British Empire: Themes and Perspectives*, ed. Sarah Stockwell (Oxford: Blackwell, 2008), 269–93; Andrew Thompson, 'Introduction', in *Britain's Experience of Empire in the Twentieth Century*, ed. Andrew Thompson (Oxford: Oxford University Press, 2012), 1–32.

[84] Kevin O'Sullivan, Matthew Hilton and Juliano Fiori, 'Humanitarianisms in Context', *European Review of History – Revue européene d'histoire* 23, No. 1–2 (2016): 3. Concerning these 'entangled' histories, see for example Rob Skinner and Alan Lester, 'Humanitarianism and Empire: New Research Agendas', *Journal of Imperial and Commonwealth History*, Special Issue: Empire and Humanitarianism (November 2012): 729–47; Johannes Paulmann, 'Humanitarianism and Empire', in *The Encyclopedia of Empire*, Volume II, ed. John M. Mackenzie (Oxford: Wiley, 2016), 1112–23; Bronwen Everill et al, 'History and Humanitarianism: A Conversation', *Past and Present* 241, Issue 1 (November 2018): 1–38.

trusteeship'.⁸⁵ British engagement with the FFHC more broadly, Bocking-Welch contends, 'shows that habits of mind associated with imperial philanthropy and trusteeship did not simply end with decolonisation, but developed in this period to coexist alongside and within newer international discourses of humanitarian aid and development'.⁸⁶ Jordanna Bailkin, similarly, posits that decolonization can be 'read generationally', highlighting the ways in which young Britons participating in Voluntary Service Overseas (VSO) during this period simultaneously forged 'new types of postimperial relationships' while preserving 'the spirit of imperial adventure'.⁸⁷

Owen's plenipotentiary in Washington, Peter Jay, clearly regarded himself, and his Foreign Secretary, as members of a distinctly post-colonial generation; a generation which, in the words of Dick Bird, was 'ready to recognise not just the inevitability, but the excitement, and yes, the justice of self-determination'.⁸⁸ As Jay stated before an audience at Harvard University in April 1978, for instance:

> What we are trying to achieve in Southern Africa is, as I have said, of special importance to people of my generation ... I did grow up at a certain stage in the history of my country, and with my contemporaries in a certain mood, when we could throw off the international complacency, the imperial nostalgia and the moral insensitivity of the past. We recognised that the systematic and unashamed oppression of one race by another was morally indefensible ... We also recognised the accelerating pace of change in the world, together with its increasing complexity, early enough, I think, to understand the interlocking nature of the global community and often the explosive interaction of events great distances apart.⁸⁹

The foreign policy implications of Owen's post-colonial vintage were also pondered by some contemporary commentators.⁹⁰ But his human rights-based approach to foreign affairs – as it pertained to Southern Africa, in any case – would not be so easily extricated from the colonial past and the ideational framework that apparently survived Britain's formal retreat from its imperial role. Indeed, by stressing, as he did on

---

[85] Anna Bocking-Welch, 'Youth Against Hunger: Service, Activism and the Mobilisation of Young Humanitarians in 1960s Britain', *European Review of History – Revue européene d'histoire* 23, No. 1–2 (2016): 158, 159.

[86] Anna Bocking-Welch, 'Imperial Legacies and Internationalist Discourses: British Involvement in the United Nations Freedom from Hunger Campaign, 1960–70', *Journal of Imperial and Commonwealth History*, Special Issue: Empire and Humanitarianism (November 2012): 892.

[87] Jordanna Bailkin, *The Afterlife of Empire* (Berkeley: University of California Press, 2012), 57.

[88] Dick Bird, *Never the Same Again: A History of the VSO* (Cambridge: Lutterworth Press, 1998), 14.

[89] Peter Jay, 'Britain and Southern Africa: A Policy for Change' (speech delivered at Harvard University), 14 April 1978, PJAY 5/3/3.

[90] See for example Fred Hauptfuhrer, 'Bio: David Owen', *People*, 6 March 1978, DOP, D709 2/7/6/9: 'Clearly, David Owen is a quick learner, a man in a hurry, the most dynamic representative of a new generation that is liberated from the agonies of losing an empire'; Leo Murray, 'Diplomatic View: "Britain is an Island"', *Liverpool Daily Post*, 24 August 1978, DOP, D709 2/9/6: 'Dr Owen is the first Foreign Secretary of a post war generation which has experienced only Britain's retreat from being a world power.'

numerous occasions, that the peaceful resolution of the Rhodesian question was Britain's 'specific responsibility', Owen was not merely suggesting that 'responsibility' entailed the establishment of self-determination in a former colony.[91] Rather, it would appear that Britain was responsible for passing on the liberal values that had developed within the colonial metropole. Before an audience of Labour members in Richmond on 21 September 1978, for example, Owen reiterated his conviction that racially discriminatory governments would find vehement opposition in the form of the Labour Party on the grounds that the 'best inheritance we could leave Africa today is our commitment to democracy and liberal values'.[92] 'The challenge to the west', he continued, 'is to project its own values in Africa, rather than to justify them in their perverted forms'.[93]

This speaks to a 'libertarian' understanding of empire that began to displace the 'authoritarian' interpretation from the early decades of the twentieth century onwards.[94] Rather than being characterized by 'the values of hierarchy and order', the identification of the Empire as an embodiment of liberal values 'has been a far more powerful and ultimately much more enduring strain of imperial identity than the pomp and circumstance so often assumed to have been the only strain'.[95] Bocking-Welch, in fact, has recently cast a spotlight on the influence that this conception of British imperial beneficence exerted within civic society spaces during the post-war period, as the 'combined processes of decolonisation and globalisation further decoupled "caring" from "ruling"', thus 'making it easier to detach "benevolence" from specifically imperial responsibilities'.[96]

Owen's attempts to situate his Rhodesian initiative within its wider historical context serve to further demonstrate the enduring quality of the liberal imperial ideal. 'In the early decades of the nineteenth century', Owen asserted, 'a more humanitarian attitude to the under-privileged, both at home and overseas, began to gain ground in Britain', yielding, in 1833, the abolition of slavery throughout the Empire.[97] Contemporaneously, in South Africa itself, Owen describes how 'the work of the London Missionary Society did much to bring home to the British Government and British public opinion their duty to defend the human rights of the native peoples'.[98] The international projection of domestic concerns surrounding race relations that

---

[91] See for example 'Speech prepared for delivery by the Rt Hon Dr David Owen MP Foreign and Commonwealth Secretary during a meeting of Commonwealth Heads of Government, Lancaster House', 9 June 1977, DOP, D709 2/7/2/1.
[92] 'Extracts from a speech to be given by the Secretary of State for Foreign and Commonwealth Affairs, Dr David Owen MP, to a public meeting arranged by Richmond Labour Party', 21 September 1978, DOP, D709 2/7/2/1.
[93] Ibid.
[94] See Peter Marshall, 'Imperial Britain', *Journal of Imperial and Commonwealth History* 23, Issue 3 (September 1995): 379–94.
[95] Ibid., 389–90. See also Richard Whiting, 'The Empire and British Politics', in *Britain's Experience of Empire in the Twentieth Century*, ed. Thompson, 161–5.
[96] Bocking-Welch, *British Civic Society at the End of Empire*, 5.
[97] Owen, *Human Rights*, 86.
[98] Ibid.

characterized Owen's framing of his Rhodesian initiative, therefore, can be seen to shed more light on the metropolitan impact of decolonization – and how this impact was felt by a generation of Britons who tended to define themselves as decidedly *post-imperial*. Moreover, it also demonstrates how the decoupling of imperial beneficence from the iniquities of British imperialism allowed this 'post-imperial' generation to repackage colonial tropes and subsume international human rights concerns within broader narratives of colonial responsibility. In turn, these issues also encourage us to appreciate the entangled histories of human rights and humanitarianism, indicating as well that the relationship between international human rights and the dissolution of empire – 'neglected' for decades by human rights historians – is deserving of more sustained scholarly engagement.[99]

As regards the rejuvenation of the Anglo–American relationship, the same desire to 'feel that our foreign policy is related to the values of our own societies' clearly exerted a galvanising influence.[100] In fact, human rights promotion during Owen's tenure as Foreign Secretary can be seen to reflect – and indeed expedite – the process of rapprochement set in motion following Labour's return to power in 1974. At the very least, the British response to President Carter's human rights policy was sufficiently accommodating, making clear to the Carter administration that cordial relations between the two countries would not be problematized by the elevation of human rights concerns within the context of US foreign policy. It could in fact be argued that, in addition to injecting fresh impetus into the Rhodesian question, Owen's contemporaneous attempts to make human rights a central pillar of British foreign policy served to bring the UK and the US closer together through a reiteration of shared values and attempts at policy coordination pursued through bilateral meetings and multilateral fora. An analysis of the UK's attempts to promote human rights through the machinery of the EC at this juncture, however, indicates that, in spite of Owen's 'Churchillian' vision and the Callaghan government's desire to strengthen Britain's relations with its European partners, human rights promotion only served to undermine European cooperation.

Transatlantic tensions

Human rights advocacy appears to have been an edifying force within the burgeoning European Community following the negotiation of the European Convention on Human Rights (ECHR). Indeed, Tom Buchanan posits that between the entry into

---

[99] Fabian Klose, 'Human Rights For and Against Empire – Legal and Public Discourses in the Age of Decolonisation', *Journal of the History of International Law* 18, Issue 2–3 (2016): 319. For examples of scholarship concerning this relationship see Burke, *Decolonization and the Evolution of International Human Rights*; Meredith Terretta, '"We Had Been Fooled into Thinking that the UN Watches over the Entire World": Human Rights, UN Trust Territories, and Africa's Decolonization', *Human Rights Quarterly* 34, No. 2 (May 2012): 329–60; Jensen, *The Making of International Human Rights*.

[100] 'Speech by Dr David Owen, Foreign Secretary, at the Pilgrims' Dinner, Savoy Hotel, London', 13 March 1978, DOP, D709 2/7/2/1.

force of the ECHR in 1953 and the signing of the Helsinki Final Act in 1975, questions of human rights promotion and the cultivation of a European identity had become 'inextricably woven'.[101] This convergence had become increasingly pronounced during the 1960s as an eruption in transnational human rights activism had made member states 'more sensitive to these issues', while the European Community had become 'increasingly willing to define itself in political as well as economic terms'.[102] The cultivation of a distinctly European approach to détente, moreover, had served to situate human rights ideals alongside a developing European identity as the apparatus of the CSCE was being established. Jeremi Suri, for instance, has illuminated the growing divergence between West European and American conceptions of détente following the publication of the Davignon Report of October 1970 – a statement of intent which 'made the formulations of a "European" foreign policy a cornerstone of a nascent European polity', while emphasizing a 'furthering of détente across the continent' and championing the civilizational values of liberty and a respect for human rights.[103] The sense of purpose encapsulated by the Report, Suri asserts, led the European Six to seize the initiative of the CSCE process during its early stages, advancing a 'much more optimistic' approach to the linking of human rights and security negotiations than that of the Nixon administration in the US.[104]

British policymakers were, according to Martin D. Brown, less enamoured than their continental allies by the prospect of codifying human rights provisions within the framework of the CSCE.[105] Nonetheless, following Britain's entry into the European Community in 1973, Foreign Office officials came to regard cooperation with their EC partners on CSCE policy as a matter of paramount importance: 'something of a test case for the development of foreign policy co-ordination among the Nine.'[106] With the imperatives of European integration in mind, British representatives working under the auspices of European Political Cooperation (EPC) would, according to Angela Romano,

---

[101] Tom Buchanan, 'Human Rights, the Memory of War and the Making of a 'European' Identity, 1945–75', in *Europeanization in the Twentieth Century: Historical Approaches*, ed. Martin Conway and Kiran Klaus Patel (Basingstoke: Palgrave Macmillan, 2010), 157.

[102] Ibid., 166. For broader coverage of the role of foreign policy cooperation in the construction of a 'European' identity, see for example Adrian Hyde-Price, 'Interests, Institutions and Identities in the Study of European Foreign Policy', in *Rethinking European Foreign Policy*, ed. Ben Tonra and Thomas Christiansen (Manchester: Manchester University Press, 2004), 99–113.

[103] Jeremi Suri, 'Détente and Human Rights: American and West European Perspectives on International Change', *Cold War History* 8, No. 4 (November 2008): 536. See also Report by the Foreign Ministers of the Member States on the Problems of Political Unification ('Davignon Report'), Luxembourg, 27 October 1970, available at https://www.cvce.eu/en/collections/unit-content/-/unit/02bb76df-d066-4c08-a58a-d4686a3e68ff/56b69a5e-3f16-4775-ba38-b4ef440fdccb/Resources#4176efc3-c734-41e5-bb90-d34c4d17bbb5_en&overlay (accessed 4 June 2020).

[104] Suri, 'Détente and Human Rights': 538.

[105] See Martin D. Brown, 'A Very British Vision of Détente: The United Kingdom's Foreign Policy During the Helsinki Process, 1969–1975', in *Visions of the End of the Cold War in Europe, 1945–1990*, ed. Frédéric Bozo, Marie-Pierre Rey and N. Piers Ludlow (New York and Oxford: Berghahn, 2012), 139–56.

[106] Mr Elliot (Helsinki) to Sir A. Douglas-Home [WDW 1/2], 13 June 1973, in *Documents on British Policy Overseas, Series III, Volume II: The Conference on Security and Cooperation in Europe, 1972–75*, ed. G. Bennett and K.A. Hamilton (London: The Stationary Office, 1997), 140. See also Steering Brief for the United Kingdom Delegation to Stage II of the CSCE [WDW 1/18], 13 September 1973, in ibid., 179–86.

make a significant contribution towards the establishment of the 'European – and British – détente' that 'differed from, and often conflicted with' the American iteration: 'The latter aimed at stabilizing the continent and consolidating bipolarity, whereas the former had a transformative intent meant to promote a gradual overcoming of the Cold War divide in Europe.'[107] Michael Clarke suggests that, in spite of this close cooperation, Britain never came to regard the CSCE with the same enthusiasm as its EC partners.[108] Even so, during the two years between the signing of the Helsinki Final Act and the follow-up conference in Belgrade, British officials pursued a 'policy that effectively put EPC as a higher priority than NATO, higher than relations with the United States over these matters, and certainly higher than its pursuit of détente as such'.[109] As regards the attitudes of British representatives concerning the CSCE, then, the harmonisation of a European approach, clearly informed by a perceived need to ingratiate themselves with their EC colleagues following Britain's entry into the Community, had been of the utmost importance. The pursuit of détente, and a commitment to human rights promotion therein, was seemingly incidental to this more pressing concern.

In anticipation of Britain's six-month presidency of the European Council, set to begin in January 1977, however, FCO officials suggested that British representatives ought to place greater emphasis on human rights promotion and play a more active role in the cultivation of a united Community policy. A report concerning the 33rd session of the UN Commission on Human Rights produced by the FCO's UN Department, for example, argued that, in view of the spotlight placed on human rights promotion by the Carter administration and an 'increasing concern for human rights in Europe', the British delegation should, 'as representative of the Presidency, be prepared to take the initiative this year in co-ordinating the Nine's support behind a more assertive and forward-looking policy on human rights'.[110] Drawing on Britain's 'close contacts with the US', the report also underscored the importance of ensuring that this approach was 'in harmony with the strategy and tactics of the United States', indicating perhaps that zero-sum 'Euro-federalist' sentiment within the FCO was not as endemic as Owen has suggested.[111] Nonetheless, this was easier said than done. By the time Owen signed the EC Joint Declaration on Fundamental Rights on behalf of the European Council on 5 April, Carter's public pronouncements on human rights had already fomented a considerable degree of animosity within the Community, particularly regarding their potentially disastrous impact on East–West relations.[112] The roles had been quickly reversed; it was now time for the European powers to call for

---

[107] Angela Romano, 'British Policy Towards Socialist Countries in the 1970s: Trade as a Cornerstone of Détente', in *The Foreign Office, Commerce and British Foreign Policy in the Twentieth Century*, ed. Fisher, Pedaliu and Smith, 467.

[108] See Michael Clarke, 'Britain and European Political Cooperation in the CSCE', in *European Détente: Case Studies of the Politics of East–West Relations*, ed. Kenneth Dyson (London: Frances Pinter, 1986), 221–36.

[109] Ibid., 249.

[110] '33rd Session of Commission on Human Rights, Human Rights: Steering Brief', 4 February 1977, TNA, FCO 30/3641.

[111] Ibid.

[112] See J. O'Connor Howe to Information Officer, 'Joint Community Declaration on Fundamental Rights', 11 May 1977, TNA, FCO 30/3643.

moderation on the part of a US President, lest his vocal support of human rights undo the progress made by the CSCE.

On 11 March, for instance, *The Times* noted that, whereas Owen's adoption of the human rights cause could be interpreted as a display of solidarity with President Carter's foreign policy approach, official French and German appraisals of Carter's human rights policy were conspicuous in their absence.[113] Weeks later, Chancellor of the Federal Republic of Germany (FRG), Helmut Schmidt, conveyed his reservations privately to Cyrus Vance. Although Schmidt told the Secretary of State that he supported Carter's stance on human rights, the Chancellor was at pains to point out the potential implications of human rights promotion in the context of East–West relations, relating specifically to his ongoing attempts to extricate millions of ethnic Germans from the Soviet Union.[114] As *The Times* later reported, 'relations between the United States and West Germany are now worse than they need be', largely on account of 'Mr Carter's vigorous stand on human rights, which some Germans feared would undermine the entire fragile structure of détente', imperilling a 'series of delicate arrangements with East Germany which have greatly increased human traffic between the two countries'.[115] French attitudes, it would appear, were no less sceptical. In preparation for an EC ministerial meeting on human rights issues scheduled for 18 April, the FCO's Reg Hibbert circulated a minute which described the French aversion to the elevation of human rights within the East–West dialogue: 'On the East Europe item it has so far proved very difficult to convince the French of the need for the Nine to consider the implications for policy toward the Soviet Union and Eastern Europe of the study carried out by the Working Group. It appears to be the human rights issue which makes them so reticent. They wish to keep their hands free and not to be swept along, as they fear might happen, in a direction chosen arbitrarily by President Carter.'[116] The apparently insurmountable nature of the East–West issue was duly noted by the Central Intelligence Agency (CIA) when it compiled its assessment of the 'Impact of the US Stand on Human Rights' in May, describing how a 'broad range of political relationships important to the US' had been 'complicated' by the administration's emphasis on human rights.[117]

---

[113] 'Handling Human Rights', *The Times*, 11 March 1977.
[114] 'My Meetings with German and British Leaders', 1 April 1977, The National Archives, College Park, MD., Central Foreign Policy Files, Record Group 59 – General Records of the Department of State, Electronic Telegrams, 1977, available at https://aad.archives.gov/aad/createpdf?rid=72880&dt=2532&dl=1629 (accessed 3 January 2020).
[115] 'Bonn at Odds with Washington', *The Times*, 18 April 1977
[116] R.A. Hibbert to PS/PUS, 'European Political Cooperation: Ministerial Meeting 18 April Human Rights', 5 April 1977, TNA, FCO 30/3643.
[117] 'Memorandum Prepared in the Central Intelligence Agency: Impact of the US Stand on Human Rights', 11 May 1977, Document No. 42 in *Foreign Relations of the United States, 1977–1980, Volume II, Human Rights and Humanitarian Affairs*, available at https://history.state.gov/historicaldocuments/frus1977-80v02/d42 (accessed 3 January 2020). A more favourable assessment of the Carter administration's human rights policies and their reception within the European Community is provided in Barbara Keys, '"Something to Boast About": Western Enthusiasm for Carter's Human Rights Diplomacy', in *Reasserting America in the 1970s: U.S. Public Diplomacy and the Rebuilding of America's Image Abroad*, ed. Hallvard Notaker, Giles Scott-Smith and David J. Snyder (Manchester: Manchester University Press, 2016), 229–44.

Figure 3.2 Owen chairing a European Community summit at Lancaster House, London, during Britain's presidency of the European Council, 18 April 1977 (Roger Jackson/Stringer/Getty images).

Such discord was certainly not what the Carter administration had wished for during the British presidency. Rather, Washington hoped that Britain, in this capacity, would be able to serve as a vital 'interlocutor' between the US and the EC on a 'broad range of foreign policy issues'.[118] Although the UK – according to the State Department's Annual Policy and Resource Assessment (PARM) – would 'continue to be a useful agent generally in developing Community positions compatible with US interests', the administration was acutely aware that, in leveraging their British connections within the EC, the US needed to proceed with caution so as not to 'confirm the fears of other Europeans that the UK is an American Trojan horse within the Community'.[119] As Stephen George notes, key policymakers within the Carter administration, including Carter himself, subscribed to the theory of trilateralism, in which the international system 'had to be managed by co-operation between the United States, Japan, and

---

[118] 'British Assume Six-Month EC Presidency', 13 January 1977, The National Archives, College Park, MD., Central Foreign Policy Files, Record Group 59 – General Records of the Department of State, Electronic Telegrams, 1977, available at https://aad.archives.gov/aad/createpdf?rid=9051&dt=2532&dl=1629 (accessed 3 January 2020).

[119] 'PARM – Annual Policy and Resource Assessment – Part 1', 31 March 1977, The National Archives, College Park, MD., Central Foreign Policy Files, Record Group 59 – General Records of the Department of State, Electronic Telegrams, 1977, available at https://aad.archives.gov/aad/createpdf?rid=63575&dt=2532&dl=1629 (accessed 3 January 2020).

Europe'.[120] The administration, therefore, wished to avoid alienating its European allies for the sake of capitalising on the access provided to them by their UK contacts, particularly in light of the fact that, in recent years, the FRG had become increasingly significant in US estimations, both economically and strategically.[121] It is eminently understandable, therefore, that Carter, whenever possible, sought to downplay any notion of a rift developing between the US and the EC on human rights issues in his interactions with the Press.[122] By the time Britain relinquished the presidency, however, it was clear that US-EC harmony would not be so easily achieved.

On 5 July, for instance, Owen met with Ambassador Brewster to discuss a broad range of foreign policy issues. Towards the end of their hour and a half discussion in Owen's office, Brewster noted that 'Owen said with some sense of insistent warning that the European situation is very disquieting ... that France and Germany are quite upset by the effect of our human rights posture on détente'.[123] It was Brewster's understanding that such reservations must have been conveyed to Owen in no uncertain terms at the recent EC summit in London.[124] Owen concluded by reiterating 'his own personal support of the US position, but seemed genuinely distressed at the growing hostility of the Germans and the French on the question of souring East–West relations'.[125] Indeed, Owen's misgivings portended a wave of European criticism directed towards the Carter administration and its heavy-handed approach to human rights within the East–West dialogue, with President Giscard d'Estaing leading the charge.[126]

Owen's enthusiastic support of Carter's human rights policy, moreover, had done little to foster transatlantic understanding. As the US Embassy in London reported, Owen's elucidation of a human rights-based approach to British foreign policy on 3 March at the annual banquet of the Diplomatic and Commonwealth Writers Association constituted a 'unilateral declaration of HMG foreign policy', that was 'not coordinated or otherwise discussed with Britain's EC partners before delivery'.[127] It

---

[120] Stephen George, *"An Awkward Partner": Britain in the European Community*, 3rd edn (Oxford: Oxford University Press, 1998), 108.

[121] See for example Bartlett, *"The Special Relationship"*, 137–8; Self, *British Foreign and Defence Policy since 1945*, 87; David Reynolds, 'A "Special Relationship"? America, Britain and the International Order since the Second World War', *International Affairs* 62, No. 1 (Winter 1985–1986): 15–16.

[122] See for example Jimmy Carter, 'International Economic Summit Meeting Exchange with Reporters Following a State Dinner at Buckingham Palace', 7 May 1977, The American Presidency Project, available at https://www.presidency.ucsb.edu/documents/international-economic-summit-meeting-exchange-with-reporters-following-state-dinner (accessed 2 January 2020).

[123] 'Luncheon Meeting with Foreign Secretary', 5 July 1977, The National Archives, College Park, MD., Central Foreign Policy Files, Record Group 59 – General Records of the Department of State, Electronic Telegrams, 1977, available at https://aad.archives.gov/aad/createpdf?rid=152259&dt=2532&dl=1629 (accessed 3 January 2020).

[124] Ibid.

[125] Ibid.

[126] See for example Ian Murray, 'Carter policy attacked by President Giscard', *The Times*, 18 July 1977; 'A Bismarckian Critique', *The Times*, 19 July 1977; Anne Sington, 'Giscard "go-it-alone" policy winning support in Europe', *Daily Telegraph*, 20 July 1977.

[127] 'Owen Speech on Détente and Human Rights', 4 March 1977, The National Archives, College Park, MD., Central Foreign Policy Files, Record Group 59 – General Records of the Department of State, Electronic Telegrams, 1977, available at https://aad.archives.gov/aad/createpdf?rid=45844&dt=2532&dl-1629 (accessed 3 January 2020).

follows, therefore, that during the course of Britain's EC presidency a perception began to develop among Britain's Community partners that the Callaghan government was too eager to position itself side-by-side with the Carter administration in the human rights field to take heed of continental anxieties.[128] Some of Owen's public statements certainly did little to disabuse Britain's EC allies of this notion, framing human rights as a distinctly *Anglophone* concept – an outgrowth of a shared philosophical inheritance which bound Britain and the United States tighter than any other Western democracies. In fact, Owen seemingly welcomed the tension that this would create within the Western alliance as Britain and the United States positioned themselves in the vanguard of the ideological struggle against communism. Consider, for example, Owen's appearance on the US television programme *Face the Nation* in July 1977:

> **Interviewer** Mr Secretary, there is no question that the Soviet Union is uneasy about the President's commitment to human rights. Do you sense that there is a sense of uneasiness as well in Western Europe about the President's campaign on human rights in so far as it has a damaging impact as seen by some on détente?
>
> **Owen** Yes, I think it would be wrong to say that there isn't a sense of unease ... I think you have to recognise ... that every country is going to handle human rights in a different way ... Britain is going to be different [than other western European countries] because it's got, in a way, the same sort of tradition to individual freedom and moral stance in foreign policy [as the United States] ... And so I find that aspect of President Carter's foreign policy deeply attractive ... France, I think has a different style on these sorts of issues, it has a different attitude to civil liberties. I don't think it's a strongly felt issue in some regards as it is for instance in Britain. It seems that Italy too has a different response.[129]

By framing human rights as not so much a common theme capable of galvanizing the European Community as a multiplicity of nation-specific discourses, Owen provides an important counterpoint to Buchanan's framing of the EC-human rights nexus, lending support to the contention that, ultimately, the European Community 'rests upon a relatively weak sense of history and identity; partly because of the diverse historical experiences of its members ... and partly because the forging of identity takes time, and comes through hard-won experience, including shared failures; it cannot be bought off the shelf'.[130]

Behind closed doors, Owen also displayed a degree of reticence when it came to the prospect of coordinating a human rights policy among 'the Nine'. In response to Michael Simpson-Orlebar's suggestion that Britain ought to discuss its ideas in the

---

[128] See for example PUS to Mr Rowlands, 'US Foreign Policy: A European View', undated (circa August 1977), TNA, FCO 58/1162: '[S]ome of our European partners consider that we have been too sensitive to American views in this field and have not taken enough account of European sensitivities and interests, particularly over human rights in East/West relations'.

[129] 'Transcript of Secretary of State's Appearance on CBS "Face the Nation"', 24 July 1977, DOP, D709 2/7/2/2.

[130] Christopher Hill and William Wallace, 'Introduction: Actors and Actions', in *The Actors in Europe's Foreign Policy*, ed. Christopher Hill (London: Routledge, 1996), 8.

human rights field with its EC allies, Owen stated that 'he wanted any British initiative to be kept in British hands'.[131] It was not, in his opinion, 'necessary to do everything with the Nine', and although he was willing to countenance a collective initiative during the British presidency, he 'would not wish the Belgian Presidency to take it over'.[132] The articulation of such reservations highlights the attenuated supranationalism of European cooperation in the foreign policy sphere – reflected not just in the outlook of member states, but also within the institutional framework of the EC – and supports Christopher Hill's assertion that, since joining the EC there has been 'no logical incompatibility' between support for European Political Cooperation and 'another defining characteristic of the British attitude, namely that Europe is a suitable forum for cooperation on some issues, but not all'.[133] Indeed, when Evan Luard echoed Owen's objection to Simpson-Orlebar's calls for greater coordination within the EC in December 1977, the debate seemingly became entangled with long-standing anxieties surrounding Britain's enduring ambivalence towards Europe and the division between ministers and Foreign Office officials as far as Britain's relationship with Europe was concerned.[134]

Reg Hibbert warned that 'if the UK were to begin to treat the Political Cooperation process in a cavalier way others, especially France, would feel much freer to do the same and the end result would be distinctly unhelpful to the UK'.[135] As far as Hibbert was concerned, the UK should not find it too difficult to marry two propositions: the development of Political Cooperation as a central tenet of British membership of the Community, and 'advocacy of action in defence of human rights' as a 'main plank of the Government's policy'.[136] 'My own belief', Hibbert concluded, 'is that the UK can in fact achieve its aims more effectively through Political Cooperation with the partners of the Nine than through going it alone. The restraint which Political Cooperation sometimes puts on the UK's freedom of action seems to me to be on the whole more apparent than real. I hope we can be authorised to ride two horses together'.[137] This response was not only rejected by Luard on the grounds that it had mischaracterized his position on human rights coordination with the Nine; his reply was accompanied by the suggestion that certain parts of the Whitehall machinery had become preoccupied with the appeasement of Britain's European partners which, in this case, ran the risk of restricting Britain's capacity for action in the human rights field:

---

[131] 'Record of an Office Meeting held by the Secretary of State on Wednesday, 25 May 1977 at 3.30 PM', TNA, FCO 58/1152.
[132] Ibid.
[133] Christopher Hill, 'Britain: A Convenient Schizophrenia', in *National Foreign Policies and European Political Cooperation*, ed. Christopher Hill (London: George Allen & Unwin, 1983), 25. See also Jakob C. Ohrgaard, 'International Relations or European Integration: Is the CFSP Sui Generis?' in *Rethinking European Foreign Policy*, ed. Tonra and Christiansen, 26–44; Reinhardt Rummel and Jörg Wiedemann, 'Identifying Institutional Paradoxes of CFSP', in *Paradoxes of European Foreign Policy*, ed. Jan Zielonka (The Hague: Kluwer Law International, 1998), 53–66.
[134] See M.K.O. Simpson-Orlebar to Mr Weir; PS/Mr Luard, 'Human Rights and Foreign Policy: Progress Report', 7 December 1977, TNA, FCO 58/1146; Evan Luard to Mr Simpson-Orlebar, 'Human Rights and Foreign Policy', 12 December 1977, TNA, FCO 58/1146.
[135] R.A. Hibbert to PS/Mr Luard, 19 December 1977, TNA, FCO 58/1146.
[136] Ibid.
[137] Ibid.

I am not against consulting with the Nine and trying to get their support for our ideas if possible but, at least in the human rights field, I do not think that it should have the absolute priority that was implied by the earlier submission to me (and, like one or two to other FCO Ministers, I believe (though a committed European) that the objective of keeping in step with the Nine at all costs perhaps plays an excessively dominant part in the thinking of officials here on many issues at present). I agree that our human rights policy and our European policy need not be in competition but on some issues they inevitably are. We are, for example, quite often in the absurd position that all the Nine are slowed down to the pace of the French. But my main point is that we should consider first what our aims are in human rights and then how far we can win support from the Nine: not vice versa.[138]

Meanwhile, the question of prioritizing UK–EC relations above all else was rapidly reaching a fever pitch in the Washington Embassy – a 'microcosm of the Foreign Office', according to the *Sunday Times*' Washington correspondent Henry Brandon – as Peter Jay repeatedly clashed with his deputy, John Robinson, a senior diplomat who had played a key role in securing Britain's entry into the European Community.[139] As a matter of fact, Jay recalls that his relationship with Robinson failed hopelessly for this very reason: 'One difficulty was the Europe theme … It appeared to me … that he not only had a passionate and overriding loyalty and commitment to Britain's relationship with the EU, but that he also believed it was a zero sum game in competition with this relationship with the United States. In other words, the one could only gain if the other was diminished.'[140] According to Jay, Robinson was so single-minded in his Europeanism that 'he seemed to think … that since there was not a lot he could do in Washington directly to strengthen the relationship with Brussels, he could best serve that cause by weakening the relationship with Washington … I began to become aware that … the things that I had been doing, which I saw as a key part of cementing the closest possible relationship with the United States, with the Administration, and political Washington, were being, in effect, undone while I was away.'[141]

Robinson was effectively exiled to New York in October 1978 once Michael Palliser became convinced that the relationship between the Ambassador and his deputy was irreparable. Still, the conflict clearly left a lasting impression on Jay, whose valedictory despatch served to press home the fundamental differences between himself and his deputy which had vitiated the attempted rejuvenation of Anglo–American relations during his time at the Embassy: 'Our world is dying; and its death is being hastened by errors and myopia in our own ranks … the framework of the West – and the security, freedoms and prosperity which depend on it – is being dangerously

---

[138] Evan Luard to R.A. Hibbert, 20 December 1977, TNA, FCO 58/1146.
[139] Henry Brandon, handwritten notes, 17 May 1977, LOC, Henry Brandon Papers, Box 56: Folder 2. The tensions between Jay and Robinson are explored in Hugo Young, *This Blessed Plot: Britain and Europe from Churchill to Blair* (London: Macmillan, 1998), 173–212.
[140] Peter Jay, interview with Malcolm McBain, 24 February 2006, BDOHP, available at https://www.chu.cam.ac.uk/media/uploads/files/Jay_Peter.pdf (accessed 18 August 2020).
[141] Ibid.

eroded.'[142] Contributing above all else to this insidious erosion was a conception of Europe 'that sees its own unity as a vehicle for a new nationalism on a sub-continental scale, as an escape from the post-war impotence of the old petty, Balkanised nationalism of France, Germany etc. into the headier league of superpower or regional nationalism'.[143] Above all, Jay concluded, 'it is the Europe that cares more about Europe than the West'.[144]

Questions regarding the appropriate degree to which the UK should consult with its EC partners on human rights issues, (and the extent to which the UK should support the approach of the Carter administration which had clearly antagonized some members of the EC), therefore, cannot be so easily extricated from larger contemporaneous debates concerning Britain's contested relationship with the rest of Europe, nor can they be separated from the Labour Party's historic tendency towards Euroscepticism.[145] Accounts that place Britain at the 'uncooperative' end of the European foreign policy continuum, or view British–EC relations through the prism of the former's distrust of the latter's supranational aspirations, however, do not tell 'the whole story'.[146] Indeed, it would certainly be unfair to suggest that Britain – an awkward partner, perhaps – was any less committed to human rights promotion within the fora of the EC than any of its Community partners during Owen's tenure as Foreign Secretary. On the contrary, following its replacement as EC Council President by representatives of the Belgian government in July 1977 – and the Cabinet's establishment of a coherent policy regarding the development of the European project – the Callaghan government would find itself facing an uphill struggle in its attempts to ensure the codification of human rights provisions within the renegotiated Lomé Convention.

The British desire to insert a human rights clause within the renegotiated Convention – signed initially in February 1975 and scheduled for renewal in 1980 – had developed as a response to the EC's inability to suspend aid to Uganda in 1976 in spite of the gross human rights abuses that were being perpetrated by the Idi Amin regime, and was raised explicitly as a policy objective in September 1977.[147] Following the confirmation

---

[142] Peter Jay, 'The West: The Peril Within', Valedictory despatch, 20 June 1979, reproduced in *Parting Shots: Undiplomatic Diplomats – The Ambassadors' Letters you were Never Meant to See*, ed. Matthew Parris and Andrew Bryson (London: Penguin, 2011), 274–5.

[143] Ibid., 276.

[144] Ibid., 276–7.

[145] See for example Vickers, *Labour's Foreign Policy since 1951*, 99: Vickers notes how Labour's historic attachment to internationalism has, at times, been a complicating factor in British–EC relations. Seen 'more in terms of having ties and commitments to the Commonwealth than Europe', Labour's internationalism, according to Vickers, has 'tended to view Britain as a world leader, not as one of many European countries'. See also Roger Broad, *Labour's European Dilemmas: From Bevin to Blair* (Basingstoke: Palgrave Macmillan, 2001).

[146] Christopher Hill, 'Convergence, Divergence and Dialectics: National Foreign Policies and the CFSP', in *Paradoxes of European Foreign Policy*, ed. Zielonka, 37; Andrew Geddes, *The European Union and British Politics* (Basingstoke: Palgrave Macmillan, 2004), 20.

[147] M.K.O. Simpson-Orlebar to Mr Weir; Mr Hibbert, 'Human Rights: Coordinated Approach with the Nine', 19 September 1977, TNA, FCO 58/1146. The EC had, in July 1977, formalized its 'Uganda guidelines', which specified that Community assistance granted to Uganda could be withdrawn if such aid was deemed capable of reinforcing or prolonging ongoing human rights violations. See Directorate-General for External Policies of the Union, 'Human Rights and Democracy Clauses in the EU's International Agreements' (Long version), 29 September 2005, available at https://www.europarl.europa.eu/RegData/etudes/etudes/join/2005/363284/EXPO-DROI_ET(2005)363284_EN.pdf (accessed 13 February 2022).

of ministerial support for the notion in November, focus turned towards securing support for the proposition within the Community, but this was hardly forthcoming.[148] French and German representatives had already articulated their misgivings over the insertion of a human rights element in Lomé II during an informal meeting of EC Foreign Ministers at Villiers le Temple in October.[149] As the debate progressed over the course of the following year, moreover, scepticism increasingly became the consensus position within the Community. As Minister for Overseas Development, Judith Hart, reported on 13 April 1978, Claude Cheysson – the French European Commissioner who controlled the management of the development portfolio – was not as concerned about potential ACP hostility towards the prospect of a human rights provision as he was by the opposition that would come from EC member states, chiefly France, Denmark and Germany.[150] Regarding the latter: 'Cheysson believed Germany was principally opposed to a human rights provision aimed at the ACP states because they thought they would be vulnerable to strong ACP criticism over their "Gastarbeiter" policy, particularly Lomé as it affects their Turkish immigrant labour ... Of our other EEC collegues, Cheysson reported that the Belgians were sceptical on the issue.'[151]

Fearing that German reticence would be reinforced by their interactions with the French, who had made their opposition to a prospective human rights provision clear at the 13 April meeting of the Committee of Permanent Representatives (COREPER), Owen and Callaghan put their case to the FRG's Foreign Minister Hans-Dietrich Genscher and Chancellor Schmidt.[152] Such efforts, however, were in vain, and by the time the subject was revisited during an EC 'Foreign Ministers Informal Weekend' in May, Owen was clearly struggling to contain his frustration, forcefully rejecting the suggestion that 'no differences of substance' could be found between the national positions of the Nine on this issue: 'Dr Owen had made clear that differences did indeed exist. He had encountered a good deal of opposition from his colleagues to anything more than a general reference (perhaps drawing on the UN Declaration) to human rights in the preamble ... it was clear that he was alone in taking a tough line on human rights/Lomé ... The Secretary of State also thought that the fact there was known to be disagreement among the Nine had weakened our negotiating position.'[153]

[148] 'Third ACP/EEC Council of Ministers, Brussels, 13/14 March', undated (circa March 1978), TNA, FCO 98/330: 'UK Ministers decided in November at CQM that one of our major objectives in renegotiation should be to secure a substantive human rights clause in a Lome II.'
[149] See ibid.
[150] Judith Hart to Secretary of State for Foreign and Commonwealth Affairs, 'EDF Aid to Uganda', 13 April 1978, TNA, FCO 98/330.
[151] Ibid.
[152] UKREP Brussels to FCO, 'Lomé Convention: Human Rights', 19 April 1978, TNA, FCO 98/330; UKREP Brussels to FCO, 'Committee of Permanent Representatives (Ambassadors): 13 April, Renegotiation of the Lomé Convention: Human Rights', 13 April 1978, TNA, FCO 98/330; M.R.H. Jenkins to Mr Fretwell; Private Secretary, 'Lomé Renegotiation: Human Rights', with attached brief: 'The Secretary of State's Meeting with Herr Genscher at Chequers on 24 April', 20 April 1978, TNA, FCO 98/330. French opposition to the insertion of an operative human rights clause within Lomé II, and its stark contrast to UK enthusiasm, is demonstrated clearly in Etienne Reuter to Mr Tickell; President, 'Lomé II', 1 May 1978, Historical Archives of the European Union, European University Institute, Florence (hereafter HAEU), CEUE_JENK-1210.
[153] W.K. Prendergast to Mr Jenkins, 'EEC Foreign Ministers Informal Weekend: Lome – Human Rights', 26 May 1978, TNA, FCO 98/331. Regarding Britain's increasingly isolated position, see also 'Meeting of Foreign Ministers and President of the Commission: Hesselet', 20 May 1978, HAEU, EN-1145.

The acceptance of a preambular reference to human rights consideration was, it seems, as far as the majority of Owen's EC colleagues were willing to go, although it must be stated that this was not for want of continued UK efforts to push for the inclusion of a more substantive human rights clause in the renegotiated Convention. At a meeting of the EC Council of Foreign Ministers on 6 June, for instance, Owen reportedly 'took the lead in pressing for some kind of language in the body of the Convention which would allow the Community to cut off aid to ACP states which violate human rights', emphasizing that its current form was 'not satisfactory in this regard, as was demonstrated last year when the Community found itself with a situation in Uganda in which its response was limited'.[154]

But even compromise solutions proved difficult to come by, in spite of growing interest in Lomé's prospective human rights dimension within the European Parliament.[155] As the US Embassy in Brussels reported following a meeting of EC Foreign Ministers on 26–7 June, 'the UK maintained its past insistence that additional language be included in body of the Convention' linking human rights with the provision of EC aid.[156] In the face of overwhelming opposition, however, 'no serious attempt was made to settle the question, and the Council agreed only on a reference in the opening statement emphasizing the importance of human rights'.[157] UK representatives were seemingly encouraged by the fact that they had, by this stage, been joined in this crusade by the Netherlands, and the two governments can be seen to coordinate their attempts to modify the Community's position during the weeks and months that followed.[158] Even still, it would appear that the UK's commitment to this endeavour far outstripped that of its Dutch collaborators. As negotiations gathered speed in the spring of 1979, Dutch support began to fade, and their reluctant acceptance of the Community's scepticism was noted with disappointment within the FCO.[159]

In light of the lack of support behind the UK's push for the insertion of an operative human rights clause in Lomé II, the fact that the renegotiated Convention contained no such provision is hardly surprising. As such, it is also misleading to suggest, as an Overseas Development Institute briefing paper does, that the EC 'wanted more than a

---

[154] 'EC Foreign Ministers Council, June 6, 1978: Lome Convention Renewal', 7 June 1978, The National Archives, College Park, MD., Central Foreign Policy Files, Record Group 59 – General Records of the Department of State, Electronic Telegrams, 1978, available at https://aad.archives.gov/aad/create pdf?rid=141742&dt=2694&dl=2009 (accessed 3 January 2020).

[155] See for example Question by Lord Reay, 'EEC-ACP Convention on Human Rights', 2 June 1978, HAEU, PE0-7442.

[156] 'EC Foreign Ministers Council, June 26–27, 1978: Renewal of Lome Convention', 29 June 1978, The National Archives, College Park, MD., Central Foreign Policy Files, Record Group 59 – General Records of the Department of State, Electronic Telegrams, 1978, available at https://aad.archives.gov/aad/createpdf?rid=141258&dt=2694&dl=2009 (accessed 3 January 2020).

[157] Ibid.

[158] See for example European Integration Department (External), 'Lome Renegotiation: Human Rights, Meeting with Dutch Officials at 10.00 on 9 November', 1978, TNA, FCO 98/333; 'Summary Record of Discussion of Lomé II/Human Rights Between the Minister of State and the Netherlands Ambassador and Officials at the FCO on 9 November 1978 at 10.15', 14 November 1978, TNA, FCO 98/333.

[159] See 'Visit to London by Mr Van Gorkum on 24 April, Lomé Renegotiation: Human Rights', 19 April 1979, TNA, FCO 98/614; R.B.R. Hervey to G.E. FitzHerbert, 'Lomé II: Human Rights', 25 April 1979, TNA, FCO 98/614.

casual reference to basic UN principles inserted in the new convention' and that the human rights clause 'was quietly dropped during the negotiations' due to the objections of the ACP countries.[160] Rather, the Callaghan government had been swimming against the tide throughout the negotiations in its attempts to codify human rights considerations within the renegotiated Convention (signed on 31 October 1979). Whereas the Callaghan government's stubbornness had been a thorn in the side of the EC during the negotiations – a solitary obstacle blocking the establishment of a unanimous negotiating position with the ACP countries – the Conservative administration of Margaret Thatcher, which came to power following the general election of May 1979, would prove to be far more attentive to the concerns of its Community partners, as was clearly indicated by this record of an exchange between the Dutch Embassy and the FCO's G.E. FitzHerbert:

> Mr Brouwer of the Dutch Embassy telephoned me this morning to ask what line British Ministers were likely to take in Brussels on 24/25 May on this issue. I said that while our new Ministers continued to attach importance to the human rights question, and would I thought in particular want to support the existing agreed Community position that the new Convention should contain at least a preambular reference to human rights, they were also well aware of the difficulties which there would be in negotiating a satisfactory outcome with the ACP. They would want to take a pragmatic line... Mr Brouwer said that while his Minister would realise that there was a difference between the present British Government and its predecessor as regards the priority to be placed on human rights issues generally, he thought that because of the past understanding between the British and Dutch Governments on this question his Minister would want to continue to keep in close touch with us about it. As Mr Hurd knows, I think it will be important for the UK not to retreat too rapidly and too openly from the very strong position taken by the previous Government on human rights in Lome.[161]

This 'pragmatic' line was duly adopted by Minister of State (and later Foreign Secretary) Douglas Hurd without objection.[162] It would, in fact, take until the entry into force of Lomé IV in 1989 for a human rights clause to feature in the Convention.[163] However, even the programmatic principles contained within Article 5 of Lomé IV have been criticized for lacking 'concrete human rights guarantees capable of being employed as

---

[160] Overseas Development Institute, 'Lomé II', Briefing Paper, No. 1 (February 1980), available at https://www.odi.org/sites/odi.org.uk/files/odi-assets/publications-opinion-files/6636.pdf (accessed 7 January 2020).
[161] G.E. FitzHerbert to PS/Mr Hurd, 'Lomé Renegotiation: Human Rights', 23 May 1979, TNA, FCO 98/615.
[162] C.T.W. Humfrey to Mr FitzHerbert, 'Lomé Renegotiation: Human Rights', 29 March 1979, TNA, FCO 98/615.
[163] See for example Bruno Simma, Jo Beatrix Aschenbrenner and Constanze Schulte, 'Human Rights Considerations in the Development Co-operation Activities of the EC', in *The EU and Human Rights*, ed. Philip Alston, Mara Bustelo and James Heenan (Oxford: Oxford University Press, 1999), 586–9.

conditions for the fulfilment of the Treaty'.[164] While the protracted development of the Convention's human rights dimension cannot be isolated from the vicissitudes of the North–South dialogue during the 1980s – the 'lost decade' of development – it ought to be noted, nonetheless, that the revival of European Political Cooperation, for which the Thatcher ministries have been partially credited, apparently came at a price as far as the prioritisation of human rights in the external agreements of the EC was concerned.[165]

Conclusion

Situating Britain's recalibration of its international role within a narrative of generational schism, Owen simultaneously rejected notions of pre-war imperial grandeur and fatalistic readings of Britain's decline from world power; disavowed the prevailing Eurocentrism of senior Foreign Office officials; held Britain's connections with the US and the EC to be mutually reinforcing; and, consequently, sought to pursue a human rights-based agenda within both 'spheres' of influence. Regarding the former, Owen's human rights initiative positioned the Callaghan government shoulder-to-shoulder with the Carter administration, and a significant degree of cooperation on human rights issues served to underscore a sense of common purpose that brought the two governments closer together. By illuminating the ways in which human rights promotion served to further UK–US rapprochement, this chapter has therefore provided a fresh perspective on Anglo-American relations during this period, challenging conventional wisdom regarding British scepticism towards the Carter administration's human rights policy.

The Callaghan government's assertive stance on human rights promotion within the EC, however, would prove to be far more problematic. Owen's enthusiastic support for Carter's human rights policy, it would appear, provoked suspicion within the Community, with many members voicing their concerns over being pushed too far on human rights promotion within the context of the East–West dialogue. This was a radical departure from the transatlantic dynamic that had emerged during the early to mid-1970s when US policymakers had called for the maintenance of the status quo in Europe and European leaders, viewing human rights as a constitutive aspect of an emerging European identity, adopted a transformative approach to détente and human rights promotion within the CSCE. By situating Owen's public support for Carter's

---

[164] Eibe Riedel and Martin Will, 'Human Rights Clauses in External Agreements of the EC', in *The EU and Human Rights*, ed. Alston, Bustelo and Heenan, 726.

[165] Gilbert Rist, *The History of Development: From Western Origins to Global Faith*, 3rd edn (London: Zed Books, 2008), 170. For analyses of the Convention's evolution, and its relationship to broader trends within the politics of development, see Ismael Musah Montana, 'The Lomé Convention from Inception to the Dynamics of the Post-Cold War, 1957–1990s', *African and Asian Studies* 2, No. 1 (2003): 63–97; Guia Migani, 'Lomé and the North–South Relations (1975–1984): From the "New International Economic Order" to a New Conditionality', in *Europe in a Globalising World: Global Challenges and European Responses in the "Long" 1970s*, ed. Claudia Hiepel (Baden-Baden: Nomos, 2014), 123–46. Regarding the role of the Thatcher governments in facilitating European Political Cooperation, see for example William Wallace, 'Introduction: Cooperation and Convergence in European Foreign Policy', in *National Foreign Policies and European Political Cooperation*, ed. Hill, 8.

policy alongside this process of role reversal, this chapter has also contributed to our understanding of Britain's complex relationship with its EC partners in the foreign policy field. Indeed, by supporting Carter's policy, Owen can be seen to effectively subvert the British approach towards the related issues of European Political Cooperation and human rights promotion within the framework of the CSCE. Whereas British delegates had, both leading up to and following the signing of the Helsinki Final Act in 1975, tended to regard human rights promotion as a mere adjunct to the more pressing objective of European cooperation, Owen saw to it that human rights promotion became much more identifiable as an end unto itself, irrespective of whether this stance would cause discord within the Community. As such, this chapter has also illuminated broader debates concerning British attitudes towards European integration.

Perhaps it could be argued that Owen's promotion of human rights during his tenure as Foreign Secretary – and the response it evoked within the EC – reflected the enduring precarity of Britain's status as a *European* power which has provided the central theme for a great deal of scholarship – *An Awkward Partner* (1998); *Reluctant Europeans* (2000); *A Stranger in Europe* (2008); *Half In, Half Out* (2018).[166] In this case, however, it would be unfair to suggest that Euroscepticism or a sense of ideological detachment was the cause. Yes, Owen exhibited, at times, a more selective approach towards the coordination of human rights policy within the EC than he did when dealing with Washington. The Callaghan government's prolonged and ultimately unsuccessful attempts to secure the codification of human rights concerns within the renegotiated Lomé Convention, and Owen's concerted efforts to bring this to fruition, however, demonstrate that the Foreign Secretary was not merely focused on the pursuit of Anglo-American initiatives in the human rights field; he also clearly viewed the EC as a valuable forum through which Britain's human rights policy could be amplified in concert with its European partners.

The Callaghan government was in fact far more proactive on this front than its ostensibly pro-European Conservative successor, which was more than willing to adopt a 'pragmatic' position in line with the majority of its EC colleagues. This divergence casts a spotlight on an important question: to what extent has the evolution of human rights promotion within the context of British foreign policy been shaped – or indeed constrained – by party-political considerations? And can we think about this question not just in terms of contested strategic imperatives, but of fundamentally disparate conceptions of human rights? The following chapter will explore these questions by focusing on the common ground occupied by David Owen and Margaret Thatcher on the situation of human rights in the East–West dialogue before analysing the ideational schism that rendered such similarities superficial.

---

[166] George, 'An Awkward Partner'; David Gowland and Arthur Turner, *Reluctant Europeans: Britain and European Integration, 1945–1998* (Harlow: Longman, 2000); Stephen Wall, *A Stranger in Europe: Britain and the EU from Thatcher to Blair* (Oxford: Oxford University Press, 2008); *Half In, Half Out*, ed. Adonis.

4

Beyond the Breakthrough

(In)divisible Human Rights and Cold War Contestations

Writing shortly after the election of Margaret Thatcher's Conservative government in May 1979, Evan Luard – who had served as Owen's Parliamentary Secretary of State and had been the chief architect of the FCO's human rights comparative assessment – noted that 'there has probably never been a time when there was so much concern about human rights questions as there is today', and commended the recent efforts of the Carter administration in the United States and 'the former Labour government in Britain' for pursuing 'active policies in this field'.[1] Indeed, as previous chapters have demonstrated, the Callaghan government's hitherto underappreciated attempts to elevate human rights concerns within the context of British foreign policy, and David Owen's influential role therein, ought to be seen as a constitutive aspect of the so-called human rights 'breakthrough' of the late 1970s.[2] There are, however, certain risks attendant to the identification of such epochal ruptures in the history of human rights that need to be underscored. In fact, in recent years scholars have increasingly begun to question the efficacy of such approaches.

Robert Brier, for example, credits revisionist scholars for showing that 'the 1970s were not merely the next step in a gradual rise of human rights, but that developments peculiar to this decade played a central role in turning human rights into the global norm they are today'.[3] Nonetheless, Brier also notes that this historiographical intervention has 'exposed something more fundamental: the historicity of human rights, i.e. the contingent, at times almost accidental nature of their emergence, their enormous malleability and adaptability', and 'the tenuousness of their position both before and after the 1970s'.[4] Human rights, in other words, 'were not simply handed down to us from the 1970s or from any other "breakthrough" moment', and our preoccupation with the identification of such moments may have reached the point of diminishing returns: 'Human rights history derives its strength precisely from its consistently historical approach. By looking for a breakthrough moment or decade, cutting it off from previous developments and collapsing the following forty years into

---

[1] Evan Luard, 'Human Rights and Foreign Policy', *International Affairs* 56, No. 4 (Autumn 1980): 579.
[2] See for example *The Breakthrough*, ed. Eckel and Moyn; Moyn, *The Last Utopia*.
[3] Brier, 'Beyond the Quest for a "Breakthrough"': 157.
[4] Ibid.

them, we are in danger of undermining what propels the exciting new project of human rights historiography.'[5]

As previously discussed, the emergence of transnational activist networks during the 1960s served to prefigure much of the human rights activism that became more readily identifiable over the course of the following decade. The legitimacy of Brier's critique, and of the like-minded contributions of Mark Philip Bradley and Stefan-Ludwig Hoffman predating his intervention, moreover, has been reinforced by numerous studies situated within the vibrant sub-section of human rights historiography focusing on the complex relationship between human rights advocacy and the ideological struggle of the Cold War.[6] Sarah Snyder, for instance, has suggested that it is possible to view human rights engagement during the Cold War not in terms of a human rights *breakthrough*, but as a more 'undulating' *process* – 'that "moments" might be a more useful framework for understanding when human rights emerged as a priority in international relations'.[7] In Snyder's view:

> We should see the Cold War as bookended by two major human rights developments – the 1948 United Nations (UN) Universal Declaration of Human Rights and the influence of human rights advocacy at the end of the Cold War. In between, attention to human rights abuses internationally was inconsistent and often overshadowed by the perceived stakes of the Cold War in political, military, ideological, and economic terms. Yet people at the time did care, and these human rights moments warrant greater attention by scholars.[8]

Rosemary Foot, likewise, maintains that human rights were clearly subsumed by the ideological contest of the Cold War, co-opted by East and West alike: 'Whereas Communist governments regarded civil and political rights as bourgeois political trappings, stating a preference for the collective rights appropriate to the social and economic goals they propounded, Western liberal capitalist governments gave priority precisely to those rights that the Soviet bloc derided.'[9] As such, while the Cold War may have 'operated in ways that kept the human rights idea alive', Foot also points out that the eventual victory of the West brought with it the 'dominance of the discourse on civil and political rights over that of economic, social, and cultural concerns, a dominance that remains controversial'.[10] This chapter will seek to shed more light on this

---

[5] Ibid.
[6] See Bradley, 'American Vernaculars': 1–21; Hoffman, 'Introduction', 1–26.
[7] Sarah B. Snyder, 'Lecture Summary – Human Rights and the Cold War: Did Anyone Care?' (an H-Diplo Essay, 9 October 2014, H-Diplo, available at https://networks.h-net.org/node/28443/discussions/47764/lecture-summary-%E2%80%9Chuman-rights-and-cold-war-did-anyone-care%E2%80%9D-h-diplo (accessed 10 January 2020). Lecture based on Sarah B. Snyder, 'Human Rights in the Cold War', in *The Routledge Handbook of the Cold War,* ed. Artemy M. Kalinovsky and Craig Daigle (New York: Routledge, 2014), 237–48.
[8] Ibid.
[9] Rosemary Foot, 'The Cold War and Human Rights', in *The Cambridge History of the Cold War, Volume 3: Endings,* ed. Melvyn P. Leffler and Odd Arne Westad (Cambridge: Cambridge University Press, 2010), 445.
[10] Ibid., 464, 465.

phenomenon by examining how the dynamics of the East–West dialogue shaped David Owen's human rights agenda at the Foreign Office, before analysing how Owen's advocacy developed in the shadow of a divergent conception of human rights championed by the Thatcher governments between 1979–90.

A striking degree of continuity can be observed between the Callaghan government and its Conservative successor as regards the weaponization of human rights within the context of the Cold War. However, while both governments sought to utilize human rights as a stick with which to beat the Soviet Union, human rights concerns would become increasingly detached from questions of socio-economic inequality following Thatcher's election in May 1979. Whereas Owen, along with fellow Labour ministers Judith Hart and Frank Judd, viewed human rights as indivisible, comprising civil and political *and* social and economic rights, British human rights policy post-1979 became ever more associated with the exclusive pursuit of the former.

Consequently, while human rights policy during the Callaghan government came to impinge upon issues concerning overseas development and Britain's constructive involvement with the politics of the North–South dialogue more broadly, the more circumscribed human rights vision that predominated during the 1980s tended to preclude British engagement with such initiatives as the New International Economic Order (NIEO) and the Right to Development championed by the 'developing' countries of the Group of 77 (G77). By the time of Thatcher's resignation as leader of the Conservative Party in 1990, moreover, the efforts of her ministries had led to this conception of human rights – tied inextricably to the imperatives of democratic promotion and free-market economics – becoming firmly embedded within the apparatus of the CSCE itself. To be sure, alternative conceptions of human rights emerged in opposition to the politics of Thatcherism. Following Owen's departure from the Labour Party and his co-founding of the Social Democratic Party (SDP) in 1981, for instance, a vision of human rights promotion that synthesized the politics of the Cold War and the North–South dialogue became part of the SDP's broader search for a viable 'third way' in British politics. However, as far as Owen's evolving personal commitment to human rights was concerned, the decoupling of human rights from issues of distributive economic justice in international discourse during the 1980s had, by the end of Thatcher's premiership, led him away from *human rights* promotion towards the adoption of a broader *humanitarian* ethos more attuned to the pressing needs of the developing world.

By exploring these developments, this chapter will not only contribute to ongoing historiographical debates concerning the chronologies of human rights history, but will also challenge the widely held view regarding Britain's indifference towards human rights promotion within the framework of the CSCE, further illuminate the significance of political parties and their respective foreign policy traditions in the context of international human rights promotion, and provide a fresh perspective on the historically contested nature of indivisible human rights in international discourse.[11]

---

[11] See Morphet, 'British Foreign Policy and Human Rights', 87–114; Vickers, *The Labour Party and the World*, Volumes I & II; Daniel J. Whelan, *Indivisible Human Rights: A History* (Philadelphia: University of Pennsylvania Press, 2010).

Furthermore, by examining how Owen's commitment to addressing the root causes of human suffering became reframed within a humanitarian optic through his engagement with the Independent Commission on International Humanitarian Issues (ICIHI) which ran from 1983–7, this chapter will draw attention to the entangled histories of human rights and humanitarianism, casting a spotlight on the emergence of rights-based approaches to humanitarian intervention – the so-called 'new humanitarianism' that would become increasingly prevalent in the post-Cold War era.

Owen, Thatcher and the weaponization of human rights within the CSCE

Writing in 1986, Philip Williams noted that the lack of scholarly attention devoted to British attitudes concerning détente and the CSCE was 'indicative of the relatively low priority given to [the] CSCE in British foreign policy throughout the 1970s'.[12] The intervening period has, if anything, witnessed the even deeper entrenchment of this narrative – the British approach to détente is widely regarded as being 'more cautious, even pedestrian, compared to other exponents of the policy during the 1960s and 1970s'.[13] British diplomats may have played a key role in establishing the human rights provisions enshrined within the August 1975 Helsinki Final Act.[14] Nonetheless, recent studies of the Helsinki Process have only served to reinforce the notion that British policymakers regarded the CSCE with suspicion, their engagement moderated by pragmatism and low expectations. Michael D. Brown, for instance, even goes so far as to invoke the British experience of détente as a means of challenging 'the pre-eminence of human rights-based analyses of the CSCE' by highlighting the diffidence of successive British governments between 1969 and 1975.[15]

President Carter's elevation of the human rights dimension within US foreign policy, it has also been suggested, did little to engender a more pro-active British approach to human rights promotion in the East–West dialogue. Rather, Brian White argues that at this point 'the British became concerned that such high-profile pressure on the Soviet system could provoke confrontation rather than promote cooperation'.[16] Thomas Robb, similarly, has recently posited that 'Carter's idea to promote international human rights was considered somewhat naïve and ultimately dangerous' by British diplomats who thought Carter's human rights agenda 'would actually contradict his stated ambition of sustaining superpower détente and lead to a far more unstable and dangerous international environment'.[17] As noted within the previous chapter, however,

---

[12] Philip Williams, 'Britain, Détente and the Conference on Security and Cooperation in Europe', in *European Détente*, ed. Dyson, 221.
[13] Sean Greenwood, *Britain and the Cold War, 1945–91* (Basingstoke: Macmillan, 2000), 175–6.
[14] See Sir Michael Alexander interview (interviewer unspecified), 25 November 1998, BDOHP, available at https://www.chu.cam.ac.uk/media/uploads/files/Alexander.pdf (accessed 10 January 2020).
[15] Brown, 'A Very British Vision of Détente', 139.
[16] Brian White, *Britain, Détente and Changing East–West Relations* (London: Routledge, 1992), 136.
[17] Robb, *Jimmy Carter and the Anglo-American 'Special Relationship'*, 26.

David Owen's public adoption of a human rights-based foreign policy following his appointment as Foreign and Commonwealth Secretary in February 1977 – and his support of President Carter's amplification of human rights concerns within the East–West dialogue – is difficult to reconcile with such accounts. In fact, upon closer inspection, Owen's attempts to weaponize human rights within the context of the ideological Cold War struggle paint an alternative picture of British engagement with human rights promotion under the auspices of the CSCE.

Owen 'despised and distrusted' the Soviet empire.[18] Indeed, the repressiveness of the Soviet system exhibited in Hungary in 1956 and in its response to the 'Prague Spring' of 1968 played a major role in shaping Owen's human rights advocacy.[19] Still, his careful handling of the human rights issue in the weeks and months following his unexpected appointment as Foreign Secretary gave little away. During his meeting with the Hungarian Foreign Minister in March 1977, Owen reportedly stressed the 'desire of the UK to be responsive to its public with respect to human rights'.[20] March would also witness Owen raising the human rights issue in 'general terms' during his meeting with the Soviet Ambassador to Britain, Nikolai Lunkov.[21] However, in June, a public rally in London in support of the Russian dissident and physicist Yuri Orlov – who had been arrested by the Soviet authorities in February – highlighted the sensitivity with which the issue of human rights within the Eastern bloc needed to be handled. Following 'considerable hand-wringing in the Foreign Office', Owen took the decision not to attend, feeling that 'this was one of those occasions when the national interest was best served by the government not associating itself with a private initiative'.[22]

This decision to distance himself, and his government, from the Orlov rally was likely influenced by the impending CSCE follow-up conference scheduled to open in Belgrade in October. While a report by the Defence and External Affairs Subcommittee urged the British delegation to 'err on the side of firmness' when conveying their dissatisfaction with the Soviets' human rights performance since the signing of the Final Act in August 1975, behind the scenes, ministers were encouraging moderation: 'there should be no hesitation in expressing criticism where Eastern countries had not fulfilled their CSCE obligations, but ... at the same time the West should not create a situation in which the East lost interest in continuing the CSCE process'.[23] Owen duly

---

[18] Owen, *Time to Declare*, 337.
[19] Carr, 'David Owen, 1977–79', 111; Owen interview, 6 December 2017: Owen recalls being particularly affected by the repression of the Hungarian uprising in 1956. He briefly contemplated travelling to Hungary himself after hearing radio reports of the uprising and the strife of the Hungarian dissidents.
[20] 'Foreign Minister Puja visits UK: His Comments on Belgrade CSCE Meeting and Human Rights', 11 March 1977, The National Archives, College Park, MD., Central Foreign Policy Files, Record Group 59 – General Records of the Department of State, Electronic Telegrams, 1977, available at https://aad.archives.gov/aad/createpdf?rid=52055&dt=2532&dl=1629 (accessed 13 January 2020).
[21] Diplomatic Staff, 'Human rights move by Owen', *Daily Telegraph*, 24 March 1977.
[22] 'London "Trial" of Yuriy Orlov', 14 June 1977, The National Archives, College Park, MD., Central Foreign Policy Files, Record Group 59 – General Records of the Department of State, Electronic Telegrams, 1977, available at https://aad.archives.gov/aad/createpdf?rid=135632&dt=2532&dl=1629 (accessed 13 January 2020).
[23] Roger Berthoud, 'MPs unhappy at the rate of progress on human rights', *The Times*, 31 May 1977; 'Record of a Meeting on Berlin Held at the Foreign and Commonwealth Office at 1100 Hours on Monday 23 May 1977', DOP, D709 2/7/15/2.

expounded upon this need for temperance as the Conference was taking place, writing in *The Times* that while human rights concerns were inextricably linked to the Helsinki Process, a 'slanging match' at Belgrade 'would be totally self-defeating'.[24] The mix of 'pragmatism and idealism' exhibited by the British delegation at Belgrade, however, raised the ire of some Soviet dissidents who felt that Owen's human rights stance, as it pertained to Belgrade, was far less committed than his previous statements on the subject had indicated.[25] This being said, Owen's visit to Moscow from 9–11 October arguably served to justify his restraint. According to the US Ambassador to the United Kingdom, Owen's audience with Foreign Minister Gromyko and an attentive Leonid Brezhnev marked 'another step in the long climb back to normalcy in Anglo–Soviet relations'.[26] Owen's belief in the efficacy of quiet diplomacy, moreover, appeared to pay dividends as the USSR provided British authorities with a status report on forty-four outstanding family reunification cases in anticipation of Owen's visit.[27]

But Owen could not hide his dissatisfaction at the sluggishness of the Helsinki Process for long. A White Paper presented to the Cabinet by Owen in March 1978 following the conclusion of the Belgrade Review Conference reveals that the experience had been largely disappointing from a British perspective: 'In the event the Soviet Union and its Allies did not respond as satisfactorily to Western criticisms as had been hoped. They refused to acknowledge shortcomings and engage in a dialogue.'[28] In summation, the 'measurable product of Belgrade is meagre ... The Soviet Union has shown that it is not yet prepared to open itself to broad or thorough implementation of the Final Act'.[29] The Soviet crackdown on the Helsinki monitoring group that followed during the summer only added fuel to the fire, leading Owen to publicly question the Soviet commitment to détente in the House of Commons on 10 July:

> The whole House will deplore the fact that the Soviet Government have now put on trial 15 members of the Helsinki monitoring group ... These trials, inasmuch as the charges relate specifically to activities fully compatible with the Helsinki Final Act, are in direct contravention of the spirit and intention of the Act. The British Government have repeatedly warned the Soviet Government of the consequences which their handling of such cases could have for the atmosphere of their relations

---

[24] David Owen, 'Why a slanging match must not get in the way of human rights', *The Times*, 6 October 1977.
[25] 'Belgrade CSCE – October 6 Afternoon Plenary Summary', 7 October 1977, The National Archives, College Park, MD., Central Foreign Policy Files, Record Group 59 – General Records of the Department of State, Electronic Telegrams, 1977, available at https://aad.archives.gov/aad/createpdf?rid=232548&dt=2532&dl=1629 (accessed 13 January 2020); Richard Beeston, 'Britain Accused of "Weak Stand" on Human Rights', *Daily Telegraph*, 29 November 1977.
[26] 'October 9–11 Visit to Moscow of Foreign Secretary Owen', 14 October 1977, The National Archives, College Park, MD., Central Foreign Policy Files, Record Group 59 – General Records of the Department of State, Electronic Telegrams, 1977, available at https://aad.archives.gov/aad/createpdf?rid=239076&dt=2532&dl=1629 (accessed 13 January 2020).
[27] Ibid.
[28] 'The Meeting held at Belgrade from 4 October to 9 March 1978 to follow up the Conference on Security and Co-operation in Europe', 9 March 1978, TNA, CAB 129/200/10.
[29] Ibid.

with the United Kingdom, and for the chances of making progress on vital issues in East–West relations generally ... There will not be an improvement in the atmosphere of detente if they continue to conduct matters like this in the way that they are showing every sign of doing.[30]

By the time Owen's *Human Rights* was published in August, then, the recent elevation of the human rights issue within the context of the CSCE had already begun to complicate British–Soviet relations. The message contained therein, furthermore, did not find a receptive audience in Moscow; the Soviet news agency Tass lambasted the book as an attempt to defend Britain's bourgeois democracy 'and to whitewash Western attempts to interfere in the internal affairs of Communist countries'.[31] Reviewing those sections of *Human Rights* concerning the East–West dialogue, it is difficult to quarrel with such a characterisation. Owen frames détente as a paradox – a process driven by increased contact and communication between East and West which, in turn, laid bare the fundamentally divergent political philosophies that breathed life into the 'ideological struggle' of the Cold War.[32] The West, with 'nothing to fear', was encouraged to embrace this competition, approaching the human rights issue as a natural extension of Western liberal philosophy that sat uncomfortably with the authoritarianism of the Soviet bloc:

> It is in human rights that we find the values which underlie our societies and give sense to Western efforts in the ideological struggle ... It is no part of our policy to promote campaigns of denunciation or to assume the role of *agents-provocateurs*. Equally, the communist countries must recognise that concern for human rights is not a diversionary tactic but an integral part of foreign policy in the Western democracies.[33]

During a BBC interview in connection with the release of *Human Rights*, Owen took the opportunity to convey this message to the Soviets by flirting with the idea of a British boycott of the Moscow Olympics in 1980. While Owen substantively echoed the view of the British Sports Council, which ruled that the decision not to participate ultimately rested with the athletes themselves, observers noted that Owen's remarks were 'noticeably sharper in tone'.[34] This implication – that the increasing weaponization of the human rights issue in the context of British–Soviet relations developed on account of Owen's initiative – is substantiated by a record of a meeting at the FCO

---

[30] 'Shcharansky And Ginzburg (USSR Trials)', 10 July 1978, *Hansard: House of Commons* Volume 953, Column 1041–4.
[31] Richard Beeston, 'Russia rages at Owen book on human rights', *Daily Telegraph*, 29 August 1978.
[32] Owen, *Human Rights*, 39.
[33] Ibid., 39, 43–51.
[34] 'Owen Remarks on Moscow Olympics in a Television Interview on August 24 in Connection with his New Book "Human Rights"...' 25 August 1978, The National Archives, College Park, MD., Central Foreign Policy Files, Record Group 59 – General Records of the Department of State, Electronic Telegrams, 1978, available at https://aad.archives.gov/aad/createpdf?rid=210432&dt=2694&dl=2009 (accessed 13 January 2020).

between the Foreign Secretary and the Chinese Foreign Minister, Huang Hua, in October 1978, which suggests that Owen had even begun to view the Rhodesian question through a Cold War lens. Owen's counterpart began a wide-ranging discussion of Cold War politics by stating that, in order to seize eventual control of Europe, 'the Soviet Union had this year stepped up its efforts on the periphery of Europe (ie the Middle East and Africa)'. Alongside continuing Soviet expansion in West and South East Asia, these developments were regarded by the Chinese Foreign Minister as 'component parts of the Soviet global strategy and not simply isolated incidents'. While Owen agreed with much of this analysis, he 'fundamentally disagreed with Mr Huang's pessimism', and 'wished to offer a more confident view'. Focusing on Africa, Owen posited that the West had learned to adopt a more 'sensitive' approach to regional disputes and was beginning to reap the rewards. This tactical recalibration, moreover, had been accompanied by a more fundamental shift: 'Another sign the West was moving off the defensive was that for the first time for 30 or 40 years it was not on the side of white racialist regimes in Africa. Britain, instead of being a colonial power and on the defensive, was now working on equal terms with countries such as Tanzania, Zambia and Zaire'. Europe may, therefore, have been in a defensive position militarily, but 'what the world did not realise was how "offensive" a human rights policy was'. The West was 'not on its back'; rather, it was in the process of putting its 'colonial past behind it and was now able to be much more aggressive in different ways'.[35]

Days later, the Prime Minister visited the Federal Republic of Germany. During a discussion with Chancellor Schmidt regarding prospective arms exports to the Chinese government, Callaghan admitted that 'relations with the Soviet Union were now in very poor shape, presumably because of the strong human rights stand taken by Owen. For this and other reasons, the British appear less reluctant to sell weapons to the PRC [People's Republic of China]'.[36] Indeed, during the New Year, Owen actively pushed for closer ties with the PRC within the Cabinet, lobbying for the export of Harrier aircraft to the Chinese government while dismissing the idea that the sale would further complicate British-Soviet relations.[37] In Owen's view, the 'stand we had taken with the Soviets on human rights had done us no harm, and they [the USSR] were beginning to grasp that détente was a two way process'.[38] As recorded by Kingman Brewster Jr, the decision to proceed with the Harrier sale served to derail burgeoning British-Soviet rapprochement: 'After shunning the Soviets for a time last summer because of human rights, HMG deliberately stepped back up to the line last fall and was waiting for a

---

[35] 'Record of a Meeting Between the Secretary of State for Foreign and Commonwealth Affairs and the Chinese Minister of Foreign Affairs, held at the Foreign and Commonwealth Office on Wednesday, 11 October 1978, at 10:45 AM', TNA, FCO 36/2201.

[36] 'Callaghan Visit to FRG: More on EMS and other Subjects', 24 October 1978, The National Archives, College Park, MD., Central Foreign Policy Files, Record Group 59 – General Records of the Department of State, Electronic Telegrams, 1978, available at https://aad.archives.gov/aad/createpdf?rid=262973&dt=2694&dl=2009 (accessed 13 January 2020).

[37] See Ed Hampshire, 'Missing the "Klondike Rush?" British Trade with China, 1971–9 and the Politics of Defence Sales', in *The Foreign Office, Commerce and British Foreign Policy in the Twentieth Century*, ed. Fisher, Pedaliu and Smith, 527–3.

[38] 'Conclusions of a Meeting of the Cabinet held at 10 Downing Street on Thursday 25 January 1979 at 10:00 am', TNA, CAB 128/65/4.

response when Harrier intervened.'[39] The record of a NATO ministerial meeting on 7 December 1978, however, reveals that any such de-escalation was by no means reflective of Owen's personal priorities:

> A substantial portion of the December 7 NATO ministerial restricted session was devoted to a broad ranging, interesting and totally unexpected discussion of human rights, the relationship of human rights and détente, and comments on how the allies might prepare for the 1980 CSCE Review Conference in Madrid... Greek Foreign Minister Rallis led off the debate by questioning certain aspects of US implementation of its human rights policies. Owen (Foreign Minister – UK) said that he agreed with a number of Rallis' points but he fundamentally disagreed with other elements of the Greek Foreign Minister's approach to human rights.[40]

Owen echoed the Greek Foreign Minister's suggestion that 'if we and our governments are seen by the East as *agents provocateurs* we could find ourselves in a dangerous situation'.[41] He also underscored the validity of Rallis' point regarding the distinction that ought to be drawn 'between private and public activities on human rights'.[42] Nonetheless, Owen argued that the West needed to seize the initiative and recognize that, in human rights, the NATO allies possessed a potent ideological weapon: 'Human rights is the most powerful way to challenge communism. The communists want to bureaucratize détente and produce endless meetings and massive paper work without concrete results. Human rights allows us to take the offensive for the first time since 1945.'[43] Although Owen tempered his statement by explaining that 'we must control our response, because the Soviets are rightly afraid of human rights', his message still managed to set alarm bells ringing: '[Dutch Foreign Minister, Chris] van der Klaauw suggested that it is dangerous to use human rights as a weapon, as Foreign Minister Owen suggested.'[44]

Contemporary commentators could be forgiven for thinking that a Conservative victory in the general election of May 1979 would bring with it a reversion to the 'hard-boiled' business of pursuing British interests overseas minus the high-minded

---

[39] 'UK-USSR Relations Not Ready to Warm Up Yet', 22 February 1979, The National Archives, College Park, MD., Central Foreign Policy Files, Record Group 59 – General Records of the Department of State, Electronic Telegrams, 1979, available at https://aad.archives.gov/aad/createpdf?rid=97633&dt=2776&dl=2169 (accessed 12 January 2020).

[40] 'NATOMIN: Human Rights, Détente, and CSCE', 8 December 1978, The National Archives, College Park, MD., Central Foreign Policy Files, Record Group 59 – General Records of the Department of State, Electronic Telegrams, 1978, available at https://aad.archives.gov/aad/createpdf?rid=324277&t=2694&dl=2009 (accessed 13 January 2020).

[41] Ibid.

[42] Ibid.

[43] Ibid.

[44] Ibid. State Department files also reveal that Owen's continued hawkishness on human rights issues within the Eastern bloc was met with hostility from Gromyko when the pair met in late November. See 'British Ambassador's Call on Gromyko; Access to Soviet Officials', 22 November 1978, The National Archives, College Park, MD., Central Foreign Policy Files, Record Group 59 – General Records of the Department of State, Electronic Telegrams, 1978, available at https://aad.archives.gov/aad/createpdf?rid=291095&dt=2694&dl=2009 (accessed 13 January 2020).

rhetoric favoured by Owen, thus rendering the Dutch Foreign Minister's concern a moot point. In the event, foreign policy issues would only play 'a minor part' in the election campaign, in keeping with an observable trend: as Britain's perceived influence in the world had diminished, so too had the significance of foreign policy issues in general elections.[45] Nonetheless, as Owen's political adviser David Stephen highlighted, while Britain's retreat from global power was an incontrovertible fact, engendering a degree of consensus on issues of foreign policy, the 'flavour' of the manifestos in the domestic sphere had, in this instance, spilled over into foreign policy.[46] Whereas the Labour manifesto, as Stephen pointed out, set its foreign policy statements 'within the context of the long-term aim, and I quote, "to create the conditions necessary to free the world from poverty, inequality and war"', the Conservative manifesto portentously entitled its section on foreign policy, '"A strong Britain in a free world"'.[47] Indeed, the possibility that a Conservative election victory would initiate a sea change in Britain's dealings with the outside world, and that this recalibration could potentially impair Anglo–American relations, was taken seriously by US policy experts, not least because the aforementioned ideological schism had already begun to manifest itself in the form of Conservative criticism of President Carter's foreign policy. As Brewster noted in June 1978:

> Conservative Party objections to Carter administration policies may cause US problems if the Party wins the coming general election … some believe that Conservative criticism of the US is at a higher point than ever since the Anglo-French invasion of Egypt in 1956 … Conservative concerns now being expressed seem to be overlaid on earlier fears some held when the new administration took office. British Conservatives shared the initial fears of many Europeans that Carter administration policy, for examole [sic] on human rights was unrealistic and naïve ('Soviet-bashing' is one thing, but pressing for majority rule in Southern Africa is quite another).[48]

Margaret Thatcher, for her part, did little to disabuse Brewster of his suspicions. For instance, when reviewing Thatcher's performance at the 1978 Conservative Party Conference, the US Ambassador felt it necessary to highlight the apparent indifference with which the Conservative leader regarded Anglo-American cooperation on foreign

---

[45] 'Foreign Policy and the New Government', The Royal Institute of International Affairs, May 1979, Chatham House Online Archive, Chatham House Briefings I. See also David Stephen, Lord Banks, and Baroness Elles, 'The British General Election: What Foreign Policy for Britain?' Chatham House, London, 24 April 1979, Chatham House Online Archive, RIIA/8/4005.

[46] Stephen, Banks, Elles, 'The British General Election'.

[47] Ibid. See also 1979 Labour Party Manifesto: 'The Labour Way is the Better Way', available at www.labour-party.org.uk/manifestos/1979/1979-labour-manifesto.shtml (accessed 10 January 2020); Conservative General Election Manifesto 1979, available at https://www.margaretthatcher.org/document/110858 (accessed 10 January 2020).

[48] 'Conservative Criticism of US Policies: Summary', 6 June 1978, The National Archives, College Park, MD., Central Foreign Policy Files, Record Group 59 – General Records of the Department of State, Electronic Telegrams, 1978, available at https://aad.archives.gov/aad/createpdf?rid=140552&dt=2694&dl=2009 (accessed 13 January 2020).

policy issues: 'an American observer at the Conference could not fail to be struck by the absence from Mrs. Thatcher's speech of a reference that used to be almost obligatory to friendship with the United States ... something that could easily have been worked into the section on foreign policy, possibly coupled with a word of praise for common goals in human rights.'[49] It was certainly not the case, however, that this omission was indicative of Thatcher's ambivalence towards human rights issues; she had in fact consistently championed the human rights cause during Callaghan's premiership, particularly with regard to the East–West dialogue.[50] Rather, her critique of the human rights policies advanced by Carter and by the Labour government was largely predicated on the notion that both were not doing *enough* to bring sufficient pressure to bear on the Soviet bloc, and that human rights demarches alone were largely impotent in the face of growing Soviet militarism.[51]

In fact, following her election victory, Thatcher's desire to keep the Soviet Union on the back foot served to keep the issue of human rights within Eastern Europe firmly on Britain's diplomatic agenda. The Prime Minister engaged with Soviet and Central European dissidents including the signatories of Charter 77, ten of whom were arrested shortly after the May general election.[52] The issue of religious freedom can also be seen to inform the first Thatcher government's diplomatic relations with Romania, with Thatcher herself exhibiting a particular concern for the plight of Jewish *refuseniks*.[53] In her letter of 26 March 1982 to Rita Eker, for example, Thatcher wrote of her 'close interest in all human rights matters' within the Soviet Union before reassuring Eker that her government had 'recently conveyed to the Soviet authorities at a senior level' its concern about a number of high-profile *refusenik* cases.[54] The following year would also see this concern reinforced within the context of Thatcher's burgeoning relationship with Carter's successor, Ronald Reagan, who had himself criticized Carter's human rights approach for exhibiting the same weaknesses Thatcher had identified within the

---

[49] 'Conservative Party Conference: Mrs Thatcher's Concluding Address', 16 October 1978, The National Archives, College Park, MD., Central Foreign Policy Files, Record Group 59 – General Records of the Department of State, Electronic Telegrams, 1978, available at https://aad.archives.gov/aad/createpdf?rid=253607&dt=2694&dl=2009 (accessed 13 January 2020).

[50] See for example Dessa Trevisan, 'Thatcher praise for Titoist system', The Times, 7 December 1977; Margaret Thatcher, 'Our first duty to freedom is to defend our own', The Times, 24 June 1978.

[51] See 'Conservative Party Conference: Mrs Thatcher's Concluding Address'; 'General Election: Thatcher Remarks on Defense and Foreign Policy', 20 April 1979, The National Archives, College Park, MD., Central Foreign Policy Files, Record Group 59 – General Records of the Department of State, Electronic Telegrams, 1979, available at https://aad.archives.gov/aad/createpdf?rid=15549&dt=2776&dl=2169 (accessed 13 January 2020).

[52] See 'Press Office: Bulletin (Letter to PM from Czech Charter 77)', 23 July 1979, Churchill Centre Archive, Ingham MSS 2/2/1, available at https://www.margaretthatcher.org/archive (accessed 13 January 2020).

[53] See for example 'Romania: FCO Letter to No.10 (Possible Government Intervention on Human Rights Cases in Romania)', 10 April 1981, TNA, PREM 19/580.

[54] 'Soviet Union: MT Letter to Rita Eker (Case of Ida Nudel)', 26 March 1982, Churchill Archive Centre, Thatcher MSS, THCR 3/2/86, available at https://www.margaretthatcher.org/archive (accessed 13 January 2020). See also Mark Hurst, *British Human Rights Organizations and Soviet Dissent, 1965–1985* (London: Bloomsbury, 2016), 100–2.

Callaghan government.[55] On 2 July 1983, Reagan informed the Prime Minister that former US Ambassador to West Germany, Walter J. Stoessel Jr., would be visiting several European countries 'to let you know of my concern about the human rights situation in the Soviet Union'.[56] Thatcher's reply articulated in the clearest terms that Reagan could count on the UK as an ally in the ideological struggle of the Cold War:

> Dear Ron, thank you for your letter of 2 July about human rights in the Soviet Union. I fully share your concern. Violations by the Soviet Union of commitments it has made about human rights call into question its behaviour in other areas ... We must certainly do all we can to help those courageous individuals who are suffering in the Soviet Union for trying to obtain or restore rights which would be taken for granted in our own countries ... We were glad to have Walter Stoessel here. [Foreign and Commonwealth Secretary] Geoffrey Howe has recently had useful discussions both with him and with [US Secretary of State] George Shultz in Washington about our policy.[57]

Reagan had initially sought to jettison the human rights emphasis of the Carter administration, reversing Carter's decision to suspend military aid to Argentina, Chile, Guatemala and Uruguay, and nominating Ernest Lefever, an outspoken critic of Carter's human rights policy, to replace Patricia Derian as Secretary of State for Human Rights and Humanitarian Affairs.[58] In the face of staunch opposition within the legislative branch of the US government, however, Reagan was forced to backtrack on the Lefever appointment, and eventually nominated Elliot Abrams in his stead.[59] In the meantime, Abrams had reportedly drafted a memo on behalf of the State Department which, according to Tamar Jacoby, 'marked the beginning of a new phase in the Reagan human rights policy; having given up its efforts to downgrade the issue, the administration now sought, in effect, to co-opt the idea and use it for its own geopolitical purposes, rather narrowly defined'.[60] In other words, President Reagan may have been unable to 'erase the 1970s' left-liberal model of human rights policy', but his

---

[55] See 'Republican Party Platform of 1980' (adopted by the Republican National Convention, 15 July 1980), The American Presidency Project, available at www.presidency.ucsb.edu/WS/index.php?pid=25844 (accessed 13 January 2020); Governor Reagan, 'Debate with Ronald Reagan', 28 October 1980, University of Virginia, Miller Center, available at https://millercenter.org/the-presidency/presidential-speeches/october-28-1980-debate-ronald-reagan (accessed 13 January 2020).

[56] 'Soviet Union: Reagan Letter to MT (Stoessel Visiting Several Countries to Express Concern about USSR Human Rights Situation)', 2 July 1983, Churchill Archive Centre, Thatcher MSS, THCR 3/1/32 (Part 2), available at https://www.margaretthatcher.org/archive (accessed 13 January 2020).

[57] 'Soviet Union: MT Letter to Reagan (USSR Human Rights Situation)', 20 July 1983, Churchill Archive Centre, Thatcher MSS, THCR 3/1/32 (Part 2), available at https://www.margaretthatcher.org/archive (accessed 13 January 2020).

[58] See Tamar Jacoby, 'The Reagan Turnaround on Human Rights', Foreign Affairs 64, No. 5 (Summer 1986): 1066–86.

[59] Sarah B. Snyder, 'The Defeat of Ernest Lefever's Nomination: Keeping Human Rights on the United States Foreign Policy Agenda', in Challenging U.S. Foreign Policy: America and the World in the Long Twentieth Century, ed. Bevan Sewell and Scott Lucas (Basingstoke: Palgrave Macmillan, 2011), 136–61.

[60] Jacoby, 'The Reagan Turnaround on Human Rights': 1071.

administration nonetheless succeeded in a long-term recasting of the 'political agenda of the sixties and seventies, not least vis-à-vis human rights and in co-opting it for conservative purposes'.[61]

By undertaking a more sustained analysis of the evolving human rights–British foreign policy nexus under Margaret Thatcher's leadership, we are able to cast a spotlight on the same phenomenon from a fresh perspective. Indeed, the foreign policies of both Reagan and Thatcher were similarly 'constrained by the newly powerful rhetoric of human rights' and were consequently 'forced to develop policies on a more complicated terrain that precluded the simple reassertion of Western or Anglo-American dominance'.[62] Nonetheless, while human rights had become somewhat embedded within the foreign policymaking processes of several Western states by the early 1980s, in Britain as in the United States, its meaning – and foreign policy application – was redefined concomitantly.[63] Decoupled from the internationalist outlook of the Callaghan government, British human rights policy under Thatcher instead became more narrowly focused on the concepts of democratic promotion and free market economics that served to galvanize the Thatcher–Reagan axis.

Competing visions of human rights in the neoliberal age

Owen and Thatcher may have been united in their belief that human rights could be used by the West as a stick with which to beat the Soviet Union. This point of consensus, it has been suggested here, goes some way towards challenging conventional wisdom regarding British engagement with human rights in the CSCE following the signing of the Helsinki Final Act. Such bipartisanship, however, belies a fundamental divergence that requires further examination. Owen viewed human rights as 'morally indivisible'; comprised of social and economic rights as well as civil and political liberties.[64] In *Human Rights*, for instance, Owen pointed out that while apartheid in South Africa and the 'continued denial of self-determination in Southern Africa' could easily be identified as 'problems of elementary human rights', the 'establishment of a dialogue between the advanced industrialized nations and those of the developing world remind us that economic deprivation, and the disease and malnutrition which go with it', should be regarded as 'equally intolerable' abuses.[65] This situation of the so-called 'North–South dialogue' within Owen's human rights agenda was accompanied by a growing concern

---

[61] Eckel, *The Ambivalence of Good*, 240. For further examples of scholarship pertaining to the Reagan-era reshaping of human rights in American foreign policy see A. Glen Mower Jr., *Human Rights and American Foreign Policy: The Carter and Reagan Experiences* (New York: Greenwood Press, 1987); Christian Philip Peterson, '"Confronting" Moscow: The Reagan Administration, Human Rights, and the Final Act', *The Historian* 74, Issue 1 (2012): 57–86; Rasmus Sinding Søndergaard, *Reagan, Congress, and Human Rights: Contesting Morality in US Foreign Policy* (Cambridge: Cambridge University Press, 2020).
[62] Cronin, *Global Rules*, 150, 151.
[63] Donnelly, 'The Social Construction of International Human Rights', 76–7.
[64] Owen, *Human Rights*, 33.
[65] Ibid., 14.

that the interconnected global order of the 1970s called for the implementation of wholesale changes in the world economy, tantamount, no less, to the creation of a New International Economic Order (NIEO). Upon receiving a letter from Fenner Brockway, who advised Owen to consult an enclosed paper on the subject in April 1978, Owen consequently informed the President of Liberation (formerly the Movement for Colonial Freedom) that he was preaching to the choir:

> Dear Fenner, It was kind of you to send me a copy of your paper 'One Hundred Nations Call for a New Economic Order' which I have now had time to read and which I found very clear and perceptive. If, in return, I send you a copy of my recent Gilbert Murray Memorial Lecture, it is so that you can see that many of the issues you raise in your paper are ones that I too am very concerned about.[66]

The sentiments expressed within Owen's lecture – which subsequently found a home in *Human Rights* – clearly attest to the broad socioeconomic scope of Owen's human rights advocacy:

> I am clear that, while much of what I advocate in establishing a new economic order is very much in this countries [sic] interests[,] self-interest will never provide a sufficient justification for that redistribution which, I believe, is a long-term necessity. There is a moral dimension that we should not be afraid to identify and draw upon. I start from the simple belief that a country that develops an attitude and an ethos which ignores poverty and equality in the world soon ignores poverty and inequality on its own doorstep.[67]

The proposals for the establishment of a New International Economic Order to which Owen and Brockway refer, had been adopted by the United Nations General Assembly in 1974 with a view to redressing the imbalances of the global economy by altering 'structures relating to trade, investment and commodity prices'.[68] Advocates of the NIEO among the 'developing' nations of the G77 and the non-aligned movement rarely made overt reference to human rights in advancing their claims.[69] According to Roland Burke, however, the NIEO nonetheless 'involved an emphatic deployment of terms and categories from the human rights milieu: equality, solidarity, and improved material conditions'.[70] NIEO language 'was human rights language, merely with a

---

[66] David Owen to Fenner Brockway, 15 May 1978, DOP, D709 2/7/1/5.
[67] 'The Gilbert Murray Memorial Lecture, Delivered by the Foreign and Commonwealth Secretary the Rt Hon Dr David Owen MP at the Oxford Union Society', 1 March 1978, DOP, D709 2/7/2/1. See also Owen, *Human Rights*, 111.
[68] Anthony Anghie, 'Whose Utopia?: Human Rights, Development, and the Third World', *Qui Parle* 22, No. 1 (Fall/Winter 2013): 73. See also 'Resolution adopted by the General Assembly, 3201 (S-VI): Declaration on the Establishment of a New International Economic Order', 1 May 1974, available at http://www.un-documents.net/s6r3201.htm (accessed 21 June 2020).
[69] Whelan, *Indivisible Human Rights*, 157.
[70] Roland Burke, 'Competing for the Last Utopia?: The NIEO, Human Rights, and the World Conference for the International Women's Year, Mexico City, June 1975', *Humanity* 6, No. 1 (Spring 2015): 47.

different chirality: its primary axis aligned to state and people'.[71] Champions of the NIEO, therefore, effectively 'reframed' human rights as 'a subordinate element of the statist development project'.[72] The demands of the NIEO, moreover, intersected with a broader revisionist trend dating back to the mid-1950s in which the nations of the Global South had sought to recalibrate the corpus of human rights, shifting the emphasis of the human rights regime away from its prevailing concern with civil and political rights towards a focus on social and economic disparities. As Daniel J. Whelan points out, the Proclamation of Tehran, which brought to a conclusion the International Conference on Human Rights in 1968, demonstrated the growing influence of the developing nations in this regard, predicating the 'full realization of civil and political rights' upon 'the enjoyment of economic, social and cultural rights'.[73] However, by the time the indivisibility rhetoric articulated at Tehran became further institutionalized in the form of UN General Assembly Resolution 32/130 (1977), a number of Western states, including the United Kingdom, had, according to Whelan, begun to express 'significant opposition to the prioritization of economic and social rights and to the suggestion that development was a prerequisite for the effective enjoyment of human rights'.[74]

Nonetheless, analysis of the Callaghan ministry's engagement with the related demands of the NIEO and debates concerning the indivisibility of the human rights complex, indicates that governmental opposition to these trends was by no means monolithic. British officials certainly maintained a degree of critical distance from the NIEO in the wake of Harold Wilson's rhetorical commitment to the establishment of a more just global economy, articulated at a Commonwealth Heads of Government meeting in Kingston, Jamaica, in May 1975.[75] However, the lack of progress made towards achieving Wilson's vision was noted with some concern during the run-up to the July 1976 Annual Conference of the Commonwealth Parliamentary Association, and Labour ministers began to develop a more sympathetic attitude towards the positions of the G77 thereafter.[76] Owen, for example, devoted a section of his maiden speech as Foreign Secretary on 1 March 1977 to the imbalances of the global economy, stating that the gap between rich and poor countries was 'not simply a matter of statistics' but a 'moral question which demands a firm and principled stand'.[77] In anticipation of a series of summits with representatives of the Global South at which

---

[71] Ibid.
[72] Ibid., 55.
[73] Whelan, *Indivisible Human Rights*, 7.
[74] Ibid., 165.
[75] Harold Wilson, 'Speech by the Prime Minister The RT Hon Harold Wilson, OBE, FRS, MP, at the Commonwealth Heads of Government Meeting, Kingston, Jamaica, 1 May 1975', in *Future Resources and World Development*, ed. Paul Rogers (New York and London: Plenum Press, 1976), 189–98. See J.A.L. Faint to Mr A.S. Fair, 'The "New International Economic Order" (NIEO)', 1 August 1975, TNA, FCO 61/1297; P.M. Maxey to Mr Statham, 'New International Economic Order', 30 September 1975, TNA, FCO 61/1297; Aid, Trade and Commodities Department, 'New International Economic Order', 22 January 1976, TNA, FCO 58/925.
[76] See J.E.S. Claydon, 'Commonwealth Parliamentary Association: Annual Conference', 26 July 1976, TNA, FCO 58/926.
[77] 'Foreign Affairs', 1 March 1977, *Hansard: House of Commons*, Volume 927, Column 199.

British representatives could 'expect the developing countries to press for measures which they believe could contribute to the establishment of a new international economic order', Owen's Minister of State, Frank Judd, encouraged the Foreign Secretary to substantiate this commitment.[78] Although 'the present state of the British economy' made it 'impossible for us to accept all their proposals', Judd argued that '[w]e should admit that there is much justice in the demands of the LDCs for a more equitable economic order', and 'stand by the Kingston commitment to remedy the disparity between rich and poor'.[79]

Perhaps the most outspoken advocate of the NIEO within the Callaghan government, however, was Minister of State for Overseas Development Judith Hart. Along with Fenner Brockway and fellow Labour MP Stan Newens, Hart played a leading role in the organisation of Liberation's campaign 'to promote the acceptance of the New International Economic Order in Britain'.[80] In this capacity, Hart took part in the planning of a March 1976 conference, the main conclusions of which she intended to forward to the upcoming United Nations Conference on Trade and Development (UNCTAD) and to the International Labour Organization (ILO).[81] In early 1976, she also participated in a parliamentary delegation that sought to impress upon the government the significance of the NIEO in the context of UNCTAD IV.[82] Furthermore, following her reappointment as Minister for Overseas Development in February 1977, Hart's attachment to the NIEO cause appeared to inform her response to the question of situating human rights concerns within Britain's aid policy. As highlighted in chapter two, the human rights dimension of development policy had taken officials by surprise when it was raised by Hart's predecessor, Reginald Prentice.[83] Hart's contributions to the debate, however, were distinctive; geared towards shifting the emphasis away from a narrow focus on civil and political liberties – evident in the FCO's human rights comparative assessment – towards a greater appreciation of the socio-economic factors which stood in the way of their realization. Prior to a ministerial meeting in the Foreign Office in May 1977, Hart brought these concerns to Owen's attention, and later reiterated her approach in a draft paper on 'Human Rights and Aid' that was discussed during a follow-up meeting in July.[84] Upon receipt of this paper, Judd wrote to Owen expressing his agreement with Hart's message. If the UK government was to be 'credible' in its commitment to human rights, Judd argued, it had

---

[78] See Frank Judd to Secretary of State, 'North/South Dialogue', 23 March 1977, TNA, FCO 68/734.
[79] Ibid.
[80] The Rt Hon Judith Hart MP to Jan Pronk, 'Conference on the New International Economic Order: March 6th and 7th 1976', 28 November 1975, PHM, HART/08/22.
[81] Ibid.
[82] See P.M. Maxey to Mr Mason; Mr Green, 'The New International Economic Order and UNCTAD IV: Call by Parliamentary Delegation on Minister of State', 3 February 1976, TNA, FCO 58/925.
[83] See R. Manning, 'Human Rights and Aid', with enclosed paper by Mr Prentice, 9 September 1976, TNA, OD/36/357. See also Hugh O'Shaughnessy, 'ODM sets civil rights criterion for aid', *Financial Times*, 22 April 1976: O'Shaughnessy suggests that while Prentice approved of 'the decision to give formal consideration to a country's respect for human rights', the idea was originally put forward by John Grant, a junior minister at the ODM before he was transferred to the Labour Ministry.
[84] See Judith Hart to David Owen, 24 May 1977, TNA, FCO 58/1152; J.M.M. Vereker, 'Human Rights and Aid', with Hart's paper enclosed, 1 July 1977, TNA, FCO 58/1152.

'no alternative but to take the economic rights argument of the G77 seriously'.[85] This was, Judd continued, 'particularly important for a democratic socialist government such as ours. To fail to respond would risk putting us in the category of egocentric evangelists'.[86]

Hart's approach was not met with unanimous approval. Her suggestions presented to the Foreign Secretary in May were regarded with suspicion by Ivor Richard, British Ambassador to the United Nations, who drew unflattering comparisons between Hart's emphasis on economic freedoms and the 'Soviet line' on human rights issues at the UN.[87] At the July meeting, moreover, Hart herself appeared more 'cautious' over human rights, and ministers and officials resolved to embrace a rather pragmatic, case-by-case approach to the human rights-overseas aid question: 'In exceptional cases (eg Chile or Uganda), we might cut off aid; in others, we should try arm twisting (Indonesia), in others, we would seek to direct funds as an inducement to restore human rights.'[88] Nonetheless, these debates – hitherto underappreciated in the existing literature devoted to UK overseas development policy – indicate that British opposition to the demands of the NIEO, although ultimately insurmountable, was seemingly more protean than conventional wisdom would suggest.[89] Indeed, in the context of overseas aid, Hart's conviction that 'the rights of man begin with breakfast' would continue to exert an influence over the Callaghan government's overseas development policy which, in spite of 1976 budget cuts, would become Labour's 'fastest rising' programme under her leadership.[90] Hart's enduring interest in human rights in the context of overseas development, officials would later acknowledge, led to the introduction of a specific Policy Guidance Note in 1978 that went some way towards embedding human rights concerns within the ODM.[91] However, while the notion of indivisible human rights was able to play a formative role in debates concerning the institutionalization of human rights during the Labour government of Jim Callaghan, its Conservative

---

[85] Frank Judd to Secretary of State, 'Human Rights and Aid', 4 July 1977, TNA, FCO 58/1152.
[86] Ibid.
[87] 'Record of an Office Meeting Held by the Secretary of State on Wednesday, 25 May, 1977 at 3.30 PM', TNA, FCO 58/1152.
[88] 'Record of a Meeting held at the Foreign and Commonwealth Office on Tuesday 5 July at 5 pm', OD 36/359.
[89] The Labour Party's post-war development policy and the establishment of the ODM in 1964 have been the subject of insightful scholarship, illuminating the ways in which Labour's attitudes to overseas aid have been shaped by colonialism and the Party's internationalist outlook. See for example Riley, 'Monstrous predatory vampires and beneficent fairy-godmothers'; Gerold Krozewski, 'Global Britain and the Post-Colonial World: The British Approach to Aid Policies at the 1964 Juncture', *Contemporary British History* 29, No. 2 (2015): 222–40. The influence exerted by human rights concerns upon the formulation of Britain's aid policy during the pivotal decade of the 1970s, however, has not yet been scrutinized, nor has it featured in broader histories of British international development policy. See for example Oliver Morrissey, Brian Smith and Edward Horesh, *British Aid and International Trade* (Buckingham: Open University Press, 1992); Barrie Ireton, *Britain's International Development Policies: A History of DfID and Overseas Aid* (Basingstoke: Palgrave Macmillan, 2013).
[90] '"The Rights of Man": The Seventh Sir David Owen Memorial Lecture, Given by the Rt Hon Mrs Judith Hart, Minister for Overseas Development, at University College, Cardiff, on Monday October 23 1978', TNA, FCO 59/1595; Judith Hart to Jenny Little, 6 April 1978, PHM, HART/08/66.
[91] See Press Cutting Section, ODA INF Dept, Labour Weekly: 'Human Rights', 1 April 1983, OD 116/9; R. Manning to Mr Browning, 'Political Aspects of Aid', 8 August 1983, TNA, OD 116/9.

successor would, in no uncertain terms, underscore the primacy of civil and political liberties over the socio-economic concerns advanced by adherents of the NIEO.

Margaret Thatcher's more circumscribed conception of human rights was clearly articulated before an audience attending the Europe Youth Rally in June 1979. The people of Europe, Thatcher maintained, had been

> divided by the differing concepts of human rights which prevail in the Western and Eastern halves of our continent. For so long as men and women are persecuted or imprisoned for their political beliefs – for daring to assert the right of every individual to dispute the official orthodoxy: for so long as people are denied the right to worship as they wish, freely and openly ... for so long as constraints are imposed on where people may go, what they may read and what they may say: for so long as dissent – the inborn right of every human being and the cherished legacy of our European individualism – is equated with treason or betrayal, the European value which live[s] in our common culture, will never be secure ... We in Western Europe ... must be fearless and outspoken in our championship of individual human rights throughout the world. We shall not provoke. But we shall clearly assert that so long as any European – and I use that term in its widest sense – is denied the right freely to develop his personality, his intellect or his creativity, there can be no true détente in Europe.[92]

For Thatcher, then, human rights encapsulated her belief that the individual was paramount, and that the rights to be cherished above all were those which enshrined the individual's freedom to pursue their fulfilment without interference from the state. The collective social and economic rights that predominated east of the Iron Curtain (and in the 'developing' world), by extension, were framed as a foreign and subversive presence. With the clarity afforded by hindsight, it could be argued that these sensibilities, which yielded the adoption of a somewhat attenuated human rights vision, were reflected in the construction of Thatcher's Cabinet and in her Sub-Cabinet Parliamentary appointees to the FCO.

For example, in Ian Gilmour, the first Thatcher government possessed a Commons Spokesman who had already publicly derided Owen's human rights approach in the *Daily Telegraph* in February 1979, deeming the internationalist scope of Owen's human rights advocacy to be symptomatic of a social democrat's self-indulgence, an indication of a politician out of touch with the exigencies of domestic social policy.[93] It was certainly not the case that Gilmour's critique was shared by all. In fact, Richard Luce, who was entrusted with a broad remit consisting of African policy, parliamentary business, passports, consular affairs, the police and Labour affairs, had encouraged the Conservatives to champion human rights in their foreign policy approach as early as

---

[92] 'Cold War: MT Speech to Europe Youth Rally ("Draft Passage for Inclusion in European Youth Rally Speech")', 2 June 1979, Churchill Archive Centre, Thatcher MSS, THCR 5/1/4/2, available at https://www.margaretthatcher.org/archive (accessed 13 January 2020).

[93] See Ian Gilmour, 'And where, in his agony, can the Social Democrat turn?' *Daily Telegraph*, 5 February 1979.

November 1977.⁹⁴ The prospective human rights agenda advanced by Luce in the pamphlet 'Human Rights and Foreign Policy', moreover, was described as being 'very similar to that of the present government' by one FCO official following a lunch meeting with Luce's co-author, John Ranelagh, in March 1978.⁹⁵ During the meeting, Ranelagh mentioned that Mrs Thatcher – 'perhaps surprisingly' to those who did not know her – was deeply 'interested in human rights'.⁹⁶ As such, she had

> recently received a delegation from Amnesty International. (The Reverend Paul Oestreicher and Mr David Simpson). She had got on well with them ... As a result of this meeting, Mrs Thatcher had asked Mr Peter Blaker MP (a former member of HM Diplomatic Service) to act as liaison with Amnesty. Mr Ranelagh thought it likely that Mr Luce would be appointed a junior FCO Minister if the Conservatives were returned to power. If so, human rights policy would probably be his responsibility.⁹⁷

In the event, however, Luce, who was 'admired for sticking to his liberal views on Southern African questions in the face of a vocal rightist minority', was given the least senior job of all of Thatcher's ministerial FCO appointees – a move 'interpreted by some as indicating a desire to remove difficult and divisive African problems from the forefront of Tory foreign policy'.⁹⁸ Furthermore, as the record of the meeting between Thatcher and the Amnesty delegation reveals, the organization was already beginning to express its concerns regarding the selectivity of Thatcher's human rights approach: 'Paul Oestreicher and David Simpson spent about 45 minutes talking to her ... They tried to persuade Margaret to look up alleged barbarities in countries such as Iran, Indonesia and South Africa in the same way as she views barbarity in Communist countries.'⁹⁹ That Thatcher should have proposed Blaker as a suitable interlocutor between her government and Amnesty International is also worth scrutinising. As the *Guardian*'s obituary of Lord Blaker recalled, although 'more diplomatic in his tone than some, during the Cold War he was a classic, well-heeled Tory defender of the US-led anti-Soviet coalition when serving Margaret Thatcher as a Foreign Office Minister'.¹⁰⁰ Chiefly responsible for the management of the East–West portfolio, Blaker's views, as the US Embassy in London reported, were undoubtedly 'in line with those of Mrs. Thatcher'.¹⁰¹ As such, it would

---

⁹⁴ See Richard Luce MP, and John Ranelagh, *Human Rights and Foreign Policy* (London: Conservative Political Centre, 1977).

⁹⁵ D. Beattie to Miss Elliot; Mr Simpson-Orlebar, 'Conservative Policy on Human Rights', 20 March 1978, TNA, FCO 58/1414.

⁹⁶ Ibid.

⁹⁷ Ibid.

⁹⁸ 'The Tory Foreign Policy Team', 15 May 1979, The National Archives, College Park, MD., Central Foreign Policy Files, Record Group 59 – General Records of the Department of State, Electronic Telegrams, 1979, available at https://aad.archives.gov/aad/createpdf?rid=223059&dt=2776&dl=2169 (accessed 13 January 2020).

⁹⁹ 'Human Rights: Sir Keith Joseph to John Davies (meeting between MT and Amnesty)', 26 May 1977, Churchill Archive Centre, Thatcher MSS, THCR 2/1/1/37, available at https://www.margaretthatcher.org/archive (accessed 9 January 2020).

¹⁰⁰ Andrew Roth, 'Obituary: Lord Blaker', *Guardian*, 9 July 2009.

¹⁰¹ 'The Tory Foreign Policy Team'.

appear that Thatcher's human rights concerns were situated firmly within the context of East–West relations. Beyond this, it could be argued that for Thatcher, and indeed for many Tories, the human rights issue was 'a bit wet'.[102]

Accordingly, the FCO human rights comparative assessment was scrapped at the behest of Conservative ministers shortly after the 1979 election.[103] The link between human rights and British overseas aid policy was subject to a more gradual demotion, as evidenced by a series of revisions appended to Hart's aforementioned policy guidance dating back to 1978.[104] The fact that the aid scheme was decimated by the Thatcher government's far-reaching budget cuts, accompanied by the swift reintegration of the ODM into the FCO, however, conveyed in more striking terms that rights-based approaches to the administration of overseas aid would not feature prominently in the formulation of policy.[105] Suspicion of the NIEO was also reinforced, and the government's approach to emerging debates surrounding a 'right to development' that grew out of the NIEO campaign was similarly rooted in a rejection of the Global South's attempts to recalibrate the human rights regime.[106]

The implementation of such striking revisions to British human rights policy was hardly surprising. Even before the axing of the human rights comparative assessment which, in spite of its limitations, had constituted a move towards the embedding of human rights criteria within the machinery of Whitehall, a Chatham House study group on 'Human Rights Criteria in British Foreign Policy' noted that the formulation of human rights policy 'did not depend on official attitudes but rather on ministers' individual predilections'.[107] Consequently, with the removal of the ministerial impetus provided not only by Owen, but also by Judd and, strikingly, by Hart at the ODM, the relationship

---

[102] 'UK-USSR Relations: A Flickering Candle', 27 November 1979, The National Archives, College Park, MD., Central Foreign Policy Files, Record Group 59 – General Records of the Department of State, Electronic Telegrams, 1979, available at https://aad.archives.gov/aad/createpdf?rid=263497&dt=2776&dl=2169 (accessed 13 January 2020).

[103] See M.K.O. Simpson-Orlebar to Sir A. Parsons, 'Human Rights Comparative Assessment', 14 June 1979, TNA, FCO 58/1706.

[104] See PGN No. 21 (Revised), 'Aid: Human Rights and Similar Considerations', February 1980, TNA, OD 108/3; 'Aid: Political and Human Rights Considerations', undated (circa 1981), TNA, OD 9/444; A.M. Archbold, 'Policy Guidance Note on Political and Human Rights Aspects of Aid', 16 December 1981, TNA, OD 108/1; PG No. 21 (Second Revision), 'Political Aspects of Aid', August 1983, TNA, OD 116/9.

[105] See The Labour Party, 'Statement by the National Executive Committee: Conservative Aid Policy', June 1980, PHM, HART/08/67. See also Morrissey, Smith and Horesh, British Aid and International Trade, 14–17; Matthew Anderson, A History of Fair Trade in Contemporary Britain: From Civil Society Campaigns to Corporate Compliance (Basingstoke: Palgrave Macmillan, 2015), 16.

[106] See K.P. O'Sullivan to Miss C. Sinclair, 'NIEO', 18 November 1981, TNA, FCO 59/1815; United Nations Department, Background Note on the Right to Development, 22 June 1982, TNA, FCO 58/2921; R.P.D. Chatterjie to Mr Roberts, 'Third Committee: Draft Resolution on the Right to Development', 29 November 1982, TNA, FCO 58/2922; H.R. Mortimer to Mr Pease, 'UN Human Rights Commission: 39th Session 21 January–11 March 1983', TNA, FCO 58/2922; S. Foulds to Mr Chatterjie, 'Human Rights Commission: 39th Session, Item 8: Question of the Realisation in all Countries of the Economic, Social and Cultural Rights Contained in the Universal Declaration of Human Rights, and Study of Special Problems which the Developing Countries Face in their Efforts to Achieve these Rights', 23 March 1983, TNA, FCO 58/3326.

[107] Cheryl Coveney, 'Study Group on Human Rights Criteria in British Foreign Policy: Report of Third Meeting – 19 February 1979', The Royal Institute of International Affairs, TNA, FCO 58/1705.

between the FCO and human rights NGOs was also downgraded. In response to an invitation to participate in a Chatham House colloquium in July 1983, for instance, FCO officials informed the organizer of the initiative, who had been encouraged by the Callaghan government's cooperation on human rights matters, that 'the enthusiasm for discussing such matters that he recalled having encountered in 1978 would not necessarily be rekindled nowadays'.[108] The 'Human Rights Network' consisting of representatives from Amnesty International, the Campaign Against the Arms Trade, the Minority Rights Group and Justice, also noted that the Thatcher government's approach towards consultation 'compared unfavourably with the previous administration's practice of holding round table meetings with interested NGOs'.[109]

Still, although 'the style was different', human rights had nonetheless remained on the foreign policy agenda at the FCO during the first Thatcher government.[110] In fact, following a colloquium on human rights and foreign policy organized by the International Commission of Jurists in October 1983, at which representatives from the UK, the US, Canada and Australia provided oral descriptions of procedures for the promotion of human rights within their respective government departments, W.J. Adams reported that the UK had 'nothing to be ashamed of in comparison with what others do, though there is no doubt that most of the governments represented, including the Americans, have a more structured and high-profile organisation of this subject than we do'.[111] In practice, Adams continued, 'our record in the field of human rights in foreign policy is quite as good as that of most other Western countries and probably better than some'.[112] Human rights also maintained their position on the Labour Party's foreign policy agenda during this period, and, on the domestic front, 'the language and politics of human rights was becoming more meaningful as a political and legal tool for non-state actors', tantamount in Michael Rask Madsen's estimation to a 'civil rights counter strategy' set against the politics of Thatcherism.[113]

As for Owen, the notion of 'opposition' took on a new dimension following his decision to leave the Labour Party and establish the Social Democratic Party (SDP) with fellow Labour defectors Roy Jenkins, Shirley Williams and Bill Rodgers in early 1981. The establishment of the SDP and Owen's rationale for breaking with Labour have been examined in great detail.[114] The ways in which the SDP's approach to foreign

---

[108] W.J. Adams to PS/Mr. Whitney, 'Chatham House Colloquium on Human Rights', 6 July 1983, TNA, FCO 58/3392.
[109] D.M. Mainwood to Mr Roberts, 'Human Rights Network', 13 February 1984, TNA, FCO 46/4260.
[110] Adams to PS/Mr. Whitney, 'Chatham House Colloquium on Human Rights'.
[111] W.J. Adams to PS; Mr Whitney, 'ICJ Colloquim on Human Rights and Foreign Policy, Chatham House, 3 to 4 October 1983', 6 October 1983, TNA, FCO 58/3392.
[112] Ibid.
[113] Moores, *Civil Liberties and Human Rights in Twentieth Century Britain*, 223; Madsen, 'France, the UK, and the "Boomerang" of the Internationalisation of Human Rights', 79. Regarding Labour's stance on human rights promotion at this juncture, see Labour Party, *The New Hope for Britain: Labour's Manifesto 1983* (London: The Labour Party, 1983), 37–9; Mark Wickham-Jones, 'Labour Party Politics and Foreign Policy', in *New Labour's Foreign Policy*, ed. Little and Wickham-Jones, 94–95.
[114] See Ivor Crewe and Anthony King, *SDP: The Birth, Life and Death of the Social Democratic Party* (Oxford: Oxford University Press, 1995), 3–117; Garnett, 'Polemic, Parliament and History': 171–88. David Owen's autobiographical offerings have also explored this pivotal moment in his political career in great depth. See David Owen, *Face the Future* (Oxford: Oxford University Press, 1981), xi–xxi; Owen, *Time to Declare*, 418–514.

policy reflected its overarching modus operandi (the establishment of a 'third way' in British politics), however, have largely evaded academic scrutiny.[115] Owen, as Chairman of the SDP's Policy Committee on International Affairs tasked with 'producing strategic proposals for debate within the Party' on foreign policy issues, oversaw much of the work undertaken in this regard. Indeed, the development of 'distinctive' foreign policy initiatives was seen as an integral part of the 'new politics' that the SDP sought to construct.[116] The promotion of human rights, moreover, featured prominently in the realization of this objective. According to David Stephen, who followed Owen to the SDP after losing his job as a political adviser in the FCO in May 1979, and became Chairman of the SDP subcommittee on the 'Formulation and Presentation of Foreign Policy', the Party soon developed an 'internationalist approach' with a 'refreshed' human rights policy, helping the SDP to break away from 'the old parties and their tramline thinking'.[117] This sense of divergence or interposition, and the role that human rights promotion might play in achieving this end, is more clearly elucidated in a policy paper – later developed into a foreign policy Green Paper – drafted by Stephen. The paper depicts a growing isolationist tendency within both the Conservative government and the increasingly influential left-wing of the Labour Party associated with Tony Benn, which supported British withdrawal from NATO and the European Community.[118] Such developments, Stephen posited, had opened up space that would allow the SDP's internationalist outlook to establish a foothold: 'Thatcherite scorn for the third world, for the niceties of multilateral diplomacy and for disarmament' was being driven 'by the conviction that those previously in charge of British foreign policy have been "soft" towards the rhetoric of third-world radicals'.[119] The 'Bennite alternative', Stephen continued,

> strangely mirrors the Thatcherite world view; Britain is called to 'give a moral lead' and existing or traditional foreign policy is represented as the advancement of the interests of squalid cabals of arms merchants and city men against 'working people' everywhere. The new Labour Party has detailed policies for El Salvador and Chile but says nothing about Poland and shows no sign of even being aware of the consequences of Soviet power and policies.[120]

In the cold light of Thatcher's realpolitik, British foreign policy was calling out for an injection of idealism. But this idealism needed to be focused: 'This is not, then, a plea

---

[115] A notable exception is Henrik Larsen, *Foreign Policy and Discourse Analysis: France, Britain and Europe* (London and New York: Routledge, 1997), although references to the SDP are cursory and sporadic.

[116] 'Keynotes No. 8: Circular to SDP Area Parties June 1982', DOP, D709 3/2/4/19; 'Foreign Affairs: Including the European Community; Defence and East–West Relations; and North–South Relations', March 1982, Social Democratic Party Archive, University of Essex Special Collections (hereafter SDP), Box 38 (a): Minutes, 19. 5. 82–23. 11. 82; Robin P. Fawcett, 'Towards a Set of Policy Sub-Committees on International Affairs', 2 June 1982, SDP, Box 38 (a): Minutes, 19. 5. 82–23. 11. 82.

[117] Stephen interview, 16 May 2019.

[118] See David Stephen, 'Towards a Re-Think of Foreign Policy', undated, SDP, Box 38 (a): Minutes, 19. 5. 82–23. 11. 82.

[119] Ibid.

[120] Ibid.

for a Labour Party-type moral-imperialist crusade. It is a plea for a re-thinking of the application of our basic values and commitments, to be done with our allies and partners.'[121]

Accordingly, the SDP's approach to the East–West dialogue was framed as being less outwardly confrontational than the Conservative government's, while also demonstrating a greater appreciation of the harshening climate of the 'second' Cold War than Labour Party policy tended to convey by entertaining the notion of unilateral nuclear disarmament – a policy position that seemed less and less realistic following the Soviet invasion of Afghanistan in 1979 and the imposition of martial law in Poland in 1981.[122] Rather, the SDP sought to pursue a measured approach on the issue of nuclear disarmament, basing its policy on the work of the Independent Commission on Disarmament and Security Issues (the Palme Commission) of which Owen was a member, and continued to value the CSCE framework as a means of reducing Cold War tensions, although direct linkage between human rights issues and progress on arms reductions was eschewed and the active destabilization of the Eastern bloc rejected.[123] This attempt to offer a genuine alternative to the two main parties in foreign affairs, moreover, shaped the SDP's approach to the pressing issues of the North–South dialogue.[124] Rooted in the Party's internationalist outlook, SDP development policy took on a moral character that precipitated engagement with the imbalances of the global economy and its attendant human costs. More specifically, the Party's Policy Group on the Third World and Development embraced the findings of the Brandt Report of 1980 (which had called for a large transfer of resources from the 'developed' countries to the Global South), advocated for an increase in the British aid budget as a means of achieving this goal, and argued for the untying of British aid from British economic interests overseas in order to provide aid to those who needed it most.[125]

---

[121] Ibid. See also 'Draft Conference Paper by David Stephen – For Discussion', undated, DOP, D709 3/2/4/19.

[122] See The Rt. Hon. Dr. David Owen MP (Plymouth-Devonport), 'Foreign Affairs and Defence' (Thursday 14th October 1982), SDP, Box 38 (a): Minutes, 19. 5. 82–23. 11. 82; 'Speech by the Rt Hon Dr David Owen MP to the Council on Foreign Relations, New York, on Monday 8 November 1982', SDP, Box 38 (f): Improving East/West Relations.

[123] See 'Draft Letter for Green Paper 8: SDP International Affairs Policy', undated, SDP, Box 38 (c); 'Minutes of the International Affairs Policy Committee', 7 June 1982, SDP, Box 38 (a): Minutes, 19. 5. 82–23. 11. 82; 'Improving East–West Relations: Notes on Meeting Held on 23rd November 1982', SDP, Box 38 (f): Improving East/West Relations; Wendy Buckley, 'East/West Relations Group: Note of Meeting Held on 23rd November 1982', 25 November 1982, SDP, Box 38 (f): Improving East/West Relations; Simon Head, 'CSCE: Latest Developments', 5 March 1983, SDP, Box 38 (f): Improving East/West Relations; Ieuan G. John, 'Political Objectives of Western Policy towards Eastern Europe', 5 March 1983, SDP, Box 38 (f): Improving East/West Relations.

[124] See for example Vincent Cable, 'British Interests and Third World Development', undated, SDP, Box 38 (h): Third World/Development, Circulated Papers, PG10/2.

[125] See Overseas Development Institute, 'The Brandt Commission', Briefing Paper No. 2 (March 1980), available at https://www.odi.org/sites/odi.org.uk/files/odi-assets/publications-opinion-files/6638.pdf (accessed 10 January 2020); C.M. Williams, 'Policy Group on the Third World and Development', 12 May 1982, with attached 'Draft Consultative Document', SDP, Box 38 (h): Third World/Development, Circulated Papers, PG10/2; C.R. Smallwood, 'Third World and Development Group', with attached brief ('The Third World and Development Aid') 26 August 1982, SDP, Box 38 (a): Minutes, 19. 5. 82–23. 11. 82; 'Minutes of the International Affairs Committee', 6 September 1982, SDP, Box 38 (a): Minutes, 19. 5. 82–23. 11. 82.

It is, therefore, important to note that human rights considerations not only continued to occupy a position on the FCO's agenda following the election of the Conservative government in May 1979 (albeit in a rather circumscribed and weaponized form), but that alternative visions and applications of human rights in the context of British foreign policy also continued to develop thereafter. Nonetheless, recent scholarship has demonstrated that the significance of the Thatcher government's recalibration of human rights policy should not be understated – Thatcher's human rights policy was, as Michael Cotey Morgan points out, constitutive of a broader phenomenon, as 'the focus on political rights to the exclusion of socioeconomic rights coincided with a crisis of Keynesian economics and a shift toward neoliberal doctrines in the West'.[126] Indeed, the relationship between human rights and neoliberalism has been subjected to a rigorous examination as of late. The two phenomena, Samuel Moyn writes, 'are clearly historical companions'.[127] But where others have inferred an insidious causal relationship – that human rights assisted the neoliberal ascendency by providing it with 'ideological mystification' – Moyn is more circumspect:

> Human rights and market fundamentalism share some negative conditions (e.g., the collapse of welfarism and socialism) as well as some ideological affinities. Putting them in the same picture, however, is interesting not because there is any significant causal relationship between them ... Rather, their companionship illustrates that if human rights languages and movements and regimes have been successful on some fronts, they have been disappointing on others.[128]

In other words, if 'human rights and market fundamentalism are *frères ennemis*, the sad fact is that human rights have failed to allow the enactment of much resistance against their more powerful sibling'.[129] The companionship between human rights and market fundamentalism, Moyn posits, may not have been 'inevitable'.[130] Nonetheless, the hegemonic influence of neoliberalism meant that shortly after their 'breakthrough' moment, 'human rights were cut off from the dream of globally fair distribution that the global South itself advocated during the 1970s'.[131] In spite of their present day ubiquity, human rights, therefore, have 'become a worldwide slogan in a time of downsized ambition'.[132] In the 'neoliberal age', the grandiose visions of global justice typified by the NIEO merely stand as memorials to 'unavailable egalitarian utopias'.[133]

---

[126] Morgan, 'The Seventies and the Rebirth of Human Rights', 250.
[127] Samuel Moyn, 'Human Rights and "Neoliberalism"', *Humanity*, blog post, 10 July 2014, available at www.humanityjournal.org/blog/human-rights-and-neoliberalism/ (accessed 13 January 2020).
[128] Ibid. C.f. Stephen Hopgood, *The Endtimes of Human Rights* (New York: Cornell University Press, 2013). See also Naomi Klein, *The Shock Doctrine: The Rise of Disaster Capitalism* (London: Penguin, 2007); Mary Nolan, 'Gender and Utopian Visions in a Post-Utopian Era: Americanism, Human Rights, Market Fundamentalism', *Central European History* 44 (2011): 13–26; Jessica Whyte, *The Morals of the Market: Human Rights and Neoliberalism* (London: Verso, 2019).
[129] Moyn, 'Human Rights and "Neoliberalism"'.
[130] Samuel Moyn, *Not Enough: Human Rights in an Unequal World* (Cambridge, MA: The Belknap Press of Harvard University Press, 2018), 8.
[131] Ibid.
[132] Ibid., 6.
[133] Ibid., 147.

An examination of David Owen's membership of the Independent Commission on International Humanitarian Issues (ICIHI) from 1983 to 1987, and of his engagement with ideas concerning global governance under the Commission's purview, however, suggests that, while human rights may have become increasingly disconnected from the demands of the NIEO as a more circumscribed conception of human rights became ever more entrenched in international discourse, a desire to address the socio-economic roots of human suffering in the developing world was able to seek fulfilment through an alternative *humanitarian* optic.

'hardly a trumpet call for freedom everywhere!'

The ICIHI was established in the light of a 1981 resolution, adopted unanimously by the UN General Assembly, relating to the creation of a 'new humanitarian order'.[134] The following year, a further resolution was adopted with unanimity, this time proposing that an international commission, operating outside of UN auspices and composed of 'leading personalities in the humanitarian field or having wide experience of government or world affairs', should be established in order to pursue this lofty ambition.[135] In January 1983, the man responsible for tabling the 1981 resolution, His Royal Highness Crown Prince Hassan bin Talal of Jordan, wrote to Owen inviting him to join the Commission. Owen jumped at the opportunity: 'I am delighted to accept and I am much looking forward to working with you and your colleagues in discussing and producing proposals for the promotion of a new international humanitarian order.'[136] Observers within the FCO, however, were more guarded in their assessment of the ICIHI's prospects.

To be sure, the Jordanians' resolution was initially well received, at least in principle.[137] But goodwill soon gave way to a more hesitant approach, rendering the FCO unwilling to put forward a British candidate for membership of the Commission.[138] This apparent scepticism, moreover, ultimately contributed towards the FCO's decision not to make a financial contribution to the ICIHI, in spite of the realization that this could raise Owen's hackles and consequently leave the government open to criticism.[139]

---

[134] 'Independent Commission on International Humanitarian Issues', undated, DOP, D709 4/3/1.

[135] Ibid. The Commission's remit was broadly defined as 'part of the continuing search of the world community for a more adequate international framework to uphold human dignity and rise to the challenge of colossal humanitarian problems arising with increasing frequency in all continents'. The 1981 resolution from which the Commission sprang recognized '[t]he importance of further improving a comprehensive international framework which takes fully into account existing instruments relating to humanitarian questions as well as the need for addressing those aspects which are not yet adequately covered' (The Independent Commission on International Humanitarian Issues, *Winning the Human Race? The Report of the Independent Commission on International Humanitarian Issues* (London and New Jersey: Zed Books, 1988), 208).

[136] 'Independent Commission on International Humanitarian Issues'.

[137] See 'Reply to the Secretary-General's Note Ref SD 2052/11 of 10 February 1982 on the Proposals for the Promotion of a New International Humanitarian Order', undated, TNA, FCO 58/3433.

[138] See 'Visit of Crown Prince Hassan of Jordan, New International Humanitarian Order: Essential Facts', undated, TNA, FCO 58/3433.

[139] See B.D. Adams to D. Mainwood, 'ICIHI', 11 August 1983, TNA, FCO 58/3433.

Two factors contributed towards the FCO's dismissal of the ICIHI's solicitation. There was certainly a widely held belief that the ICIHI's mission statement was somewhat ill defined and consequently liable to stray into territory already covered by UN initiatives. More instructive than these misgivings was an understanding that the FCO, and the departments for whom the proposals of the ICIHI would be particularly germane (chiefly the Overseas Development Administration), were severely hamstrung by recent budget cuts, and were therefore required to focus on maintaining their pre-existing commitments with regard to international humanitarian assistance.[140] On 21 September 1983, David Peate of the UN Department somewhat regretfully conveyed to Richard Fursland at UKMIS (New York) that these factors constituted an insuperable obstacle.[141]

As debates concerning the efficacy of the ICIHI's endeavours continued into 1984 with no significant alteration in the FCO's position, however, the unfolding humanitarian catastrophe wrought by widespread famine in Ethiopia was serving to underscore the value of its operations.[142] Indeed, while Michael Buerk's October 1984 report may have brought the untold suffering of millions of Ethiopians into the living rooms of Britain, triggering an outpouring of humanitarian solidarity that would reach its apogee in the landmark Live Aid concerts of 13 July 1985, the ICIHI had already been grappling with the scourge of famine in Africa since the Commission's establishment in 1983.[143] This work culminated in the publication in May 1985 of *Famine: A Man-Made Disaster?* Owen, who played a key role in the development of the report, bemoaned the seemingly transient appeal of the Brandt Commission's recommendations and urged the international community to discard the fallacy that famine was an unavoidable consequence of nature's capriciousness and to increase its efforts to tackle the problem at its roots.[144] As such, while the Thatcher government was, according to Andrew Jones, unable to fully embrace Live Aid – Thatcher's appreciation for the 'Victorian' value of philanthropy conflicting with the government's determination not to kowtow to public pressure to reassess overseas development policy – Owen was able to position himself as a natural champion of the event:

---

[140] N.C.R. Williams to Mr Adams, 'Independent Commission on International Humanitarian Issues', 15 September 1983, TNA, FCO 58/3433.
[141] D.J. Peate to R.C. Fursland, 'Independent Commission on International Humanitarian Issues (ICIHI)', 21 September 1983, TNA, FCO 58/3433.
[142] See Sadruddin Aga Khan to Timothy Raison, 13 March 1984, TNA, FCO 58/3849; Timothy Raison to Sadruddin Aga Khan, 18 April 1984, TNA, FCO 58/3849; N.C.R. Williams to D.J. Moss, 'Independent Commission on International Humanitarian Issues (ICIHI)', 15 March 1984, TNA, FCO 58/3849.
[143] For examples of scholarship situating this explosion of humanitarian philanthropy in its broader historical context see Tehila Sasson, 'In the Name of Humanity: Britain and the Rise of Global Humanitarianism' (PhD thesis, UC Berkeley, 2015); Sasson & Vernon, 'Practising the British Way of Famine': 860–72; Kevin O'Sullivan, 'A "Global Nervous System": The Rise and Rise of European Humanitarian NGOs, 1945–1985', in *International Organizations and Development, 1945–1990*, ed. Marc Frey, Sönke Kunkel and Corinna R. Unger (Basingstoke: Palgrave Macmillan, 2014), 196–219.
[144] The Independent Commission on International Humanitarian Issues, *Famine: A Man-Made Disaster? A Report for the Independent Commission on International Humanitarian Issues* (London and Sydney: Pan Books, 1985).

There is a message in Live Aid for this Government – where the British people have given generously to famine relief, this Government has not found a single extra pound for the Aid budget to handle famine relief. A public relations exercise based on deceit has given the impression, with fairly frequent announcements of extra grants to Ethiopia or Sudan, that the Aid budget has actually expanded. Whereas all that has actually happened is that money has been transferred from one part of the Development budget to another. Our young people put to shame the official expression of concern.[145]

In October, Owen reiterated these concerns, taking the opportunity presented by Fight World Poverty's lobby of Parliament, which witnessed an unprecedented 20,000 concerned Britons descend upon Westminster, to underline the pertinence of the ICIHI's recommendations.[146] Although Owen acknowledged that it would be a mistake to turn such an event into a vote touting exercise, he was nonetheless at pains to point out that, in light of the SDP's moral commitment to international development, an SDP government under his leadership – now in alliance with the Liberal Party – could in no circumstances have 'lived through the famine of the last year or so without increasing substantially the British aid budget'.[147]

The focus on long-term strategies of humanitarian assistance exhibited by Owen and the ICIHI carries historiographical significance, speaking to broader debates concerning the evolution of humanitarian practice and its response to questions of international development. During the first UN 'Development Decade' of the 1960s, humanitarianism's traditional emphasis on the immediate alleviation of human suffering 'at the expense of a critical response to the causes of conflict or poverty' became increasingly scrutinized, with major organizations such as Oxfam leading the way in the redefinition of humanitarian engagement from 'the provision of emergency aid to a more "alchemical" type of assistance'.[148] In other words, humanitarian activists began to move away 'from the short-term relief of poverty to the long-term attempt to tackle its underlying causes', a commitment articulated emphatically by a group of British humanitarian NGOs in the Haselmere Declaration of 1968.[149] This reorientation, moreover, paved the way for the growing embrace of a human rights framework within which the grassroots work of humanitarian NGOs could be 'translated into a global

---

[145] 'Live Aid: Statement by David Owen', 13 July 1985, DOP, D709 3/17/1/5/97. See also Andrew Jones, 'Band Aid Revisited: Humanitarianism, Consumption and Philanthropy in the 1980s', *Contemporary British History* 31, No. 2 (2017): 189–209.

[146] See 'Speech by the Rt Hon Dr David Owen MP, Leader of the Social Democratic Party, Addressing the Fight World Poverty Lobby in Methodist Central Hall, Westminster, at 3.20 PM on Tuesday, 22 October 1985', DOP, D709 3/17/1/5/141.

[147] Ibid.

[148] Bronwyn Leebaw, 'The Politics of Impartial Activism: Humanitarianism and Human Rights', *Perspectives in Politics* 5, No. 2 (June 2007): 227; Matthew Hilton, 'Charity and the End of Empire: British Non-Governmental Organizations, Africa, and International Development in the 1960s', *The American Historical Review* 123, Issue 2 (April 2018): 493.

[149] Hilton, 'Charity and the End of Empire': 493; The Haselmere Group, *The Haselmere Declaration* (London: The Haselmere Committee, 1968), 4. See also Peter Van Dam, 'No Justice Without Charity: Humanitarianism After Empire', *The International History Review* (2020): 1–22.

agenda'.[150] As Matthew Hilton notes, traditional concepts of faith-based and secular humanitarianism had, by the end of the twentieth century, 'given way to a model of development based on human rights'.[151] It is now difficult, Hilton maintains, 'to escape the focus on human rights that now dominates the core missions of [humanitarian] NGOs'.[152]

Upon examining the ICIHI's final report, which laid bare the philosophical underpinnings of its operations when it was published in 1988, it is clear to see that the organization reflected this ideational recalibration, its humanitarian remit shaped profoundly by an appreciation of human rights discourse. 'Winning the human race', so stated Prince Sadruddin's foreword, 'is the challenge faced by contemporary society. It cannot be met in our view without placing human welfare at the centre of national and international policymaking'.[153] In this regard, the ICIHI was not starting from scratch. Rather, the Commission viewed itself as a continuation of a 'process' that began with the Universal Declaration of Human Rights, was subsequently carried forward by a number of conventions, and which 'ought to be further strengthened by a declaration of Humanitarian Principles in order to guide policies and actions at [the] global level'.[154] Indeed, the report went on to define humanitarianism as 'the bridge between ethics and human rights, both of which are needed to make global society healthy and secure for the present and future generations'.[155] The ICIHI's synthesis of human rights and humanitarianism vis-à-vis the imperatives of international development, therefore, does more than shed light on the entangled histories of human rights and humanitarianism; the organisation can also be seen, more specifically, to contribute to the development of the 'New Humanitarianism' – a rights-based approach to humanitarian engagement that has become increasingly prominent in international discourse.[156]

However, looking back upon the ambitious vision of distributive economic justice that was buttressed by this merger of humanitarian and human rights discourse in the dim light of the more palliative conception of human rights that we have become accustomed to, the ICIHI and its talk of a 'New International Humanitarian Order',

---

[150] Matthew Hilton, 'International Aid and Development NGOs in Britain and Human Rights since 1945', *Humanity* 3, No. 3 (December 2012): 455. For further scholarly coverage of this convergence, see for example Michael Barnett, *Empire of Humanity: A History of Humanitarianism* (Ithaca: Cornell University Press, 2011); Richard Ashby Wilson and Richard D. Brown, 'Introduction', in *Humanitarianism and Suffering*, ed. Richard Ashby Wilson and Richard D. Brown (Cambridge: Cambridge University Press, 2009), 1–28; David Chandler, *From Kosovo to Kabul: Human Rights and International Intervention* (London: Pluto Press, 2002); Larry Minear, *The Humanitarian Enterprise: Dilemmas and Discoveries* (Bloomfield, CT: Kumarian, 2002).

[151] Hilton, 'International Aid and Development NGOs in Britain and Human Rights since 1945': 449.

[152] Ibid.

[153] The Independent Commission on International Humanitarian Issues, *Winning the Human Race?* ix.

[154] Ibid., x.

[155] Ibid., 186.

[156] This development has not been met with unanimous approval, both in terms of the lack of analytical clarity brought about by the widespread conflation of the two concepts and its practical consequences. See for example Samuel Moyn, 'Theses on Humanitarianism and Human Rights', *Humanity*, blog post, 23 September 2016, available at http://humanityjournal.org/blog/theses-on-humanitarianism-and-human-rights/ (accessed 24 June 2020); B.S. Chimni, 'Globalization, Humanitarianism and the Erosion of Refugee Protection', *Journal of Refugee Studies* 13, No. 3 (2000): 243–63.

like that of the New International Economic Order before it, reminds us of roads not travelled; of alternative visions of human rights that were ultimately stifled during the 'neoliberal age'.[157] It could perhaps be argued that the agenda of the ICIHI helps to support the notion that the legacy of the NIEO can be thought of as one of 'unfailure' – a paradox that can be used to refer to 'many seemingly failed political and social movements' which, 'even though they did not realize their ambitions in their own moment, often live on as prophetic visions, available as an idiom for future generations to articulate their own hopes and dreams'.[158] Seen from this perspective, the ICIHI's ambitious vision played a part in incubating the 'NIEO imaginary', providing a discursive space within which concepts of distributive economic justice and the recalibration of the global economy could survive amid what Mark Mazower has labelled the 'real new international economic order' of neoliberal ascendency.[159] Nonetheless, in the final analysis, Owen's involvement with the ICIHI serves to cast an unforgiving spotlight on the 'lost decade' of development in which concepts of human rights were forcibly decoupled from issues concerning the North–South dialogue while becoming increasingly fused to the politics of the East–West conflict.[160]

Although human rights had played a formative role in the construction of the Commission's agenda, it would appear that the development of human rights discourse beyond the ICIHI's sphere of influence meant that the term was, in common parlance, no longer suited to the attainment of the grandiose vision that the Commissioners strove towards. Rather, human rights, as Owen posited during a speech before a meeting of the ICIHI in New York on 21 January 1987, had become, through its close association with the East–West dialogue and the polarized debate surrounding the North–South divide, increasingly politicized and devoid of deeper meaning.[161] As such, Owen opined: 'Humanitarianism might prove to be a more acceptable umbrella within which to examine the inter-relationships between human rights, human needs and human obligations.'[162] By the time the ICIHI's final report was published, it became clear that the etymological significance of this development was something that Owen had continued to explore during the intervening period: 'Humanitarianism as a word will replace human rights in the international lexicon over the next decade.'[163]

Certainly, the contemporaneous development of human rights policy within Whitehall reflected the calcification of a narrow understanding of the concept that prohibited engagement with the socio-economic debates that the ICIHI sought to

---

[157] See for example Nils Gilman, 'The New International Economic Order: A Reintroduction', *Humanity* 6, No. 1 (Spring 2015): 1–2.
[158] Ibid.: 10.
[159] Kevin O'Sullivan, 'The Search for Justice: NGOs in Britain and Ireland and the New International Economic Order, 1968–82', *Humanity* 6, No. 1 (Spring 2015): 173; Mazower, quoted in ibid.: 183.
[160] Rist, *The History of Development*, 170.
[161] '"Humanitarianism": A Speech by the Rt. Hon. Dr David Owen MP, Leader of the British Social Democratic Party in an Address to a Meeting of the Independent Commission on International Humanitarian Issues in New York on Wednesday, 21 January 1987', DOP D709 3/7/1/7/149.
[162] Ibid.
[163] 'Statement by the Rt Hon Dr David Owen MP at the Presentation of the Final Report "Winning the Human Race", from the Independent Commission on International Humanitarian Issues', 12 October 1988, DOP, D709 3/17/1/7/149.

address. This much became abundantly clear to one FCO official upon consulting a briefing paper which summarized human rights practices in the Foreign Office in April 1984: 'I am glad we are not issuing this publicly. It is hardly a trumpet call for freedom everywhere!'[164] The following year, officials also began to note 'a number of recent signs of disquiet about the Government's approach to human rights questions', including letters of protest from MPs and members of the public which 'drew unfavourable comparisons between the Secretary of State's espousal of human rights causes on his visits to Eastern Europe and the Government's attitude to human rights in other countries'.[165] Notably, Sir Anthony Williams, leader of the UK delegation to the UN Commission on Human Rights, along with the UK's Deputy Permanent Representative in New York, expressed 'concern about our "hand to mouth" and over-politicized approach to human rights questions in the UN context', which had begun to erode Britain's 'standing on human rights issues' to such a degree that 'we no longer play a leading role in upholding the cause of human rights at the UN'.[166] In any case, long-standing UK opposition to proposals concerning the establishment of a 'right to development' endured – as did a broader scepticism surrounding the 'so-called "third generation" or collective rights' which were becoming 'an increasing, and unwelcome, feature of discussion on human rights in the UN and elsewhere'.[167] When the time finally came to vote on the Right to Development at the Third Committee of the 41st UN General Assembly in 1986, the UK delegation abstained, taking issue with 'the cause and effect relationship implied between violations of human rights and development'; rejecting the notion that 'human rights are indivisible and inter-dependent' (while accepting that certain rights were 'inter-related'); and disavowing 'any link between the promotion and protection of human rights and the establishment of a new international economic order'.[168]

This approach was not accepted with unanimity within Whitehall.[169] Moreover, it is important to note that additional steps were in fact taken to institutionalize human

---

[164] J. Houston to Mr Williams, 'Human Rights in Foreign Policy', 30 April 1984, TNA, FCO 58/3767.
[165] P. Lever to Mr O'Neill; PUS/Mr Renton, 'Human Rights: Consistency and Principle in HMG's Approach', 14 June 1985, TNA, FCO 58/4067.
[166] Ibid.
[167] N.C.R. Williams to Mr Adams, 'Parliamentary Human Rights Group', 17 May 1984, TNA, FCO 58/3767. See also R.B. Janvrin to Mr O'Neill, 'Council of Europe: Meeting of the Ad Hoc Committee of Experts to Exchange views on Human Rights in Relation to Development', 27 December 1984, TNA, FCO 58/3721; United Nations Department, '41st Session of the United Nations Commission on Human Rights, Geneva, 4 February–15 March 1985, Agenda Item No. 8: Question of the Realisation in All Countries of Economic, Social and Cultural Rights', February 1985, TNA, FCO 58/4025; S. Foulds to Mr Jones, 'Human Rights Commission: 41st Session Item 8', 20 May 1985, TNA, FCO 58/4024; United Nations Department, 'Essential Facts: Declaration on a Right to Development', September 1985, TNA, FCO 58/4025.
[168] 'UNGA 41, Third Committee, Explanation of Vote by the United Kingdom on L. 4: Draft Declaration on the Right to Development', 28 November 1986, TNA, FCO 58/4434.
[169] See for example Sally Morphet to Mr Jones, 'United Kingdom Policy on Human Rights', 23 October 1985, TNA, FCO 58/4067: 'I have written at length on the relationship between civil and political and economic and social rights in my 1978 paper on the balance between the two ... Basically we argue that the arguments put forward by some in the west for the priority of civil and political rights over economic and social rights are not persuasive as the categorical distinctions between the two sets of rights do not stand up to careful analysis ... we should take a positive attitude to the rights in both covenants.'

rights policy within the FCO during this period with the establishment of a Human Rights Unit in 1986.[170] According to Alan Clark, who served as Minister of State for Trade between 1986–9, human rights concerns had become deeply rooted in the FCO's agenda, a development that Clark recorded with a considerable degree of consternation:

> I am blighted by the Foreign Office at present. Earlier today a creepy official, who is 'in charge' (heaven help us) of South America, came over to brief me ahead of a trip to Chile. All crap about Human Rights. Not one word about the UK interest; how we saw the balance, prospects, pitfalls, opportunities in the Hemisphere. I'm Minister of Trade, for Christ's sake, what's the point of keeping an expensive mission in Santiago if they can't even tell me what to push? When I questioned him, he was evasive on all policy matters other than his own *Guardian*esque [sic] obsession.[171]

It ought to be reiterated, therefore, that the story of international human rights promotion under the Thatcher governments is not so easily reducible to one of emphatic demotion. Even if they so desired, Conservative ministers were seemingly unable to return to a narrow conception of the 'national interest' that precluded engagement with human rights norms. It is nonetheless important to stress, however, that continuing British engagement with human rights promotion in the international sphere during this period was undoubtedly characterized by an elevation of the individual's civil and political liberties above conceptions of collective rights, pertaining to social and economic issues. As a matter of fact, the remainder of the decade would witness the codification of Thatcher's decidedly neoliberal human rights vision within the apparatus of the CSCE itself.

Although less outwardly hawkish than the first when it came to East–West issues, the second and third Thatcher governments remained steadfast in their support of the Helsinki Process, and as the Cold War hurtled towards its unexpected denouement, Thatcher – embracing the role of superpower interlocutor – continued to press the Soviet leadership on the human rights issue.[172] Thatcher, it seems, was not prepared to compromise. Further reconciliation between East and West would be contingent upon the continued improvement of the human rights situation in the Soviet bloc.[173] Indeed, in response to Soviet Foreign Minister Eduard Shevardnadze's suggestion that Moscow should be considered as the setting for a CSCE conference on human rights in the near future, Thatcher voiced her misgivings in no uncertain terms, refusing even to

---

[170] See P.K. Williams to PS/Mr Eggar, 'Policy on Human Rights', 8 January 1988, TNA, FCO 58/4952; J.W. Watt, 'Human Rights Coordination Meeting, 8 November', 18 October 1989, TNA, FCO 58/5144.

[171] Alan Clark, *Diaries* (London: Phoenix, 1994), 161 (diary entry from 14 April 1987).

[172] See for example Ilaria Poggiolini, 'Thatcher's Double-Track Road to the End of the Cold War: The Irreconcilability of Liberalization and Preservation', in *Visions of the End of the Cold War in Europe*, ed. Bozo, Rey, Ludlow and Rother, 266–79; Archie Brown, 'The Change to Engagement in Britain's Cold War Policy: The Origins of the Thatcher–Gorbachev Relationship', *Journal of Cold War Studies* 10, No. 3 (Summer 2008): 3–47.

[173] See 'Soviet Union: FCO Minute for Powell ("Prime Minister's Message to Gorbachev")', 21 November 1986, TNA, PREM 19/3548.

'contemplate a conference on human contacts in Moscow while the Soviet Union's record on human rights remains as bad as it is'.[174] As Charles Powell, Thatcher's Private Secretary, relayed: 'Only when we have a much clearer idea of what commitments the Russians are ready to undertake on human rights and contacts – and in [the Prime Minister's] view, they would have to be much firmer than anything hitherto seen – should we be prepared even to consider it.'[175]

In respect to the close attention she paid to the human rights issue in the context of the East–West dialogue, Thatcher was, at this point, actually taking the lead within NATO. In fact, it was Thatcher who urged President Reagan not to commit to the Moscow human rights conference until the Soviets 'match[ed] words with actions', and although the New Year witnessed her government grant its assent, 'in principle', to the Moscow conference, doubts regarding the commitment of Britain's allies persisted within Thatcher's Private Office.[176] Correspondence between Thatcher and Powell, moreover, bears witness to the fact that the Prime Minister raised these concerns in Washington, and hoped to lay the foundations of an Anglo-American bulwark with a view to establishing the Western position on the subject of the Moscow conference.[177] Although Britain's NATO allies would eventually lend their support to the Anglo-American approach that Thatcher had orchestrated, her attempts to enlist the support of other allied leaders in this endeavour were seemingly complicated by her perceived inflexibility.[178]

Though the collapse of the Berlin Wall and the dissolution of the bi-polar Cold War order was not something Thatcher thought she would have to grapple with during her premiership, it is therefore unsurprising to find that she was quick to identify the opportunities this presented regarding the consolidation of her human rights vision within the apparatus of the CSCE.[179] In anticipation of Thatcher's speech marking the fortieth anniversary of the Aspen Institute in August 1990, for instance, Powell described the Prime Minister's far-reaching ambitions. 'The purpose' of the speech, he confided in Stephen Wall, 'will be to set out a wider vision of Europe and its role, the

---

[174] C.D. Powell to Lyn Parker, 'CSCE: Western Strategy', 2 October 1987, TNA, PREM 19/3174.
[175] Ibid.
[176] 'Cold War: Ridgeway Briefing for Shultz ("Your Meeting with Prime Minister Thatcher, 16 December at 11:00am")', 15 December 1987, US State Dept FOI 2006-01579, available at https://www.margaretthatcher.org/archive (accessed 13 January 2020); Cabinet Office to White House, 'Moscow Human Rights Conference', 3 January 1988, TNA, PREM 19/3174; C.D. Powell to Prime Minister, 'CSCE: Moscow Conference', 13 October 1988, TNA, PREM 19/3174.
[177] See C.D. Powell to Prime Minister, 'CSCE: Moscow Human Rights Conference', 19 October 1988, TNA, PREM 19/3714; Margaret Thatcher to Ronald Reagan, undated (c. October 1988), TNA, PREM 19/3174; White House to Cabinet Office, 28 October 1988, TNA, PREM 19/3714; J.S. Wall to C.D. Powell, 'CSCE: Moscow Human Rights Conference', 10 November 1988, TNA, PREM 19/3174.
[178] See 'Europe: US State Dept Briefing (Fact Sheet: Conference on Security and Cooperation in Europe (CSCE)', 15 November 1988, US State Dept FOI 2006-01579, available at https://www.margaretthatcher.org/archive (accessed 13 January 2020); 'Italy: Charles Powell Conversation Record (MT – De Mita, Howe and Andreotti Joining Later)', 21 October 1988, TNA, PREM 19/3410.
[179] McNally interview: 'On the day the Berlin Wall fell I was in a conference in Berlin where we had been discussing the future of East–West relations ... our Foreign Office briefing which was very much the line Mrs Thatcher took at the time was that German unity was a 21st-century issue.'

direction in which we want to see Europe move and how we see relations between Europe and the United States. It should relate [to] developments in the Community or those in NATO, the CSCE and East/West relations more generally, to present an overall vision of – or design for – the future of Europe'.¹⁸⁰ As John Hibbs reported in the *Daily Telegraph* after the event, Thatcher's Aspen address – which she regarded as 'her most important foreign policy speech since taking office' – outlined 'an agenda for international co-operation in the next century based on extending the principles of free trade, democracy and the rule of law into the former Communist bloc'.¹⁸¹ To this end, the Prime Minister had 'called on the leaders of the 35 nations who will assemble for the East–West summit in the autumn, including the Soviet Union, to sign a European "Magna Carta"'.¹⁸² This reframing of a deeply rooted British cultural landmark within a broader European setting – which once again attests to the existence of specific human rights vernaculars reflective of distinctive national debates and traditions – caught the attention of Michael Howard, who suggested that this historical reference was ill advised, carrying as it did certain political connotations:

> The American setting explains much, including no doubt the reference to Magna Carta: an archaic and ambiguous document that means little to our European partners but has long been an indispensable part of Anglo-Saxon political myth ... But as Magna Carta was concerned with limiting the powers of the central government rather than enhancing them, it was an appropriate reference point for the prime minister. 'A Europe which rejects central control and its associated bureaucracy' is language of which the barons at Runnymede would thoroughly have approved. Yet when she presents her ideas at the autumn summit on co-operation and security in Europe, Mrs Thatcher should think of a historical analogy more intelligible in Paris, Prague, Warsaw and Rome.¹⁸³

But Thatcher was not particularly interested in utilising human rights as a means of unifying disparate political cultures. Rather, as her visits to Eastern Europe that followed shortly thereafter made abundantly clear, her vision of a post-Cold War Europe – and the European 'Magna Carta' in which its guiding principles were to be enshrined – was very much in keeping with the neoliberal preoccupations that had animated her ministries since her election in 1979. Indeed, as Thatcher explained, first in Czechoslovakia and then in Hungary, any financial aid akin to a European Marshall

---

[180] C.D. Powell to J.S. Wall, 'Aspen Institute: Prime Minister's Speech', 2 May 1990, TNA, PREM 19/3136.
[181] John Hibbs, 'Thatcher proposes EC membership and Magna Carta for new democracies', *Daily Telegraph*, 6 August 1990.
[182] Ibid.
[183] Michael Howard, 'Thatcher vision in need of deeds', *The Times*, 7 August 1990. Regarding the significance of nation-specific ideational frameworks in which human rights debates have become situated, see for example Bradley, 'American Vernaculars'; Patrick Schmidt and Simon Halliday, 'Introduction: Socio-Legal Perspectives on Human Rights in the National Context', in *Human Rights Brought Home*, ed. Schmidt and Halliday, 1–21; Moores, *Civil Liberties and Human Rights in Twentieth Century Britain*.

Plan would only be provided to the former Soviet states if they were to move towards the establishment of market economies and 'push ahead with privatisation'.[184]

Following Powell's insistence that Thatcher's public statements concerning the European Magna Carta ought to be fleshed out prior to the CSCE Summit to be held in Paris (19–21 November), a draft document, the 'Charter of European Human Rights and Freedoms', was circulated in October.[185] The aim of this exercise, Richard Gozney relayed, 'has been to draft a short, politically binding statement ... to build a bridge between the CSCE and the [European] Convention [on Human Rights]'.[186] Upon viewing the draft, however, Thatcher commented that the language of the draft was 'too sterile', and the 'list of freedoms more restrictive' than those mentioned in her Aspen speech.[187] There was 'no mention, for example, of the freedom of the market place, freedom to maintain nationhood, and freedom from fear of an over-mighty State'.[188] With this criticism in mind, Gozney pushed forward, determined to 'graft this Charter onto the CSCE text on "Democracy and the Rule of Law", replacing the major part of the existing text with our own'.[189] To 'secure a separate section with its own heading, within the Summit document' would be 'a distinctly British achievement which we could justifiably refer to as a European Magna Carta'.[190]

Following lengthy negotiations, the British delegation, headed by Brian Crowe, succeeded in doing just that.[191] As such, the Summit Final Document, 'the vehicle for the leaders of the 34 to give formal endorsement to the principles which have been supported by the peoples of Central and Eastern Europe', enumerated not only 'political rights', but also committed 'the 34 to liberal economic values, and to the continued transformation of command economies into market economies, thereby facilitating integration of the reforming economies of Eastern Europe and the international economic system'.[192] Although Thatcher's attendance at the Paris Summit at which the 'Charter of Paris for a

---

[184] See George Jones, 'Thatcher points way forward to Czechs', *Daily Telegraph*, 18 September 1990; George Jones, 'Thatcher resists Marshall Plan for East', *Daily Telegraph*, 21 September 1990. Regarding the establishment of a connection between human rights and free-market economics within Whitehall, see also A.R. Brenton, 'Human Rights and Democratic Development', 14 February 1990, TNA, FCO 58/5546; W.R. Tomkys to Mr Brenton, 'Human Rights Guidance for Posts', with attached excerpt from policy guidelines draft, 9 April 1990, TNA, FCO/5546; J.W. Watt, 'Human Rights in Foreign Policy: Guidelines for Posts and Departments', with attached draft, 27 July 1990, TNA, FCO/5546.

[185] C.D. Powell to Richard Gozney, 'CSCE: European Magna Carta', 25 September 1990, TNA, PREM 19/3314.

[186] Richard Gozney to C.D. Powell, 'CSCE: European Magna Carta', 11 October 1990, TNA, PREM 19/3314.

[187] Charles Powell to R.H.T. Gozney, 'CSCE: European Magna Carta', 14 October 1990, TNA, PREM 19/3314.

[188] Ibid.

[189] R.H.T. Gozney to C.D. Powell, 'CSCE: European Magna Carta', 18 October 1990, TNA, PREM 19/3314.

[190] Ibid.

[191] See R.H.T. Gozney to C.D. Powell, 'CSCE European Magna Carta', 29 October 1990, TNA, PREM 19/3314; Brian Crowe, Vienna to FCO Telno 368, 'CSCE Paris Summit', 13 November 1990, TNA, PREM 19/3314.

[192] J.S. Wall to C.D. Powell, 'CSCE Summit: Paris, 19–21 November', 16 November 1990, TNA, PREM 19/3314.

New Europe' was signed will forever be associated with her inglorious departure from domestic politics, as it pertains to the trajectory of human rights in international relations, the Paris Charter perhaps ought to be remembered as her final triumph – the unequivocal reinstatement of the individual's civil and political rights above concepts of collective socio-economic rights, and the consummation of the relationship between human rights and free-market economics following a decade of unwavering commitment to the elevation of human rights considerations within the CSCE.[193]

Conclusion

It is a widely held belief that the CSCE, and the human rights provisions codified therein, played a key role in expediting the Western victory in the Cold War. This interpretation of events has been upheld by diplomats who worked within the CSCE framework and, somewhat unsurprisingly, by the CSCE's successor, the Organization for Security and Cooperation in Europe (OSCE).[194] Nicolas Badalassi and Sarah Snyder's recently published co-edited volume on the CSCE does not deviate from this received wisdom, positing that 'the CSCE succeeded in giving human rights a prominent place in international relations', allowing the 'Soviet powers to recognize the legitimacy of a dialogue on a subject that went against the values and practices of the Eastern bloc'.[195] This chapter, it could be argued, has gone some way towards supporting this notion, or the very least illuminating it from a hitherto underappreciated perspective. The idea that human rights could be used as a stick with which to beat the Soviet Union clearly appealed both to David Owen during his tenure as Foreign Secretary, and to Margaret Thatcher during her occupancy of No. 10 Downing Street. This point of consensus, it has been suggested, not only had the effect of elevating human rights among Britain's diplomatic imperatives; it served to keep them on the agenda, irrespective of the Conservative reorientation of foreign policy that followed the general election of 1979. The preceding paragraphs, however, have hopefully demonstrated that we ought to specify what *kind* of human rights victory the CSCE achieved, and *at what cost*?

Looking beyond their common weaponization of human rights within the context of the CSCE, it is clear that within the Callaghan government, human rights held a different meaning than it did within the Thatcher ministries. Owen, alongside fellow Labour ministers Frank Judd and Judith Hart, viewed human rights – both civil/

---

[193] While Thatcher was in Paris, she received the news that she had not secured enough votes in the first round of the Conservative Party's leadership election to maintain her position. A further round of voting was required. Realizing that her position was untenable in the face of growing internal opposition, Thatcher resigned as Prime Minister shortly thereafter.

[194] See for example Andrew Carter interview with Jimmy Jamieson, 20 October 2006, BDOHP, available at https://www.chu.cam.ac.uk/media/uploads/files/Carter.pdf (accessed 10 January 2020); Alexander, BDOHP interview; Organization for Security and Cooperation in Europe, '35 years from the Helsinki Final Act', 31 March 2011, available at https://www.osce.org/secretariat/104605 (accessed 10 January 2020).

[195] Nicolas Badalassi and Sarah B. Snyder, 'Conclusion', in *The CSCE and the End of the Cold War*, ed. Badalassi and Snyder, 354.

political and social/economic – as being indivisible, a conception that necessitated engagement with the East–West *and* North–South dialogues. Margaret Thatcher, however, clearly held civil and political rights to be paramount and consequently exhibited a more circumscribed human rights agenda, focusing unerringly on its Cold War applications. As the 1980s progressed, and the association between human rights and the East–West dialogue became more exclusive, partly on account of the policies pursued by the Thatcher governments, Owen came to embrace humanitarianism as a movement more capable of furthering a common understanding of humanity by tackling the pressing issues facing the developing world. The ways in which the ICIHI's operations both drew from human rights discourse and reflected the emergence of the 'new humanitarianism', moreover, serve to shed light on the 'entangled' histories of human rights and humanitarianism. Recent explorations of the relationship between the twin trajectories of human rights and neoliberalism since the human rights 'breakthrough' of the 1970s, however, have demonstrated that the grandiose visions of economic distributive justice advanced, in part, through the language of human rights by the ICIHI – and formerly by proponents of the NIEO – belong to a bygone era. Although the broad scope of this chapter has precluded a forensic post-mortem investigation into the demise of such aspirational human rights visions, it would appear that the institutionalization of Thatcher's human rights vision within the apparatus of the CSCE, at the very least, should be regarded as a portentous development – a harbinger of the era of 'downsized ambition' in which human rights has 'conformed to the political economy of the age, not defining it but reflecting it'.[196]

Indeed, the intersection of human rights and free market ideals has been clearly observed in the construction of the Paris Charter. Adopted at the CSCE summit in November 1990, this document was, in many respects, symbolic of a post-Cold War optimism that envisaged human rights – albeit infused with neoliberal presuppositions – occupying a more prominent role in interstate relations. Academics affiliated with the OSCE, however, have recently reflected on the transitory nature of such hopes: 'The vision of a new European security architecture, based on cooperative and inclusive security and partnership between the former Cold War enemies, did not stand the test of the 1990s, with the Soviet Union collapsing and ethnic conflicts leading to the Balkan Wars and protracted conflicts in the post-Soviet sphere.'[197] The following chapter will address the human rights implications of these cataclysmic changes, exploring through Owen's eyes the protracted development of a so-called 'New World Order' during the post-Cold War period. Owen, it shall be demonstrated, was not merely reflective of the times; he can in fact be identified as a key actor within an emerging zeitgeist that, by the turn of the new century, had shaped concepts of global governance and established the centrality of collective security and human rights protections therein.

---

[196] Moyn, *Not Enough*, 8.
[197] Christian Nunlist (principal author), Juhana Aunesluoma, Benno Zogg, 'The Road to the Charter of Paris: Historical Narratives and Lessons for the OSCE Today', OSCE Network of Think Tanks and Academic Institutions, Vienna, December 2017, 4, available at http://osce-network.net/file-OSCE-Network/Publications/Road_to_the_Charter_of_Paris_final_report.pdf (accessed 20 November 2019).

5

Lessons from the Balkans

On the Protracted Development of a New World Order

Beginning on 24 March 1999, the airstrikes undertaken by North Atlantic Treaty Organization (NATO) forces in Kosovo in order to bring an end to the ethnic cleansing of the Albanian population by Yugoslav forces quickly came to be seen as a turning point in international relations, ushering in a 'new era' in the enforcement of human rights.[1] This was, in Václav Havel's estimation, 'probably the first war ever fought ... in the name of certain principles and values ... an important precedent for the future'.[2] It is unsurprising, therefore, to find that Stefan-Ludwig Hoffmann's attempt to 'push the historiographical revisionism of Moyn and others even further' by arguing that human rights only became an 'irreplaceable and consequential concept of global politics' during the 1990s cites Operation Allied Force as a symptom of this epochal rupture.[3] According to Hoffmann, the conflict in Kosovo not only represented 'the first test case for the new belief in military intervention in the name of human rights' – the 'most important motifs for the new human rights idealism' can also be identified in the justifications underpinning NATO's operations, namely, 'the pre-eminence of individual human rights over the rights of states; reference to the genocidal policies of the Second World War', and 'global claims of human rights and the humanitarian state of emergency that, broadcast in the media, demand a reaction here and now'.[4]

The fundamental changes wrought to the global system by the collapse of the Cold War created an environment in which the notion of military intervention predicated on the violation of human rights abroad could achieve an unprecedented degree of influence in Western capitals.[5] Nonetheless, the development of what has been labelled

---

[1] Thorsten Gromes, 'A Humanitarian Milestone? NATO's 1999 Intervention in Kosovo and Trends in Military Responses to Mass Violence', *Peace Institute Frankfurt/Leibniz Institut Hessische Stiftung Friedens – und Konfliktforschung* (PRIF Reports, 35), 2019, 1. See also Chandler, *From Kosovo to Kabul*; Aiden Hehir, *Humanitarian Intervention After Kosovo: Iraq, Darfur and the Record of Global Civil Society* (Basingstoke: Palgrave Macmillan, 2008).
[2] Václav Havel, 'Address to the Senate and the House of Commons of the Parliament of Canada', 29 April 1999, quoted in Gromes, 'A Humanitarian Milestone?' 1.
[3] Stefan-Ludwig Hoffmann, 'Human Rights and History', *Past and Present* 232 (August 2016): 282.
[4] Ibid.: 295–6.
[5] See for example Jan Eckel, 'Humanitarian Intervention as Global Governance: Western Governments and Suffering "Others" Before and After 1990', in *Human Rights and Humanitarian Intervention: Legitimizing the Use of Force since the 1970s*, ed. Norbert Frei, Daniel Stahl and Annette Weinke (Göttingen: Wallstein Verlag, 2017), 64–88.

the 'humanitarian interventionist norm' during the post-Cold War period was undoubtedly a painful and drawn-out process.[6] As Hoffmann duly points out, the urgency with which Western democracies embraced intervention in Kosovo can only be explained by the 'protracted hesitation of the European Union and the United States to intervene in the bloody break-up of Yugoslavia (as well as by past failed interventions and the reluctance to intervene in other humanitarian catastrophes of the 1990s in Somalia, Rwanda and East Timor)'.[7] Indeed, whereas Tony Blair's prominent leadership role in the midst of the Kosovo conflict was seen by some contemporary commentators as a reflection of the 'aura of moral authority' and 'sense of mission' he and his government wished to portray on the international stage ('a self-image of the ethical new Britain bestriding the world'), coverage of British policy during the break-up of the former Yugoslavia earlier in the decade makes clear that pretentions to moral leadership did not feature prominently in the machinations of Whitehall.[8] For example, in their recently published study, Mark Garnett, Simon Mabon and Robert Smith contend that while Britain's reluctance to intervene in the face of Serbian aggression and expansionism in the Balkans (which resulted in the deaths of approximately 80,000 Bosnian Muslims and Bosnian Croats between 1992-5) was symptomatic of a much broader international ambivalence, 'it is entirely proper to note that its role was characterised by a singular lack of heroism'.[9] Brendan Simms provides an even more pointed analysis of the 'particularly disastrous role' played by Britain during the disintegration of the former Yugoslavia.[10] According to Simms, Britain's political leaders became afflicted with a 'disabling form of conservative pessimism which disposed them not only to reject military intervention themselves, but to prevent anybody else, particularly the Americans, from intervening either'.[11] In light of these excoriating commentaries, David McCourt's suggestion that British policymakers merely decided to 'drag their feet over the use of force in Bosnia from 1992' seems decidedly charitable.[12]

Owen, who was appointed as EU Co-Chairman of the International Conference on the Former Yugoslavia (ICFY) by the Major government in August 1992, witnessed this inertia and its paralysing effect at close quarters. The diplomatic initiatives pursued by Owen in this capacity, which largely revolved around his attempts to construct a peace settlement based on the division of Bosnia into several ethnic 'cantons' with his Co-Chairman Cyrus Vance, however, have also been subjected to harsh criticism. Indeed, Simms posits that between Owen's impassioned calls for the West to intervene militarily in Bosnia during the summer of 1992 and his decision to extricate himself

---

[6] Stephen Wertheim, 'A Solution from Hell: The United States and the Rise of Humanitarian Interventionism, 1991-2003', *Journal of Genocide Research* 12, No. 3-4 (September-December 2010): 154.
[7] Hoffmann, 'Human Rights and History': 293.
[8] Mick Hume, '"The war against the Serbs is about projecting a self-image of the new ethical Britain bestriding the world. It is a crusade"', *The Times*, 12 April 1999.
[9] Garnett, Mabon and Smith, *British Foreign Policy since 1945*, 250.
[10] Brendan Simms, *Unfinest Hour: Britain and the Destruction of Bosnia* (London: Penguin, 2002), xvii.
[11] Ibid.
[12] David McCourt, 'Embracing Humanitarian Intervention: Atlanticism and the UK Interventions in Bosnia and Kosovo', *British Journal of Politics and International Relations* 15, Issue 2 (May 2013): 246.

from the labyrinthine peace process in June 1995, Owen had accepted the conventional wisdom passed down from his political masters in Whitehall. He had, in other words, 'transmogrified' from a 'leading apostle' of limited but decisive military intervention to an embodiment of the prevailing realism – 'the personification of the West's broad diplomatic failure and moral surrender'.[13] While it is not the aim of this chapter to quarrel with Simms' characterization of the peace process and the role that Owen played in advancing, or indeed setting back the negotiations, as the case may be, it shall nonetheless be posited that a different picture of Owen's 'Balkan Odyssey' emerges when it is placed within its broader context.

Owen was certainly one of the most vocal proponents of Western military intervention in Bosnia during the early stages of the conflict – a conviction that was buttressed by his continued engagement with concepts of global governance following the dissolution of the Independent Commission on International Humanitarian Issues in 1987 and the Palme Commission on Disarmament and Security Issues in 1989. Although Owen certainly moderated his interventionist position during his tenure as EU Co-Chairman, the insidious 'education' he received courtesy of Her Majesty's Government did not serve to fully extinguish the crusading moralism he had exhibited prior to his appointment.[14] Rather, following his ignominious departure from the Balkans, Owen can clearly be situated within a broader interventionist milieu in which it is possible to observe the development of a protean 'Responsibility to Protect' (R2P) ethic. The lobbying efforts undertaken by Owen on behalf of the Carnegie Commission on Preventing Deadly Conflict (which ran from 1994–8), moreover, exerted a perceptible influence on key figures within the New Labour government of Tony Blair following its landslide victory in the general election of May 1997, shaping its attitudes towards conflict prevention and the reform of the United Nations' security architecture.

By exploring these developments, this chapter will, first and foremost, contribute to ongoing historiographical debates concerning chronologies of human rights history and the emergence of human rights norms in international affairs during the post-Cold War period. In so doing, this chapter will also continue to illuminate the complex relationship between concepts of human rights and humanitarianism in both theory and practice while highlighting the significant role played by international commissions and 'norm entrepreneurs' in the development of ethical considerations in the foreign policy arena.[15] Furthermore, by investigating how Owen sought to impart the lessons he had learned from his experiences in the Balkans upon the New Labour government, this chapter will offer a fresh perspective on debates surrounding the development of the R2P ethic within the context of British foreign policy, providing a crucial link between the shortcomings of British policy during the Bosnian War and the proactive liberal interventionist outlook that would later characterize New Labour's engagement with the global community.

---

[13] Simms, *Unfinest Hour*, 136, 137; Michael Sheridan, 'Mediators demand Serbs withdraw today', *Independent*, 12 August 1993, cited in ibid., 167–8.
[14] Simms, *Unfinest Hour*, 139.
[15] Dunne and Hanson, 'Human Rights in International Relations', 54.

'A "New World Order" was buried in the rubble of Vukovar'

As Owen recalls in his memoirs, he looked across St James's Park from the window of his London office on Wednesday 29 July 1992 with a sense of new-found freedom. Since the dissolution of the SDP two years earlier following a string of disastrous by-election results, Owen had continued to serve as an independent MP, but he had 'deliberately kept out of politics' since leaving the House of Commons prior to the April general election and was contemplating with some enthusiasm the prospect of a new career in international business.[16] As such, when Owen picked up the telephone to hear a young BBC researcher inviting him to comment on the discovery of Serbian prison camps in Bosnia-Herzegovina, he was reluctant to offer his perspective. Nonetheless, Owen – somewhat 'weakened' by the researcher's solicitation – left the door ajar by telling him to call back in the evening.[17] During the intervening period, Owen slowly began to reassess his self-imposed political exile: 'The researcher had mentioned in particular the *Guardian* story on the camps which I had read with shock that morning but had not fully absorbed, and so I read the *Guardian* exposé again and with more attention. It was a horrifying tale and as I read it I became angry.'[18] During a conversation with Foreign Secretary Douglas Hurd at a mutual friend's house in May, Owen had advised Hurd against putting British troops into Bosnia-Herzegovina, encouraging the Foreign Secretary to prioritize international diplomatic and peacekeeping initiatives through the European Community and the UN respectively.[19] Owen's position, however, was shifting in light of the grim reality laid bare by Maggie O'Kane's deeply affecting article: 'I was still against putting in troops on the ground, but the revelations coming from the camps showed that we were witnessing grotesque abuses of humanitarian law and that the Bosnian Serb leadership was failing to act to curb them despite the clamour of world condemnation.'[20]

In pondering the contradictory impulses with which Owen wrestled during this afternoon of introspection, it is worth highlighting that Owen's 'one exception to withdrawal from political activity' had been his chairmanship of Humanitas – a charity that Owen had established following the disbanding of the Independent Commission on International Humanitarian Issues (ICIHI) with the intention of 'building on' its achievements.[21] The work undertaken by Humanitas was largely educational in nature, including the development of major television documentaries and the planning of

---

[16] Owen, *Balkan Odyssey*, 5.
[17] Ibid.
[18] Ibid. For the story in question, see Maggie O'Kane, 'Muslims' nightmare under the hot Yugoslav sun', *Guardian*, 29 July 1992.
[19] Owen, *Balkan Odyssey*, 5–6.
[20] Ibid., 6.
[21] Ibid.; Bates, Wells & Braithwaite to The Charity Commission, 'Re: Humanitas', 15 October 1990, DOP, D709 5/4/2. Lord Owen recounted the establishment of Humanitas and detailed its genesis in the final days of the ICIHI at a 2017 event commemorating the thirtieth anniversary of the publication of the ICIHI's final report. See 'Winning Back the Human Race: The Legacy of the ICIHI', Chatham House, 14 November 2017, available at http://ibhi.org/wordpress1/conference-materials/ (accessed 19 November 2019).

school programmes on humanitarian issues.[22] The charity's 1990 'Report on Activities', however, also detailed a more ambitious policy-shaping aspect of its remit, which sought to facilitate communication between academic specialists, members of the media, and humanitarian practitioners. To this end, Humanitas established a series of seminars 'for journalists and documentary makers to meet with specialists on particular humanitarian issues for background briefings and exchanges of views', the first of which was held in April 1991.[23] Indeed, as Owen recalls, while he may have been reluctant to wade into the debate concerning the break-up of Yugoslavia, he was nonetheless 'mentally engaged in analysing what could be done in Bosnia' as a consequence of these activities.[24] It could also be argued that Owen's work with Humanitas was a constitutive aspect of a broader engagement with ideas concerning global governance, and that these ideas had been imbued with greater significance as the stifling orthodoxy of superpower rivalry gave way to a new 'unipolar' era.[25] In this respect, the significance of Owen's membership of the Palme Commission on Disarmament and Security Issues is also worth taking into consideration.

In Geoffrey Wiseman's estimation, the Palme Commission could justifiably claim to be a successful 'blue-ribbon commission' on account of its pioneering work surrounding the concept of 'common security', which attracted the attention of 'significant players in the policymaking process', not least Soviet Premier Mikhail Gorbachev.[26] As such, although the Commission – which published its report in 1982 – was a 'product of a particularly virulent chapter of the Cold War', Wiseman suggests that 'its ideas played no small part in helping to find a way out of that lamentable period in international affairs'.[27] Understandably, the Commission's final statement, issued in Stockholm on 14 April 1989, was at pains to point out the stark contrast between the frosty environment in which the Commission put down roots and the decidedly more propitious atmosphere in which its membership parted company:

> The Palme Commission on Disarmament and Security Issues concludes its work at a time when reason and common sense seem at last to be taking hold in the world. Long and bloody conflicts in several regions have been ended ... There seems to be a greater spirit of cooperation among countries. The United Nations has gained new respect and is again being used as an important instrument for peace. The current situation stands in striking contrast to the state of the world in 1980, when the Commission was established under the leadership of the late Prime Minister of Sweden, Olof Palme. At that time, relations between the United States

---

[22] 'Humanitas: Report on Activities, Fiscal Year 1990', DOP, D709 5/4/2.
[23] Ibid.
[24] Owen, *Balkan Odyssey*, 6.
[25] Charles Krauthammer, 'The Unipolar Moment', *Foreign Affairs* 70, No. 1 (1990–1): 23.
[26] Geoffrey Wiseman, 'The Palme Commission: New Thinking about Security', in *International Commissions and the Power of Ideas*, ed. Ramesh Thakur, Andrew F. Cooper and John English (New York: United Nations University Press, 2005), 67.
[27] Ibid., 69.

and the Soviet Union were deteriorating rapidly, heading toward a struggle reminiscent of the darkest moments of the Cold War.[28]

Far from resting on its laurels, however, the Commission urged its supporters to seize the opportunity to build on this prevailing spirit of international cooperation: 'In our opinion humanity in the final decade of the Twentieth Century has a historic opportunity to create a radically more peaceful and more humane world. This opportunity must not be missed; it may not reappear.'[29] Writing in the *Guardian* shortly thereafter, Owen echoed this sentiment. Appreciative of the Commission's contributions to international discourse yet wary of the potential transience of its message, Owen opined: 'many obstacles must be surmounted as the current sense of international opportunity is turned into concrete achievements. International hostilities and suspicions derived from decades of conflict and warfare cannot be erased overnight. But as they fade into history, a far better world – one with far less violence and far greater security for all – can be created'.[30]

It is possible to infer from these pronouncements a hint of the same millenarian optimism encapsulated by Francis Fukuyama's influential and divisive essay 'The End of History', published in *The National Interest* during the summer of 1989. Although Fukuyama did not mean to suggest that 'there will no longer be events to fill the pages of *Foreign Affairs*', his article posited that the soon-to-be confirmed triumph of the Western powers over the Soviet Union signalled the Hegelian 'end point of mankind's ideological evolution and the universalization of Western liberal democracy as the final form of human government'.[31] Humanity, Fukuyama suggested, had repudiated the 'paroxysm of ideological violence' that absolutist ideologies had inflicted upon the twentieth century and was heading towards a world based on a state system that is 'liberal insofar as it recognizes and protects through a system of law man's universal right to freedom, and democratic insofar as it exists only with the consent of the governed'.[32] Although, as we shall see, it did not take long for the shadow of ideological violence and the recapitulation of ancient rivalries to shroud such triumphalism, it nonetheless exerted an influence on the discourse of international relations that extended beyond the pages of academic journals and arcane periodicals. Indeed, during the first Gulf War of 1990–1, the US-led 'coalition of the willing' that successfully repelled Saddam Hussein's forces following his invasion of Kuwait was framed by President George H.W. Bush as the guarantor of a 'new world order – a world where the

---

[28] The Palme Commission on Disarmament and Security Issues, 'A World at Peace: Common Security in the Twenty-first Century', Stockholm, April 1989, DOP, D709 4/1/16.
[29] Ibid.
[30] David Owen, 'How to grasp the chance of peace', *Guardian*, 17 April 1989. For similar contributions from other members of the Palme Commission, see for example Cyrus Vance and James Leonard, 'The Palme Commission Showed the Way', *International Herald Tribune*, 31 May 1989, DOP, D709 4/1/7.
[31] Francis Fukuyama, 'The End of History?' *The National Interest* (Summer 1989): 1, available at https://www.embl.de/aboutus/science_society/discussion/discussion_2006/refl-22june06.pdf (accessed 20 November 2019).
[32] Ibid.: 1, 3.

rule of law, not the law of the jungle, governs the conduct of nations'.³³ Bush called upon the United Nations to embrace its peacekeeping role in order 'to fulfil the promise and vision of the UN's founders'.³⁴ In Europe, meanwhile, efforts were already being made to breathe life into the 'aspiration for a pan-European security architecture', with the FRG's Foreign Minister, Hans-Dietrich Genscher, and French President François Mitterand providing much of the impetus.³⁵

By dint of his engagements with Humanitas and the Palme Commission, Owen can therefore be situated within a much broader international zeitgeist which sought to capitalize upon the seismic shifts in the international order that accompanied the conclusion of the Cold War, believing (or at the very least *hoping*) that a more harmonious and secure global system was within reach. Therefore, when he was forced to scrutinize the stark reality of the bloody break-up of the former Yugoslavia on that Wednesday afternoon in July 1992, it is reasonable to suggest that Owen began to view the escalating crisis not in a vacuum, but as a litmus test of sorts for the humanitarian ethic and the concept of collective security that would hopefully flourish in the post-Cold War era. This would at least go some way towards explaining the verve with which Owen committed himself to a reassessment of the Bosnian problem after receiving the second telephone call from the BBC researcher. Owen accepted the invitation to appear on the *Today* programme the following morning and, with another emotive article concerning the situation in the camps fresh in his memory, used the broadcast to call upon John Major to bring NATO air power to bear on the Bosnian Serbs and impose a ceasefire.³⁶ 'Immediately afterwards', Owen recalls, 'I dictated a letter to John Major over the phone to my secretary and sent the final version by fax direct to No. 10 Downing Street, the *Evening Standard* and the Press Association, all before nine o'clock in the morning'.³⁷

This was not the first time that Owen had sought to impress his interventionist outlook upon the Prime Minister. He had, following the allied intervention in the Gulf, written to Major about 'the grotesque abuse of human rights' being carried out by Saddam Hussein's forces in Iraqi Kurdistan, begging the Prime Minister to 'uphold the good name and honour of the United Kingdom' by once again calling the Western allies into action.³⁸ Owen duly credited Major for putting sufficient pressure on the US administration to implement and enforce 'safe zones' in which Iraqi Kurds were spared further persecution.³⁹ In fact, in his letter of 30 July 1992, Owen invoked Major's

---

³³ George H.W. Bush, 'Address to the Nation Announcing Allied Military Action in the Persian Gulf', 16 January 1991, *Public Papers of the Presidents of the United States: George Bush, 1991, Book One* (Washington, DC: Government Printing Office, 1992), 44. For President Bush's first recorded reference to the creation of a 'new world order', see George H.W. Bush, 'The President's News Conference on the Persian Gulf Crisis', 30 August 1990, *Public Papers of the Presidents of the United States: George Bush, 1990, Book Two* (Washington, DC: Government Printing Office, 1991), 1179. Additional references can be found in ibid., 1219, 1332, 1669.
³⁴ Bush, 'Address to the Nation', 44.
³⁵ Nunlist, Aunesluoma and Zogg, 'The Road to the Charter of Paris'.
³⁶ 'BBC Radio Four Today Programme – 30 July 1992', DOP, D731 8/4/1. The article in question was featured in the *Daily Express*, 30 July 1992.
³⁷ Owen, *Balkan Odyssey*, 15.
³⁸ David Owen to John Major, 3 April 1991, DOP, D709 3/16/3/7.
³⁹ See for example David Owen, 'Building on Major's triumph', *The Times*, 12 April 1991.

Kurdish intervention as an honourable precedent before underscoring the gravity of the situation unfolding in the Balkans:

> Dear Prime Minister, Almost a year ago I wrote to you about the then threatened genocide of the Kurds in Northern Iraq. At that time the world community was wringing its hands and saying that nothing could be done. Fortunately you overrode the advice of the fainthearts, and championed the safe haven policy enforced by allied military power outside Iraq and then reinforced by a military presence inside Iraq. It is a sad commentary on our world that a situation even worse in humanitarian terms has now developed in what was Yugoslavia ... It is not an exaggeration to say that we are witnessing, 50 years on, scenes in Europe that mirror the early stages of the Nazi holocaust under the dreadful description of 'ethnic cleansing'. I urge you not to accept the conventional wisdom that nothing can be done militarily to stop the escalation of fighting and the continuation of such grotesque abuses of human rights.[40]

Owen's invocation of World War Two-era imagery was undoubtedly a hallmark of much media commentary during the summer of 1992, when the 'scenes of emaciated and terrified men confined to detention camps in north-western Bosnia and Herzegovina' were 'first discovered by Western reporters'.[41] While the 'dismal' history of genocide prevention since the signing of the Genocide Convention in 1948 had left little doubt that the lessons learned from the Holocaust – the 'never again' mentality – could be all too easily forgotten, such images revealed a harsh truth for Western spectators: 'What made Bosnia shocking was the revelation that the pledge was not even meant for Europeans.'[42]

Analogies concerning Operation Desert Storm and its aftermath, however, were – as Owen would later come to realize – of limited relevance and utility. As Matt Beech and Timothy J. Oliver point out, because the war raging in Bosnia was being contested by several competing factions battling for the control of the country, it presented a scenario 'loaded with humanitarian implications' that could not be reduced to a simple narrative of victims and aggressors.[43] As such, in 'comparison with the relative moral clarity and unity which evidenced itself in the response of the Conservative Party to the Gulf War, Bosnia would throw light on deep internal divisions within the party on the question of humanitarian intervention'.[44] Indeed, as Percy Cradock – who served as

---

[40] David Owen to John Major, 30 July 1992, reprinted in Owen, *Balkan Odyssey*, 15.
[41] Christian Axboe Nielsen, 'Surmounting the myopic focus on genocide: the case of the war in Bosnia and Herzegovina', *Journal of Genocide Research* 15, No. 1 (2013): 24. See also Stephen Harper, '"History is Screaming at Us": Humanitarian Interventionism and the Popular Geopolitics of the Bosnian War in Leigh Jackson and Peter Kominsky's *Warriors*', *Journal of European Popular Culture* 2, No. 1 (2011): 47–8.
[42] Scott Straws, 'Genocide and Human Rights', in *Human Rights*, ed. Goodhart, 352; Richard Falk, 'The Challenge of Genocide and Genocidal Politics in an Era of Globalisation', in *Human Rights in Global Politics*, ed. Dunne and Wheeler, 184.
[43] Matt Beech and Timothy J. Oliver, 'Humanitarian Intervention and Foreign Policy in the Conservative-led Coalition', *Parliamentary Affairs* 67, Issue 1 (January 2014): 106.
[44] Ibid.

John Major's Foreign Policy Adviser – recalls, simple answers to the Bosnian question were hard to come by:

> Could we talk in Iraq-Kuwait terms, in which case the predominant threat was Serbian aggression? Or were we still looking at a multi-faceted civil war with no clear lines of responsibility? ... I came to the unsatisfactory conclusion that while we were ready to concede that the federation was irretrievably fragmented, we still recoiled from the conclusion that international aggression was occurring.[45]

British interests, moreover, 'were not seriously threatened'.[46] Although rarely articulated in these stark terms, it did not take long for the Whitehall establishment to bring this reality to Owen's attention.

In fact, what Simms describes as Owen's insidious 'education' at the hands of the Major government began before the contents of his letter could be carefully considered by the Prime Minister. By the time Owen sat down for a lunch meeting with Stephen Wall, now Major's Private Secretary, a matter of hours had passed since he had dictated his message to the Prime Minister. Nonetheless, as the conversation between the two friends – who had worked in close proximity during Owen's tenure as Foreign Secretary – turned towards the topic of Yugoslavia, an atypical butting of heads resulted in Owen and Wall parting company after 'what diplomats would call a vigorous exchange of views'.[47] As Owen records: '[w]e normally agreed on major issues: but on this occasion we were at opposite poles.'[48] Wall, it would appear, provided a stern and convincing counterargument against Owen's calls for greater Western involvement.[49] The record of a meeting that took place between Major and Hurd that afternoon, moreover, makes clear that the official response to Owen's letter – and indeed to a similar letter sent by Margaret Thatcher – would be very much in keeping with Wall's cautionary tone and with Cradock's verdict that the complexities of the situation and its factional nature needed to be fully appreciated when formulating an approach.[50] This message was clearly conveyed in Major's reply, issued on 3 August:

---

[45] Percy Cradock, *In Pursuit of British Interests: Reflections on Foreign Policy under Margaret Thatcher and John Major* (London: John Murray, 1997), 187.
[46] Ibid.
[47] Owen, *Balkan Odyssey*, 18.
[48] Ibid., 17.
[49] Ibid.: 'We did not agree, but he undoubtedly dented some of my arguments. For instance, I did not have a good answer to the question [of] what NATO's response should be if Bosnian Serb soldiers, who were in some instances operating outside the formal command structure, ignored NATO air strikes and continued ethnic cleansing, killing Muslim prisoners.'
[50] 'Bosnia: Stephen Wall Record of Conversation (Major-Hurd)', 30 July 1992, TNA, PREM 19/3992: 'The Prime Minister and the Foreign Secretary discussed Yugoslavia this afternoon, particularly in the light of the letter which the Prime Minister had received from Lord Owen and the letter which the Foreign Secretary had received from Lady Thatcher ... The Foreign Secretary said that we were not dealing with an aggressive army pushing into Bosnia from Belgrade. We were dealing with local commanders, influenced by but not controlled by, nationalist leaders. We were not dealing with the armies or terrain that lent itself to the kind of response Lady Thatcher and Lord Owen had in mind.'

We have of course professionally studied the military implications which are more serious than you suggest. Air power would be unlikely to be enough. The numbers of forces involved, the likely length of operations and the level of casualties (civilian as well as military) would all be higher than you suggest. We are not dealing with an orthodox war, a single enemy, a front line, or clearly identifiable targets. Nor do I detect any support in Parliament or in public opinion for operations which would tie down large numbers of British forces in difficult and dangerous terrain for a long period.[51]

Although Whitehall's reluctance to become embroiled in Bosnia was at this stage deeply entrenched, across the Atlantic the debate surrounding intervention was far more protean. The question of what line to take over the Balkans would in fact become a prominent feature of the presidential election campaign in which President Bush was roundly criticized for his adoption of an isolationist position; his earlier proclamations of a 'New World Order' sounding decidedly hollow in retrospect.[52] Bush's Democratic opponent, Governor of Arkansas Bill Clinton, seized the initiative by making the case for US intervention. Prior to receiving the Democratic nomination, Clinton had been advised by foreign policy analyst (and later US Ambassador to NATO) Robert Hunter in June 1992 to take a stand on Bosnia. 'The continuing civil war in Yugoslavia', Hunter wrote, 'is posing a serious challenge, not just for US foreign policy, but for the promise contained at the end of the Cold War'.[53] While Western leaders seemed to hope that the conflict would somehow resolve itself, Hunter argued that 'there is a strong case for investing Yugoslavia with overwhelming military force – US-led, with forces being drawn from other NATO nations and even from the East, in order to stop the fighting'.[54] Days later, Clinton issued a public statement calling upon the Bush administration to reassess its approach.[55] This message was amplified on 4 August 1992: 'I am outraged by the revelations of concentration camps in Bosnia and urge immediate action to stop this slaughter ... The United States and the international community must take action. If the horrors of the Holocaust taught us anything, it is the high cost of remaining silent and paralyzed in the face of genocide.'[56] The United Nations, Clinton continued, 'should demand the release of all non-combatants into the custody of the ICRC and [the] immediate closing of any detention centers'.[57] These demands, moreover, 'should be backed up by collective action, including the use of force, if necessary. The United States should be prepared to lend appropriate support, including military, to such an operation'.[58]

---

[51] John Major to David Owen, 3 August 1992, reprinted in Owen, *Balkan Odyssey*, 19.
[52] See for example Anthony Lewis, 'The New World Order', *New York Times*, 17 May 1992.
[53] Memorandum from Robert Hunter to Bill Clinton, 23 June 1992, LOC, Anthony Lake Papers, Box 10, Folder 6.
[54] Ibid.
[55] See 'Statement by Governor Bill Clinton on the Crisis in Bosnia', 26 July 1992, LOC, Anthony Lake Papers, Box 10, Folder 7.
[56] 'Statement by Governor Bill Clinton on Killings in Serbian Camps', 4 August 1992, LOC, Anthony Lake Papers, Box 10, Folder 7.
[57] Ibid.
[58] Ibid.

Time, however, was very much of the essence – as Hunter confided to Clinton days prior to the opening of the London conference which established the ICFY, this would be 'the last chance for the outside world to take a stand'.[59] In hindsight, Hunter imbued the London conference, which took place across 26–7 August, with undue significance. It was, as one Washington insider present at the negotiations reported, little more than 'a face-saving charade for the United States, the United Nations and the European Community (in particular, Great Britain)'.[60] This interpretation of events was also shared by the State Department's former desk officer for Yugoslav affairs, who had recently resigned from this post 'in protest over the Administration's handling of this issue'.[61] It was becoming ever clearer that the political will simply did not exist in Western capitals to countenance military involvement in the former Yugoslavia. In the words of David Rieff, who spent a great deal of time in the Balkans during the conflict, the Bosnians would have to learn 'that there was no world order, old or new', that 'the principles developed half a century earlier when the UN was founded ... were really just a joke'.[62] This realization had seemingly not yet dawned on Owen by the time of his unlikely appointment as EU Co-Chairman of the ICFY in Lord Carrington's stead on 28 August. The writing, however, had long since been on the wall. In a reference to the shelling of a town in eastern Croatia from August to November 1991 by the Yugoslav People's Army which had failed to illicit any meaningful reaction among the Western allies, Owen would later lament that the promise of a more just, secure and humane global system that accompanied the Cold War's demise, had be rendered illusory long before that fateful afternoon of 29 July 1992. 'A "New World Order"', Owen expounded, 'was buried in the rubble of Vukovar'.[63]

'who better than me to take the flak?'

When Owen met with Lord Carrington on 30 August to discuss what lay ahead, his predecessor clearly spelled out the Sisyphean nature of the task he had just inherited: Carrington, 'even more than the press over the weekend, emphasized the scale of the problem facing me. Almost everyone believed that not much could be done to halt the fighting. The task was being labelled "mission impossible"'.[64] As Carrington discussed his dealings with European Foreign Ministers, and the decision that had been taken during a fractious European Community summit in December 1991 to recognize the

---

[59] 'Memorandum from Robert Hunter to Bill Clinton', 22 August 1992, LOC, Anthony Lake Papers, Box 10, Folder 7.
[60] 'Memorandum from Mike Chapman to Governor Clinton', 30 August 1992, LOC, Anthony Lake Papers, Box 10, Folder 7.
[61] Ibid. The State Department official mentioned here was George D. Kenney, who laid out the reasoning behind his resignation in an op-ed for the *Washington Post*. See George D. Kenney, 'Bosnia – Appeasement in Our Time', *Washington Post*, 30 August 1992.
[62] David Rieff, *Slaughterhouse: Bosnia and the Failure of the West* (New York: Touchstone, 1995), 21.
[63] 'Speech by the Rt Hon the Lord Owen to the Jerusalem Foundation Conference on "conflict resolution at the end of the 20th century – the international dimension"', 7 November 1994, DOP, D709 5/2/16 (part 1 of 2).
[64] Owen, *Balkan Odyssey*, 31.

independence of Croatia and Slovenia, Owen recalls that 'a hard edge came into his voice'.[65] His replacement would soon be able to empathize, as Owen too was forced to face up to the implications of an EC policy that would render the implementation of a swift and effective peace process all the more difficult. At the Hague, Owen received a briefing on the rejection of a Dutch proposal arguing for boundary changes that had been brought to the attention of EC Foreign Ministers during the Dutch presidency on 13 July 1991. This proposal, as Peter van Walsum explained to Owen during their meeting, 'was unanimously rejected' by ministers on the grounds that it was 'out of date to draw state borders along ethnic lines', and that to do so would potentially 'open a Pandora's box'.[66]

In Owen's view, the rejection of this proposal which effectively put paid to any suggestion of adopting a flexible approach to the border question, was 'a profound mistake' that would place severe limitations on negotiations moving forward: 'The refusal to make these borders negotiable greatly hampered the EC's attempt at crisis management in July and August 1991 and subsequently put all peacekeeping from September 1991 onwards within a straitjacket that greatly inhibited compromises between the parties in dispute'.[67] The decision to recognize the independence of Croatia and Slovenia – the result of a unilateral German initiative – had certainly flown in the face of conventional wisdom and the West's stated preference for keeping Yugoslavia intact.[68] The rejection of the Dutch proposal, however, would prove to be even more deleterious to the peace process as far as Owen was concerned:

> If the EC had launched a political initiative in August 1991 to address the key problem facing the parties to the dispute, namely the republics' borders, and had openly been ready to see an orderly and agreed secession of separate states in revised borders, then in conjunction with NATO a credible call could have been made for an immediate ceasefire ... It is in the first few days and weeks of a conflict developing that conflict resolution has its greatest chance of success. In July 1991 there was such an opportunity; once missed, it took until 1995 for war exhaustion to become the determining factor.[69]

To be sure, the EC's rejection of the Dutch proposal is noteworthy for the ways in which it served to vitiate diplomatic initiatives henceforth. But it is also possible to

---

[65] Ibid.
[66] A.P. van Walsum to Paul Sizeland, 3 September 1992, in *Bosnia-Herzegovina: The Vance/Owen Peace Plan*, ed. David Owen (Liverpool: University of Liverpool Press, 2013), 26. For a copy of the Dutch proposal, see The Hague COREU, 'The Second Stage of EPC Involvement', 13 July 1991, in ibid., 27–9.
[67] Owen, *Balkan Odyssey*, 34.
[68] See for example Beverly Crawford, 'Explaining Defection from International Cooperation: Germany's Unilateral Recognition of Croatia', *World Politics* 48, No. 4 (July 1996): 482–521; Stanley Hoffmann, 'Humanitarian Intervention in the Former Yugoslavia', in Stanley Hoffmann (with contributions from Robert C. Johansen, James P. Sterba and Raimo Väyrynen), *The Ethics and Politics of Humanitarian Intervention* (Notre Dame, Indiana: University of Notre Dame Press, 1996), 39. These anxieties are illuminated from a British perspective in Cradock, *In Pursuit of British Interests*, 185–7.
[69] Owen, *Balkan Odyssey*, 375–6.

draw a broader conclusion from this decision, which cast a spotlight on the lack of influence that appeals to human rights violations were able to exert within interventionist discourse at this juncture, highlighting the subservience of human rights imperatives to the well-established norm of Westphalian sovereignty.

It has been suggested that the dynamics of the Helsinki Process – which effectively pitted the Soviet preference for state sovereignty and the inviolability of borders against the Western insistence that a concern for human rights transcended national boundaries – not only expedited the Cold War's unexpected denouement, but also continued to exhibit a normative effect thereafter. Indeed, as posited recently by Nicholas Badalassi and Sarah Snyder, the significance of the CSCE and its codification of human rights concerns can only be appreciated fully in light of subsequent events which have continued to reflect the 'triumph of the transnational logic on which the Helsinki Process had been founded'.[70] As responses to the war in the former Yugoslavia demonstrated, however, far from representing an outdated impediment to the international protection of human rights, the sovereignty principle constituted an insurmountable obstacle that led to the prolongation of the conflict. Consequently, although clear-cut solutions to territorial questions in the Balkans were always fated to be illusory, the response of the international community has since been roundly criticized for its lack of 'flexibility' on the border issue, and for failing to 'offer ingredients for a compromise solution that would have given the nationalist leaders of the republics reasons to end the fighting'.[71]

In the 'infernal triangle' of sovereignty, self-determination and human rights, there were, in the words of Stanley Hoffmann, 'only bad choices' to be made.[72] Still, the Vance–Owen Peace Plan (VOPP) presented to the warring parties by Owen and his Co-Chairman representing the UN, Cyrus Vance, on 31 January 1993, constituted a 'valiant attempt to square the circle and rescue what could be rescued'.[73] In his efforts to implement the VOPP, which sought to establish ten semi-autonomous ethnic regions or 'cantons' within Bosnia-Herzegovina, however, Owen would find himself bereft of much-needed leverage.[74] The threat of force had been taken well and truly off the table by the decision to prioritize palliative humanitarian assistance – part of a 'compromise course' undertaken by the Major government when faced with the reality that intervention in the former Yugoslavia would likely mean the 'deployment of massive forces in very difficult terrain for an indefinite period' in what was deemed to be the 'Balkan equivalent of Northern Ireland'.[75]

---

[70] Nicholas Badalassi and Sarah B. Snyder, 'Introduction', in *The CSCE and the End of the Cold War*, ed. Badalassi and Snyder, 10.
[71] Raimo Väyrynen, 'Introduction: How Much Force in Humanitarian Intervention?' in Hoffmann et al, *The Ethics and Politics of Humanitarian Intervention*, 3.
[72] Hoffmann, 'Humanitarian Intervention in the Former Yugoslavia', 56.
[73] Simms, *Unfinest Hour*, 142.
[74] 'Text of the VOPP – 30 January 1993', University of Liverpool Special Collections & Archives, Balkan Odyssey Digital Archive (BODA), 1/3/4, available at https://sca-archives.liverpool.ac.uk/Record/5428#tree-5428 (accessed 1 December 2019).
[75] Craddock, *In Pursuit of British Interests*, 187-8.

Figure 5.1 The eponymous architects of the Vance–Owen Peace Plan (VOPP), 2 February 1993. Owen (left) had established a close working relationship with former US Secretary of State Cyrus Vance (right) during his tenure as Foreign Secretary (Rick Maiman/Getty Images).

The primacy of the humanitarian effort had been clearly underscored by Hurd during the London conference in August.[76] While he called for the closure of the detention camps, it was unclear how or why the Foreign Secretary thought this could be achieved by merely issuing strongly worded statements. 'While they do continue to exist', however, the Foreign Secretary was at pains to point out that 'international humanitarian agencies, notably the Red Cross, should, as UN Security Council Resolution 771 puts it, have "immediate, unimpeded and constant access" to them'.[77] This emphasis on the application of palliative humanitarian assistance in the face of unmistakable abuses of human rights was not merely symptomatic of a deeply entrenched realism in British foreign policy that had seemingly endured in spite of the steps taken by the Major government to further institutionalize human rights promotion as a diplomatic priority within the FCO.[78] Nor, for that matter, was this policy simply the latest manifestation of the historical reticence that European powers have exhibited when faced with Balkan conflicts.[79] Rather, it was also illustrative of the

[76] See 'Statement by Mr. Douglas Hurd, the Foreign Secretary of the United Kingdom', 26 August 1992, in *The International Conference on the Former Yugoslavia, Official Papers: Volume I*, ed. B.G. Ramcharan (The Hague/London/Boston: Kluwer Law International, 1997), 88.
[77] Ibid.
[78] See for example Gaskarth, 'Ethical Policies or Empty Promises?': 49–55.
[79] See for example Owen, *Balkan Odyssey*, 18: Owen recalls a telephone conversation with his godson, Andrew Gimson, which took place during the summer of 1992 in which Gimson reminded Owen of Otto von Bismarck's famed ambivalence towards the region. 'The Balkans', Bismarck stated, 'were not worth the healthy bones of a single Pomeranian grenadier'.

complex relationship between human rights and humanitarianism and how, in the words of Andrew Thompson, 'the promotion of the one has sometimes been (or at least perceived to have been) at the expense of the other'.[80]

As highlighted in the previous chapter, while the fundamental ideational separation of the two concepts is well established, recent years have nonetheless witnessed much gnashing of teeth over what many consider to be the insidious conflation of human rights and humanitarianism – a development that became particularly pronounced in Western responses to the terror attacks of 11 September 2001.[81] When it comes to justifying war, the 'ideology of our times', writes Jean Bricmont, 'is no longer Christianity, nor Kipling's "white man's burden" or the "civilizing mission" of the French Republic, but is a certain discourse on human rights and democracy, mixed in with a particular representation of the Second World War'.[82] If nothing else, the emphasis placed on the humanitarian effort in the Balkans by the Western powers was reflective of the fact that this controversial weaponization of human rights had not yet been normalized. Western recourse to humanitarian assistance also served to shed light on the human rights–humanitarian dialectic from an operational standpoint, as the prospect of military intervention was consistently ruled out in the belief that it would jeopardize the fulfilment of the humanitarian operation already taking place on the ground.[83] In the event, those administering the relief effort soon encountered the harsh reality that in such intra-state conflicts, and in the absence of an agreed ceasefire, 'local powerholders can obstruct the delivery of humanitarian aid and unduly benefit by confiscating it'.[84] As Sadako Ogata, UN High Commissioner for Refugees (UNHCR) reported to the UN Secretary-General on 15 January 1993, the delivery of humanitarian aid to those most in need was becoming increasingly problematic, with UNHCR workers encountering verbal and physical intimidation, arbitrary arrests, vehicle theft and harassment at checkpoints with increasing regularity.[85] Such misgivings, however,

---

[80] Andrew Thompson, 'Humanitarian Interventions, Past and Present', in *The Emergence of Humanitarian Intervention: Ideas and Practices from the Nineteenth Century to the Present*, ed. Fabian Klose (Cambridge: Cambridge University Press, 2016), 342.

[81] This development is encapsulated most poignantly in the writing of David Rieff who, having witnessed the carnage in Bosnia and lamented the unwillingness of the Western powers to intervene, later became a leading critic of intervention and its neo-colonial implications. See for example David Rieff, 'Save us from the rescuers', *Los Angeles Times*, 18 May 2008.

[82] Jean Bricmont, *Humanitarian Imperialism: Using Human Rights to Sell War* (New York: Monthly Review Press, 2006), 20.

[83] For an overview of the tension between the protection of human rights and the provision of humanitarian assistance – and a brief analysis of how these contradictory dynamics were illustrated by the international response to the Bosnian conflict – see Alan J. Kuperman, 'Humanitarian Intervention', in *Human Rights*, ed. Goodhart, 370–88. See also Richard K. Betts, 'The Delusion of Impartial Intervention', *Foreign Affairs* 73, No. 6 (November/December 1994): 20–33.

[84] Väyrynen, 'Introduction', 8. For more sustained coverage of the humanitarian dilemmas (both relating to issues of principle and logistical concerns) that peacekeepers were increasingly confronted by during the intra-state conflicts of the post-Cold War era, see also Norrie MacQueen, 'Cold War Peacekeeping versus Humanitarian Intervention: Beyond the Hammarskjöldian Model', in *The Emergence of Humanitarian Intervention*, ed. Klose, 250–1; Alex J. Bellamy and Paul D. Williams with Stuart Griffin, *Understanding Peacekeeping*, 2nd edn (Cambridge: Polity Press, 2010), 93–111.

[85] 'Letter from Sadako Ogata, UN High Commissioner for Refugees to UN Secretary-General, 15 January 1993', in *Bosnia-Herzegovina*, ed. Owen, 233–4.

did not provoke a change of policy – the humanitarian effort, it would appear, provided a useful shield that could deflect public outrage and calls for a greater degree of Western military involvement in the crisis. This became particularly apparent in the official response to those advocating air strikes to back up the diplomatic effort – an idea that David Owen would repeatedly champion.

In anticipation of the VOPP's unveiling, for example, Owen pressed Major to consider the possibility that military measures could be taken in order to curb the aggression of the Bosnian Serb forces, forcing them to reconsider their reluctance to engage with the peace process. Such measures would not extend to the use of ground troops – there were already 'more than enough forces fighting each other'.[86] All that was needed to 'tilt the balance against the Serbs and in favour of the Muslim and Croatian forces on the ground', Owen opined, was the 'selective use of air power'.[87] Owen went on to state this position publicly on several occasions as he sought to drum up support for the peace plan bearing his name.[88] This was a proposition, moreover, that developed considerable momentum during the spring of 1993, due in no small part to the support it received from Baroness Thatcher, who had been conspicuously absent from public discourse since her resignation as leader of the Conservative Party in November 1990. When asked by the BBC's Peter Sissons on 13 April whether a 'Western ultimatum' supported by a 'clear threat of military intervention' should be delivered to the Serbs, Thatcher responded enthusiastically in the affirmative: 'The present policy of humanitarian aid plus negotiation plus trying to get a ceasefire clearly hasn't worked ... We can't go on with this policy: namely feeding people but leaving ... the innocent to be massacred ... The West, by not doing more, has been a little like an accomplice to massacre.'[89] Thatcher's intervention had, according to journalist David Wastell, 'contributed to a shift in terms of the argument' pertaining to military intervention.[90] Indeed, her example was invoked in a Commons debate that took place the following day – she had, in the words of Labour MP Tony Banks, 'articulated the deep anger and frustration' that many people felt towards the apparent inability of current policy to engender any improvement of the situation in Bosnia.[91] Secretary of State for Defence Malcolm Rifkind, however, was unmoved, citing in his defence of government policy the principle of humanitarian impartiality.[92]

Nonetheless, it appeared that international opinion, too, was beginning to entertain the notion of limited military intervention in order to break the deadlock. On 18 April,

---

[86] 'Draft Letter from David Owen to Prime Minister John Major', prepared on 18 January 1993 but not sent, in *Bosnia-Herzegovina*, ed. Owen, 260. Although this message was not sent, it was used as a speaking note by Lord Owen for a seminar that took place at 10 Downing Street on 22 January 1993.
[87] Ibid.
[88] See for example Anthony Lewis, interview with David Owen, 3 February 1993, LOC, Anthony Lewis Papers, Box II: 575; 'The Future of the Balkans: An Interview with David Owen', *Foreign Affairs* 72, No. 3 (Spring 1993): 1–9.
[89] '"Europe has been like an accomplice to massacre"', *The Times*, 14 April 1993 (edited transcript of Thatcher's BBC interview with Peter Sissons, broadcast on 13 April 1993).
[90] David Wastell, 'The grand old lady stirs it up', *Sunday Telegraph*, 18 April 1993.
[91] 'Bosnia debate in Commons Chamber', 14 April 1993, *Hansard: House of Commons*, Volume 222, Column 836.
[92] Ibid.

the British Embassy in Washington reported that a meeting of senior US policymakers had been 'sympathetic to Lord Owen's call for air strikes', which he had coincidentally reiterated that day during an interview with David Frost.[93] This was followed on 19 April by a report from the UK's Embassy in Brussels detailing the alteration of the Belgian Foreign Minister's position, which now countenanced the possibility of limited military involvement as a means of countering Serbian intransigence.[94] This sentiment was also echoed by Spanish ministers and by the EC Commissioner, Hans van den Broek.[95] Such momentum, however, would not prove to be decisive in 'crucial capitals like London, Washington or Paris'.[96] As Douglas Hurd contemporaneously sought to underscore the humanitarian implications of the suggested alternatives, UK policy remained unchanged:

> There have been calls for removal of the mandatory United Nations arms embargo against the Bosnian Government ... There are also advocates of air strikes against selected Serb targets as a way of putting further pressure on the Serbs to sign the Vance–Owen plan and, indeed, to reduce the risk of attacks on further Muslim enclaves ... We have considered the options again this morning. We must take account of the view of our military advisers that such strikes would probably have only limited military value unless supported by troops on the ground, given the nature of the terrain and the nature of the conflict. We must take into account the high risk of civilian casualties ... We shall stay in touch with our allies and partners, but we should not go down this or any other route without a reasonable judgement that it would do more good than harm. We should not lightly jeopardise the continued humanitarian role played by the United Nations and by our own forces.[97]

Such argumentation clearly chimes with David Rieff's critique of Western policy. From his vantage point at the epicentre of the Balkan conflict, Rieff quickly developed an understanding that this emphasis on the humanitarian efforts undertaken by aid workers under the banner of the UN and myriad NGOs was serving 'as a pretext behind which the great powers – aka the international community could hide'.[98] Whenever the call was made for greater military involvement, be it in France, Britain or the United States, 'the government ministers of the countries in question, and, with more authority, representatives of the United Nations, who were perceived as having an objectivity about Bosnia ... would quickly insist that the reason no intervention was

---

[93] 'Report from UK Embassy, Washington, on US Administration view on Bosnia, 18 April 1993', in *Bosnia-Herzegovina*, ed. Owen, 388; 'Extract of Lord Owen's interview on BBC "Breakfast with Frost"', 18 April 1993', in ibid., 382.
[94] 'Report by UK Embassy, Brussels, on Belgian views on Bosnia, 19 April 1993', in ibid., 395.
[95] See 'Report from UK Embassy, Madrid, on possible Spanish participation in air strikes against the Serbs, 19 April 1993', in ibid., 397; 'Report from UKREP, Brussels on comments by EC Commissioner, Van den Broek, on use of force, 19 April 1993', in ibid., 398.
[96] David Owen, editorial note in ibid., 292.
[97] 'Bosnia debate in Commons Chamber', 19 April 1993, *Hansard: House of Commons*, Volume 223, Column 22-3.
[98] Rieff, *Slaughterhouse*, 14.

possible was that it – we soon assimilated the phrase as one might a mantra – "would compromise the humanitarian effort".[99] The Western powers' convenient championing of the humanitarian effort was also castigated by leading humanitarians such as Secretary-General of Médecins Sans Frontières, Alain Destexhe. 'In short', Destexhe argued, 'humanitarianism has served as an alibi for political impotence. It has never been further removed from what it asserts itself to be: a significant gesture of fraternity and hope. When the accounts are drawn up, when we finally know Bosnia's fate, humanitarianism will find itself sitting in the dock with the accused'.[100] In Destexhe's reckoning, the crimes against humanity committed in Yugoslavia were compounded by another grievous offence: 'the major European political authorities have committed a crime against humanitarianism itself that they will never have to account for by using it to play a role diametrically opposed to its real vocation and principles'.[101]

Owen's enduring commitment to the principle of enforcing his peace treaty with the threat of air strikes should at the very least absolve him of these charges. Indeed, his hawkishness was such that it raised the hackles of the Bosnian-Serb leadership, who called for the EU to remove Owen from his post and find a less bellicose replacement.[102] It came to Owen's great surprise, therefore, to learn that the VOPP was rapidly falling out of favour in Washington; regarded by many as an unsatisfactory agreement that favoured the Serbs by recognizing much of their war gains.[103] Although it was the Serbs themselves who eventually torpedoed the VOPP in June 1993 when the Serbian parliament voted to overturn the decision of its president Radovan Karadzic to accede to the agreement, Owen nonetheless places a great deal of responsibility at the feet of the Clinton administration (which had taken office in January 1993) for depriving it of much-needed support.[104] Cyrus Vance resigned as UN negotiator following the demise of the VOPP, but Owen remained a representative of the EU's diplomatic efforts in partnership with Vance's replacement, Thorvald Stoltenberg. The pair continued in their attempts to broker a peace deal, firstly in the shape of the EU Action Plan, finalized in December 1993, and subsequently by offering their support to the Contact Group made up of the US, the UK, France, Germany and Russia, which ran through to the summer of 1994. Owen, however, became an increasingly peripheral figure whose influence on proceedings diminished to such an extent that when he finally bowed out in June 1995, the *Financial Times* reported that his protracted resignation 'may have surprised some who did not realise he was still in the job'.[105]

---

[99] Ibid., 14–15.
[100] Dr. Alain Destexhe, 'Yugoslavia: The Placebo Effect, Looking at the Crisis from a Humanitarian Point of View' (translation by Alison Marschner of 'Yougoslavie: la politique de la bande velpeau' from *L'Humanitaire Impossible ou deux siecles d'ambiguite* by Alain Destexhe, published by Armand Collin, Paris, 1993), Brussels, June 1993, LOC, Anthony Lewis Papers, Box II: 606, Folder 2.
[101] Ibid. A similar analysis can be found in 'A text book written in blood', *Economist*, 26 February 1994.
[102] 'Political Sitrep from UK Embassy, Belgrade, 20/21 April 1993', in *Bosnia-Herzegovina*, ed., Owen, 403.
[103] See for example 'To Stand Against Aggression: Milosevic, The Bosnian Republic, and The Conscience of the West', A Report to the Committee on Foreign Relations, United States Senate, by Senator Joseph R. Biden, Jr., April 1993 (Washington, DC: US Government Printing Office, 1993), 1–9.
[104] See Owen, *Balkan Odyssey*, particularly Chapter Four: The Ditching of the VOPP.
[105] Edward Mortimer, 'Lord Owen: interview. An exit with one regret', *Financial Times*, 2 June 1995, cited in Simms, *Unfinest Hour*, 172.

By this point, moreover, Owen had well and truly become a scapegoat for the systemic failure of the Western nations to intervene in Bosnia. In the words of Jim Hoagland of the *Washington Post*, 'Owen will be the person we remember whenever the West's betrayal of Bosnia is mentioned in the future – even though many others deserve that honor as well'.[106] It is therefore to Owen's credit that he embraced this role with such equanimity in view of the fact that he was 'given the weakest possible hand to play' by his political masters: 'now I have no political ambitions[,] if a dirty deal has to be done and hundreds of thousands of lives saved, who better than me to take the flak?'[107] This is not to say that Owen's diplomatic efforts were beyond reproach; that his failings can be explained away or justified entirely by referring to the limitations placed on the peace process by UK policy or by Western passivity in a much broader sense. While there can be no doubt that Owen, in calling for greater British (and allied) involvement in the region, faced an insurmountable degree of inertia, it certainly took him a long time to realize 'something which any vaguely intelligent student of diplomacy could have told him in the beginning', namely, that without the 'stick' of military backing, any 'carrots' he would dangle in front of the warring parties would not have the desired effect.[108] If Lord Carrington had not sufficiently impressed upon his successor the unwillingness of the Major government to support his negotiations with the threat of force, Owen had begun to demonstrate an awareness of his isolated position by December 1992, when, exhibiting his famous capacity for bluntness, he beseeched the Bosnian public moments after landing at Sarajevo airport: 'Don't, don't, don't live under this dream that the West is going to come in and sort this problem out. Don't dream dreams.'[109] Owen, with the clarity afforded by hindsight, should have resigned, as Carrington had, as soon as this realization dawned, understanding that the task ahead was not merely impossible, but that he would inevitably become a lightning rod for criticism largely intended for those responsible for his appointment.

Owen, however, was determined to learn from his experiences in the Balkans and would continue to push back against the lethargy that had undermined his diplomatic endeavours between 1992 and 1995. In fact, long before Owen took the decision to step down as Co-Chairman of the ICFY, he had begun to contextualize his 'Balkan Odyssey' within much broader debates concerning humanitarian intervention and the effective resolution of armed conflicts. Such concerns were clearly present when Owen wrote to Anthony Lewis on 26 November 1993, extending an invitation to the *New York Times* journalist who had covered the Bosnian conflict with scarcely concealed moral outrage:

> I am writing to you in my capacity as chairman of HUMANITAS which is a small charitable trust, based in the UK, which has carried forward the work of the Independent Commission on International Humanitarian Issues – of which I was

---

[106] Jim Hoagland, 'Lord Owen's Betrayal', *Washington Post*, 10 August 1993.
[107] Ibid.; David Owen to Sir Derek Birkin, 14 September 1993, DOP, D709 5/2/10.
[108] Hoffmann, 'Humanitarian Intervention in the Former Yugoslavia', 49.
[109] Michael Adler, 'Owen Fear Beirut-Style Division of Sarajevo', Agence France-Presse, 19 December 1992, cited in Samantha Power, *A Problem from Hell: America and the Age of Genocide*, 2nd edn (London: Flamingo, 2003), 327.

a member – and which met from 1983–86... The Trustees of HUMANITAS have decided that a conference on the break up of [the] former Yugoslavia would be worth holding and to concentrate on people who were active participants in the peace process at some stage during the conflict, either as negotiators, politicians, peacekeepers, aid workers, diplomats or commentators.[110]

The primary function of this conference, Owen continued, was to uncover 'what mistakes were made and how can we learn from the experience for any future regional conflicts'.[111]

The 'high-water mark of humanitarian interventionism'

Representatives of several leading international humanitarian institutions made the journey to Leeds Castle, Kent, to attend the Humanitas summit that took place from 25–7 February 1994. Interspersed with prominent media representatives, academics, diplomats and policy experts, the list of conference delegates included Kofi Annan (then serving as UN Under-Secretary General for Peacekeeping Operations); Director of Operations for the International Committee of the Red Cross (ICRC), Jean de Courten; Wilbert Van Hovell, Senior Protection Officer for the UNHCR Special Operation on the Former Yugoslavia; and the aforementioned Secretary-General of Médecins Sans Frontières, Alain Destexhe. Reading Lewis's conference notes, one is immediately struck by the anger and incredulity that characterized participants' initial reflections on the passivity of the Western nations and their failure to support the peace process militarily. As the conference progressed, however, the implications of the conflict for the theory and practice of humanitarian intervention became more clearly visible.

Destexhe, who reiterated his contention that the humanitarian emphasis of allied operations had been 'little more than an alibi for not undertaking political or military intervention', was supported by Rosalyn Higgins, Professor of International Law at LSE, who had opposed 'humanitarian intervention from the start, because it would prevent forceful – more robust action'.[112] The deployment of armed escorts to accompany humanitarian conveys was also called into question on the grounds of efficacy and principle. 'The use of armed escorts for humanitarian convoys is very disturbing to us', stated De Courten on behalf of the ICRC: 'Open, independent + impartial – neutral... to all the combatants: Those are the principles for humanitarian relief – threatened by armed escorts. Mixing political negot[iations] + humanitairian[ism] will only politicize the latter'.[113] Destexhe, on the other hand, questioned the value of military protection for

---
[110] David Owen to Anthony Lewis, 26 November 1993, LOC, Anthony Lewis Papers, Box II: 606, Folder 3.
[111] Ibid.
[112] Anthony Lewis, 'Notes on Humanitas Conference on Former Yugoslavia, Leeds Castle, Great Britain, 25–27 February 1994', LOC, Anthony Lewis Papers, Box II: 606, Folder 2.
[113] Ibid.

convoys, painting them as impotent bystanders in the conflict: 'Force was in fact never used, so what was the point?'[114] This was also the verdict reached by Humanitas Trustee – and later speech-writer to Kofi Annan during his tenure as UN Secretary-General – Edward Mortimer, who concluded portentously: 'Three kinds of ops ... humanitarian, peacekeeping, mil[itary] intervention ... they suffer when mixed up. In Bosnia, sh[oul]d be more separate ... "Hum[anitarian] intervention" sh[oul]d mean strong mil[itary]-political intervention on hum[anitarian] grounds, not confining yourself to hum[anitarian] means.'[115]

In a sense, the Leeds Castle conference can be viewed, if not as a watershed moment in and of itself, at least as an indication of an incipient sea change in the discourse of humanitarian intervention. Indeed, Mortimer's desire to break free from the confines of humanitarian 'means' by normalizing military action on humanitarian 'grounds' can be seen to gain a great deal of international traction shortly thereafter. It was certainly the case that a 'turning point in the international debate over humanitarian intervention' was brought about by the climax of the conflict in the former Yugoslavia itself.[116] Following the massacre of thousands of Bosnian Muslims at the UN 'safe haven' at Srebrenica in July 1995 and the bombing of a crowded Sarajevo market weeks later, NATO launched a bombing campaign that would tilt the balance of power away from the Bosnian Serbs and bring about the signature of the Dayton Agreement in November 1995. Although military intervention had been long overdue, henceforth, 'Bosnia held out a vision of a "good intervention", the use of military power in defence of the defenceless, and the use of bombs to stop evil and genocide'.[117]

It would appear, however, that a more fundamental (albeit protracted) change to the discourse had already been set in motion by the genocide in Rwanda, and by the international community's struggle to come to terms with its inadequate response to the slaughter of approximately 800,000 Tutsi by the Hutu majority between April and July 1994. Whereas Samantha Power's seminal polemic *A Problem from Hell* (2002) lays bare a US political 'system' that had militated against intervention in the former Yugoslavia, Stephen Wertheim reveals that the horrors of the Rwandan genocide ushered in a new orthodoxy; one that not only normalized military intervention as a means of ameliorating suffering and tackling human rights abuses, but one that concomitantly came to underestimate the risks and difficulties inherent in such operations.[118] As this interventionist norm became more deeply entrenched, it brought together an unlikely alliance of humanitarians and hawkish neoconservatives, united in their calls for 'what might be called "transformative invasions"', and in the assumption

---

[114] Ibid.
[115] Ibid.
[116] Rory Stewart and Gerald Knaus, *Can Intervention Work?* (New York: W.W. Norton & Company, 2012), 118.
[117] Ibid., 119.
[118] See Power, *A Problem from Hell*, xx: 'A few diplomats at the State Department and several lawyers on Capitol Hill relentlessly tried to convince an intransigent bureaucracy to bomb Serb ethnic cleansers in Bosnia. These men watched the sanitization of cables, the repackaging of the conflict as "intractable" and "ancient", and the maintenance of an arms embargo against Bosnia's outgunned Muslims.' See also Wertheim, 'A Solution from Hell', 149–72.

that 'military force could easily transform foreign polities'.[119] Moreover, by the time that intervention in Kosovo came to mark the culmination of this normative shift – the first war to be fought in the name of human rights – their ranks had been joined by a cadre of greying student radicals of the 1968 vintage; the ideological trajectory of these erstwhile revolutionaries supporting Stefan-Ludwig Hoffmann's assertion that while human rights may not have been 'the decisive catalyst' behind the Cold War's collapse, the human rights ideal later became wrapped up in 'the promise that the events around 1990 should acquire historical meaning'.[120]

In light of such galvanizing capabilities, it is unsurprising that Glynne Evans, who served as Head of the UN Department at the FCO from 1990 to 1996, retrospectively views the period that separated the Rwandan genocide and the intervention in Kosovo as the 'high-water mark of humanitarian interventionism'.[121] Any attempts to explain the enthusiasm with which Tony Blair would advocate for NATO's operations in Kosovo, therefore, certainly ought to take into consideration the development of this transatlantic zeitgeist. As David McCourt argues, 'Britain's embrace of intervention cannot be reduced to an effect of Blair and New Labour alone because it was underpinned by wider changes in attitudes towards the appropriateness of military force in humanitarian crises'; ideational shifts that had been 'set in train before 1997, in Washington not London'.[122] Nonetheless, it has also been suggested that while parliamentary responses to the war in Bosnia between 1992 and 1995 may have witnessed 'the first signs of a distinctly Conservative argument in *favour* of humanitarian intervention', the debate concerning intervention took a 'distinctly path-dependent step' following the election of the New Labour government in May 1997.[123] By following the methods of discourse analysis, Ann Schreiner has attempted to underscore the significance of New Labour's ascension in this regard by highlighting the striking similarities between the interventionist stance encapsulated by 'left-wing' editorials printed in the *New Statesman* and the *Observer* between 1991 and 1995 and 'the actual speeches and policies of Labour Party politicians' leading up to the implementation of Operation Allied Force.[124] Although conceding that the 'issue of cause and effect' cannot be measured with 'fine precision' by this methodology, Schreiner maintains that the 'overall direction in which official Labour policy evolved is clear'.[125] Documents from the Labour Research Department, moreover, lend support to the contention that the New Labour government, or at the very least influential voices therein, were particularly receptive to broader international trends favouring a

---

[119] Wertheim, 'A Solution from Hell': 150.
[120] Hoffmann, 'Human Rights and History': 13. See also Paul Berman, *Power and the Idealists: Or, the Passion of Joschka Fischer, and its Aftermath* (New York & London: W.W. Norton & Company, 2005).
[121] Dame Glynne Evans, interview with the author, 2 May 2019.
[122] McCourt, 'Embracing Humanitarian Intervention': 246.
[123] Beech and Oliver, 'Humanitarian Intervention and Foreign Policy in the Conservative-led Coalition': 107, 108.
[124] Ann Schreiner, 'Humanitarian Intervention, the Labour Party and the Press: The Break-up of Yugoslavia in the 1990s', in *The British Labour Party and the Wider World*, ed. Corthorn and Davis, 194.
[125] Ibid., 208.

more assertive approach to humanitarian intervention and the protection of human rights worldwide.

As evidenced by a report of a November 1994 meeting of the Socialist International Committee on Human Rights (SICOHR) convened in Geneva, Labour's Domestic and International Policy Committee – whose membership included Robin Cook, Gordon Brown, Harriet Harman, Clare Short, Jack Straw and Margaret Beckett – had begun to situate its activities amongst emerging international debates concerning UN reform and the promotion of human rights in the post-Cold War era well in advance of the Party's landslide general election victory.[126] David Mepham, who represented the Labour Party at the SICOHR meeting, also acted as Party representative during a conference on conflict prevention and resolution in July 1995. Hosted by the Olof Palme International Center in Sweden, the conference sought to illuminate inter alia the humanitarian issues raised by the conflict in the former Yugoslavia, providing a forum for 'a number of experts on the region', including Owen's erstwhile collaborator Thorvald Stoltenberg.[127] In Mepham's view, attendance at this conference had been 'beneficial to the Labour Party' for the following reasons: 'As a policy-focused conference, it was an ideal opportunity to discuss a range of policy ideas with Swedish and other international participants – ideas that will be very useful for the work of the party's Policy Commission on Foreign Affairs and Security. The issues covered included: early warning systems, preventive diplomacy, UN peacekeeping, post-conflict reconciliation, democracy-building, and the strengthening of international institutions.'[128] The Domestic and International Policy Committee's engagement with these issues and debates is particularly noteworthy bearing in mind its recent integration into the Party's centralized policymaking machinery. According to one policy directive circulated in March 1995, the Committee had been made a constitutive element of the National and Regional Policy Forums strategy, implemented with a view to stimulating debate within the party and adding clarity to its approach during the 'pre-general election period'.[129] Mepham's pre-eminence within the Committee, moreover, is worth highlighting. Indeed, following his untimely death in November 2018 – at which time he was working as the UK Director of Human Rights Watch – the *Guardian* noted that Mepham 'helped develop Robin Cook's ideas about an ethical foreign policy' before becoming an influential figure in the Department of International Development (DfID – the successor organization to the Ministry of Overseas Development).[130]

It was with a sense of well-placed optimism, therefore, that Owen wrote to the newly elected Prime Minister on 3 September 1997, accompanying his note of congratulations with an invitation to consider his latest foray into the politics of global

---

[126] See 'Report of the Socialist International Committee on Human Rights (SICOHR), Geneva, 8 November 1994', PHM, LP/RD/1/1.
[127] 'Report of Conference Organised by Olof Palme International Centre in Sweden on 17–18 July 1995', PD(I)3822/November 1995, PHM, LP/RD/1/5.
[128] Ibid.
[129] 'Policy Directorate: Domestic and International Policy Committee, Conference and Forum Co-operation', PD3740/March 1995, PHM, LP/RD/1/2.
[130] Julian Borger, 'David Mepham obituary', *Guardian*, 7 November 2018.

governance – his membership of the Carnegie Commission on Preventing Deadly Conflict, which was in the process of concluding its final report:

> You may remember when we talked last summer that I mentioned the UN and the work I was doing with the Carnegie Commission on Preventing Deadly Conflict. Our final report will hopefully come out on 10 December coinciding with the anniversary of the Universal Declaration of Human Rights at an event in Washington ... At this stage I would like to interest you in one particular aspect, namely, as soon as possible, committing the UK to earmarked forces and to participate in a UN Rapid Reaction Force ... The powerful emotive argument for such a UN force is that if 5,000 specifically equipped and trained troops had been deployed rapidly in April 1994 the genocide in Rwanda could have been stopped. To recommit the UK Government will, I suspect, require a Prime Ministerial push. I suggest it would be a powerful substantive action which could put yourself and the UK in a leading role on the whole question of UN reform.[131]

Although Owen's engagement with the theory and practice of humanitarianism had continued under the auspices of Humanitas following the conference at Leeds Castle, it was his membership of the Carnegie Commission (which began its deliberations in May 1994) that placed him in the vanguard of the interventionist movement and provided him with the opportunity to impress his outlook upon key policymakers in Whitehall.[132]

The Commission consisted of sixteen 'international leaders and scholars with long experience and path-breaking accomplishments in conflict prevention and conflict resolution', many of whom – Owen included – had tried to 'help resolve very bitter conflicts, often at a late stage'.[133] The Commission, therefore, began by asking 'what might have been done at an early stage to avert mass violence and achieve a just outcome', before constructing 'a vision of a worldwide system of conflict prevention' that would blaze a trail into the twenty-first century.[134] Clearly, the Commission's Co-Chairman David Hamburg and Cyrus Vance conceded, the world had been 'unprepared for the genocidal slaughters of Bosnia and Rwanda'.[135] After the horrors of two world wars and the threat of nuclear annihilation during the Cold War, it was, as Hamburg and Vance recalled, 'reasonable to assume (wishfully) that mass killing would go away by the close of the century'.[136] In the event, however, policymakers 'of

---

[131] David Owen to the Rt Hon Tony Blair MP, 3 September 1997, DOP, D709 5/4/4 (2 of 3).
[132] Between the Leeds Castle conference and the eventual dissolution of Humanitas in 2000, the charity's activities were increasingly geared towards supporting a diploma scheme in international humanitarian assistance that Owen had put together with Kevin Cahill of the Centre for International Health and Cooperation. See for example Maggie Smart to Mrs Kathleen Newland, 3 May 2000, DOP, D709 5/4/2; David Owen to The Rt Hon Christopher Patten CH, 7 September 2001, DOP, D709 5/4/2.
[133] Carnegie Commission on Preventing Deadly Conflict, *Preventing Deadly Conflict: Executive Summary of the Final Report* (Washington, DC: Carnegie Commission on Preventing Deadly Conflict, 1997), vii.
[134] Ibid., vii, viii.
[135] Ibid., x.
[136] Ibid.

good will and human decency were confounded and often paralyzed by the rush of murderous events in the 1990s', with deep 'perplexity' leading to 'hesitation'.[137] With these systemic failures in mind, the Commission concluded that 'the prevention of deadly conflicts is, over the long term, too hard – intellectually, technically, and politically – to be the responsibility of a single institution or government, no matter how powerful. Strengths must be pooled, burdens shared, and labor divided among actors'.[138]

Owen's letter to Blair was not the first attempt he had made to attract Prime Ministerial support for this cooperative undertaking – he had written to John Major in November 1996 with the same objective in mind.[139] However, whereas Major dismissed Owen's suggestion that the UK government earmark 1,000 troops to support the UN's rapid reaction capabilities, Blair was far more receptive to the notion, stating that he 'would be happy to consider associating the British Government' with the Carnegie Commission's agenda while ensuring that the issue of earmarking UK forces for UN rapid reaction capabilities would be 'looked at afresh as part of the Strategic Defence Review' – a commitment that reflected the Labour Government's determination to 'play a full part in reinvigorating the UN system'.[140] With these words of encouragement ringing in his ear, Owen reported back to the Commission's Executive Director Jane Holl, and, in anticipation of the final report's European launch in the New Year, lobbied for London to be considered the most appropriate setting.[141] Owen's argument, which highlighted not only the Prime Minister's amenability, but also the fact that Britain would assume the EU presidency in January 1998, thereby increasing the chances of the report's dissemination among its European allies, clearly impressed the Joint Chairmen of the Commission and, following subsequent correspondence between the Commission and the FCO, a 'definite commitment' was made by the Blair government to provide 'a venue in London, logistics support for the meeting, a senior Minister to chair the event, and assistance in developing an audience'.[142] The Commission's final report was duly unveiled in the Locarno suite of the Foreign and Commonwealth Office on 8 January with Foreign Secretary Robin Cook in attendance.

As far as issues of global governance were concerned, however, the Carnegie Commission was not the only game in town. A commission established by the United Nations Association of the United States and headed by Lord Carrington had also chosen that week to come to London and present its findings. As Edward Mortimer reported for the *Financial Times*, although there was 'a lot of overlap' between the two commissions, Carrington's panel was more sceptical than the Carnegie Commission as regards the UN's peacekeeping capabilities: 'It does not think UN member states will be ready "anytime soon" to consider the establishment of "a standing or even standby UN force"... The crucial point, it concludes, is not the existence of a ready-made force

---

[137] Ibid.
[138] Ibid.
[139] David Owen to John Major, 12 November 1996, DOP, D709 5/2/34.
[140] Tony Blair to David Owen, 24 September 1997, DOP, D709 5/4/4 (2 of 3).
[141] David Owen to Jane Holl, 29 September 1997, DOP, D709 5/4/4 (2 of 3).
[142] Maggie Smart to Jonathan Powell, 16 October 1997, DOP, D709 5/4/4 (2 of 3).

but the willingness of one or more of the big powers to take the lead'.[143] Nonetheless, having already established the willingness of the New Labour government to consider his suggestions, Owen would continue to force the issue and ensure that the more optimistic outlook of the Carnegie Commission would be the one reflected in government policy.

Acting upon the pleas of the Commission's Executive Director to harness the 'good deal of momentum' that the final report had generated and to 'capitalize on the interest and enthusiasm of governments and other official audiences', Owen reached out to Robin Cook and Secretary of State for Defence George Robertson in May, enclosing in his letters a copy of a paper by Colonel Scott R. Feil making 'the military arguments for a rapid reaction force in the context of Rwanda'.[144] This emphasis on the Rwandan genocide – also present in Owen's letter to Blair – and the notion that the crisis could have been averted by the introduction of a small, well-trained security force in the region, was certainly not unique to the Carnegie Commission. As Wertheim points out, 'it took four years for inaction in Rwanda to be represented as cowardice in the face of preventable evil ... the war that wasn't'.[145] In the construction of this narrative, moreover, Wertheim suggests that it is possible to identify 'the blindspots' that developed within the humanitarian movement more broadly, as the West began to overcorrect for its inglorious passivity during the genocide itself and underestimate the difficulties of the operations it began to advocate more readily in its aftermath.[146] Indeed, Glynne Evans, who had been in Rwanda in 1994, and had 'talked to many of the key players and military', was dubious of the Commission's suggestion that a peacekeeping force of approximately 5,000 troops would have been able to effectively interpose itself between the Hutu and Tutsi populations, believing instead that nothing 'less than a serious US-led intervention would have stopped the carnage in the particular circumstances of the time'.[147]

Still, it would appear that the Commission's reading of the Rwandan genocide found a receptive audience among a New Labour Cabinet eager to stamp its (moral) authority on British foreign policy. Robertson was the first to respond to Owen's letter, informing him that 'we have examined thoroughly the role of our Armed Forces in support of UN Peace Keeping as part of the Strategic Defence Review' before inviting further dialogue on the subject following the publication of the relevant White Paper.[148] Cook's response was even more promising:

---

[143] Edward Mortimer, 'New world order?' *Financial Times*, 14 January 1998.

[144] Jane E. Holl to David Owen, 2 March 1998, DOP, D709 5/4/4 (1 of 3); David Owen to the Rt Hon George Robertson MP, 19 May 1998, DOP, D709 5/4/4 (1 of 3); David Owen to the Rt Hon Robin Cook MP, 19 May 1998, DOP, D709 5/4/4 (1 of 3). For the report enclosed in these letters, see Scott R. Feil, 'Preventing Genocide: How the Early Use of Force Might Have Succeeded in Rwanda', A Report to the Carnegie Commission on Preventing Deadly Conflict, April 1998, available at https://www.carnegie.org/media/filer_public/02/45/0245add3-b6aa-4a08-b9fc-6eb91f4e2975/ccny_report_1998_genocide.pdf (accessed 3 December 2019)

[145] Wertheim, 'A Solution from Hell': 158.

[146] Ibid.: 151.

[147] M.G.D. Evans to Lord Owen, 22 January 1998, DOP, D709 5/4/4 (1 of 3).

[148] George Robertson to David Owen, 31 May 1998, DOP, D709 5/4/4 (1 of 3).

The analysis and recommendations set out in the Carnegie Commission's report on Preventing Genocide are particularly coherent and thoughtful. As Colonel Scott Feil and others have concluded, the genocide in Rwanda in 1994 could perhaps have been prevented, or at least largely contained, had the international community responded differently. With hindsight, other options could have been tried that may not have been so evident at the time. We cannot change history, but we are determined to learn from the mistakes made, and to ensure as far as possible that they are never repeated.[149]

As this correspondence was followed by an apparent break in contact between Owen and the New Labour government, Owen could have been forgiven for thinking that a familiar pattern was repeating itself; words of encouragement and expressions of sympathy that would, in the final analysis, give way to an appreciation of strategic imperatives. This time, however, things were different. In a development Owen regarded as a 'significant victory for the Commission in terms of our recommendations', an FCO press release announced on 25 June 1999 that 'crack UK peacekeeping troops, able to go anywhere in the world at a moment's notice', were to be made available to the United Nations in order to prevent the escalation of regional conflicts as per the 'new Memorandum of Understanding (MOU) on peacekeeping with the UN'.[150] The press release also revealed that the French government would be signing a similar agreement contemporaneously. As such, the UK and France became the first Permanent Members of the UN Security Council to commit a proportion of their respective armed forces to the reinforcement of the UN's rapid reaction capabilities.

It is, of course, impossible to discern with complete certainty the extent to which this announcement was reflective of Owen's intervention. David Hamburg was certainly effusive in his appraisal of Owen's influence in the aftermath of the FCO's announcement.[151] There are, however, myriad factors that ought to be appreciated in any analysis of the New Labour government's foreign policy approach and the enthusiasm with which key policymakers sought to shape its trajectory. Strategic considerations, for instance the desire of the newly elected government to 'overcome Labour's historic image problem of being seen as "weak"' on issues of foreign policy should be carefully considered.[152] Oliver Daddow has suggested that Blair, contrary to popular wisdom, lacked a clear foreign policy vision by the time he embraced intervention in

---

[149] Robin Cook to David Owen, 8 June 1998, DOP, D709 5/4/4 (1 of 3).
[150] David Owen to Ms Jane Holl, 1 July 1999, DOP, D709 5/4/4 (1 of 3); Foreign and Commonwealth Office, Press Release: 'Crack UK Troops Available for UN Peacekeeping', 25 June 1999, DOP, D709 5/4/4 (1 of 3).
[151] David Hamburg to David Owen, 29 September 1999, DOP, D709 5/4/4 (1 of 3): 'I gather that you have continued to have a formidable effect on the British government with respect to preventing deadly conflict, with special attention to the UN ... In any event I am delighted that you are having continuing influence in these matters of great importance ... I do think it is vitally important that the UK be one of the principal leadership countries in this effort.'
[152] Oliver Daddow, '"Tony's War"? Blair, Kosovo and the Interventionist Impulse in British Foreign Policy', *International Affairs* 85, No. 3 (2009): 550. See also John Kampfner, *Blair's Wars* (London: Free Press, 2004), 8–11.

Kosovo, and was instead shaped 'into the leader he was previously wary of becoming' as a consequence of Operation Allied Force: 'a more confident, proactive leader genuinely committed to grounding British foreign policy in the theory of liberal interventionism.'[153] Dan Bulley, however, contends that 'tracing British claims to ethical foreign policy as humanitarian intervention from 1997 onwards shows a remarkable continuity'.[154] Bulley suggests that Labour's outlook developed *in parallel with* the work of the International Commission on Intervention and State Sovereignty (ICISS); it was not *a consequence of* the ICISS's activities which culminated in the publication of its highly influential 2001 report, 'The Responsibility to Protect'.[155] As such, it may be impossible to extricate Owen's lobbying efforts from these extraneous factors and to quantify precisely his influence on the development of New Labour's interventionist policies. In any case, as regards the evolution of British governmental attitudes concerning conflict prevention and the reform of the UN's security apparatus, the significance of Owen's lobbying of the New Labour government on behalf of the Carnegie Commission on Preventing Deadly Conflict should not be understated. Taking place at a particularly propitious and highly contingent moment when the crystallization of the interventionist norm in international discourse coincided with the election of a government in the UK that was far more receptive to this message than its immediate predecessors, Owen's attempts to impart the lessons of his Balkan Odyssey upon key policymakers within Tony Blair's ministry provide a crucial link between the failures of British policy in Bosnia and the liberal internationalism that would come to define New Labour's approach to foreign affairs.

Conclusion

NATO's intervention in Kosovo marked a turning point that gave hopes for a global order based on collective security and the protection of human rights in international politics – hopes that had been so prevalent at the beginning of the decade – a new lease on life. As these principles became codified in international law through the 'Responsibility to Protect' during the early years of the twenty-first century, they concomitantly put down roots in British political discourse, as the New Labour government sought to substantiate Tony Blair's Doctrine of the International Community.[156] Unveiled in Chicago in April 1999 as NATO forces were undertaking

---

[153] Daddow, '"Tony's War"?': 548.
[154] Dan Bulley, 'The Politics of Ethical Foreign Policy: A Responsibility to Protect Whom?' *European Journal of International Relations* 16, No. 3 (2010): 456.
[155] See ibid.: 447–56. For the ICISS report, see 'The Responsibility to Protect', Report of the International Commission on Intervention and State Sovereignty, International Development and Research Centre, Ottawa, Canada, December 2001, available at http://responsibilitytoprotect.org/ICISS%20Report.pdf (accessed 3 December 2019).
[156] The ICISS's recommendations were adopted unanimously by UN member states at the 2005 World Summit with the aim of addressing four key concerns: genocide prevention, war crimes, ethnic cleansing and crimes against humanity. See United Nations, 2005 World Summit Outcome, available at http://www.globalr2p.org/media/files/wsod_2005.pdf (accessed 3 December 2019).

an aerial bombardment of Yugoslav forces, the Blair Doctrine asserted that '[w]e are all internationalists now, whether we like it or not. We cannot refuse to participate in global markets if we want to prosper. We cannot ignore new political ideas in other countries if we want to innovate. We cannot turn our backs on conflicts and the violation of human rights within other countries if we want still to be secure.'[157] As this chapter has made clear, however, the emergence of such concepts of international responsibility, and the attendant normalization of military intervention as a means of preventing human rights violations, has very much been a protracted development. It was, in fact, born out of the failure of Britain, in concert with the other Western powers to intervene sufficiently in the humanitarian crises that emerged soon after the collapse of the Soviet Union – crises which put paid to the optimistic rhetoric of a 'New World Order' that accompanied the end of the Cold War. If David Owen's 'Balkan Odyssey' began in the summer of 1992 with the cultivation of such utopian visions in mind, he would leave the region three years later having witnessed the collective failure of the Western powers to guide it to fruition, and having become the face of Western passivity and duplicity in the process.

While it has not been the aim of this chapter to provide a hagiographic reassessment of Owen's time in Bosnia-Herzegovina and to undo some of the damage that Owen's involvement in the Balkan conflict did to his political reputation, it has, by adopting a broader perspective, demonstrated that Owen was by no means the 'Hobbesian' diplomat that his harshest critics have maintained.[158] Rather, following his frustrated attempts to lobby for greater military involvement in the Bosnian crisis, Owen was seemingly determined to overcome the inertia he had faced in Whitehall and elsewhere. This undertaking was provided with much-needed leverage by Owen's membership of the Carnegie Commission on Preventing Deadly Conflict which, during the course of its operations (1994–8), took its place in the vanguard of a burgeoning transatlantic zeitgeist – the incipient 'interventionist norm' which had become a matter of orthodoxy by the century's close. As the Commission's Co-Chair David Hamburg conveyed to Owen as the Commission was closing down its operations:

> It is fair to say that five years ago, when we began our enterprise, only a few voices could be heard in support of prevention. Today, it has become impossible to discuss violent conflict without some reference to how such conflict might be prevented. Our discussions with world leaders in governments, international organizations, in the private sector – among religious, media, business, scientific and educational communities – clearly reflect the growing global awareness that we are not powerless in the face of incipient outbreak[s] of violence. We can act, and act with effect to prevent its occurrence. The Commission can rightly take its place as a founding influence in the field ... Where has our work taken hold? Notably in the United Nations, especially in the office of the Secretary General

---

[157] Tony Blair, 'The Blair Doctrine', 22 April 1999, reproduced by the Global Policy Forum, available at https://www.globalpolicy.org/component/content/article/154/26026.html (accessed 30 June 2020).
[158] Susan Welsh, 'The Hobbesian diplomatic world of Britain's Lord David Owen', *Executive Intelligence Review* 23, No. 17 (April 1996): 18–28.

where Kofi Annan has made prevention a centerpiece of his tenure in office. His 1999 report to the Organization directly challenges member states to take up the prevention mission ... Governments, too, have begun to demonstrate a determination to pursue the prevention agenda. Canada, the Scandinavian countries, Germany, the UK and Japan lead the way, and important work has also begun in the US State Department ... Policy leaders have embraced the idea as well, among them, Kofi Annan, Boutros-Boutros Ghali ... Jimmy Carter ... Warren Christopher, Hillary Clinton, Sadako Ogata ... Mikhail Gorbachev ... and many others.[159]

Indeed, it was through his membership of the Carnegie Commission that Owen would exert a perceptible influence over the development of the New Labour government's approach to conflict prevention and the reform of the UN's security architecture, leading policymakers to earmark, for the first time, British troops to buttress the UN's rapid reaction capabilities. In light of this achievement, it could therefore be argued that although a New World Order conceived on the promise of collective security and the international protection of human rights had been buried during the bloody break-up of Yugoslavia, Owen had, by the century's close, assisted in its partial excavation.

---

[159] David A. Hamburg and Jane E. Holl to David Owen, 31 December 1999, DOP, D709 5/4/4 (1 of 3).

Conclusion

Engagement with the diplomatic fora of the United Nations notwithstanding, human rights promotion was not considered to be the *raison d'être* of British foreign policy until David Owen's unexpected appointment as Foreign Secretary following the untimely death of Anthony Crosland in February 1977.[1] Certainly, Owen's appointment was preceded by significant developments in the relationship between British foreign policy and the international promotion of human rights. By imposing a series of punitive measures on the Pinochet regime in Chile, for instance, the Labour government had responded to the concerns of a growing human rights network in Britain that began to coalesce in the aftermath of Salvador Allende's deposition in 1973. In fact, the decision to implement an arms embargo on Chile, in addition to accepting Chilean refugees, cutting off export credits and removing the British Ambassador from Santiago, can be seen as a resumption of a process set in motion by the first Wilson government (1964–70), which had taken steps towards the establishment of an incipient human rights bureaucracy in Whitehall, and adopted a more positive interpretation of Articles 55 and 56 of the UN Charter than the defensive stance favoured by British diplomats hitherto.

Nonetheless, this study has demonstrated a step-change in British human rights policy following Owen's promise to take a 'stand on human rights in every corner of the globe', identifying the human rights considerations that came to impinge upon a multiplicity of foreign policy issues facing the Callaghan government.[2] As regards Britain's bilateral relations with governments guilty of significant human rights abuses, the question of British arms sales to the repressive governments of El Salvador and Iran was examined by utilizing a case-study-based approach. Regarding the former, analysis of the decision to cancel an armoured vehicles contract in early 1978 revealed the growing influence that religious pressure groups – a constitutive aspect of Britain's burgeoning human rights network – were able to exert over the foreign policymaking process by subverting traditional modes of policy formulation. As for the Republic of Iran, however, concerned onlookers who voiced their opposition to Britain's support of Shah Mohammad Reza Pahlavi found that they were not afforded the same luxury; Iran's economic and geopolitical significance was too great to risk unsettling the Shah and the lucrative business he provided for the British arms industry. Steps had been

---

[1] Eckel, *The Ambivalence of Good*, 192.
[2] Annual Banquet of the Diplomatic and Commonwealth Writers Association speech, 3 March 1977

taken during the weeks and months that preceded Owen's appointment to institutionalize human rights concerns within the British foreign policymaking process in the form of the FCO's human rights comparative assessment. But hopes that this exercise would result in the establishment of a consistent and objective policy on human rights promotion proved to be illusory as an appreciation of entrenched economic and strategic interests – and subjective judgements made at the ministerial level – resulted in a strikingly ad hoc approach to human rights promotion.

Under Owen's leadership of the FCO, human rights promotion also impacted Britain's relationships with its allies across the Atlantic and across the Channel. Owen's adoption of a human rights-based approach to foreign affairs positioned the Callaghan government shoulder-to-shoulder with the Carter administration, and a significant degree of cooperation on human rights issues served to underscore a sense of common purpose that brought the two government's closer together. This was observed vis-à-vis the joint Anglo-American approach that the two nations would pursue in Rhodesia, the CSCE, and in the fora of the United Nations. A sense of shared commitment to the promotion of human rights internationally also led to the moderation of US criticism of British policies in Northern Ireland. The Callaghan government's prolonged and ultimately unsuccessful attempts to codify human rights provisions within the renegotiated Lomé Convention demonstrated that the Foreign Secretary was not focused solely on the pursuit of Anglo-American initiatives in the human rights field; clearly he also viewed the EC as a valuable forum through which Britain's human rights policy could be amplified in concert with its European partners.

The Callaghan government's assertive stance on human rights promotion within the EC, however, exerted a schismatic influence as Owen's enthusiastic support for Carter's human rights policy provoked suspicion within the Community, with many members voicing their concerns over being pushed too far on human rights promotion within the context of the East–West dialogue. This was a significant departure from the transatlantic dynamic that had emerged during the early-to-mid-1970s when US policymakers had called for the maintenance of the status quo in Europe, and European leaders, viewing human rights as a constitutive aspect of an emerging European identity, adopted a transformative approach to détente and human rights promotion within the CSCE. Moreover, by supporting Carter's policy, Owen recalibrated the British approach towards the related issues of European Political Cooperation and human rights promotion within the CSCE framework. Whereas British delegates had, both leading up to and following the signing of the Helsinki Final Act in 1975, tended to regard human rights promotion as a mere adjunct to the more pressing objective of European cooperation, Owen saw to it that human rights promotion became much more identifiable as an end unto itself, irrespective of whether this stance would cause discord within the Community.

Human rights concerns did not disappear from British foreign policy following the election of the first Thatcher government in May 1979. Rather, this study has revealed a striking degree of continuity between the Callaghan government and its Conservative successor as regards the weaponization of human rights within the context of the Cold War. However, while both governments sought to utilize human rights as a stick with which to beat the Soviet Union, human rights concerns became increasingly detached from questions of global socio-economic inequality during Thatcher's premiership. Whereas Owen, along with fellow Labour ministers Judith Hart and Frank Judd, viewed human rights as indivisible, comprising civil and political *and* social and economic rights, British human rights policy under Thatcher became ever more associated with the exclusive pursuit of the former. Consequently, while human rights policy during the Callaghan government touched upon issues concerning overseas development and Britain's constructive involvement with the politics of the North–South dialogue more broadly, the more circumscribed human rights vision that predominated during the 1980s tended to preclude British engagement with the human rights initiatives favoured by the Global South. Even still, although the tone and emphasis of Britain's human rights policy shifted post-1979, the institutionalization of human rights concerns within Whitehall continued nonetheless, much to the chagrin of some Conservatives who felt that the pursuit of Britain's 'national interests' (narrowly defined) was being hampered by superfluous moral posturing. By the time of Thatcher's resignation as leader of the Conservative Party in 1990, moreover, her steadfast commitment to keeping the Soviet Union on the back foot by emphasising the human rights aspects of the Helsinki Process had ensured that her understanding of human rights – tied inextricably to the imperatives of democratic promotion and free-market economics – became embedded within the apparatus of the CSCE itself in the form of the Paris Charter.

While this document – a 'European Magna Carta' – sought to place human rights at the centre of the post-Cold War reconstruction of Europe, such optimistic hopes were swiftly shattered by the recapitulation of ethnic conflicts that accompanied the collapse of the Soviet Union during the early 1990s. Indeed, the policy of benign neglect favoured by the Major government in response to the Bosnian War of 1992–5 demonstrated that concepts of collective security and the use of military force to prevent human rights abuses overseas were unable to exert a meaningful influence within Whitehall. Owen's ill-fated attempts to implement the peace plan bearing his name during his time as EU Co-Chairman of the Conference on the Former Yugoslavia (ICFY) cast a spotlight on the paralysing effects of this diplomatic inertia. By placing Owen's 'Balkan Odyssey' in its wider context, however, it has been possible to explore the development of the 'humanitarian interventionist norm' within international discourse from a fresh perspective.[3] Prior to Tony Blair's articulation of the Doctrine of the International Community during NATO's intervention in Kosovo in 1999, Owen, through his chairmanship of Humanitas and later his membership of the Carnegie Commission on Preventing Deadly Conflict, had not only played a part in cultivating an incipient Responsibility to Protect (R2P) ethic; he had also impressed this outlook upon key members of the New Labour government following its election victory in 1997.

In the process of examining these developments, this book has – by utilizing an innovative periodization, spanning the late Cold War and early post-Cold War periods – been able to further illuminate ongoing debates concerning the chronology of human

---

[3] Wertheim, 'A Solution from Hell': 154.

rights history. Much of the analysis has supported the notion, well established within the existing literature, that the 1970s constituted a pivotal moment in the history of human rights, revealing how Owen both responded and contributed to the elevation of human rights norms within international discourse by raising human rights concerns within British foreign policymaking to a level of prominence and influence hitherto unseen during his tenure as Foreign and Commonwealth Secretary. This study, however, has also emphasized that there are certain risks attendant to the identification of such epochal ruptures in the history of human rights; that we ought to qualify the 1970s 'breakthrough' by acknowledging the ways in which human rights advocacy had been shaped by previous developments, and continued to develop subsequently.

For instance, we perhaps ought to regard the assertion that human rights 'emerged in the 1970s seemingly from nowhere' which a degree of caution, noting that the human rights activism that would become increasingly prevalent over the course of decade had been prefigured by the emergence of transnational activist networks during the 1960s.[4] Similarly, we need to be attentive to consequences of the conservative reframing of human rights during the 1980s, even if Margaret Thatcher and Ronald Reagan were unable to completely 'erase the left-liberal model' of human rights that had put down roots on either side of the Atlantic.[5] Indeed, the persistent weaponization of human rights in the context of the East–West dialogue – and the concomitant conflation of human rights with concepts of democratic promotion and free-market economics – further indicates that human rights should not be regarded as a crystalline concept 'handed down to us from the 1970s or from any other "breakthrough" moment'.[6] The validity of this injunction has also been supported by an analysis of emerging human rights norms in international relations following the collapse of the bipolar global order that had calcified during the Cold War – a seismic shift in international politics that opened up space in which concepts of collective security and militarized humanitarianism became normalized in the wake of ethnic conflict in the former Yugoslavia and genocide in Rwanda.[7] In other words, although the 1970s undoubtedly constituted a period of striking 'transformation' in the history of human rights and international relations, we nonetheless ought to be careful as human rights historians of 'cutting it off from previous developments and collapsing the following forty years into them'.[8]

Analysis of David Owen's sustained engagement with the related concepts of human rights and humanitarianism has, therefore, shed new light on the fragmented, asynchronous development of human rights ideas within international politics, lending credence to the assertion that 'what human rights were understood to be by actors in the historical moment was always a considerably messier process' than 'breakthrough' narratives tend to suggest.[9] Furthermore, by exploring the remaking of British foreign

---

[4] Moyn, *The Last Utopia*, 3.
[5] Eckel, *The Ambivalence of Good*, 240.
[6] Brier, 'Beyond the Quest for a "Breakthrough"': 157.
[7] Hoffmann, 'Human Rights and History': 279–310.
[8] Eckel, *The Ambivalence of Good*, 8; Brier, 'Beyond the Quest for a "Breakthrough"': 157.
[9] Bradley, 'American Vernaculars': 4–5.

policy in response to the evolution of the international human rights system, analysis has reinforced the contention that the study of human rights and their chronology 'should no longer be considered as a historiographical field in isolation', but should instead be 'investigated as part of broader political ideologies and practices' – a concept that enables historians 'better to understand relations between developments at the local and translocal level, and domestic and foreign policies'.[10]

It ought to be stressed that by adopting a biographical focus this book cannot claim to provide a comprehensive history of British foreign policy initiatives in the human rights field during the period in question. Indeed, the limitations of such an approach are noted in Lora Wildenthal's study of human rights in West Germany, which offers the reader 'a set of stories', each of which sheds more light on the plasticity of human rights concepts in a specific context: 'they are far from the only stories. More could be added, like pages to a loose-leaf binder, from the West German era as well as from the years since [the] unification of West and East Germany in 1990'.[11] The same can be said of this project – it is possible to envisage similarly illustrative studies being undertaken on different subjects. Judith Hart's engagement with human rights, for example, has only been discussed briefly, although her attempts to spearhead rights-based approaches to development policy during her time as Minister for Overseas Development are certainly deserving of much more sustained coverage, as is Frank Judd's long-standing engagement with human rights and humanitarianism.[12] And what about Robin Cook? One can imagine that a study tracing the development of his involvement with human rights issues from his campaigns against the arms sales policy of the Callaghan government though to his articulation of an 'ethical dimension' to foreign policy in 1997 would be equally revelatory.

By focusing on *Owen's* human rights advocacy, however, this study has not only highlighted the intersections between British foreign policy, broader international developments concerning human rights promotion, and domestic debates surrounding the reorientation of Britain's role in the world during his political career; it has also been able to provide a reappraisal of the political philosophy of one of the most recognizable – and enigmatic – parliamentarians of recent British history. For instance, in the process of contextualizing Owen's public adoption of the human rights cause, this study has revealed the impact of Mervyn Stockwood's Christian socialism on the development of Owen's political outlook. Rooted in the conviction that politics – and particularly the politics of British democratic socialism – suffered when it became uprooted from its moral foundations, Owen's dissatisfaction with the first Wilson government was not, therefore, symptomatic of a general detachment from the intellectual foundations of Labourism as has often been suggested. Notwithstanding his association with political lost causes, a connection that was forged by his sustained but ultimately unsuccessful efforts to carve out a 'third way' in British politics with the

---

[10] Van Trigt, 'Beyond the Last Utopia' About the Historiography of Human Rights': 327.
[11] Wildenthal, *The Language of Human Rights in West Germany*, 167.
[12] Judd served as Director of Voluntary Service Overseas from 1980–5 and then became Director of Oxfam UK (1985–91). Judd later became a member of the Advisory Board at the LSE Centre for the Study of Human Rights and participated in the House of Lords Human Rights Joint Committee between 2003–07.

SDP, Owen was clearly a prescient thinker, attuned to the currents of public opinion. This was clearly evidenced by his identification of a burgeoning internationalist sentiment percolating within extra-parliamentary forums during the 1970s, and his subsequent attempts to bind this internationalist spirit to the state by championing human rights in British foreign policy.

At times, the impact that Owen's political outlook had on the trajectory of British human rights policy proved more difficult to ascertain. It certainly appears that Owen's principled stance on human rights facilitated the cancellation of the armoured vehicles contract with El Salvador in early 1978. The decision to continue to support the Shah of Iran as his authority was crumbling, on the other hand, reflected Owen's limited capacity to challenge the widespread acceptance of the geopolitical and economic significance of a pro-Western Iran. Nonetheless, even as Owen's human rights policy came up against insurmountable economic and strategic obstacles, another aspect of his political philosophy revealed itself: a compromise ethic influenced by the value pluralism of Isaiah Berlin. If nothing else, Owen's response to the harsh reality of compromise that became increasingly clear during the Iranian Revolution – to immerse himself in works of history, theology, and philosophy pertaining to the 'morality' of compromise – supports Stephen Wall's assessment of Owen's meditative nature, which stands in stark contrast to the managerialism that has prevailed within Whitehall in more recent years.[13]

The situation of Owen's human rights agenda within an ambitious conception of Britain's overseas role, however, did appear to influence the application of human rights policy in relation to the United States and the European Community during his tenure as Foreign Secretary. Owen, it was demonstrated, cleaved to an essentially 'Churchillian' understanding of Britain's global influence. This worldview, moreover, reflected the specificities of Owen's political generation: post-imperial, yet unable to completely extricate itself from the legacies of Britain's colonial history. This notion of generational schism was indeed supported by Owen himself, and by his plenipotentiary in Washington, Peter Jay. In fact, the appointment of Jay to the Washington Embassy revealed another aspect of this generational division as Owen and Jay clashed with senior diplomats in the FCO and the Washington Embassy; officials whose thwarted attempts to secure British membership of the EC during the 1960s had imbued them with a single-minded Eurocentrism fundamentally at odds with Owen's conception of a global Britain in which the relationships between the UK, the United States and the EC, were regarded as mutually reinforcing.

We do not have to overstate Owen's overt influence over the trajectory of British human rights policy in order to appreciate the ways in which his evolving advocacy reflected his personalized conception of human rights, and how this reflected broader developments in the international human rights regime. For instance, the concept of indivisible rights espoused by Owen – and also by fellow Labour ministers Hart and

---

[13] Wall interview: 'The thing that struck me ... maybe this is just because, you know, as you get older you always think that the past is better, but I did think to myself, are there any of today's politicians who, as ministers, would make those kinds of reflective speeches? I can't think of a speech in recent times of that kind where a minister stands up and actually talks about issues in those ways.'

Judd – may have fallen increasingly by the wayside during the Thatcher years, and the ambitious *humanitarian* agenda that Owen was consequently drawn towards during his time on the Independent Commission on International Human Issues (ICIHI) was similarly unable to leave much of an impression on the FCO in spite of his best efforts. Nonetheless, through his appreciation of human rights-related initiatives pursued by the Global South, such as the New International Economic Order, we are able to paint a more complete picture of Western governmental attitudes towards indivisible human rights. And, by exploring Owen's adoption of a humanitarian optic through which the pressing development needs of the Global South could be addressed more effectively, this study has been able to shed more light on the entangled nature of the histories of human rights and humanitarianism and the emergence of the rights-based 'new humanitarianism'.

But Owen's influence on the evolution of the British foreign policy-human rights relationship should not be so readily discounted either. Although he was, at times, a marginal figure, unable to secure the changes to the international human rights-humanitarian regime that he campaigned for, in the related spheres of collective security and militarized humanitarian intervention Owen played an important role in shaping British governmental attitudes at a crucial juncture. Indeed, having witnessed, at close quarters, the diplomatic inertia that militated against British military involvement in the Bosnian War (1992–5), Owen redoubled his efforts to realize the promises of a 'new world order' based on the principles of collective security and the protection of human rights through his membership of the Carnegie Commission on Preventing Deadly Conflict. In this respect, Owen ought to be regarded as an influential 'norm entrepreneur', whose lobbying efforts helped to shape the liberal internationalist outlook of Tony Blair's New Labour government, impressing upon key policymakers the importance of buttressing the UN's rapid response capabilities with British forces.[14]

This study of the evolving relationship between international human rights norms and institutions and the formulation of British foreign policy through the historical lens provided by David Owen's long-standing commitment to the promotion of human rights – and humanitarianism – within the international order, therefore, has underscored the conclusion of Wildenthal's study: 'Human rights norms do not unfold or evolve over time in any necessary way, and they do not represent increasing moral progress. This is because people, and not norms, are the true subject of the history of human rights.'[15] By continuing to place the individual at the centre of human rights history, 'listening to their words, but not necessarily taking them at their word', we may be able to inject yet more vigour into this rich historiography by being attentive to its fragmented chronology (or, indeed, *chronologies*), identifying, with greater acuity, the emergence of specific human rights 'vernaculars' in the historical moment, and illuminating broader political ideologies and practices from hitherto underappreciated perspectives.[16]

---

[14] Dunne and Hanson, 'Human Rights in International Relations', 54.
[15] Wildenthal, *The Language of Human Rights in West Germany*, 169.
[16] Ibid., 174.

Bibliography

Archival material

Chatham House Online Archive
David Owen Papers, University of Liverpool Special Collections & Archives
Historical Archives of the European Union, European University Institute, Florence
The Library of Congress, Washington DC., Manuscript Division
    Henry Brandon Papers
    Anthony Lake Papers
    Anthony Lewis Papers
Margaret Thatcher Foundation
The National Archives, Kew
    Cabinet Office
    Colonial Office
    Foreign Office
    Foreign and Commonwealth Office
    Home Office
    Ministry of Overseas Development
    Prime Minister's Office
People's History Museum, Manchester, Labour History Archive & Study Centre
    Chile Solidarity Campaign
    Judith Hart Papers
    Labour Research Department
Peter Jay Papers, Churchill College, Cambridge, Churchill Archives Centre
Records of the US State Department
Social Democratic Party Archive, University of Essex Special Collections

Published collections of primary sources

Ahlberg, K.L., ed., *Foreign Relations of the United States, 1977–1980, Volume I, Foundations of Foreign Policy, 1974–1980*. Washington, DC: Government Printing Office, 2014.
Bennett, G., and K.A. Hamilton, ed., *Documents on British Policy Overseas, Series III, Volume II: The Conference on Security and Cooperation in Europe, 1972–75*. London: The Stationery Office, 1997.
Hansard (Official Report of Debates in Parliament).
Owen, D., ed., *Bosnia-Herzegovina: The Vance/Owen Peace Plan*. Liverpool: University of Liverpool Press, 2013.
Parris, M., and A. Bryson, ed., *Parting Shots: Undiplomatic Diplomats – The Ambassadors' Letters You Were Never Meant to See*. London: Penguin, 2011.
Public Papers of the Presidents of the United States: George Bush, 1990, Book Two. Washington, DC: Government Printing Office, 1991.

194   *Bibliography*

Public Papers of the Presidents of the United States: George Bush, 1991, Book One.
    Washington, DC: Government Printing Office, 1992.
Public Papers of the Presidents of the United States, Jimmy Carter, 1977, Book One.
    Washington, DC: United States Government Printing Office, 1977.
Ramcharan, B.G., ed., *The International Conference on the Former Yugoslavia, Official Papers: Volume I.* The Hague/London/Boston: Kluwer Law International, 1997.
Suri, J., ed., *The Global Revolutions of 1968: A Norton Casebook in History.* New York: W.W. Norton & Company, 2007.

Newspaper and magazine archives

Daily Mirror Archive
Economist Historical Archive
The Financial Times Historical Archive, 1888–2016
Guardian and Observer Archive
The Listener Historical Archive, 1929–91
Los Angeles Times Archive
New York Times Archive
The Sunday Times Digital Archive, 1822–2006
Telegraph Historical Archive, 1855–2000
The Times Digital Archive
Washington Post Archive

Oral histories

Association for Diplomatic Studies and Training Foreign Affairs Oral History Project (ADST):
    Ward Barmon, interview with Charles Stuart Kennedy, 27 July 1998, available at https://www.adst.org/OH%20TOCs/Barmon,%20Ward.toc.pdf (accessed 14 January 2020).
    John W. Kimball, interview with Charles Stuart Kennedy, 24 May 1999, available at https://www.adst.org/OH%20TOCs/Kimball,%20John%20W.toc.pdf (accessed 14 January 2020).
    Robert S. Steven, interview with Charles Stuart Kennedy, 3 August 2001, available at https://www.adst.org/OH%20TOCs/Steven,%20Robert%20S.toc.pdf (accessed 14 January 2020).
British Diplomatic Oral History Programme (BDOHP), Churchill College, Cambridge:
    Sir Michael Alexander (interviewer unspecified), 25 November 1998, available at https://www.chu.cam.ac.uk/media/uploads/files/Alexander.pdf (accessed 10 January 2020).
    Andrew Carter, interview with Jimmy Jamieson, 20 October 2006, available at https://www.chu.cam.ac.uk/media/uploads/files/Carter.pdf (accessed 10 January 2020).
    Sir John Coles, interview with Malcolm McBain, 24 November 1999, available at https://www.chu.cam.ac.uk/media/uploads/files/Coles.pdf (accessed 9 December 2019).
    Sir Brian Lee Crowe, interview with Gwenda Scarlett, 15 October 2003, available at https://www.chu.cam.ac.uk/media/uploads/files/Crowe.pdf (accessed 9 January 2020).

Peter Jay, interview with Malcolm McBain, 24 February 2006, available at https://www.chu.cam.ac.uk/media/uploads/files/Jay_Peter.pdf (accessed 28 August 2017).
Sir Anthony (Derrick) Parsons, interview with Jane Barder, 22 March 1996, available at https://www.chu.cam.ac.uk/media/uploads/files/Parsons_Anthony.pdf (accessed 20 May 2020).
Sir Stephen Wall, interview with Thomas Raineau (Universite de Paris – Sorbonne), part 1, 12 December 2010; part 2, 28 February 2012, available at https://www.chu.cam.ac.uk/media/uploads/files/Wall.pdf (accessed 1 September 2017).

Interviews conducted by the author:
Dame Glynne Evans, 2 May 2019.
Julian Filochowski, 17 May 2019.
Lord Frank Judd, 15 January 2018.
Lord Tom McNally, 19 February 2019.
Lord David Owen, 6 December 2017; 19 March 2019.
David Stephen, 15 October 2018; 16 May 2019.
Sir Stephen Wall, 23 August 2018.

Diaries and memoirs

Brown, G., *In My Way.* London: Victor Gollancz, 1971.
Clark, A., *Diaries.* London: Phoenix, 1994.
Cradock, P., *In Pursuit of British Interests: Reflections on Foreign Policy under Margaret Thatcher and John Major.* London: John Murray, 1997.
Crossman, R., *The Diaries of a Cabinet Minister, Volume I: Minister of Housing, 1964–66.* London: BCA, 1976.
Donoughue, B., *Downing Street Diary, Volume II: with James Callaghan in No. 10.* London: Jonathan Cape, 2008.
Hain, P., *Outside In.* London: Biteback, 2012.
Jenkins, R., *A Life at the Centre.* London: Macmillan, 1991.
Lucas, I., *A Road to Damascus: Mainly Diplomatic Memoirs from the Middle East.* London: The Radcliffe Press, 1997.
Owen, D., *Balkan Odyssey*, 2nd edn. London: Indigo, 1996.
Owen, D., *Personally Speaking to Kenneth Harris.* London: Weidenfeld and Nicolson, 1987.
Owen, D., *Time to Declare.* London: Penguin, 1992.
Parsons, D., *The Pride and the Fall: Iran, 1974–79.* London: Jonathan Cape, 1984.
Sullivan, W.H., *Mission to Iran.* New York & London: W.W. Norton & Company, 1981.

Digitized resources

American Presidency Project:
Carter, J., 'London, England: Remarks on Arrival at Heathrow Airport', 5 May 1977, The American Presidency Project, available at https://www.presidency.ucsb.edu/documents/london-england-remarks-arrival-heathrow-airport (accessed 3 January 2020).
Carter, J., 'Newcastle-Upon-Tyne, England – Remarks at the Newcastle Civic Centre', 6 May 1977, The American Presidency Project, available at https://www.presidency.

ucsb.edu/documents/newcastle-upon-tyne-england-remarks-the-newcastle-civic-centre (accessed 3 January 2020).

Carter, J., 'International Economic Summit Meeting Exchange with Reporters Following a State Dinner at Buckingham Palace', 7 May 1977, The American Presidency Project, available at https://www.presidency.ucsb.edu/documents/international-economic-summit-meeting-exchange-with-reporters-following-state-dinner (accessed 2 January 2020).

'Republican Party Platform of 1980' (adopted by the Republican National Convention 15 July 1980), The American Presidency Project, available at www.presidency.ucsb.edu/WS/index.php?pid=25844 (accessed 13 January 2020).

Blair, T., 'The Blair Doctrine', 22 April 1999, reproduced by the Global Policy Forum, available at https://www.globalpolicy.org/component/content/article/154/26026.html (accessed 30 June 2020).

Brown, T.S., '1968. Transnational and Global Perspectives', *Docupedia-Zeitgeschichte*, June 11, 2012, available at www.docupedia.de/zg/1968 (accessed 9 December 2019).

Brzezinski, Z., 'The New Dimensions of Human Rights', Fourteenth Morgenthau Memorial Lecture on Ethics and Foreign Policy, May 26, 1995, available at https://www.carnegiecouncil.org/publications/archive/morgenthau/269 (accessed 9 January 2020).

Charter of the United Nations, Chapter IX: International Economic and Social Co-operation (Articles 55–60), available at https://www.un.org/en/sections/un-charter/chapter-ix/index.html (accessed 9 December 2019).

'Cold War: Ridgeway Briefing for Shultz ("Your Meeting with Prime Minister Thatcher, 16 December at 11:00am")', 15 December 1987, US State Dept FOI 2006-01579, available at https://www.margaretthatcher.org/archive (accessed 13 January 2020).

Conservative General Election Manifesto 1979, available at https://www.margaretthatcher.org/document/110858 (accessed 10 January 2020).

Corrigan, P., '1968: Year of Human Rights', Amnesty International UK/blogs, available at https://www.amnesty.org.uk/blogs/belfast-and-beyond/1968-year-human-rights (accessed 9 December 2019).

Crowder, G., 'Pluralism, Relativism and Liberalism in Isaiah Berlin', refereed paper presented to the Australasian Political Studies Association Conference, University of Tasmania, Hobart, 29 September–1 October 2003, available at http://berlin.wolf.ox.ac.uk/ (accessed 9 January 2020).

'Decision Making in Foreign Policy', FCO Historians and Oxford University Press Learning from History Seminar, 21 February 2013, available at https://issuu.com/fcohistorians/docs/learning_from_history_seminar (accessed 18 May 2020).

Directorate-General for External Policies of the Union, 'Human Rights and Democracy Clauses in the EU's International Agreements' (Long version), 29 September 2005, available at https://www.europarl.europa.eu/RegData/etudes/etudes/join/2005/363284/EXPO-DROI_ET(2005)363284_EN.pdf (accessed 13 February 2022).

'Europe: US State Dept Briefing (Fact Sheet: Conference on Security and Cooperation in Europe (CSCE))', 15 November 1988, US State Dept FOI 2006-01579, available at https://www.margaretthatcher.org/archive (accessed 13 January 2020).

Feil, S.R., 'Preventing Genocide: How the Early Use of Force Might Have Succeeded in Rwanda', A Report to the Carnegie Commission on Preventing Deadly Conflict, April 1998, available at https://www.carnegie.org/media/filer_public/02/45/0245add3-b6aa-4a08-b9fc-6eb91f4e2975/ccny_report_1998_genocide.pdf (accessed 3 December 2019).

Governor Reagan, 'Debate with Ronald Reagan', 28 October 1980, University of Virginia, Miller Center, available at https://millercenter.org/the-presidency/presidential-speeches/october-28-1980-debate-ronald-reagan (accessed 13 January 2020).

Hall, S., 'Life and Times of the First New Left', *New Left Review* 61 (January/February 2010), available at https://newleftreview.org/issues/II61 (accessed 8 December 2019).

1979 Labour Party Manifesto: 'The Labour Way is the Better Way', available at www.labour-party.org.uk/manifestos/1979/1979-labour-manifesto.shtml (accessed 10 January 2020).

'Memorandum Prepared in the Central Intelligence Agency: Impact of the US Stand on Human Rights', 11 May 1977, Document No. 42 in *Foreign Relations of the United States, 1977–1980, Volume II, Human Rights and Humanitarian Affairs*, available at https://history.state.gov/historicaldocuments/frus1977-80v02/d42 (accessed 3 January 2020).

Moyn, S., 'Human Rights and "Neoliberalism"', *Humanity*, blog post, 10 July 2014, available at www.humanityjournal.org/blog/human-rights-and-neoliberalism/ (accessed 13 January 2020).

Moyn, S., 'Theses on Humanitarianism and Human Rights', *Humanity*, blog post, 23 September 2016, available at www.humanityjournal.org/blog/theses-on-humanitarianism-and-human-rights/ (accessed 13 January 2020).

Nunlist C., (principal author), J. Auesluoma and B. Zogg, 'The Road to the Charter of Paris: Historical Narratives and Lessons for the OSCE Today', OSCE Network of Think Tanks and Academic Institutions, Vienna, December 2017, available at http://osce-network.net/file-OSCE-Network/Publications/Road_to_the_Charter_of_Paris_final_report.pdf (accessed 20 November 2019).

'On This Day, 1960: Thousands protest against H-bomb', 18 April 1960, BBC News, available at http://news.bbc.co.uk/onthisday/hi/dates/stories/april/18/newsid_2909000/2909881.stm (accessed 3 May 2020).

Organization for Security and Cooperation in Europe, '35 years from the Helsinki Final Act', 31 March 2011, available at https://www.osce.org/secretariat/104605 (accessed 10 January 2020).

Overseas Development Institute:
  'Lome II', Overseas Development Institute, Briefing Paper, No. 1 (February 1980), available at https://www.odi.org/sites/odi.org.uk/files/odi-assets/publications-opinion-files/6636.pdf (accessed 7 January 2020).
  'The Brandt Commission', Overseas Development Institute, Briefing Paper, No. 2 (March 1980), available at https://www.odi.org/sites/odi.org.uk/files/odi-assets/publications-opinion-files/6638.pdf (accessed 10 January 2020).

'PD-13: Conventional Arms Transfer Policy', 13 May 1977, The Jimmy Carter Presidential Library and Museum, available at https://www.jimmycarterlibrary.gov/assets/documents/directives/pd13.pdf (accessed 20 May 2020).

Report by the Foreign Ministers of the Member States on the Problems of Political Unification ('Davignon Report'), Luxembourg, 27 October 1970, available at https://www.cvce.eu/en/collections/unit-content/-/unit/02bb76df-d066-4c08-a58a-d4686a3e68ff/56b69a5e-3f16-4775-ba38-b4ef440fdccb/Resources#4176efc3-c734-41e5-bb90-d34c4d17bbb5_en&overlay (accessed 4 June 2020).

'Resolution adopted by the General Assembly, 3201 (S-VI): Declaration on the Establishment of a New International Economic Order', 1 May 1974, available at http://www.un-documents.net/s6r3201.htm (last accessed 21 June 2020).

'The Responsibility to Protect', Report of the International Commission on Intervention and State Sovereignty, International Development and Research Centre, Ottawa, Canada, December 2001, available at http://responsibilitytoprotect.org/ICISS%20Report.pdf (accessed 3 December 2019).

Snyder, S.B., 'Lecture Summary – Human Rights and the Cold War: Did Anyone Care?' (an H-Diplo Essay, 9 October 2014, H-Diplo, available at https://networks.h-net.org/

node/28443/discussions/47764/lecture-summary-%E2%80%9Chuman-rights-and-cold-war-did-anyone-care%E2%80%9D-h-diplo (accessed 10 January 2020).

'Text of the VOPP – 30 January 1993', University of Liverpool Special Collections & Archives, Balkan Odyssey Digital Archive, 1/3/4, available at https://sca-archives.liverpool.ac.uk/Record/5428#tree-5428 (accessed 1 December 2019).

The UNESCO Courier, '1968: International Year for Human Rights', XXI (January 1968), available at https://unesdoc.unesco.org/ark:/48223/pf0000078234 (accessed 8 January 2020).

United Nations, 2005 World Summit Outcome, available at http://www.globalr2p.org/media/files/wsod_2005.pdf (accessed 3 December 2019).

Wicks, N., 'Defining the Boundary within the Executive: Ministers, Special Advisers and the Permanent Civil Service', The ninth report of the Committee on Standards in Public Life, April 2003, available at https://www.gov.uk/government/publications/defining-the-boundaries-within-the-executive-ministers-special-advisers-and-the-permanent-civil-service (accessed 19 May 2020).

Wilson, H., Leader's Speech at the Labour Party Conference, Blackpool, 1 October 1968, available at http://www.britishpoliticalspeech.org/speech-archive.htm?speech=166 (accessed 12 May 2020).

'Winning Back the Human Race: The Legacy of the ICIHI', Chatham House, 14 November 2017, available at http://ibhi.org/wordpress1/conference-materials/ (accessed 19 November 2019).

Articles

Acheson, D., 'Our Atlantic Alliance: The Political and Economic Strands', speech delivered at the United States Military academy, West Point, New York, 5 December 1962. Reprinted in *Vital Speeches of the Day* 29, No. 6 (1 January 1963): 162–6.

Anghie, A., 'Whose Utopia?: Human Rights, Development, and the Third World', *Qui Parle* 22, No. 1 (Fall/Winter 2013): 63–80.

Atkins, J., 'A Renewed Social Democracy for an "Age of Internationalism": An Interpretivist Account of New Labour's Foreign Policy', *BJPIR* 15 (2013): 175–91.

Axboe Nielsen, C., 'Surmounting the myopic focus on genocide: the case of the war in Bosnia and Herzegovina', *Journal of Genocide Research* 15, No. 1 (2013): 21–39.

Baughan, E., 'The Imperial War Relief Fund and the All British Appeal: Commonwealth, Conflict and Conservatism within the British Humanitarian Movement, 1920-1925', *Journal of Imperial and Commonwealth History* 40, No. 5 (December 2012): 845–61.

Beech, M., and T.J. Oliver, 'Humanitarian Intervention and Foreign Policy in the Conservative-led Coalition', *Parliamentary Affairs* 67, Issue 1 (January 2014): 102–18.

Betts, R.K., 'The Delusion of Impartial Intervention', *Foreign Affairs* 73, No. 6 (November/December 1994): 20–33.

Black, L., '"Still at the Penny-Farthing Stage in a Jet-Propelled Era": Branch Life in 1950s Socialism', *Labour History Review* 65 (2000): 202–26.

Blackburn, D., 'Facing the Future? David Owen and Social Democracy in the 1980s and Beyond', *Parliamentary Affairs* 64, No. 4 (2011): 634–51.

Bocking-Welch, A., 'Imperial Legacies and Internationalist Discourses: British Involvement in the United Nations Freedom from Hunger Campaign, 1960-70', *Journal of Imperial and Commonwealth History, Special Issue: Empire and Humanitarianism* (November 2012): 879–96.

Bocking-Welch, A., 'Youth Against Hunger: Service, Activism and the Mobilisation of Young Humanitarians in 1960s Britain', *European Review of History: Revue européenne d'histoire* 23, Issue 1–2 (2016): 154–70.

Borshoff, I., 'What is a Human Rights Foreign Policy: Definitions, Double Standards, and the Carter Administration', *Historian* 78, Issue 4 (Winter 2016): 710–32.

Bouwman, B., 'From Religious Freedom to Social Justice: The Human Rights Engagement of the Ecumenical Movement from the 1940s to the 1970s', *Journal of Global History* 13, Issue 2 (2018): 252–73.

Brack, D., 'David Owen and the Social Market Economy', *The Political Quarterly* 61, Issue 4 (October 1990): 463–76.

Bradley, M.P., 'American Vernaculars: The United States and the Global Human Rights Imagination', *Diplomatic History* 38, No. 1 (2014): 1–21.

Brier, R., 'Beyond the Quest for a "Breakthrough": Reflections on the Recent Historiography on Human Rights', *European History Yearbook* 16 (2015): 155–74.

Brown, A., 'The Change to Engagement in Britain's Cold War Policy: The Origins of the Thatcher–Gorbachev Relationship', *Journal of Cold War Studies* 10, No. 3 (Summer 2008): 3–47.

Buchanan, T., 'Amnesty International in Crisis, 1966-7', *Twentieth Century British History* 15, No. 3 (2004): 267–89.

Buchanan, T., '"The Truth Will Set You Free": The Making of Amnesty International', *Journal of Contemporary History* 37, No. 4 (2002): 575–97.

Buettner, E., '"This is Staffordshire not Alabama": Racial Geographies of Commonwealth Immigration in Early 1960s Britain', *The Journal of Imperial and Commonwealth History* 42, No. 4 (2014): 710–40.

Bulley, D., 'The Politics of Ethical Foreign Policy: A Responsibility to Protect Whom?' *European Journal of International Relations* 16, No. 3 (2010): 441–61.

Burke, R., 'From Individual Rights to National Development: The First UN International Conference on Human Rights, Tehran, 1968', *Journal of World History* 19 (2008): 275–96.

Burke, R., 'Competing for the Last Utopia?: The NIEO, Human Rights, and the World Conference for the International Women's Year, Mexico City, June 1975', *Humanity* 6, No. 1 (Spring 2015): 47–61.

Castiglioni, C., 'No Longer a Client, Not Yet a Partner: The US-Iranian Alliance in the Johnson Years', *Cold War History* 15, No. 5 (2015): 491–509.

Chimni, B.S., 'Globalization, Humanitarianism and the Erosion of Refugee Protection', *Journal of Refugee Studies* 13, No. 3 (2000): 243–63.

Colls, R., 'The Forgotten World of Christian Socialism', *History Today* 65, Issue 3 (March 2015): 37–9.

Conway, M., 'The Rise and Fall of Western Europe's Democratic Age, 1945–1973', *Contemporary European History* 13, No. 1 (February 2004): 67–88.

Craig, M. M., '"I Think We Cannot Refuse the Order": Britain, America, Nuclear Non-Proliferation, and the Indian Jaguar Deal', *Cold War History* 16, No. 1 (2016): 61–81

Crawford, B., 'Explaining Defection from International Cooperation: Germany's Unilateral Recognition of Croatia', *World Politics* 48, No. 4 (July 1996): 482–521.

Daddow, O., '"Tony's War"? Blair, Kosovo and the Interventionist Impulse in British Foreign Policy', *International Affairs* 85, No. 3 (2009): 547–60.

Davis, M., 'Arguing Affluence: New Left Contributions to the Socialist Debate 1957–63', *Twentieth Century British History* 23, No. 4 (2012): 496–528.

Davis, M., 'Can One Nation Labour Learn from the New Left?' *Renewal* 21, Issue 1 (Spring 2013): 5–8.
Davis, M., 'Edward Thompson's Ethics and Activism 1956–1963: Reflections on the Political Formation of The Making of the English Working Class', *Contemporary British History* 28, No. 4 (2014): 438–56.
Davis, M., '"Among the Ordinary People": New Left Involvement in Working-Class Political Mobilization 1956–68', *History Workshop Journal* 86 (Autumn 2018): 133–59.
Deighton, A., 'Don and Diplomat: Isaiah Berlin and Britain's Early Cold War', *Cold War History* 13, No. 4 (2013): 525–40.
Dexter, B., 'Morley and Compromise', *Foreign Affairs* 26, No. 2 (January 1948): 335–48.
Drezner, D.W., 'Ideas, Bureaucratic Politics, and the Crafting of Foreign Policy', *American Journal of Political Science* 44, No. 4 (October 2000): 733–49.
Ellis, C., 'The Younger Generation: The Labour Party and the 1959 Youth Commission', *Journal of British Studies* 41, No. 2 (April 2002): 205–31.
Everill, B., et al, 'History and Humanitarianism: A Conversation', *Past and Present* 241, Issue 1 (November 2018): 1–38.
Facchini, M., '"The Millstone Around Our Necks": Harold Wilson and the HMS Fearless Conference (9–13 October 1968)', *Contemporary British History* 28, No. 3 (2014): 274–93.
Felci, V., '"A Latter-Day Hitler": Anti-Shah Activism and British Policy towards Iran, 1974–1976', *Diplomacy and Statecraft* 30, No. 1 (2019): 515–35.
Fukuyama, F., 'The End of History?' *The National Interest* 16 (Summer 1989): 3–18.
'The Future of the Balkans: An Interview with David Owen', *Foreign Affairs* 72, No. 2 (Spring 1993): 1–9.
Gains, F., and Stoker, G., 'Special Advisers and the Transmission of Ideas from the Policy Primeval Soup', *Policy & Politics* 39, No. 4 (2011): 485–98.
Gardner, N., 'The Harold Wilson Government, Airwork Services Limited, and the Saudi Arabian Air Defence Scheme, 1965–1973', *Journal of Contemporary History* 42, No. 2 (2007): 345–63.
Garnett, M., 'Polemic, Parliament and History: Michael Foot versus David Owen', *Parliamentary History* 35, pt. 2 (2016): 171–88.
Gaskarth, J., 'Ethical Policies or Empty Promises? New Labour and Human Rights in British Foreign Policymaking', *The International Journal of Human Rights* 10, No. 1 (March 2006): 45–60.
Gaskarth, J., 'Interpreting Ethical Foreign Policy: Traditions and Dilemmas for Policymakers', *BJPIR* 15 (2013): 192–209.
Gilman, N., 'The New International Economic Order: A Reintroduction', *Humanity* 6, No. 1 (Spring 2015): 1–16.
Gilmore, J., 'Still a "Force for Good"? Good International Citizenship in British Foreign and Security Policy', *BJPIR* 17 (2015): 106–29.
Gilmour, J., 'The Uncertain Merger of Values and Interests in UK Foreign Policy', *International Affairs* 90 (2014): 541–57.
Goode, J.F., 'Assisting Our Brothers, Defending Ourselves: The Iranian Intervention in Oman, 1972–75', *Iranian Studies* 47, Issue 3 (May 2014): 441–62.
Grant, K., 'The British Empire, International Government, and Human Rights', *History Compass* 11, Issue 8 (August 2013): 573–83.
Hall, S., 'Protest Movements in the 1970s: The Long 1960s', *Journal of Contemporary History* 43, No. 4 (2008): 655–72.

Harper, S., '"History is Screaming at Us": Humanitarian Interventionism and the Popular Geopolitics of the Bosnian War in Leigh Jackson and Peter Kominsky's Warriors', *Journal of European Popular Culture* 2, No. 1 (2011): 43–63.

Hilton, M., 'International Aid and Development NGOs in Britain and Human Rights since 1945', *Humanity* 3, No. 3 (December 2012): 449–72.

Hilton, M., 'Ken Loach and the Save the Children Film: Humanitarianism, Imperialism, and the Changing Role of Charity in Postwar Britain', *The Journal of Modern History* 87 (June 2015): 357–94.

Hilton, M., 'Charity and the End of Empire: British Non-Governmental Organizations, Africa, and International Development in the 1960s', *The American Historical Review* 123, Issue 2 (April 2018): 493–517.

Hoffmann, S.L., 'Human Rights and History', *Past and Present* 232 (August 2016): 279–310.

Jacoby, T., 'The Reagan Turnaround on Human Rights', *Foreign Affairs* 64, No. 5 (Summer 1986): 1066–86.

Jones, A., 'Band Aid Revisited: Humanitarianism, Consumption and Philanthropy in the 1980s', *Contemporary British History* 31, No. 2 (2017): 189–209.

Jones, T., 'The SDP's Ideological Legacy', *Journal of Liberal Democratic History* 18 (1998): 4–7.

Keck, M.E., and Sikkink, K., 'Transnational Advocacy Networks in International and Regional Politics', *International Social Science Journal* 68, Issue 227–228 (March-June 2018), (reprinted from *International Social Science Journal* 51, Issue 159 (March 1999): 89–101).

Kelly, P.W., 'The 1973 Chilean Coup and the Origins of Transnational Human Rights Activism', *Journal of Global History* 8, Issue 1 (2013): 165–86.

Kirby, D., 'Anglo-American Relations and the Religious Cold War', *Journal of Transatlantic Studies* 10, No. 2 (June 2012): 167–81.

Klose, F., 'Human Rights For and Against Empire – Legal and Public Discourses in the Age of Decolonisation', *Journal of the History of International Law* 18, Issue 2–3 (2016): 317–38.

Krauthammer, C., 'The Unipolar Moment', *Foreign Affairs* 70, No. 1 (1990–91): 22–33.

Krozewski, G., 'Global Britain and the Post-Colonial World: The British Approach to Aid Policies at the 1964 Juncture', *Contemporary British History* 29, No. 2 (2015): 222–40.

Leebaw, B., 'The Politics of Impartial Activism: Humanitarianism and Human Rights', *Perspectives in Politics* 5, No. 2 (June 2007): 223–9.

Luard, E., 'Human Rights and Foreign Policy', *International Affairs* 56, No. 4 (Autumn 1980): 579–606.

Marshall, P., 'Imperial Britain', *Journal of Imperial and Commonwealth History* 23, Issue 3 (September 1995): 379–94.

Marwick, A., 'The Cultural Revolution of the Long Sixties: Voices of Reaction, Protest, and Permeation', *The International History Review* 27, No. 4 (2005): 780–806.

McCourt, D., 'Embracing Humanitarian Intervention: Atlanticism and the UK Interventions in Bosnia and Kosovo', *BJPIR* 15, Issue 2 (May 2013): 242–62.

McGlinchey, S., and Murray, R.W., 'Jimmy Carter and the Sales of the AWACS to Iran in 1977', *Diplomacy and Statecraft* 8, No. 2 (2017): 254–76.

Montana, I.S., 'The Lomé Convention from Inception to the Dynamics of the Post-Cold War, 1957–1990s', *African and Asian Studies* 2, No. 1 (2003): 63–97.

Moores, C., 'The Progressive Professionals: The National Council for Civil Liberties and the Politics of Activism in the 1960s', *Twentieth Century British History* 20, Issue 4 (2009): 538–60.

Moores, C., 'Solidarity for Chile, Transnational Activism and the Evolution of Human Rights', *Moving the Social: Journal of Social History and the History of Social Movements* 51 (2017): 115-36.
Morris, J., 'The Strange Death of Christian Britain: Another Look at the Secularization Debate', *Historical Journal* 46, No. 4 (2003): 963-76.
Murphy, P., 'Britain and the Commonwealth: Confronting the Past – Imagining the Future', *The Round Table* 100, No. 414 (June 2011): 267-83.
Nolan, M., 'Gender and Utopian Visions in a Post-Utopian Era: Americanism, Human Rights, Market Fundamentalism', *Central European History* 44 (2011): 13-26.
O'Sullivan, K., 'The Search for Justice: NGOs in Britain and Ireland and the New International Economic Order, 1968-82', *Humanity* 6, No. 1 (Spring 2015): 173-87.
O'Sullivan, K., M. Hilton and J. Fiori, 'Humanitarianisms in Context', *European Review of History – Revue européene d'histoire* 23, No. 1-2 (2016): 1-15.
Pedaliu, E.G.H., 'Human Rights and Foreign Policy: Wilson and the Greek Dictators, 1967-1970', *Diplomacy and Statecraft* 18 (2007): 185-214.
Pendas, D.O., 'Towards a New Politics? On the Recent Historiography of Human Rights', *Contemporary European History* 21, No. 1 (2012): 95-111.
Peterson, C.P., '"Confronting" Moscow: The Reagan Administration, Human Rights, and the Final Act', *The Historian* 74, Issue 1 (2012): 57-86.
Posnett, E., 'Treating His Imperial Majesty's Warts: British Policy towards Iran, 1977-79', *Iranian Studies* 45, No. 1 (January 2012): 119-37.
Reynolds, D., 'A "Special Relationship"? America, Britain and the International Order since the Second World War', *International Affairs* 62, No. 1 (Winter 1985-1986): 1-20.
Russell, M., and R. Serban 'The Muddle of the "Westminster Model": A Concept Stretched Beyond Repair', *Government and Opposition* (2020): 1-21.
Sasson, T., and J. Vernon, 'Practising the British way of Famine: Technologies of Relief, 1770-1985', *European Review of History: Revue européenne d'histoire* 22, Issue 6 (2015): 860-72.
Schwarz, B., '"The Only White Man in There": The Re-Racialisation of England, 1956-1968', *Race and Class* 38, No. 1 (1996): 65-78.
Skinner, R., and Lester, A., 'Humanitarianism and Empire: New Research Agendas', *Journal of Imperial and Commonwealth History, Special Issue: Empire and Humanitarianism* (November 2012): 729-47.
Slaughter, J.R., 'Hijacking Human Rights: Neoliberalism, the New Historiography, and the End of the Third World', *Human Rights Quarterly* 40, No. 4 (November 2018): 735-75.
Suri, J., 'Détente and Human Rights: American and West European Perspectives on International Change', *Cold War History* 8, No. 4 (November 2008): 527-45.
Terretta, M., '"We Had Been Fooled into Thinking that the UN Watches over the Entire World": Human Rights, UN Trust Territories, and Africa's Decolonization', *Human Rights Quarterly* 34, No. 2 (May 2012): 329-60.
Trenta, L., 'The Champion of Human Rights meets the King of Kings: Jimmy Carter, the Shah, and Iranian Illusions and Rage', *Diplomacy and Statecraft* 24, No. 3 (2013): 476-98.
Van Dam, P., 'No Justice Without Charity: Humanitarianism After Empire', *The International History Review* (2020): 1-22.
Van Trigt, P., 'Beyond the Last Utopia: About the Historiography of Human Rights', *Tijdschrift voor Geschiedenis* 131, Issue 2 (June 2018): 327-40.
Wallace, W., 'After Berrill: Whitehall and the Management of British Diplomacy', *International Affairs* 54, Issue 2 (1978): 220-39.

Welsh, S., 'The Hobbesian diplomatic world of Britain's Lord David Owen', *Executive Intelligence Review* 23, No. 17 (April 1996): 18–28.
Wertheim, S., 'A Solution from Hell: The United States and the Rise of Humanitarian Interventionism, 1991–2003', *Journal of Genocide Research* 12, No. 3–4 (September–December 2010): 149–72.
Wheeler, N.J., and Dunne, T., 'Good International Citizenship: a Third Way for British Foreign Policy', *International Affairs* 74, No. 4 (1998): 847–70.

Books and edited collections

Acland, R., MP, F. Brockway, MP, L. Hale, MP, *Waging Peace: The Need for a Change in British Policy*. London: Halcyon Press, 1953.
Ali, T., *The Coming British Revolution*. London: Jonathan Cape, 1972.
Alvandi, R., *Nixon, Kissinger, and the Shah: The United States and Iran in the Cold War*. New York: Oxford University Press, 2014.
Anderson, M., *A History of Fair Trade in Contemporary Britain: From Civil Society Campaigns to Corporate Compliance*. Basingstoke: Palgrave Macmillan, 2015.
Bailkin, J., *The Afterlife of Empire*. Berkeley: University of California Press, 2012.
Barnett, M., *Empire of Humanity: A History of Humanitarianism*. Ithaca: Cornell University Press, 2011.
Bartlett, C.J., *"The Special Relationship": A Political History of Anglo-American Relations since 1945*. Harlow: Longman, 1992.
Bates, E., *The Evolution of the European Convention on Human Rights from its Inception to the Creation of a Permanent Court of Human Rights*. Oxford: Oxford University Press, 2010.
Beckett F., and T. Russell, *1956: The Year that Changed Britain*. London: Biteback, 2015.
Bell, P., *The Labour Party in Opposition, 1970–1974*. London: Routledge, 2004.
Bellamy, A.J., and P.D. Williams, with S. Griffin, *Understanding Peacekeeping*, 2nd edn. Cambridge: Polity Press, 2010.
Bennett, H., *Fighting the Mau Mau: The British Army and Counter-Insurgency in the Kenya Emergency*. Cambridge: Cambridge University Press, 2012.
Berlin, I., *Russian Thinkers*, revised edn. London: Penguin, 2008.
Berman, P., *Power and the Idealists: Or, the Passion of Joschka Fischer, and its Aftermath*. New York & London: W.W. Norton & Company, 2005.
Bird, D., *Never the Same Again: A History of the VSO*. Cambridge: Lutterworth Press, 1998.
Black, L., *The Political Culture of the Left in Affluent Britain, 1951–64*. Basingstoke: Palgrave Macmillan, 2003.
Bocking-Welch, A., *British Civic Society at the End of Empire Decolonisation, Globalisation, and International Responsibility*. Manchester: Manchester University Press, 2018.
Bricmont, J., *Humanitarian Imperialism: Using Human Rights to Sell War*. New York: Monthly Review Press, 2006.
Broad, R., *Labour's European Dilemmas: From Bevin to Blair*. Basingstoke: Palgrave Macmillan, 2001.
Brown, C.G., *The Battle for Christian Britain: Sex, Humanists and Secularisation, 1945–1980*. Cambridge: Cambridge University Press, 2019.
Brown, C.G., *The Death of Christian Britain: Understanding Secularisation, 1800–2000*. London: Routledge, 2001.
Bruce, S., *Religion in the Modern World: From Cathedrals to Cults*. Oxford: Oxford University Press, 1996.

Buchanan, T., *Amnesty International and Human Rights Activism in Postwar Britain, 1945–1977*. Oxford: Oxford University Press, 2020.
Burke, R., *Decolonization and the Evolution of International Human Rights*. Philadelphia: University of Pennsylvania Press, 2010.
Burkett, J., *Constructing Post-Imperial Britain: Britishness, 'Race' and the Radical Left in the 1960s*. Basingstoke: Palgrave Macmillan, 2013.
Byrne, P., *The Campaign for Nuclear Disarmament*. London: Routledge, 1988.
Caine, B., *Biography and History*. New York: Palgrave Macmillan, 2010.
Chandler, D., *From Kosovo to Kabul: Human Rights and International Intervention*. London: Pluto Press, 2002.
Cobain, I., *Cruel Britannia: A Secret History of Torture*. London: Portobello Books, 2012.
Coles, J., *Making Foreign Policy: A Certain Idea of Britain*. London: John Murray, 2000.
Crewe, I., and A. King, *SDP: The Birth, Life and Death of the Social Democratic Party*. Oxford: Oxford University Press, 1995.
Crines, A., and K. Hickson, ed. *Harold Wilson: The Unprincipled Prime Minister? Reappraising Harold Wilson*. London: Biteback, 2016.
Cronin, J.E., *Global Rules: America, Britain and a Disordered World*. New Haven, Connecticut & London: Yale University Press, 2014.
De-La-Noy, M., *Mervyn Stockwood: A Lonely Life*. Mowbray: London, 1996.
Dickie, J., *Inside the Foreign Office*. London: Chapman, 1992.
Dickie, J., *'Special' No More, Anglo-American Relations: Rhetoric and Reality*. London: Weidenfeld & Nicolson, 1994.
Dickson, B., *The European Convention on Human Rights and the Northern Ireland Conflict*. Oxford: Oxford University Press, 2010.
Dimbleby, D., and D. Reynolds, *An Ocean Apart: The Relationship Between Britain and America in the Twentieth Century*. London: Hodder & Stoughton, 1988.
Dobson, A.P., *Anglo-American Relations in the Twentieth Century: of Friendship, Conflict and the Rise and Decline of Superpowers*. New York: Routledge, 1995.
Donnelly, J., *Universal Human Rights: In Theory and Practice*, 2nd edn. New York: Cornell University Press, 2003.
Drohan, B., *Brutality in an Age of Human Rights: Activism and Counterinsurgency at the End of the British Empire*. Ithaca and London: Cornell University Press, 2017.
Dumbrell, J., *A Special Relationship: Anglo-American Relations from the Cold War to Iraq*. Basingstoke: Palgrave Macmillan, 2006.
Duranti, M., *The Conservative Human Rights Revolution: European Identity, Transnational Politics, and the Origins of the European Convention*. Oxford: Oxford University Press, 2017.
Eckel, J., *The Ambivalence of Good: Human Rights in International Politics Since the 1940s*. Oxford: Oxford University Press, 2019.
Eley, G., *Forging Democracy: The History of the Left in Europe, 1850–2000*. Oxford: Oxford University Press, 2002.
Field, C.D., *Britain's Last Religious Revival? Quantifying Belonging, Behaving, and Believing in the Long 1950s*. Basingstoke: Palgrave Pivot, 2015.
Fielding, S., *The Labour Governments 1964–1970, Volume I: Labour and Cultural Change*. Manchester: Manchester University Press, 2003.
Fink, C., P. Gassert and D. Junker, eds, *1968: The World Transformed* (Cambridge: Cambridge University Press, 1999).
Foote, G., *The Labour Party's Political Thought: A History*. Basingstoke: Palgrave Macmillan, 1985.

Fraser, R., *1968: A Student Generation in Revolt*. London: Chatto and Windus, 1988.
Galbraith, J.K., *The Affluent Society*. Boston: Houghton Mifflin, 1958.
Garnett, M., S. Mabon and R. Smith, *British Foreign Policy since 1945*. London & New York: Routledge, 2018.
Gaskarth, J., *British Foreign Policy*. London: Polity, 2013.
Geddes, A., *The European Union and British Politics*. Basingstoke: Palgrave Macmillan, 2004).
George, S., *"An Awkward Partner": Britain in the European Community*, 3rd edn. Oxford: Oxford University Press, 1998.
Gorman, D., *Imperial Citizenship: Empire and the Question of Belonging*. Manchester: Manchester University Press, 2006.
Gowland G., and A. Turner, *Reluctant Europeans: Britain and European Integration, 1945-1998*. Harlow: Longman, 2000.
Grant, K., *A Civilised Savagery: Britain and the New Slaveries in Africa, 1884-1926*. New York: Routledge, 2005.
Greenwood, S., *Britain and the Cold War, 1945-91*. Basingstoke: Macmillan, 2000.
Haines, J., *The Politics of Power*. London: Jonathan Cape, 1977.
Harrison, B., *Finding a Role? The United Kingdom, 1970-1990*. Oxford: Oxford University Press, 2010.
Harrison, B., *Seeking a Role: The United Kingdom 1951-1970*. Oxford: Oxford University Press, 2009.
Heater, D., *Britain and the Outside World*. London: Longman, 1976.
Hehir, A., *Humanitarian Intervention After Kosovo: Iraq, Darfur and the Record of Global Civil Society*. Basingstoke: Palgrave Macmillan, 2008.
Henderson, N., *The Private Office: A Personal View of Five Foreign Secretaries and of Government from the Inside*. London: Weidenfeld and Nicolson, 1984.
Hennessy, P., *Never Again: Britain, 1945-51*. London: Jonathan Cape, 1992.
Hilton, M., J. McKay, N. Crowson, and J.F. Mouhot, *The Politics of Expertise: How NGOs Shaped Modern Britain*. Oxford: Oxford University Press, 2013.
Hopgood, S., *The Endtimes of Human Rights*. New York: Cornell University Press, 2013.
Hudson, K., *CND: Now More than Ever: The Story of a Peace Movement*. London: Vision, 2005.
Hurst, M., *British Human Rights Organizations and Soviet Dissent, 1965-1985*. London: Bloomsbury, 2016.
Ireton, B., *Britain's International Development Policies: A History of DfID and Overseas Aid*. Basingstoke: Palgrave Macmillan, 2013.
Iriye, A., *Global Community: The Role of International Organizations in the Making of the Contemporary World*. Berkeley: University of California Press, 2002.
Jackson, B., *Equality and the British Left*. Manchester: Manchester University Press, 2007.
Jensen, S.L.B., *The Making of International Human Rights: The 1960s, Decolonization, and the Reconstruction of Global Values*. Cambridge: Cambridge University Press, 2016.
Jones, I., *The Local Church and Generational Change in Birmingham, 1945-2000*. Woodbridge: Boydell Press, 2012.
Jones, P.D., *The Christian Socialist Revival, 1877-1914: Religion Class, and Social Conscience in Late Victorian England*. Princeton: Princeton University Press, 1968.
Keck, M.E., and K. Sikkink, *Activists Beyond Borders: Advocacy Networks in International Politics*. Ithaca: Cornell University Press, 1998.
Keys, B., *Reclaiming American Virtue: The Human Rights Revolution of the 1970s*. Cambridge, MA: Harvard University Press, 2014.

Klein, N., *The Shock Doctrine: The Rise of Disaster Capitalism*. London: Penguin, 2007.
Klotz, A., *Norms in International Relations: The Struggle Against Apartheid*. Ithaca: Cornell University Press, 1995.
Klug, F., *Values for a Godless Age: The Story of the United Kingdom's New Bill of Rights*. London: Penguin, 2000.
Klug, F., *A Magna Carta for all Humanity*. London: Routledge, 2015.
Kyle, K., *Suez: Britain's End of Empire in the Middle East*. London & New York: I.B. Tauris, 2011.
Lake, A., *The 'Tar Baby' Option: American Policy Toward Southern Rhodesia*. New York: Colombia University Press, 1976.
Larsen, H., *Foreign Policy and Discourse Analysis: France, Britain and Europe*. London and New York: Routledge, 1997.
Lee, M., *Utopia and Dissent in West Germany: The Resurgence of the Politics of Everyday Life in the Long 1960s*. Abingdon and New York: Routledge, 2019.
LeoGrande, W.M., *Our Own Backyard: The United States in Central America, 1977-1992*. Chapel Hill: University of North Carolina Press, 1998.
Livingstone, G., *Britain and the Dictatorships of Argentina and Chile, 1973-82: Foreign Policy, Corporations and Social Movements*. Basingstoke: Palgrave Macmillan, 2018.
Luce R., MP, and J. Ranelagh, *Human Rights and Foreign Policy*. London: Conservative Political Centre, 1977.
Magee, B., *Men of Ideas*. New York: The Viking Press, 1978.
Martin, D., and P. Johnson, *The Struggle for Zimbabwe: The Chimurenga War*. London: Faber & Faber, 1981.
Marwick, A., *The Sixties: Social and Cultural Transformation in Britain, France, Italy and the United States, 1958-74*. Oxford: Oxford University Press, 1998.
McKie, D., and C. Cook, eds, *Decade of Disillusion: British Politics in the Sixties*. Basingstoke: Palgrave Macmillan, 1972.
McPherson, A., *Intimate Ties, Bitter Struggles: The United States and Latin America since 1945*. Washington, DC: Potomac Books, 2006.
Minear, L., *The Humanitarian Enterprise: Dilemmas and Discoveries*. Bloomfield: Kumarian, 2002.
Mitchell, N., *Jimmy Carter in Africa: Race and the Cold War*. Washington, DC: Woodrow Wilson Press, 2016.
Moores, C., *Civil Liberties and Human Rights in Twentieth-Century Britain*. Cambridge: Cambridge University Press, 2017.
Moorhouse, G., *The Diplomats: The Foreign Office Today*. London: Jonathan Cape, 1977.
Morgan, A., *Harold Wilson*. London: Pluto, 1992.
Morgenthau, H.J., *Human Rights and Foreign Policy*. New York: Council on Religion and Foreign Affairs, 1979.
Morrissey, O., B. Smith, and E. Horesh, *British Aid and International Trade*. Buckingham: Open University Press, 1992.
Mower Jr., A.G., *Human Rights and American Foreign Policy: The Carter and Reagan Experiences*. New York: Greenwood Press, 1987.
Moyn, S., *The Last Utopia: Human Rights in History*. Cambridge, MA: Harvard University Press, 2010.
Moyn, S., *Christian Human Rights*. Philadelphia: University of Pennsylvania Press, 2015.
Moyn, S., *Not Enough: Human Rights in an Unequal World*. Cambridge, MA: The Belknap Press of Harvard University Press, 2018.

Muravchik, J., *The Uncertain Crusade: Jimmy Carter and the Dilemmas of Human Rights Policy*. Washington, DC: American Enterprise Institute for Public Policy Research, 1991.

Nartzizenfield Sneh, I., *The Future Almost Arrived: How Jimmy Carter Failed to Change U.S. Foreign Policy*. New York: Peter Lang, 2008.

Nehring, H., *The Politics of Security: British and West German Protest Movements and the Early Cold War, 1945–1970*. Oxford: Oxford University Press, 2013.

Owen, D., *Human Rights*. London: Jonathan Cape, 1978.

Owen, D., *Face the Future*. Oxford: Oxford University Press, 1981.

Parkinson, C.O.H., *Bills of Rights and Decolonization: The Emergence of Domestic Human Rights Instruments in Britain's Overseas Territories*. Oxford: Oxford University Press, 2007.

Perry, K.H., *London is the Place for Me: Black Britons, Citizenship and the Politics of Race*. Oxford: Oxford University Press, 2015.

Phillips, P.T., *A Kingdom on Earth: Anglo-American Social Christianity, 1880–1940*. University Park: The Pennsylvania State University Press, 1996.

Pimlott, B., *Harold Wilson*. London: HarperCollins, 1992.

Power, S., *A Problem from Hell: America and the Age of Genocide*, 2nd edn. London: Flamingo, 2003.

Pythian, M., *The Politics of British Arms Sales Since 1964*. Manchester: Manchester University Press, 2000.

Reynolds, D., *Britannia Overruled: British Policy and World Power in the Twentieth Century*, 2nd edn. Harlow: Pearson, 2000.

Rhodes, R.A.W., *Network Governance and the Differentiated Polity: Selected Essays, Volume I*. Oxford: Oxford University Press, 2017.

Rieff, D., *Slaughterhouse: Bosnia and the Failure of the West*. New York: Touchstone, 1995.

Rist, G., *The History of Development: From Western Origins to Global Faith*, 3rd edn. London: Zed Books, 2008.

Robb, T.K., *Jimmy Carter and the Anglo-American 'Special Relationship'*. Edinburgh: Edinburgh University Press, 2017.

Rosati, J.A., *The Carter Administration's Quest for Global Community: Beliefs and their Impact on Behaviour*. Columbia, SC: University of South Carolina Press, 1987.

Sanders, D., *Losing an Empire, Finding a Role: British Foreign Policy since 1945*. Basingstoke: Palgrave Macmillan, 1990.

Schumaker, K., *Troublemakers: Students' Rights and Racial Justice in the Long 1960s*. New York: New York University Press, 2019.

Self, R., *British Foreign and Defence Policy since 1945: Challenges and Dilemmas in a Changing World*. Basingstoke: Palgrave Macmillan, 2010.

Shannon, M.K., *Losing Hearts and Minds: American-Iranian Relations and International Education during the Cold War*. Ithaca, New York and London: Cornell University Press, 2017.

Shaw, C., *Britannia's Embrace: Modern Humanitarianism and the Imperial Origins of Refugee Relief*. Oxford: Oxford University Press, 2015.

Simms, B., *Unfinest Hour: Britain and the Destruction of Bosnia*. London: Penguin, 2002.

Simpson, A.W.B., *Human Rights and the End of Empire: Britain and the Genesis of the European Convention*. Oxford: Oxford University Press, 2001.

Skinner, R., *The Foundations of Anti-Apartheid: Liberal Humanitarianism and Traditional Activists in Britain and the United States, c. 1919–64*. Basingstoke: Palgrave Macmillan, 2010.

Snyder, S.B., *Human Rights Activism and the End of the Cold War: A Transnational History of the Helsinki Network*. Cambridge: Cambridge University Press, 2011.
Snyder, S.B., *From Selma to Moscow: How Human Rights Activists Transformed US Foreign Policy*. New York: Columbia University Press, 2018.
Søndergaard, R.S., *Reagan, Congress, and Human Rights: Contesting Morality in US Foreign Policy*. Cambridge: Cambridge University Press, 2020.
Stockwood, M., *Cambridge Sermons*. London: Hodder and Stoughton, 1959.
Stockwood, M., *The Cross and the Sickle*. London: Sheldon Press, 1978.
Stewart R., and G. Knaus, *Can Intervention Work?* New York: W.W. Norton & Company, 2012.
Sylvest, C., *British Liberal Internationalism, 1880–1930*. Manchester: Manchester University Press, 2009.
Thomas, D.C., *The Helsinki Effect: International Norms, Human Rights, and the Demise of Communism*. Princeton: Princeton University Press, 2001.
Thörn, H., *Anti-Apartheid and the Emergence of a Global Civil Society*. Basingstoke: Palgrave Macmillan, 2006.
Tulli, U., *A Precarious Equilibrium: Human Rights and Détente in Jimmy Carter's Soviet Policy*. Manchester: Manchester University Press, 2020.
Vickers, R., *The Labour Party and the World, Volume 1: The Evolution of Labour's Foreign Policy, 1900–51*. Manchester: Manchester University Press, 2003.
Vickers, R., *The Labour Party and the World, Volume II: Labour's Foreign Policy since 1951*. Manchester: Manchester University Press, 2011.
Vincent, R.J., *Human Rights and International Relations*. Cambridge: Cambridge University Press, 1986.
Wall, S., *A Stranger in Europe: Britain and the EU from Thatcher to Blair*. Oxford: Oxford University Press, 2008.
Wallace, W., *The Foreign Policy Process in Britain*. London: Royal Institute of International Affairs, 1977.
Whelan, D.J., *Indivisible Human Rights: A History*. Philadelphia: University of Pennsylvania Press, 2010.
White, B., *Britain, Détente and Changing East–West Relations*. London: Routledge, 1992.
Whyte, J., *The Morals of the Market: Human Rights and Neoliberalism*. London: Verso, 2019.
Wildenthal, L., *The Language of Human Rights in West Germany*. Philadelphia: University of Pennsylvania Press, 2012.
Wilkinson, A., *Christian Socialism: Scott Holland to Tony Blair*. London: SCM Press, 1998.
Woollacott, W., *After Suez: Adrift in the American Century*. London & New York: I.B. Tauris, 2006.
Young, H., *This Blessed Plot: Britain and Europe from Churchill to Blair*. London: Macmillan, 1998.
Ziegler, P., *Wilson: The Authorised Life of Lord Wilson of Rievaulx*. London: Wiedenfeld and Nicolson, 1993.

Chapters in edited collections

Ashby Wilson, R., and R.D. Brown, 'Introduction'. In *Humanitarianism and Suffering*, edited by Richard Ashby Wilson and Richard D. Brown, 1–28. Cambridge: Cambridge University Press, 2009.

Badalassi, N., and S.B. Snyder, 'Conclusion'. In *The CSCE and the End of the Cold War: Diplomacy, Societies and Human Rights, 1972–1990,* edited by Nicholas Badalassi and Sarah B. Snyder, 350–5. New York & Oxford: Berghahn, 2019.

Badalassi, N., and S.B. Snyder, 'Introduction'. In *The CSCE and the End of the Cold War: Diplomacy, Societies and Human Rights, 1972–1990,* edited by Nicholas Badalassi and Sarah B. Snyder, 1–14. New York & Oxford: Berghahn, 2019.

Beech, M., 'David Owen'. In *Labour's Thinkers: The Intellectual Roots of Labour from Tawney to Gordon Brown,* edited by Matt Beech and Kevin Hickson, 196–219. London: I.B. Tauris, 2007.

Berman, P., 'The Dream of a New Society'. In *The Great Revolutions of 1968,* edited by Jeremi Suri, 301–08. New York: W.W. Norton & Company, 2007.

Blackledge, P., 'The New Left: Beyond Stalinism and Social Democracy'?. In *Against the Grain: The British Far Left from 1956,* edited by Evan Smith and Matthew Worley, 45–61. Manchester: Manchester University Press, 2014.

Bradley, M.P., 'The Origins of the 1970s Global Human Rights Imagination'. In *The Long 1970s: Human Rights, East–West Détente and Transnational Relations,* edited by Paol Villaume, Rasmus Mariager, and Helle Porsdam, 15–32. London: Routledge, 2016.

Brown, M.D., 'A Very British Vision of Détente: The United Kingdom's Foreign Policy During the Helsinki Process, 1969–1975'. In *Visions of the End of the Cold War in Europe, 1945–1990,* edited by Frédéric Bozo, Marie-Pierre Rey, N. Piers Ludlow and Bernd Rother, 139–56. New York/Oxford: Berghahn Books, 2012.

Buchanan, T., 'Human Rights Campaigns in Modern Britain'. In *NGOs in Modern Britain: Non-State Actors in Society and Politics since 1945,* edited by Nick Crowson, Matthew Hilton and James McKay, 113–24. Basingstoke: Palgrave Macmillan, 2009.

Buchanan, T., 'Human Rights, the Memory of War and the Making of a "European" Identity, 1945–75'. In *Europeanization in the Twentieth Century: Historical Approaches,* edited by Martin Conway and Kiran Klaus Patel, 151–71. Basingstoke: Palgrave Macmillan, 2010.

Carr, F., 'David Owen: Foreign Secretary, 1977–79'. In *British Foreign Secretaries since 1974,* edited by Kevin Theakston, 93–116. London: Routledge, 2004.

Clarke, M., 'Britain and European Political Cooperation in the CSCE'. In *European Détente: Case Studies of the Politics of East–West Relations,* edited by Kenneth Dyson, 221–36. London: Frances Pinter, 1986.

Cmiel, K., 'The Recent History of Human Rights'. In *The Human Rights Revolution: An International History,* edited by Akira Iriya, Petra Goedde and William I. Hitchcock, 27–53. Oxford: Oxford University Press, 2012.

Connelly, M., 'Future Shock: The End of the World as They Knew it'. In *The Shock of the Global: The 1970s in Perspective,* edited by Niall Ferguson, Charles S. Maier, Erez Manela and Daniel J. Sargent, 337–50. Cambridge, MA: The Belknap Press of Harvard University Press, 2011.

Cotey Morgan, M., 'The Seventies and the Rebirth of Human Rights'. In *The Shock of the Global: The 1970s in Perspective,* edited by Niall Ferguson, Charles S. Maier, Erez Manela and Daniel J. Sargent, 237–50. Cambridge, MA: The Belknap Press of Harvard University Press, 2011.

Davis, M., '"Labourism" and the New Left'. In *Interpreting the Labour Party: Approaches to Labour Politics and History,* edited by John Callaghan, Steven Fielding and Steve Ludlam, 39–56. Manchester: Manchester University Press, 2003.

Donnelly, J., 'The Social Construction of International Human Rights'. In *Human Rights in Global Politics*, edited by Tim Dunne and Nicholas J. Wheeler, 71–102. Cambridge: Cambridge University Press, 1999.

Doyle, M.W., 'Ethics and Foreign Policy: A Speculative Essay'. In *New Labour's Foreign Policy*, edited by Richard Little and Mark Wickham-Jones, 49–60. Manchester: Manchester University Press, 2000.

Dunne, T., and M. Hanson, 'Human Rights in International Relations'. In *Human Rights: Politics and Practice*, edited by Michael Goodhart, 3rd edn, 44–59. Oxford: Oxford University Press, 2016.

Eckel, J., 'Allende's Shadow, Leftist Furor, and Human Rights: The Pinochet Dictatorship in International Politics'. In *European Solidarity with Chile, 1970s–1980s*, edited by Kim Christiaens, Idesbald Goddeeris and Magaly Rodriguez Garcia, 67–92. Frankfurt: Peter Lang, 2014.

Eckel, J., 'Humanitarian Intervention as Global Governance: Western Governments and Suffering "Others" Before and After 1990'. In *Human Rights and Humanitarian Intervention: Legitimizing the Use of Force since the 1970s,* Norbert Frei, Daniel Stahl and Annette Weinke, 64–88. Göttingen: Wallstein Verlag, 2017.

Falk, R., 'The Challenge of Genocide and Genocidal Politics in an Era of Globalisation'. In *Human Rights in Global Politics*, edited by Tim Dunne and Nicholas J. Wheeler, 177–94. Cambridge: Cambridge University Press, 1999.

Fisher, J., E. Pedaliu and R. Smith, 'Introduction'. In *The Foreign Office, Commerce and British Foreign Policy in the Twentieth Century*, edited by John Fisher, Effie Pedaliu and Richard Smith, 1–24. Basingstoke: Palgrave Macmillan, 2016.

Foot, R., 'The Cold War and Human Rights'. In *The Cambridge History of the Cold War, Volume 3: Endings*, edited by Melvyn P. Leffler and Odd Arne Westad, 445–65. Cambridge: Cambridge University Press, 2010.

Forsythe, D.P., 'Introduction'. In *Human Rights and Comparative Foreign Policy: Foundations of Peace*, edited by David P. Forsythe, 1–18. New York: UN University, 2000.

Fowler, D., 'From "Danny the Red" to British Student Power: Labour and the International Student Revolts of the 1960s'. In *The British Labour Party and the Wider World*, edited by Paul Corthorn and Jonathan Davis, 167–89. London and New York: Tauris Academic Studies, 2008.

Garnett, J., et al, 'Introduction'. In *Redefining Christian Britain: Post-1945 Perspectives*, edited by Jane Garnett, Matthew Grimley, Alana Harris, William Whyte and Sarah Williams, 1–18. London: SCM Press, 2006.

Gilcher-Holtey, I., 'May 1968 in France: The Rise and Fall of a New Social Movement'. In *1968: The World Transformed*, edited by Carole Fink, Philipp Gassert and Detlef Junker, 253–76. Cambridge: Cambridge University Press, 1998.

Hampshire, E., 'Missing the "Klondike Rush?" British Trade with China, 1971–9 and the Politics of Defence Sales'. In *The Foreign Office, Commerce and British Foreign Policy in the Twentieth Century*, edited by John Fisher, Effie Pedaliu and Richard Smith, 527–53. Basingstoke: Palgrave Macmillan, 2016.

Heerten, L., 'The Dystopia of Postcolonial Catastrophe: Self-Determination, the Biafran War of Secession, and the 1970s Human Rights Movement'. In *The Breakthrough: Human Rights in the 1970s*, edited by Jan Eckel and Samuel Moyn, 15–32. Philadelphia: University of Pennsylvania Press, 2014.

Hill, C., 'Britain: A Convenient Schizophrenia'. In *National Foreign Policies and European Political Cooperation*, edited by Christopher Hill, 19–33. London: George Allen & Unwin, 1983.

Hill, C., 'Convergence, Divergence and Dialectics: National Foreign Policies and the CFSP'. In *Paradoxes of European Foreign Policy*, edited by Jan Zielonka, 35–51. The Hague: Kluwer Law International, 1998.

Hill, C., and W. Wallace, 'Introduction: Actors and Actions'. In *The Actors in Europe's Foreign Policy*, edited by Christopher Hill, 1–16. London: Routledge, 1996.

Hirsch, S., 'The United Kingdom: Competing Conceptions of Internationalism'. In *European Solidarity with Chile, 1970s–1980s*, edited by Kim Christiaens, Idesbald Goddeeris and Magaly Rodriquez Garcia, 145–62. Frankfurt: Peter Lang, 2014.

Hoffmann, S., 'Humanitarian Intervention in the Former Yugoslavia'. In *The Ethics and Politics of Humanitarian Intervention*, edited by Stanley Hoffmann (with contributions from Robert C. Johansen, James P. Sterba and Raimo Väyrynen), 38–60. Notre Dame, IN: University of Notre Dame Press, 1996.

Hoffman, S.L., 'Introduction: Genealogies of Human Rights'. In *Human Rights in the Twentieth Century*, edited by Stefan-Ludwig Hoffmann, 1–26. Cambridge: Cambridge University Press, 2011.

Hopkins, M.F., 'Introduction'. In *The Washington Embassy: British Ambassadors to the United States, 1939–77*, edited by Michael F. Hopkins, Saul Kelly and John W. Young, 1–13. Basingstoke: Palgrave Macmillan, 2009.

Hyde-Price, A., 'Interests, Institutions and Identities in the Study of European Foreign Policy'. In *Rethinking European Foreign Policy*, edited by Ben Tonra and Thomas Christiansen, 99–113. Manchester: Manchester University Press, 2004.

Jensen S.L.B., and R. Burke, 'From the Normative to the Transnational: Methods in the Study of Human Rights History'. In *Research Methods in Human Rights: A Handbook*, edited by Bärd A. Andreassen, Hans-Otto Sano and Siobhán McInerney-Lankford, 117–40. Cheltenham: Edward Elgar, 2017.

Keys, B., '"Something to Boast About": Western Enthusiasm for Carter's Human Rights Diplomacy'. In *Reasserting America in the 1970s: U.S. Public Diplomacy and the Rebuilding of America's Image Abroad*, edited by Hallvard Notaker, Giles Scott-Smith and David J. Snyder, 229–44. Manchester: Manchester University Press, 2016.

Klose, F., '"Source of Embarrassment": Human Rights, State of Emergency, and the Wars of Decolonization'. In *Human Rights in the Twentieth Century*, edited by Stefan-Ludwig Hoffmann, 237–57. Cambridge: Cambridge University Press, 2011.

Kuperman, A.J., 'Humanitarian Intervention'. In *Human Rights: Politics and Practice*, edited by Michael Goodhart, 3rd edn, 370–88. Oxford: Oxford University Press, 2016.

Lane, A., 'Foreign and Defence Policy'. In *New Labour, Old Labour: The Wilson and Callaghan Governments, 1974–79*, edited by Anthony Seldon and Kevin Hickson, 154–69. London: Routledge, 2004.

MacQueen, N., 'Cold War Peacekeeping versus Humanitarian Intervention: Beyond the Hammarskjöldian Model'. In *The Emergence of Humanitarian Intervention: Ideas and Practice from the Nineteenth Century to the Present*, edited by Fabian Klose, 231–52. Cambridge: Cambridge University Press, 2016.

Madsen, M.R., 'France, the UK, and the "Boomerang" of the Internationalisation of Human Rights (1945–2000)'. In *Human Rights Brought Home: Socio-Legal Perspectives on Human Rights in the National Context,* edited by Patrick Schmidt and Simon Halliday, 57–86. Oxford and Portland, OR: Hart Publishing, 2004.

Migani, G., 'Lomé and the North–South Relations (1975–1984): From the "New International Economic Order" to a New Conditionality'. In *Europe in a Globalising World: Global Challenges and European Responses in the 'Long' 1970s*, edited by Claudia Hiepel, 123–46. Baden-Baden: Nomos, 2014.

Morphet, S., 'British Foreign Policy and Human Rights: From Low to High Politics'. In *Human Rights and Comparative Foreign Policy: Foundations of Peace*, edited by David P. Forsythe, 87–114. New York: UN University, 2000.

Müller, J.W., 'Introduction: Concepts, Character, and the Specter of New Cold Wars'. In *Isaiah Berlin's Cold War Liberalism*, edited by Jan-Werner Müller, 1–10, Singapore: Palgrave Macmillan, 2019.

Nehring, H., '"The Long Night is Over": The Campaign for Nuclear Disarmament, "Generation" and the Politics of Religion (1957–1964)'. In *Redefining Christian Britain: Post-1945 Perspectives*, edited by Jane Garnett et al, 138–47. London: SCM Press, 2006.

Nehring, H., 'Great Britain'. In *1968 in Europe: A History of Protest and Activism, 1956–1977*, edited by Martin Klimke and Joachim Scharloth, 125–36. Basingstoke: Palgrave Macmillan, 2008.

Ohrgaard, J.C., 'International Relations or European Integration: Is the CFSP Sui Generis?'. In *Rethinking European Foreign Policy*, edited by Ben Tonra and Thomas Christiansen, 26–44. Manchester: Manchester University Press, 2004.

O'Sullivan, K., 'A "Global Nervous System": The Rise and Rise of European Humanitarian NGOs, 1945–1985'. In *International Organizations and Development, 1945–1990*, edited by Marc Frey, Sönke Kunkel and Corinna R. Unger, 196–219. Basingstoke: Palgrave Macmillan, 2014.

Owen, D., 'James Callaghan'. In *Half In, Half Out: Prime Ministers on Europe*, edited by Andrew Adonis, 111–32. London: Biteback, 2018.

Paulmann, J., 'Humanitarianism and Empire'. In *The Encyclopedia of Empire, Volume II*, edited by John M. Mackenzie, 1112–23. Oxford: Wiley, 2016.

Poggiolini, I., 'Thatcher's Double-Track Road to the End of the Cold War: The Irreconcilability of Liberalization and Preservation'. In *Visions of the End of the Cold War in Europe, 1945–1990*, edited by Frédéric Bozo, Marie-Pierre Rey, N. Piers Ludlow and Bernd Rother, 266–79. New York/Oxford: Berghahn Books, 2012.

Preston, A., 'Introduction: The Religious Cold War'. In *Religion and the Cold War: A Global Perspective*, edited by Philip E. Muelenbeck, xi–xxii. Nashville: Vanderbilt University Press, 2012.

Renders, H., and B. de Haan, 'Introduction: The Challenges of Biographical Studies'. In *Theoretical Discussions of Biography: Approaches from History, Microhistory, and Life Writing*, edited by Hans Renders and Binnie de Haan, 1–8. Leiden: Brill, 2004.

Renders, H., B. de Haan, and J. Harmsma, J., 'The Biographical Turn: Biography as Critical Method in the Humanities and in Society'. In *The Biographical Turn: Lives in History*, edited by Hans Renders, Binnie de Haan and Jonne Harmsma, 3–11, New York: Routledge, 2017.

Rex, J., 'The Race Relations Catastrophe'. In *Matters of Principle: Labour's Last Chance*, edited by Tyrell Burgess et al, 70–83, London: Penguin, 1968.

Riedel, E., and M. Will, 'Human Rights Clauses in External Agreements of the EC'. In *The EU and Human Rights*, edited by Philip Alston, Mara Bustelo and James Heenan, 723–56. Oxford: Oxford University Press, 1999.

Riley, J., 'Liberal Pluralism and Common Decency'. In *Isaiah Berlin's Cold War Liberalism*, edited by Jan-Werner Müller, 57–91. Singapore: Palgrave Macmillan, 2019.

Romano, A., 'British Policy Towards Socialist Countries in the 1970s: Trade as a Cornerstone of Détente'. In *The Foreign Office, Commerce and British Foreign Policy in the Twentieth Century*, edited by John Fisher, Effie Pedaliu and Richard Smith, 465–85. Basingstoke: Palgrave Macmillan, 2016.

Rummel, R., and I. Wiedemann, 'Identifying Institutional Paradoxes of CFSP'. In *Paradoxes of European Foreign Policy*, edited by Jan Zielonka, 53–66. The Hague: Kluwer Law International, 1998.

Sargent, D.J., 'The United States and Globalization in the 1970s'. In *The Shock of the Global: The 1970s in Perspective*, edited by Niall Ferguson, Charles S. Maier, Erez Manela and Daniel J. Sargent, 49–64. Cambridge, MA: The Belknap Press of Harvard University Press, 2011.

Schreiner, A., 'Humanitarian Intervention, the Labour Party and the Press: The Break-up of Yugoslavia in the 1990s'. In *The British Labour Party and the Wider World*, edited by Paul Corthorn and Jonathan Davis, 190–208. London & New York: Tauris Academic Studies, 2008.

Sedgwick, P., 'Farewell, Grosvenor Square'. In *The Left in Britain, 1956–1968*, edited by David Widgery, 19–41. London: Penguin, 1976.

Sedgwick, P., 'The Two New Lefts'. In *The Left in Britain, 1956–1968*, edited by David Widgery, 131–51. London: Penguin, 1976.

Schmidt, P., and S. Halliday, 'Introduction: Socio-Legal Perspectives on Human Rights in the National Context'. In *Human Rights Brought Home: Socio-Legal Perspectives on Human Rights in the National Context*, edited by Patrick Schmidt and Simon Halliday, 1–21. Oxford and Portland, OR: Hart Publishing, 2004.

Simma, B., J.B. Aschenbrenner and C. Schulte, 'Human Rights Considerations in the Development Co-operation Activities of the EC'. In *The EU and Human Rights*, edited by Philip Alston, Mara Bustelo and James Heenan, 586–9. Oxford: Oxford University Press, 1999.

Smith, K.E., and M. Light, 'Introduction'. In *Ethics and Foreign Policy*, edited by Karen E. Smith and Margot Light, 1–11. Cambridge: Cambridge University Press, 2001.

Smith, E., and M. Worley, 'Introduction: The Far Left in Britain from 1956'. In *Against the Grain: The British Far Left from 1956*, edited by Evan Smith and Matthew Worley, 1–22. Manchester: Manchester University Press, 2014.

Smith, R., '"Paying Our Way in the World": The FCO, Export Promotion and Iran in the 1970s'. In *The Foreign Office, Commerce and British Foreign Policy in the Twentieth Century*, edited by John Fisher, Effie Pedaliu and Richard Smith, 487–506. Basingstoke: Palgrave Macmillan, 2016.

Snyder, S.B., 'The Defeat of Ernest Lefever's Nomination: Keeping Human Rights on the United States Foreign Policy Agenda'. In *Challenging U.S. Foreign Policy: America and the World in the Long Twentieth Century*, edited by Bevan Sewell and Scott Lucas, 136–61. Basingstoke: Palgrave Macmillan, 2011.

Snyder, S.B., 'Human Rights in the Cold War'. In *The Routledge Handbook of the Cold War*, edited by Artemy M. Kalinovsky and Craig Daigle, 237–48. New York: Routledge, 2014.

Spelling, A., 'Ambassadors Richardson, Armstrong and Brewster, 1975–81'. In *The Embassy in Grosvenor Square: American Ambassadors to the United Kingdom, 1938–2008*, edited by Alison R. Holmes and J. Simon Rofe, 189–214. Basingstoke: Palgrave Macmillan, 2012.

Stevens, S., 'Why South Africa? The Politics of Anti-Apartheid Activism in the Long 1970s'. In *The Breakthrough: Human Rights in the 1970s*, edited by Jan Eckel and Samuel Moyn, 204–25. Philadelphia: University of Pennsylvania Press, 2014.

Stockwell, S., 'Ends of Empire'. In *The British Empire: Themes and Perspectives*, edited by Sarah Stockwell, 269–93. Oxford: Blackwell, 2008.

Straws, S., 'Genocide and Human Rights'. In *Human Rights: Politics and Practice*, edited by Michael Goodhart, 3rd edn, 351–69. Oxford: Oxford University Press, 2016.

Theakston, K., 'New Labour and the Foreign Office'. In *New Labour's Foreign Policy*, edited by Michael Goodhart, 112-27. Manchester: Manchester University Press, 2000.

Thompson, A., 'Humanitarian Interventions, Past and Present'. In *The Emergence of Humanitarian Intervention: Ideas and Practice from the Nineteenth Century to the Present*, edited by Fabian Klose, 331-56. Cambridge: Cambridge University Press, 2016.

Thompson, A., 'Introduction'. In *Britain's Experience of Empire in the Twentieth Century*, edited by Andrew Thompson, 1-32. Oxford: Oxford University Press, 2012.

Townshend, C., 'Northern Ireland'. In *Foreign Policy and Human Rights: Issues and Responses*, edited by R.J Vincent, 119-40. Cambridge: Cambridge University Press, 1986.

Väyrynen, R., 'Introduction: How Much Force in Humanitarian Intervention?'. In *The Ethics and Politics of Humanitarian Intervention*, edited by Stanley Hoffmann (with contributions from Robert C. Johansen, James P. Sterba and Raimo Väyrynen), 1-11. Notre Dame, IN: University of Notre Dame Press, 1996.

Wallace, W., 'Introduction: Cooperation and Convergence in European Foreign Policy'. In *National Foreign Policies and European Political Cooperation*, edited by Christopher Hill, 1-16. London: George Allen & Unwin, 1983.

Whiting, R., 'The Empire and British Politics'. In *Britain's Experience of Empire in the Twentieth Century*, edited by Andrew Thompson, 161-210. Oxford: Oxford University Press, 2012.

Wickham-Jones, M., 'Labour Party Politics and Foreign Policy'. In *New Labour's Foreign Policy*, edited by Richard Little and Mark Wickham-Jones, 93-111. Manchester: Manchester University Press, 2000.

Widgery, D., 'The Double Exposure: Suez and Hungary'. In *The Left in Britain, 1956-1968*, edited by David Widgery, 43-65. London: Penguin, 1976.

Williams, P., 'Britain, Détente and the Conference on Security and Cooperation in Europe'. In *European Détente: Case Studies of the Politics and East-West Relations*, edited by Kenneth Dyson, 221-36. London: Frances Pinter, 1986.

Wilson, H., 'Speech by the Prime Minister The RT Hon Harold Wilson, OBE, FRS, MP, at the Commonwealth Heads of Government Meeting, Kingston, Jamaica, 1 May 1975'. In *Future Resources and World Development*, edited by Paul Rogers, 189-98. New York and London: Plenum Press, 1976.

Wiseman, G., 'The Palme Commission: New Thinking about Security'. In *International Commissions and the Power of Ideas*, edited by Ramesh Thakur, Andrew F. Cooper and John English, 46-75. New York: United Nations University Press, 2005.

Wrigley, C., 'Now you See it, Now you Don't: Harold Wilson and Labour's Foreign Policy 1964-70'. In *The Wilson Government, 1964-1970*, edited by Richard Coopey, Steven Fielding and Nick Tiratsoo, 123-35. London: Pinter Publishers, 1993.

Dissertations

Brivati, L., 'The Campaign for Democratic Socialism 1960-1964' (PhD thesis, Queen Mary University of London, 1992).

Erciyas, O., 'British Dilemmas: Arms Sales and Human Rights in Anglo-Iranian relations (1968-1979)' (PhD thesis, University of Leicester, 2020).

Hanney, R., 'Special Advisers: Their Place in British Government' (PhD thesis, Brunel University, February 1993).

Lakin, M., 'David Owen, New Labour and the Social Market Economy', Master's Dissertation published online by the Social Market Foundation, 2009, available at https://www.yumpu.com/en/document/read/51594306/david-owen-new-labour-and-the-social-market-economy-the- (accessed 26 March 2020).

Riley, C.L., 'Monstrous predatory vampires and beneficent fairy-godmothers: British post-war colonial development in Africa' (PhD thesis, UCL, 2013) available at https://discovery.ucl.ac.uk/id/eprint/1389424/1/Final%2520Thesis.pdf (accessed 25 March 2020).

Sasson, T., 'In the Name of Humanity: Britain and the Rise of Global Humanitarianism' (PhD thesis, UC Berkeley, 2015).

Published reports, papers and manifestos

Biden, J. R., Jr., 'To Stand Against Aggression: Milosevic, The Bosnian Republic, and The Conscience of the West', A Report to the Committee on Foreign Relations, United States Senate, April 1993 (Washington, DC.: US Government Printing Office, 1993).

Carnegie Commission on Preventing Deadly Conflict, *Preventing Deadly Conflict: Executive Summary of the Final Report* (Washington, DC: Carnegie Commission on Preventing Deadly Conflict, 1997).

Gromes, T., 'A Humanitarian Milestone? NATO's 1999 Intervention in Kosovo and Trends in Military Responses to Mass Violence', *Peace Institute Frankfurt/Leibniz Institut Hessische Stiftung Friedens – und Konfliktforschung* (PRIF Reports, 35), 2019, 1–35.

The Haselmere Group, *The Haselmere Declaration* (London: The Haselmere Committee, 1968).

The Independent Commission on International Humanitarian Issues, *Famine: A Man-Made Disaster? A Report for the Independent Commission on International Humanitarian Issues* (London and Sydney: Pan Books, 1985).

The Independent Commission on International Humanitarian Issues, '*Winning the Human Race? The Report of the Independent Commission on International Humanitarian Issues* (London and New Jersey: Zed Books, 1988).

Labour Party, *The New Hope for Britain: Labour's Manifesto 1983* (London: The Labour Party, 1983).

Index

Abrams, Elliot 130
Academics for Chile 37
Acland, Sir Richard 20
Adams, W.J. 139
Aden 33
Afghanistan 140
African, Caribbean and Pacific Countries (ACP) 9, 87, 114–16
Aitkin, Ian 11
Ali, Tariq 38–40
Allaun, Frank 80
Allende, Salvador 12, 37, 40, 41, 46, 49, 61, 185
Amin, Idi 113
Amnesty International 2, 23, 37, 45, 55, 71, 72, 74, 137, 139
Anglo-American relations 3, 9, 12, 72–3, 87–8, 90–9, 104, 108–10, 112, 113, 117–18, 128–31, 150–1, 186
Anglo-Iranian relations 8, 69–75, 78, 80–3
Annan, Kofi 174, 175, 184
Anti-Apartheid Movement (AAM) 8, 13, 19, 20, 21, 25, 28–30, 39, 42, 45–6
Argentina 2, 60, 130
Australia 139

Ballantrae, Lord 86
Banks, Tony 170
Beckett, Dame Margaret 177
Belgium 111, 113, 171
Belize 59–61, 68, 82
Benenson, Peter 23, 37
Benn, Tony 140
Berlin, Isaiah 8, 77–9, 83, 190
Berrill Report (CPRS Report) 69, 86, 91
Biafra 33, 35
Blair, Tony 5, 10, 156, 157, 176, 179, 180, 181, 182, 183, 187, 191
Blaker, Lord Peter 137

Bosnia 4, 9, 156, 157, 158, 162, 164, 167, 171–2, 173, 175, 176, 182, 183, 187, 191
Brandt Commission 141, 144
Brewster, Kingman Jr. 94, 109, 124, 126, 128
British Council for Aid to Refugees 37
British Embassy
 Brussels 171
 San Salvador 60
 Santiago 40, 41
 Tehran 70–1, 72, 74
 Washington 54, 90, 95, 112, 171
British Sports Council 125
Brockway, Lord Fenner 20, 132, 134
Brown, Gordon 177
Brown, Lord George 57
Brzezinski, Zbigniew 83
Buerk, Michael 144
Bush, George H.W. 160–1, 164
Butler of Brockwell, Lord 58

Cabinet Committee on Defence and Overseas Policy (DOP) 61–3, 65
Callaghan, Jim (Baron Callaghan) 4, 54, 63–5, 70, 75, 82, 92–4, 99, 114, 126
 government of 4, 8, 9, 41, 54, 69, 70, 82, 87, 91–2, 97, 104, 110, 113, 116–18, 119, 121, 129–30, 131, 133–5, 139, 153, 185–7, 189
Campaign Against the Arms Trade 139
Campaign for Nuclear Disarmament (CND) 8, 13, 19, 20, 21, 25, 28–30, 39, 45–6
Canada 139, 184
Cardiff Justice and Peace Group 64
Carnegie Commission on Preventing Deadly Conflict 10, 157, 178–81, 182, 183, 184, 187, 191

Carrington, Lord Peter 100, 165, 173, 179
Carter, Jimmy 54, 55, 82, 85, 92–4, 99, 104, 107–9, 129, 184
   administration of 9, 50, 54, 58, 72–3, 80, 82, 85, 87, 90, 92–9, 100, 104, 106–10, 113, 117–18, 119, 122–3, 128, 129–30, 186
Catholic Institute for International Relations (CIIR) 8, 37, 41, 51, 61–7, 82
Central Intelligence Agency (CIA) 107
Central Policy Review Staff (CPRS) 86, 91
Central Treaty Organization (CENTO) 71, 76
Charter 77 129
Charter of Paris for a New Europe 151–4, 187
Chatham House 86, 138–9
Cheysson, Claude 114
Chile 2, 8, 12, 14, 37–44, 46, 49, 55, 60, 130, 135, 140, 149, 185
Chile Solidarity Campaign 2, 6, 37–42, 46
China, People's Republic of (PRC) 126
Chitnis, Lord Pratap 62, 64
Christian Aid 37
Christopher, Warren 184
Churchill, Sir Winston 91
Clark, Alan 149
Clinton, Bill 164–5
   administration of 172
Clinton, Hillary 184
Cohn-Bendit, Daniel 38
Coles, Sir John 32
Collins, Canon John 20, 21
Colonial Office 32
Committee of Permanent Representatives (COREPER) 114
Commonwealth, The 88, 91, 133
Communist Party of Great Britain (CPGB) 15–16, 37
Conference on Security and Cooperation in Europe (CSCE) 9, 49, 95, 105–7, 117–18, 121, 122–7, 141, 149–54, 167, 186–7
   Belgrade Conference 123–5
   and Helsinki Final Act 105–6, 118, 122, 123, 124, 131, 186
   Helsinki monitoring group 123–5
   Madrid Conference 127

Conservative Party 5, 9, 14, 18, 66, 128, 137, 162
Convention on the Prevention and Punishment of the Crime of Genocide 162
Cook, Robin 3–4, 41, 71, 177, 180, 189
CPRS Report, see Berrill Report
Craddock, Sir Percy 162, 163
Croatia 165, 166, 170
Crosland, Anthony 11, 52, 58, 64, 70–1, 97, 185
Crowe, Sir Brian L. 56, 152
CSCE, see Conference on Security and Cooperation in Europe
Czechoslovakia 35, 38, 123, 151

Darlington, Roger 66
Davignon Report 105
Dayton Agreement 175
De Courten, Jean 174
Dell, Edmund 61
Denmark 114
Department of International Development (DfID) 177
Derian, Patricia 95–6, 130
Destexhe, Alain 172, 174
Dimbleby, David 58
Driberg, Tom 20
Dutschke, Rudi 38

East Germany 107, 189
East Timor 156
Eden, Anthony 15, 23
Egypt 68, 128
Eker, Rita 129
El Salvador 8, 51, 59–65, 67–8, 82, 140, 185, 190
Ennals, David 55
Ennals, Martin 45, 46, 55, 74
Ethiopia 145
European Commission on Human Rights 97
European Community (EC) 6, 9, 12, 87–90, 104–6, 108–18, 140, 158, 165, 166, 186, 190
European Convention on Human Rights 24, 32, 104–5
European Council 106, 110

European Political Cooperation (EPC) 105–6, 111, 117–18, 186
European Union (EU) 157, 172, 179
Evans, Dame Glynne 176, 180

Fay, Stephen 43
Feil, Colonel Scott R. 180–1
Fight World Poverty 145
Filochowski, Julian 37, 41, 61–7
Fischer, Joschka 38
FitzHerbert, G.E. 116
Foreign and Commonwealth Office (FCO) 2, 3, 6, 11, 30, 40, 41, 51–2, 54–5, 57–8, 60–64, 67–9, 71–5, 82, 87, 89, 90–3, 95, 106–7, 115–16, 119, 121, 123, 125, 134, 136–137, 138–139, 142, 143–144, 148–149, 168, 179, 181, 185, 190–1
Foreign Office (pre-1968) 31–33
France 15, 31, 35, 109–11, 113–14, 172
Frost, David 171
Fukuyama, Francis 160
Fursland, Richard 144

Gaitskell, Hugh 16, 18, 26
Galbraith, J.K. 18
Gardiner, Gerald 32
Genscher, Hans-Dietrich 114, 161
Germany 166, 172, 184
Germany, Federal Republic of (FRG) 39, 107, 109, 113, 114, 126, 130, 161, 189
Ghali, Boutros-Boutros 184
Gilmour, Ian 136
Giscard d'Estaing, Valery 109
Gorbachev, Mikhail 159, 184
Goronwy-Roberts, Lord 62
Gozney, Sir Richard 152
Greece 33, 127
Griffiths, Peter 101
Gromyko, Andrei 124
Group of 77 (G77) 121, 132, 133, 135
Guatemala 59–60, 130

Hain, Lord Peter 38–9
Haines, Joe 57
Hale, Lord Leslie 20
Hall, G.E. 64, 68
Hamburg, David 178, 181, 183
Harlech, Lord (David Ormsby-Gore) 86

Harmann, Harriet 177
Hart, Judith (Baroness Hart) 6, 9, 38–9, 114, 121, 134–5, 138, 153, 187, 189–90
Haselmere Declaration 145
Hassan bin Talal, Crown Prince 143
Havel, Václav 155
Hawkes, Nigel 11
Heath, Sir Edward 40, 88, 92
Helsinki Process, see Conference on Security and Cooperation in Europe
Henderson, Nicholas (Nico) 58
Henderson, V.J. 61
Hibbert, Sir Reginald 107, 111
Hibbs, John 151
Higgins, Rosalyn 174
Hoagland, Jim 173
Holl, Jane 179
Home, Lord (of the Hirsel) 86
House of Commons 6, 12, 52, 81, 93, 124, 136, 170, 158
House of Lords 6, 62, 86
Howard, Michael 151
Howe, Geoffrey 130
Hua, Huang 126
Huddleston, Trevor 21
Humanitas 158, 159, 161, 173–4, 175, 178, 187
Human Rights Commission of the Organization of American States 65, 96
Hume, Cardinal Basil 62–4
Hungary 15–16, 17, 38, 123, 151
Hunter, Robert 164–5
Hurd, Lord Douglas 116, 158, 163, 168, 171
Hussein, Saddam 160, 161

Independent Commission on Disarmament and Security Issues (Palme Commission) 141, 157, 159–60, 161
Independent Commission on International Humanitarian Issues (ICIHI) 9, 122, 143–7, 157, 158, 173, 191
Indonesia 135, 137
International Commission of Jurists 139

International Commission on
    Intervention and State Sovereignty
    (ICISS) 182
International Conference on Human
    Rights (Tehran, 1968) 133
International Conference on the Former
    Yugoslavia (ICFY) 9, 156, 165, 173,
    187
International Labour Organization 134
International Marxist Group (IMG)
    38, 40
Iran 8, 51, 68–71, 137, 185, 190
Iraq 162, 163
Irvine, Rev. Murray 17
Israel 15
Italy 110

Jamaica 133
James, Michael 71
Japan 94, 108, 184
Jay, Peter 6, 88, 90–2, 102, 112–13, 190
Jenkins, Peter 11, 73
Jenkins, Roy 5, 42, 139
Johnson, Paul 76, 78
Jordan 68, 143
Joseph Rowntree Trust 62
Judd, Lord Frank 7, 9, 72–4, 96, 121, 134–5,
    138, 153, 187, 189, 191
Justice (non-governmental organization)
    23, 139

Karadzic, Radavan 172
Keatley, Patrick 53
Kewley, Vanya 74
Khomeini, The Ayatollah 75, 80–1
Kierkegaard, Søren 78
Kimball, John W. 98
Kosovo 155, 156, 176–7, 182, 187
Kuwait 160, 163

Labour Party 3, 5, 6, 9, 12, 14, 16, 18, 25, 26,
    37, 38, 42–3, 46, 66, 128, 139, 140–1,
    176, 177
Lancaster House Agreement 100
Lefever, Ernest 130
Lewis, Anthony 173, 174
Liberal Party 26, 43, 66, 145
Liberation (formerly the Movement for
    Colonial Freedom) 132, 134

Little, Jenny 74
Live Aid 144–5
Lomé Convention 9, 87, 113–18, 186
London Missionary Society 103
Luard, Evan 55–6, 58, 67–8, 96, 111, 119
Lucas, Ivor 73–4, 76
Luce, Richard 136–7
Lunkov, Nikolai 123

Mackintosh, John 20
Macmillan, Harold 20
McNally, Lord Tom 64, 66, 75
Major, B.A. 72
Major, Sir John 161, 163, 170, 179
    government of 156, 163, 167, 168, 173,
    179, 187
Marquand, David 26
Maxey, P.M. 55
Médicins Sans Frontières 172
Mepham, David 177
MI5 67
Ministry of Defence (MOD) 60–1
Ministry of Overseas Development
    (ODM) 6, 55, 135, 138
Minority Rights Group 139
Mitterand, Francois 161
Mondale, Walter 100
Morgenthau, Hans J. 50, 83
Morley, John 78–9
Mortimer, Edward 175, 179
Moscow Olympics (1980) 125
Mulley, Fred 60–1

National Council for Civil Liberties
    (NCCL) 2, 36–7, 42
National Executive Committee (NEC) 70
Netherlands 115–16
Newens, Stan 80, 134
New International Economic Order
    (NIEO) 121, 132–6, 138, 142–3,
    147, 154, 191
New Labour 3, 10, 157, 176, 179, 180, 181,
    182, 184, 187, 191
Nigeria 33, 35, 68
Nixon, Richard 69, 88, 105
North Atlantic Treaty Organization
    (NATO) 95, 106, 127, 140, 150–1,
    155, 161, 164, 166, 175–6, 182,
    187

Northern Ireland 20, 35, 97–8, 167, 186
Nossiter, Bernard D. 53

Oestreicher, Reverend Paul 137
Ogata, Sadako 169, 184
O'Kane, Maggie 158
Oman 68–9
OPEC 88
Operation Allied Force 155, 176, 182
Operation Desert Storm 162
Organization for Security and Cooperation in Europe (OSCE) 153–4
Orlov, Yuri 123
O'Shaughnessy, Hugh 61
Overseas Development Institute (ODI) 115
Owen, Lord David
    appointment as Foreign Secretary 4, 11–12, 34, 41, 44, 46
    childhood and schooling 14–15
    'Churchillian' diplomacy 88–90
    Co-Chairman of the International Conference on the Former Yugoslavia (ICFY) 165–74
    Cold War weaponization of human rights 122–8
    disaffection with the first Wilson government 26–8
    engagement with the 'new left' 43–5
    the Independent Commission on International Humanitarian Issues (ICIHI) 143–7
    the Independent Commission on Disarmament and Security Issues (Palme Commission) 159–60
    on indivisible human rights 131–2
    joining the Labour Party 16–25
    membership of the Carnegie Commission on Preventing Deadly Conflict 178–83
    on the 'morality of compromise' 75–9
    opposition to the sale of armoured vehicles to El Salvador 59–61, 63–5
    Rhodesian initiative 99–104
    the SDP 139–41, 145
    University of Cambridge 15–18, 21–3, 77–8
Owen, John 14–15
Owen, Molly 15
Oxfam 45, 145

Pakistan 68
Palliser, Sir Michael 56, 71, 112
Palme Commission, *see* Independent Commission on Disarmament and Security Issues
Papadopolous, Achilles 69
Paris Charter, *see* Charter of Paris for a New Europe
Parsons, Sir Anthony 70, 72–4
Peate, David 144
PEN (non-governmental organization) 23
Pinochet, Augusto 12, 37, 38, 40, 185
Poland 140, 141
Portugal 23
Powell, Lord Charles 150, 152
Power, Samantha 175
Prentice, Reginald 55, 134
Proudhon, Pierre 43

Rallis, Georgios 127
Ramsbotham, Peter 90–2, 94
Ranelagh, John 137
Reagan, Ronald 92, 129–31, 150, 188
Red Cross 168, 174
Rees, Lord Merlyn 66
Responsibility to Protect (R2P) 10, 157, 182, 187
Rhodesia 9, 28, 33, 42, 99–104, 126, 186
Richard, Ivor 135
Rieff, David 165, 171
Rifkind, Sir Malcolm 170
Robertson, Lord George 180
Robinson, John 112
Rodgers, Lord Bill 5, 139
Romania 129
Romero, Carlos Humberto 51, 61
Roosevelt, Franklin D. 26
Rowlands, Lord Ted 59–60, 67
Russia 172
Rwanda 4, 156, 175–6, 180–1, 188

Sadruddin, Prince 146
Sanjabi, Dr. Karim 81
Saudi Arabia 69
SAVAK 70
Schmidt, Helmut 107, 114, 126
Schultz, George 130
Schwelb, Egon 30–1
SDP, *see* Social Democratic Party
Shah Mohammad Reza Pahlavi 8, 51, 69–70, 72–5, 79, 81, 83, 185, 190
Shakespeare, J.W.R. 60
Shevardnadze, Eduard 149
Short, Clare 177
Simpson, David 137
Simpson-Orlebar, Michael 54, 95, 110–11
Sissons, Peter 170
Slovenia 166
Smart, Maggie 64
Smith, Ian 28, 33, 99, 100
Smythe, Tony 36
Social Democratic Party (SDP) 5, 6, 121, 139–41, 145, 158, 190
Socialist International Committee on Human Rights (SICOHR) 177
Somalia 156
Soper, Donald 20
South Africa 12, 20, 28, 31, 39, 55, 103, 131, 137
Soviet Union (USSR) 20, 22, 35, 107, 110, 121, 123–31, 140, 149–51, 153, 159, 160, 183, 186–7
Spain 23, 171
Squire, Christopher 95
State Department (US) 6, 55, 94, 95, 98, 108, 130, 165, 184
Stephen, David 7, 37, 63–6, 81, 128, 140
Stockwood, Mervyn 7, 13, 16–23, 25, 46, 189
Stoessel, Walter J. Jr. 130
Stoltenberg, Thorvald 172, 177
Straw, Jack 177
Sudan 145
Suez Crisis 15–16, 17, 21

Tanzania 68, 126
Thatcher, Margaret (Baroness Thatcher) 6, 9, 91, 100, 118, 128–31, 136–8, 144, 149–50, 151, 152, 153, 154, 163, 170, 187, 188
governments of 9, 116, 117, 119, 121, 136–9, 140, 142, 144–5, 148–54, 186–7, 191

Uganda 12, 113, 115, 135
UN Covenants on Human Rights 12, 50
Unilateral Declaration of Independence (UDI) 99
United Nations (UN) 2, 9, 10, 12, 23, 29, 30–5, 41, 96, 101–2, 132, 133, 134, 143, 144, 145, 148, 157, 158, 159, 161, 164–5, 167, 168, 171, 175, 177, 178, 179, 181, 183, 185, 186, 191
United States (US) 12, 13, 15, 20, 35, 49, 50, 83, 87–8, 89, 94, 106, 107, 108–10, 112, 129, 131, 139, 151, 156, 160, 164, 165, 171, 190
Universal Declaration of Human Rights 12, 21, 24, 31, 34, 114, 120, 146
Uruguay 130
US Embassy (Brussels) 115
US Embassy (London) 35, 53, 72, 93, 94, 98, 109, 137

Vance, Cyrus 90, 92, 98–9, 107, 156, 167, 168, 172, 178
Vance-Owen Peace Plan 167, 170, 171, 172
Van den Broek, Hans 171
Van der Klaauw, Chris 127
Van Hatten, Margaret 73
Van Horell, Wilbert 174
Van Walsum, Peter 166
Vietnam 34
Voluntary Service Overseas (VSO) 102

Walden, Brian 80–1
Walker, David 5
Walker, Patrick Gordon 30
Wall, Sir Stephen 7, 63, 89, 150, 163, 190
War on Want 37
Wastell, David 170
Weber, Max 27
Weir, M.S. 56, 71
Williams, Sir Anthony 148

Williams, Shirley (Baroness Williams) 5, 139
Wilson, Lord Harold 26–8, 40, 70, 99, 133
   first government of (1964–70) 7, 12, 13, 26–34, 46, 57, 185, 189
   second government (1974–76) 2, 12, 40–1, 70, 185

Yarnold, Patrick 73
Young, Andrew 96
Youth Against Hunger (YAH) 101

Zaire 126
Zambia 68, 126
Zimbabwe 100

www.ingramcontent.com/pod-product-compliance
Lightning Source LLC
Chambersburg PA
CBHW062220300426
44115CB00012BA/2146